6th Workshop on NLP for Conversational AI (NLP4ConvAI 2024)

Bangkok, Thailand
16 August 2024

ISBN: 979-8-3313-0171-2

Printed from e-media with permission by:

Curran Associates, Inc.
57 Morehouse Lane
Red Hook, NY 12571

Some format issues inherent in the e-media version may also appear in this print version.

Association for Computational Linguistics
209 N. Eighth Street
Stroudsburg, Pennsylvania 18360

Phone: 1-570-476-8006
Fax: 1-570-476-0860

acl@aclweb.org

Additional copies of this publication are available from:

Curran Associates, Inc.
57 Morehouse Lane
Red Hook, NY 12571 USA
Phone: 845-758-0400
Fax: 845-758-2633
Email: curran@proceedings.com
Web: www.proceedings.com

NLP4ConvAI 2024

The 6th Workshop on NLP for Conversational AI

Proceedings of the Workshop

August 16, 2024

Association for Computational Linguistics (ACL)
317 Sidney Baker St. S
Suite 400 - 134
Kerrville, TX 78028
USA
Tel: +1-855-225-1962
acl@aclweb.org

Introduction

We are excited to welcome you to NLP4ConvAI 2024, the 6th Annual Workshop on NLP for Conversational AI, co-located with ACL 2024 at Bangkok, Thailand.

The goal of this workshop is to bring together NLP researchers and practitioners in different fields, alongside experts in speech and machine learning, to discuss the current state-of-the-art and new approaches in conversational AI, and to shed light on future directions. Following the success of the five previous editions of NLP for Conversational AI workshops at ACL & EMNLP, NLP4ConvAI 2024 is a one-day workshop including keynotes, oral presentations and posters.

We received 37 submissions this year, consisting of 25 long papers and 12 short papers. We had a total of 68 program committee (PC) members. At least three PC members reviewed each of the papers. We accepted 14 papers: 14 long papers and 0 short papers. These numbers give an overall acceptance rate of 38%, with the long and short papers acceptance rate being 56% and 0% respectively. Out of the 14 accepted papers, 6 are being presented as oral presentations and the remaining in a poster session. We have also identified one best paper (Revealing User Familiarity Bias in Task-Oriented Dialogue via Interactive Evaluation) and one outstanding paper (Engineering Conversational Search Systems: A Review of Applications, Architectures, and Functional Components).

In addition, the workshop program consists of invited talks given by leading practitioners in industry and academia. We would also like to thank all the authors for submitting their work at the workshop, the program committee members for diligently reviewing the submissions and giving valuable feedback to the authors, and the ACL organizing committee for supporting us throughout the process.

We hope you will enjoy NLP4ConvAI 2024 at ACL and contribute to the future success of our community!

NLP4ConvAI 2024 Organizers
Elnaz Nouri, General and Sponsorship Chair
Abhinav Rastogi, General Chair
Georgios Spithourakis, Program Chair
Bing Liu, Publication chair
Yun-Nung (Vivian) Chen, Publication chair
Yu Li, Diversity & Publicity Chair
Alon Albalak, Shared Task Chair
Hiromi Wakaki, Shared Task Chair
Alexandros Papangelis, Advisory Board

Organizing Committee

General Chair and Sponsorship Chair

Elnaz Nouri, Microsoft Research

General Chair

Abhinav Rastogi, Google Research

Program Chair

Georgios Spithourakis, ex-PolyAI, Entrepreneur First

Publication Chair

Bing Liu, Meta

Publication Chair

Yun-Nung Chen, National Taiwan University

Diversity and Publicity Chair

Yu Li, Columbia University

Shared Task Chair

Alon Albalak, University of California, Santa Barbara

Shared Task Chair

Hiromi Wakaki, Sony Group Corporation

Advisory Board

Alexandros Papangelis, Amazon Alexa AI

Program Committee

Reviewers

Divyanshu Aggarwal
Renat Aksitov, Google
Alon Albalak
Raghuram Mandyam Annasamy, Google
Abhinav Arora, Facebook
Mukul Bhutani, Google
Simone Caldarella
Jie Cao
Simral Chaudhary
Maximillian Chen
Parag Pravin Dakle
Nina Dethlefs, University of Hull
Daniel Elkind
Ashwinkumar Ganesan, Amazon
Ananya Ganesh
Shubham Garg, Amazon
Alborz Geramifard, Meta
Parker Glenn, Fidelity Investments
Xiaojie Guo, International Business Machines
Ruohao Guo, Georgia Institute of Technology
Meiqi Guo, Google
Vivek Gupta, University of Pennsylvania, United States
Raghav Gupta, Research, Google
Shachi H. Kumar, Intel Labs
Richang Hong, Hefei University of Technology
Songbo Hu, Language Technology Lab, University of Cambridge
Chao-Wei Huang, National Taiwan University
Mihir Kale, Google
HyeongSik Kim
Abi Komma
Nitish Kulkarni, Google
Harsh Lara, Research, Google
Stefan Larson, Vanderbilt University
Benjamin Levin, PolyAI Limited
Hsien-chin Lin
Yen-Ting Lin, National Taiwan University
Wolfgang Maier, Mercedes Benz Research & Development
Dana Moukheiber
Seyed Mahed Mousavi
Lin Ning, Google
Naoki Otani, Megagon Labs
Alexandros Papangelis, Amazon
Udita Patel, Amazon
Wei Peng, Huawei Technologies Ltd.
Shiva Kumar Pentyala, SalesForce.com
Samrat Phatale, Google DeepMind

Evgeniia Razumovskaia, University of Cambridge
Giuseppe Riccardi, University of Trento
Lina Maria Rojas-Barahona
Igor Shalyminov, Amazon
Akshat Shrivastava
Lei Shu, Google
Shubham Shukla
Georgios P. Spithourakis
Anirudh Sundar, Georgia Institute of Technology
Anh Duong Trinh, National College of Ireland and Technological University Dublin
Yi-Lin Tuan, UC Santa Barbara
Gokhan Tur, University of Illinois at Urbana-Champaign
Stefan Ultes, Otto-Friedrich Universität Bamberg
David Vandyke
Ivan Vulić, University of Cambridge and PolyAI Limited
Peidong Wang
Peratham Wiriyathammabhum
Jiaxing Wu, Google
Longfei Yang, Tokyo Institute of Technology, Tokyo Institute of Technology
Qiusi Zhan, University of Illinois Urbana-Champaign
Jianguo Zhang, SalesForce AI Research

Table of Contents

Program

Friday, August 16, 2024

09:00 - 09:10	*Opening Remarks*
09:10 - 09:40	*INVITED SPEAKER (Scott Yih)*
09:40 - 10:10	*INVITED SPEAKER (Prof. Mausam)*
10:10 - 10:30	*Revealing User Familiarity Bias in Task-Oriented Dialogue via Interactive Evaluation (Best Paper)*
10:30 - 10:50	*Coffee Break*
10:50 - 12:00	*Poster Session*
12:00 - 13:30	*Lunch Break*
13:30 - 14:00	*INVITED SPEAKER (Xiang Gao)*
14:00 - 14:20	*Engineering Conversational Search Systems: A Review of Applications, Architectures, and Functional Components (Outstanding Paper)*
14:20 - 14:40	*Visualizing Dialogues: Enhancing Image Selection through Dialogue Understanding with Large Language Models*
14:40 - 15:00	*SOLID: Self-seeding and Multi-intent Self-instructing LLMs for Generating Intent-aware Information-Seeking Dialogs*
15:00 - 15:30	*INVITED SPEAKER (Ben Athiwaratkun)*
15:30 - 15:50	*Coffee Break*
15:50 - 16:20	*SHARED TASK*
16:20 - 16:40	*Aligning to Thousands of Preferences via System Message Generalization*
16:40 - 17:00	*Evaluating Robustness of Open Dialogue Summarization Models in the Presence of Naturally Occurring Variations*

Friday, August 16, 2024 (continued)

17:00 - 17:10 *Closing Remarks*

On the Benchmarking of LLMs for Open-Domain Dialogue Evaluation

John Mendonça[1,2], **Alon Lavie**[3,4] and **Isabel Trancoso**[1,2]
[1] INESC-ID, Lisbon
[2] Instituto Superior Técnico, University of Lisbon
[3] Carnegie Mellon University, Pittsburgh
[4] Phrase, Pittsburgh
{john.mendonca, isabel.trancoso}@inesc-id.pt, alavie@cs.cmu.edu

Abstract

Large Language Models (LLMs) have showcased remarkable capabilities in various Natural Language Processing tasks. For automatic open-domain dialogue evaluation in particular, LLMs have been seamlessly integrated into evaluation frameworks, and together with human evaluation, compose the backbone of most evaluations. However, existing evaluation benchmarks often rely on outdated datasets and evaluate aspects like *Fluency* and *Relevance*, which fail to adequately capture the capabilities and limitations of state-of-the-art chatbot models.

This paper critically examines current evaluation benchmarks, highlighting that the use of older response generators and quality aspects fail to accurately reflect modern chatbot capabilities. A small annotation experiment on a recent LLM-generated dataset (SODA) reveals that LLM evaluators such as GPT-4 struggle to detect actual deficiencies in dialogues generated by current LLM chatbots.

Context: **A:** I am chatting with clients on the internet. **B:** What kind of service are you providing them?
Mitsuku Response: Is there only one? **Fluency:** 5 **Relevance:** 2 **Overall Score:** 2
Claude-3 Response: Ah, well you see, I'm what you might call a... digital concierge, of sorts. My role is to engage with clients online, understand their needs and preferences and provide them with personalised assistance and recommendations. **Fluency:** 5 **Relevance:** 5 **Overall Score:** 5
LLama3 Response: I'm offering technical support and answering questions about software products. **Fluency:** 5 **Relevance:** 5 **Overall Score:** 4

Table 1: Responses given example context obtained from the FED benchmark. Responses are generated by benchmark's chatbot (Mitsuku), a contemporary closed-source (Claude-3-haiku) and open-source (Llama-3-70B-instruct) chatbot. Scores provided by GPT-4.

1 Introduction

The emergence of Large Language Models has brought about a significant transformation in the field of Natural Language Processing (NLP). Through advancements in model and data scale and clever prompting strategies that leverage In Context Learning and Chain-of-Thought reasoning (Wei et al., 2022), these models have exhibited remarkable capabilities, marking a notable shift in the landscape of NLP research and development.

For the task of dialogue evaluation in particular, several works have proposed the use of LLMs as a standalone or as part of a dialogue evaluation framework for direct assessment of a response or full dialogue (Liu et al., 2023; Mendonça et al., 2023; Lin and Chen, 2023). By simply providing inside the prompt the quality aspects under evaluation, together with a few examples, these models achieve state of the art correlations with human judgements on several benchmarks.

Despite the promising results heralded by this recent approach, we argue that the methods used to benchmark dialogue evaluation are not adequate to accurately assess the evaluation capabilities of current open-domain dialogue evaluation metrics.

In this paper, we investigate existing commonly used human-annotated datasets and identify their shortcomings when used as benchmarks for assessing LLM-based evaluators. In particular, these datasets often rely on the use of weak chatbots to evaluate the proposed framework/metric (as illustrated in Table 1). Consequently, the commonly probed quality aspects have as a primary focus issues such as **Fluency** (*Is the response written correctly?*) and **Relevance** (*Is the response relevant given the context?*). With the introduction of LLMs, the evaluation of these aspects is rendered mostly useless. Yet, existing benchmarks continue

Proceedings of the 6th Workshop on NLP for Conversational AI (NLP4ConvAI 2024), pages 1–12
August 16, 2024

Annotation	Dataset	Type	Lang	Quality Aspects	Generation Models
FED	Meena, Mitsuku, Human-Machine	Turn	EN	Interesting, Engaging, Specific, Relevant, Correct, Semantically Appropriate, Understandable, Fluent, Overall	Human, Meena, Mitsuku
		Dial	EN	Coherent, Recover, Consistent, Diverse, Depth, Likeable, Understanding, Flexible, Informative, Inquisitive, Overall	
USR	PersonaChat TopicalChat	Turn Turn	EN EN	Understandable, Natural, Maintains Context, Interesting, Uses Knowledge, Overall	Transformer, Seq2Seq, LSTM,KV-MemNN
DSTC10	Mixture	Turn	EN	Appropriateness, Content, Grammatical, Relevance	LSTM, HRED, BlenderBot, DialoGPT, T5, GPT-3
DSTC11	Mixture	Turn+Dial	EN,ES,ZH	Appropriateness, Content Richness, Grammatical Correctness, Relevance, Coherence, Engageness/Likeability, Informativeness, Overall	DSTC10, GPT-3.5, ChatGPT, BlenderBot3, Xiaoice, PlatoXL

Table 2: Human annotation benchmarks used to evaluate LLM-based open-domain dialogue evaluators.

to prioritise these outdated criteria, leading to a disconnect between evaluation practices and the capabilities of modern chatbots.

In support of our argument, we present a small qualitative analysis of evaluations provided by these models on dialogues that better approximate current chatbot performance. On the one hand, our analysis shows that dialogues that lack *Fluency* are both easy to detect, and hard to find. On the other hand, LLMs struggle to correctly identify *Coherence* and *Commonsense* issues, which are aspects where the current generation of chatbots still underperform and where better detection and evaluation would be desirable.

With these contributions, we seek to highlight the following:

1. There is an urgent need for new and more meaningful benchmarks. In particular, the release of more human annotations of responses and dialogues generated by contemporary LLMs is necessary to provide a better benchmarking framework for new evaluation methodologies.

2. Evaluation methodologies must be informed by current chatbot capabilities. Open-domain evaluation should focus on identifying novel frontiers in dialogue generation. We argue that aspects such as *Coherence* and *Commonsense* should take the forefront in evaluation instead of *Fluency* or *Relevance*.

2 Benchmark datasets

This section presents a brief survey of datasets that have been used as a benchmark for LLM-based open-domain dialogue evaluation metrics. These datasets are summarised in Table 2 for ease of reference.

The **FED dataset (Mehri and Eskenazi, 2020a)** consists of turn level and dialogue level annotations of conversations conducted between a Human (40 dialogues) and two chatbot engines (**Meena** with 40 dialogues (Adiwardana et al., 2020) and 44 from **Mitsuku** [1]) targeting eighteen quality aspects. Each conversation received one annotation at the dialog level and three annotations at the turn level, randomly selected from the conversation. In total, the FED dataset comprises 3,348 turn-level and 1,364 dialog-level data points, amounting to 4,712 annotations.

For **USR (Mehri and Eskenazi, 2020b)**, annotations were collected for models trained on the TopicalChat (Gopalakrishnan et al., 2019) and PersonaChat (Zhang et al., 2018) dialogue datasets. Generated responses were obtained from models including **Transformer** (Vaswani et al., 2017), **RNN Seq2Seq** (Shang et al., 2015), **LSTM** (Hochreiter and Schmidhuber, 1997), and **KV-MemNN** (Miller et al., 2016). For each dialog context, an additional human response was also collected. Human annotation was then carried out on sixty dialog contexts, with six responses per context for Topical-Chat (four transformer outputs with different decoding strategies, one newly-annotated human output, and the original ground-truth response) and five for PersonaChat (Seq2Seq, LSTM, KV-MemNN, one newly-annotated human output, and the original ground-truth response).

DSTC10 (Zhang et al., 2021). The principal goal of the "Automatic Evaluation and Moderation of Open-domain Dialogue Systems" track was to offer a competitive venue for participants in this challenge to design robust automatic dialogue evaluation metrics that correlate well with human judgements across multiple dialogue domains as well as across different quality aspects. For the development set, 14 publicly available

[1]Mitsuku blogpost

datasets were collected: (1-3) GRADE Datasets (Huang et al., 2020), (4-5) DailyDialog/Persona-Zhao (Zhao et al., 2020), (6) DailyDialog-Gupta (Gupta et al., 2019), (7-8) USR, (9) HUMOD (Merdivan et al., 2020), (10) Twitter-DSTC6 (Hori and Hori, 2018), (11) Reddit-DSTC7 (Galley et al., 2019), (12) Persona-See (See et al., 2019) and (13-14) FED. In total, over 35k turn-level human annotations were compiled. For testing, 3 sources of data were used: (1) CHANEL-JSALT2020, (2) ChatEval (Sedoc et al., 2019) and (3) an additional annotation conducted on TopicalChat (Gopalakrishnan et al., 2019) and PersonaChat (Zhang et al., 2018). Eight systems, a human baseline, and a random utterance were used as response generators. Specifically, the eight systems are **LSTM Seq2Seq**, **Attention-based LSTM Seq2Seq** (Sutskever et al., 2014), **HRED** (Serban et al., 2016), **VHRED**, **BlenderBot (400M-Distill)** (Roller et al., 2021), **DialoGPT-medium** (Zhang et al., 2020), **T5-base** (Raffel et al., 2020), and **GPT-3** (Brown et al., 2020).

DSTC11 (Rodríguez-Cantelar et al., 2023). Similar to DSTC10, the "Robust and Multilingual Automatic Evaluation Metrics for Open-Domain Dialogue Systems" track is split into development and test sets. For the development set, the organisers provide data from two clusters of datasets from DSTC10 and 4,470 dialogues (approximately 130k turns) open-domain human-human dialogues which are originally in Chinese. Since the goal of the shared task was to evaluate mulitlingual-ity and robustness of metrics, development data is translated into English, Chinese, Spanish, and back-translated. For testing, the organisers combine a portion of the DSTC10 test set, and include new Human-Chatbot dialogues generated by SotA chatbots. These are: **ChatGPT** (a platform powered by GPT-3.5-Turbo), **GPT-3.5** (Ouyang et al., 2022) and **BlenderBot3** (Shuster et al., 2022). Similar to the development set, the test set was also translated. In total, 4,839 turn level and 277 dialogue level annotations were conducted.

3 LLMs as evaluators

Most automatic evaluation in the literature up until recently was conducted with word-overlap metrics or encoder-based metrics trained using self-supervised training objectives (Yeh et al., 2021). Mehri and Eskenazi (2020a) proposed an alternative approach called **FED** (fine-grained evaluation of dialog), which measures dialogue quality by computing the likelihood that DialoGPT (Zhang et al., 2020) will respond to it with a particular set of follow-up utterances that are constructed.

Despite the unsupervised nature, it was only with the introduction of LLMs that these approaches fully replaced encoder-based metrics.

The first documented systematic evaluation of LLMs was conducted by Huynh et al. (2023), where they evaluate training and few-shot strategies for this task. The authors evaluate several LLMs including BLOOM (Workshop, 2023), OPT (Zhang et al., 2022), GPT-3, Flan-T5 (Chung et al., 2022), InstructDial (Gupta et al., 2022) and TNLGv2 (Smith et al., 2022b) on the **DSTC10** and **FED** benchmarks. The authors report good correlation results with human judgements and confirm the appropriateness of few-shot learning for dialogue evaluation.

GPTScore (Fu et al., 2023) is based on the assumption that a generative pre-training model will assign a higher probability to high-quality generated text than low quality one following a given instruction and context. Several LLMs are tested, including GPT-3 and Flan-T5 on the **FED-turn** dataset.

G-Eval (Liu et al., 2023) studies GPT-3.5-Turbo and GPT-4 for the evaluation of generation models. In detail, the framework comprises (1) a prompt defining the evaluation task and criteria, (2) a Chain-Of-Thoughts step containing intermediate instructions generated by the LLM outlining evaluation steps, and (3) a scoring function based on return token probabilities estimated by generating multiple times. For the task of dialogue evaluation, G-Eval is benchmarked on the **USR-TopicalChat** dataset covering naturalness, coherence, engagingness and groundedness.

DialEvalML (Mendonça et al., 2023) is a hybrid framework combining encoder-based models (in this case XLM-RoBERTa-large (Conneau et al., 2020)) trained with self-supervised objectives and direct prompting and score extraction from GPT-3.5-Turbo. The authors combine the predictions using a correlation rescaling method obtained from the development set, achieving first place in all tracks of **DSTC11** (Rodríguez-Cantelar et al., 2023).

LLM-Eval (Lin and Chen, 2023) is a single-prompt-based evaluation method that leverages a unified evaluation schema to cover multiple dimensions of conversation quality in a forward pass. The authors evaluate Claude-v1.3 (Anthropic, 2023), ChatGPT and GPT-3.5 on the **DSTC10** hidden set.

XDial-Eval (Zhang et al., 2023) focuses on probing the evaluation capabilities of several open access LLMs against GPT-3.5-Turbo. The authors focus on context relevance and coherence by combining a selection of subsets from **DSTC11** development set. They additionally translate the original English data to 9 additional languages. Unlike other approaches, the LLMs were evaluated in (1) zero and few shot learning scenario; (2) instruction finetuning; and (3) ensemble with a strong encoder-based framework.

Zhang et al. (2024) conduct a comprehensive study of 30 recently emerged LLMs for automatic dialogue evaluation using a smaller subset than the one from XDial-Eval. In particular, the authors assess *Relevance*, *Understandability*, *Specificity*, *Interestingness*, and *Overall quality* at the turn level, while at the dialogue level, they evaluate *Coherence*, *Engagingness*, *Informativeness*, *Diversity*, and *Overall quality*.

4 Limitations in Current Benchmarking

Given the datasets identified in Section 2 used to assess LLM-based evaluators (Section 3), we identify several limitations in the benchmarking of automatic open-domain dialogue evaluation, which we enumerate below.

Use of Outdated Generative Models With the exception of DSTC11-test (which was only used as a benchmark by `DialEvalML`), most benchmarks contain responses from older generative models such as LSTMs or HRED. As a result, a substantial amount of low quality responses are easily identifiable (lacking basic quality aspects such as fluency, contextual relevance or specificity). Concurrently, responses that are relevant but contain contradictions, coherence issues or are factually incorrect are overvalued by evaluators due to biased guidelines. This tendency to rate flawed responses can skew the perception of evaluator performance, leading to misleading conclusions about their effectiveness in practice.

Irrelevance of Quality Aspects in Current Chatbots Dialogue evaluation guidelines are focused on detecting issues that were prevalent in older generation models. For instance, all benchmarks have a quality aspect that targets *Fluency* and *Relevance*. Given current LLM-based chatbots, these quality aspects are no longer informative to differentiate output quality between different contemporary dialogue systems: most if not all models now output fluent and relevant responses (e.g., Table 1).

Focus on English An overarching trend on the benchmarks being used is that they exclusively focus on the English language. Although DSTC11 does provide annotations in Chinese and Spanish, they are only partially available for the test set. Moreover, in the development set, only translated versions of the original English dialogues are included, thereby introducing English bias into the assessment of quality. This bias further extends to the test set, where, even if evaluated by native annotators, the aspects being measured fall short of capturing the linguistic and cultural nuances present in dialogues. These nuances can include the use of formal versus informal language, expressions of politeness, cultural references, and idiomatic expressions[2] that may not directly translate into English.

5 Qualitative Analysis

Informed by the issues highlighted in Section 4, we conduct a small scale annotation experiment. The goal of this annotation is twofold. Firstly, we aim to understand whether annotations such as *Fluency* are still relevant. Secondly, the annotation of more complex aspects such as *Coherence* or *Commonsense* in this dataset allows us to understand the performance of LLMs when evaluating responses generated by SoTA chatbots on quality aspects that require a stronger understanding of conversational dynamics.

We use SODA (Kim et al., 2023) as our dialogue dataset since it leverages a LLM (in this case GPT-3.5) for the generation of dialogues. As such, SODA will exhibit most of the typical issues associated with LLMs, thereby making its use as a contemporary benchmark more relevant than benchmarks relying on weaker response generators (as identified in Section 4). Human evaluation conducted on SODA shows that its dialogues are more consistent, specific, and natural than DailyDialog (Li et al., 2017), a frequently used dialog dataset used for the development of evaluation metrics (Yeh et al., 2021). Table 6 presents an example of the SODA dataset, where a *Coherence* issue is highlighted.

[2]Visit Cultural Atlas for a centralised repository of various cultures and corresponding communication practices.

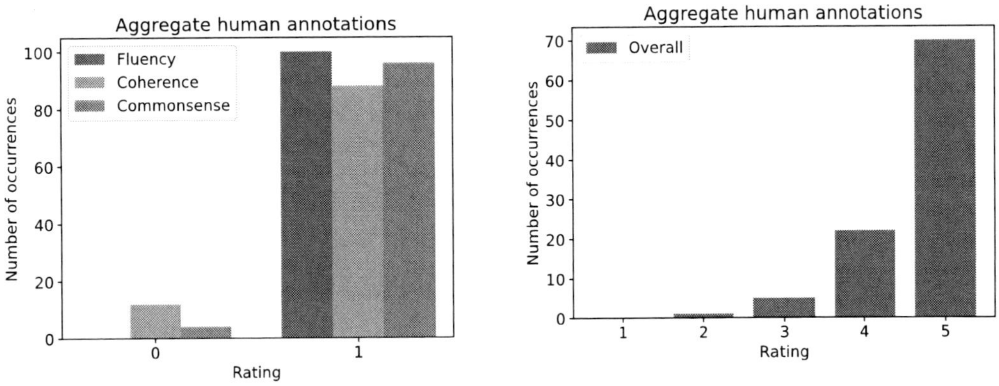

Figure 1: Aggregate human annotations on SODA. Annotations for *Overall* rounded down to the nearest integer.

5.1 Annotation

We recruited 3 expert annotators [3] to rate the first 100 dialogues[4] of the test set in terms of:

- *Fluency (0,1):* The dialogue is written correctly and has no grammatical errors.
- *Coherence (0,1):* The dialogue is coherent and does not contain contradictions within itself.
- *Commonsense (0,1):* The dialogue does not contain common sense issues. It is logical, makes sense and is aware of basic facts and effects.
- *Overall quality [1,5]:* Overall impression of the dialogue.

Aspect	Spearman
Fluency	-
Coherence	0.7025
Commonsense	0.6534
Overall	0.7425

Table 3: Inter annotator agreement for each aspect studied. All correlations p<0.05.

Following Mehri and Eskenazi (2020a), we report inter annotator agreement results in Table 3, corresponding to the correlation between each annotation and the mean of the annotations for the same quality aspect. For *Fluency*, all annotators reported 0 dialogues with issues. As such, the correlation (and most other agreement metrics) is undetermined. For the other annotations, agreement is high, and in line with other works (Mehri and Eskenazi (2020a) reports correlations as low as 0.562 for *Consistency*.). Figure 1 presents the aggregate annotations for the SODA dataset. These aggregate ratings are computed using majority voting for the binary aspects and simple average (rounded down) for *Overall*.

With respect to the annotations that target specific aspects of quality, the majority of dialogues

Your task is to evaluate dialogues in terms of Fluency, Coherence, Commonsense and Overall Quality.

Fluency (0-bad,1-good): The dialogue is written correctly and has no grammatical errors.

Coherence (0-bad,1-good): The dialogue is coherent and does not contain contradictions within itself. E.g.: Someone saying they are flying to London for the first time and then saying they went there before in a subsequent turn.

Commonsense (0-bad,1-good): The dialogue does not contain common sense issues. It is logical, makes sense and is aware of basic facts and effects. E.g. Drinking a coffee as a refreshment for the summer lacks commonsense.

Overall (1 (poor) up to 5 (excellent)): Overall impression of the dialogue.

Please present your evaluation into the following json format:
{"Fluency": _, "Coherence": _, "Commonsense": _, "Overall": _}

Dialogue:
[Dialogue]

Table 4: Dialogue evaluation instruction template (denoted as *Ours* in the experiments).

[3] All annotators are members of our research lab.

[4] The evaluated dialogues have a turn distribution similar to the one of the full SODA dataset (average of 4 turns per dialogue, minimum 2 and maximum 8).

Evaluator	Fluency (Acc.)	Coherence (r_{pb})	Commonsense (r_{pb})	Overall (ρ)
G-EVAL 3.5 (2023)	0.99	0.2283	*0.0425*	0.2716
G-EVAL 4	0.97	0.1749	**0.4348**	0.3789
LLM-EVAL 3.5 (2023)	**1.00**	0.1834	0.1993	0.2435
LLM-EVAL 4	**1.00**	0.2489	0.4054	**0.3811**
Ours GPT-3.5	0.99	0.2721	0.3353	0.1857
Ours GPT-4	0.99	0.1659	0.3440	0.3782
Ours Llama-3-8B	0.99	0.1155	*0.0205*	0.1953
Ours Llama-3-70B	0.99	**0.2722**	*0.0205*	0.2115

Table 5: Evaluation results with human judgements on SODA. Performance for *Fluency* is reported using Accuracy, *Coherence* and *Commonsense* using Point-biserial correlation and *Overall* with Spearman correlation. **Bold** denotes best performance. All correlations p<0.05 unless *italicised.*

were annotated as *fluent*, *coherent* and with *commonsense*. In particular, the annotations did not identify **any** *Fluency* issues in all dialogues. This supports our argument that annotating *Fluency* has limited value given current chatbot capabilities.

5.2 Baseline Evaluators

As a baseline for the analysis, we evaluate two typically used closed-source LLMs: GPT-3.5-Turbo and GPT-4 [5], using the prompting strategies of G-Eval (Liu et al., 2023), LLM-EVAL (Lin and Chen, 2023), and our own contribution. Additionally, we probe the performance of Llama-3 (AI@Meta, 2024), an open access model with benchmark performances [6] similar to the closed source ones:

- **G-Eval** calculates an average score sampled from 20 generations with high temperature. We obtain a binary decision for *Fluency* when s > 0.5.
- **LLM-EVAL** outputs a score from 1-100. Similar to G-Eval, we consider a dialogue to be fluent when s > 50.
- **Our contribution** directly probes the LLM using the same guidelines provided to the annotators, therefore the scores are extracted directly. The template used is presented in Table 4.

We provide in the prompt the full dialogue and ask the LLM to rate the dialogue according to the probed aspects. We follow the hyperparameters of the original work whenever available. For our method, we employ a *temperature* of 0.3 for GPT models and 0.6 for Llama, and generate a single output.

For evaluation, we employ metrics adapted to the aggregate labels. For *Fluency*, since all dialogues are rated as being fluent, we use simple accuracy; for *Coherence* and *Commonsense*, we report results using point-biserial correlation (r_{pb}) since the labels provided are binary (0,1); finally, *Overall* results are presented using Spearman (ρ) correlation (1-5 Likert score).

5.3 Results

We present the evaluation results for our annotated subset in Table 5.

Fluency With the exception of LLM-EVAL, all evaluators failed to correctly identify all dialogues as being fluent. One dialogue in particular contains a hallucination that affects the understanding of the dialogue, but is still strictly fluent. As such, the performance of LLM-EVAL can be attributed to the 0-100 scoring scale, which allows for a more fine grained evaluation of the dialogue. In fact, LLM-EVAL outputs a much lower score (still above the decision threshold of 50) to this dialogue when compared to other ones. In any case, we consider this to be an edge case of a failed evaluation that could be resolved by providing a more comprehensive prompt and/or including examples.

Coherence Generally speaking, LLM evaluators struggle with correctly identifying responses that lack *Coherence*, with the best approaches only achieving **.2722** correlation (LLama-3-70B). Using our prompting strategy, we note that these ap-

[5] `gpt-3.5-turbo-0125` and `gpt-4-1106-preview` accessed via OpenAI's API in early April.

[6] `Llama-3` reported evaluation

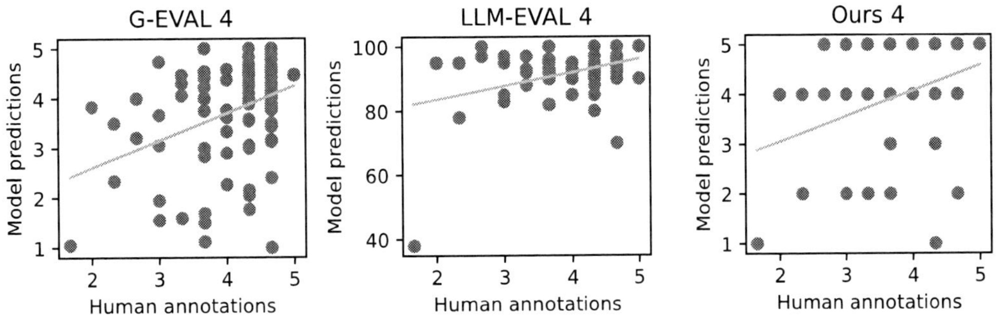

Figure 2: Scatter plots and corresponding correlations for each prompting strategy using GPT-4.

proaches were only able to correctly classify 1 (GPT-3.5-Turbo) and 2 (GPT-4) out of 12 incoherent dialogues, underlining the difficulty these models have in identifying coherence issues. In fact, GPT-3.5-Turbo only rated a single dialogue as lacking coherence (against the 6 dialogues rated by GPT-4), which explains why it has larger correlations than GPT-4 (lower false positives). Table 6 presents an example of such failed prediction.

Commonsense When compared to *Coherence*, LLMs have much larger variability in performance for *Commonsense*. For instance, GPT-4 achieves over .4 correlation using G-Eval and LLM-EVAL prompting strategies, whereas the LLama-3 model evaluations and G-EVAL 3.5 are mostly uncorrelated. The low score for LLama-3 could be attributed to a difficulty in understanding the evaluation task. Given GPT-3.5 worked reasonably well for the other prompting strategies, the performance is explained by the disagreement between individual sampled scores. In any case, the predictions are generally better for *Commonsense* than with *Coherence*, which could be explained by the fact that illogical actions can be mostly identified directly, and without taking into account prior contextual details found in the dialogue. This contrasts with *Coherence*, which requires a deeper contextual analysis to detect inconsistencies, which is a known limitation of LLMs (Han et al., 2023).

Overall Similar to *Commonsense*, *Overall* predictive performance is stronger when using GPT-4 as the base LLM evaluator, with the best correlations being achieved using LLM-EVAL 4 at **.3811**. Nevertheless, this correlation rate is still subpar when compared against reported dialogue-level correlations on other benchmark datasets – for instance, LLM-EVAL reports a 0.71 correlation on **FED-dialogue** (*Overall Quality*). Figure 2 presents scatter plots for GPT-4 predictions across the probed prompting strategies.

A: I've been thinking a lot lately about moving back to my home country.

B: Really? Why?

A: I miss my family a lot. And I want to be closer to them as they get older. I can provide support and assistance to them more easily if I am living nearby.

B: I can understand that. But what about us?

A: We can still visit each other. And it's not like we're moving to different countries. We'll still be in the same region.

B: True, But it's going to be a big adjustment for both of us.

A: I know it will be tough at first, but I think it will be worth it in the long run. Plus, you could always come visit me in my home country!

B: Hmmm...I don't know if I'm ready for that kind of commitment just yet. But I'm willing to try it if you are.

Human annotation:
Fluency: 1 **Coherence:** 0 **Commonsense:** 0 **Overall:** 2

Ours GPT-4:
Fluency: 1 **Coherence:** 1 **Commonsense:** 1 **Overall:** 5

Table 6: Example dialogue extracted from SODA, together with Human and GPT-4 rating. The underline text identifies a coherence issue.

5.4 Discussions

Model size Overall, we note that the larger models (GPT-4 vs GPT-3.5, LLama-3-70B vs LLama-3-8B) consistently outperform their corresponding smaller models for both Coherence and Commonsense. This may be attributed to breakthrough performance thanks to model scaling, which has also

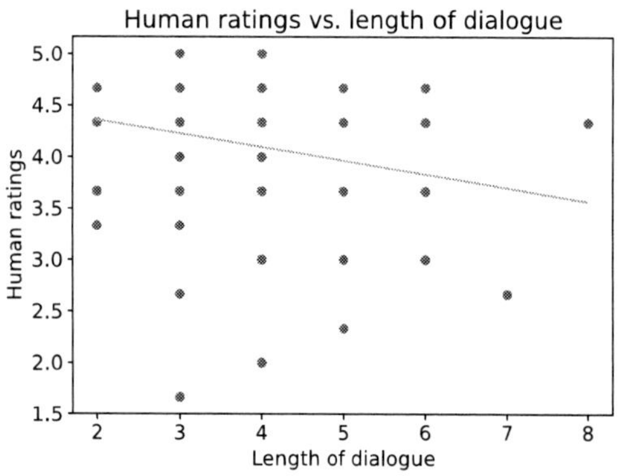

Figure 3: Scatter plots of human ratings against dialogue length.

been reported as "emergent abilities" in complex reasoning tasks (Zoph et al., 2022). This observation contrasts with Fluency, where no difference has been noted between model size.

External Expert Knowledge Surprisingly, we find instances where the model considers a high quality dialogue to be low quality. Upon further inspection, these ratings appear to have been influenced by external expert knowledge, something the annotators did not take into account. For instance, in one of the dialogues, one of the participants is asking for advice to patent a catalytic converter they invented. This is picked up by the evaluator when asked for an explanation: *"there is a significant commonsense issue: the catalytic converter is not a new invention."*. This is an incorrect evaluation within the framework of our study since it is not commonsense knowledge. Nevertheless, this topic is of significant interest for evaluation and is not explicitly studied in many benchmarks. In fact, it might be one type of evaluation LLMs can excel at, especially when individual annotator knowledge is limited.

Dialogue length The limitations of LLM reasoning and understanding over long contexts is well documented in the literature (Bai et al., 2024; Kuratov et al., 2024). As such, one possible reason for issues in the dialogue could be attributed to dialogue length. With this in mind, we calculate the Point-biserial correlation (r_{pb}) between *Coherence*/*Commonsense* and the length of the dialogue. For *Coherence*, we report a correlation of -0.228, which denotes a small to medium correlation; for *Commonsense*, correlation is non-significant (0.006). We additionally present the scatter plot for *Overall* in Figure 3. Similarly to *Coherence*, we report a Spearman correlation of -0.251. Firstly, as expected, commonsense issues are mostly independent to dialogue length, which makes sense since commonsense knowledge is drawn from model training and not from context. For coherence, its correlation with dialogue length is small. However, we acknowledge that the small sample size of larger dialogues does not allow for more definitive conclusions.

6 Conclusion

This paper conducts an inventory of open domain dialogue evaluation benchmarks being currently used by LLM evaluation frameworks. We show that these benchmarks have several limitations that hinder the progress in the field. In particular, we argues they lack (1) responses generated by strong LLM chatbots; (2) aspects that identify their weaknesses; (3) representation of other languages and cultures. In order to illustrate these limitations, we also conducted a small scale experiment on SODA and show that even GPT-4 shows limitations in the detection of low quality responses.

However, these findings underscore one critical limitation in how direct assessment benchmarks are currently being developed: they are mostly concerned with evaluating contemporary chatbot capabilities. As it stands, the current evaluation research environment is one where the driver of progress is the advancement in generation, and not the converse. Ultimately, evaluation benchmarks should possess the flexibility to remain relevant as newer chatbots emerge, thereby pushing the envelope of dialogue generation. Embracing this goal would not only foster greater comparability and reproducibility in research, but also facilitate continuous improvement in the field, leading to the development of better chatbots.

7 Limitations

Pairwise Comparisons Our study is focused on metrics that predict human judgements on singular responses or dialogues. We acknowledge other methodologies such as pairwise comparisons exist, and that they mostly circumvent the limitations we highlight. Nevertheless, given the documented interest in the literature of metrics that are optimised to predict direct assessments provided by humans, we argue our study is still valuable. Furthermore, direct assessments provide a more granular assessment of response quality that pairwise comparisons lack, especially when comparing models that differ only slightly in quality but are otherwise similar (Smith et al., 2022a).

SODA Unlike the majority of benchmarks studied, where chatbots generate a response given seed human-human interaction or conducts a full conversation with a human, SODA dialogues are entirely synthetic. As such, one might argue this approach may hide possible limitations of chatbots since they are in control of the whole conversation, thereby excluding human feedback within the conversation which can be used to aid evaluation (Petrak et al., 2023). However, there are very few open source open-domain dialogue datasets that contain LLMs as one of the participants[7].

Self-evaluation biases One consideration in the current LLM-based evaluation paradigm is that self-evaluation biases may arise. This bias is more evident in subjective assessments such as "Overall Quality", which is more pronounced in pairwise comparisons (Panickssery et al., 2024). While this bias can be reduced by employing more objective quality aspects such as the ones we propose in this work, it is still possible that models will erroneously overlook their own errors. As such, it is important to complement automated direct assessment with human judgements.

Monolingual We identified English-centric evaluation as one the issues in current benchmarking. However, our experiment is conducted on SODA, which is exclusively in English. The aim of our annotation is not to propose a novel benchmark for the evaluation community (hence only 100 dialogues), but as an artefact to highlight the limitations of current datasets being used to benchmark automatic dialogue evaluation. Nevertheless, our annotations are based on generations that better approximate current chatbot capabilities. Furthermore, our analysis show that these dialogues still contain language and culture-agnostic issues that evaluators ought to be able to detect. As such, our annotations may be used as a compliment to current benchmarks, and most importantly, as an example for future annotation efforts.

[7]In fact, most recent user-LLM chatbot interaction datasets are conversational QA (Zheng et al., 2024; Zhao et al., 2024).

8 Ethical Considerations

Expert Annotations All annotators are fluent in English and graduate level professionals in the field of Computation Linguistics (two of which authors of this work) and volunteered to conduct the annotation. Notwithstanding the diverse backgrounds, the annotation may still contain biases in evaluation process. For instance, given the expertise of these annotators in this field, their assessment of quality might differ from other groups. A larger, more diverse pool of annotators may reduce this bias, which was not considered in this work due to its small scale.

Monolingual As identified in the Limitation section, our work, despite arguing for multilingual and multicultural benchmarks, conducts its experimentation in English. Additionally, all annotators share similar western cultural background. As such, it's conclusions are biased towards the evaluation of English dialogues, which may not extend to other cultures, specifically non-western ones. For instance, high context cultures (Hall, 1959) privilege non-verbal methods of communication, which is typically not transcribed into text (Nishimura et al., 2008).

Acknowledgments

This research was supported by the Portuguese Recovery and Resilience Plan through project C645008882-00000055 (Responsible.AI) and by national funds through *Fundação para a Ciência e a Tecnologia* (FCT) with references PRT/BD/152198/2021 and DOI: 10.54499/UIDB/50021/2020.

References

Daniel Adiwardana, Minh-Thang Luong, David R. So, Jamie Hall, Noah Fiedel, Romal Thoppilan, Zi Yang, Apoorv Kulshreshtha, Gaurav Nemade, Yifeng Lu, and Quoc V. Le. 2020. Towards a human-like open-domain chatbot. *CoRR*, abs/2001.09977.

AI@Meta. 2024. Llama 3 model card.

Anthropic. 2023. Model card and evaluations for claude models.

Yushi Bai, Xin Lv, Jiajie Zhang, Hongchang Lyu, Jiankai Tang, Zhidian Huang, Zhengxiao Du, Xiao Liu, Aohan Zeng, Lei Hou, Yuxiao Dong, Jie Tang, and Juanzi Li. 2024. Longbench: A bilingual, multitask benchmark for long context understanding.

Tom Brown, Benjamin Mann, Nick Ryder, Melanie Subbiah, Jared D Kaplan, Prafulla Dhariwal, Arvind Neelakantan, Pranav Shyam, Girish Sastry, Amanda Askell, et al. 2020. Language models are few-shot learners. *Advances in neural information processing systems*, 33:1877–1901.

Hyung Won Chung, Le Hou, Shayne Longpre, Barret Zoph, Yi Tay, William Fedus, Yunxuan Li, Xuezhi Wang, Mostafa Dehghani, Siddhartha Brahma, Albert Webson, Shixiang Shane Gu, Zhuyun Dai, Mirac Suzgun, Xinyun Chen, Aakanksha Chowdhery, Alex Castro-Ros, Marie Pellat, Kevin Robinson, Dasha Valter, Sharan Narang, Gaurav Mishra, Adams Yu, Vincent Zhao, Yanping Huang, Andrew Dai, Hongkun Yu, Slav Petrov, Ed H. Chi, Jeff Dean, Jacob Devlin, Adam Roberts, Denny Zhou, Quoc V. Le, and Jason Wei. 2022. Scaling instruction-finetuned language models.

Alexis Conneau, Kartikay Khandelwal, Naman Goyal, Vishrav Chaudhary, Guillaume Wenzek, Francisco Guzmán, Edouard Grave, Myle Ott, Luke Zettlemoyer, and Veselin Stoyanov. 2020. Unsupervised cross-lingual representation learning at scale. In *Proceedings of the 58th Annual Meeting of the Association for Computational Linguistics*, pages 8440–8451, Online. Association for Computational Linguistics.

Jinlan Fu, See-Kiong Ng, Zhengbao Jiang, and Pengfei Liu. 2023. Gptscore: Evaluate as you desire.

Michel Galley, Chris Brockett, Xiang Gao, Jianfeng Gao, and Bill Dolan. 2019. Grounded response generation task at dstc7.

Karthik Gopalakrishnan, Behnam Hedayatnia, Qinlang Chen, Anna Gottardi, Sanjeev Kwatra, Anushree Venkatesh, Raefer Gabriel, and Dilek Hakkani-Tür. 2019. Topical-chat: Towards knowledge-grounded open-domain conversations. In *Interspeech 2019*.

Prakhar Gupta, Cathy Jiao, Yi-Ting Yeh, Shikib Mehri, Maxine Eskenazi, and Jeffrey Bigham. 2022. InstructDial: Improving zero and few-shot generalization in dialogue through instruction tuning. In *Proceedings of the 2022 Conference on Empirical Methods in Natural Language Processing*, pages 505–525, Abu Dhabi, United Arab Emirates. Association for Computational Linguistics.

Prakhar Gupta, Shikib Mehri, Tiancheng Zhao, Amy Pavel, Maxine Eskenazi, and Jeffrey Bigham. 2019. Investigating evaluation of open-domain dialogue systems with human generated multiple references. In *Proceedings of the 20th Annual SIGdial Meeting on Discourse and Dialogue*, pages 379–391, Stockholm, Sweden. Association for Computational Linguistics.

Edward T. Hall. 1959. *The silent language*. Doubleday, Garden City, N. Y.

Ridong Han, Tao Peng, Chaohao Yang, Benyou Wang, Lu Liu, and Xiang Wan. 2023. Is information extraction solved by chatgpt? an analysis of performance, evaluation criteria, robustness and errors.

Sepp Hochreiter and Jürgen Schmidhuber. 1997. Long short-term memory. *Neural Comput.*, 9(8):1735–1780.

Chiori Hori and Takaaki Hori. 2018. End-to-end conversation modeling track in dstc6.

Lishan Huang, Zheng Ye, Jinghui Qin, Liang Lin, and Xiaodan Liang. 2020. GRADE: Automatic graph-enhanced coherence metric for evaluating open-domain dialogue systems. In *Proceedings of the 2020 Conference on Empirical Methods in Natural Language Processing (EMNLP)*, pages 9230–9240, Online. Association for Computational Linguistics.

Jessica Huynh, Cathy Jiao, Prakhar Gupta, Shikib Mehri, Payal Bajaj, Vishrav Chaudhary, and Maxine Eskenazi. 2023. Understanding the effectiveness of very large language models on dialog evaluation.

Hyunwoo Kim, Jack Hessel, Liwei Jiang, Peter West, Ximing Lu, Youngjae Yu, Pei Zhou, Ronan Bras, Malihe Alikhani, Gunhee Kim, Maarten Sap, and Yejin Choi. 2023. SODA: Million-scale dialogue distillation with social commonsense contextualization. In *Proceedings of the 2023 Conference on Empirical Methods in Natural Language Processing*, pages 12930–12949, Singapore. Association for Computational Linguistics.

Yuri Kuratov, Aydar Bulatov, Petr Anokhin, Ivan Rodkin, Dmitry Sorokin, Artyom Sorokin, and Mikhail Burtsev. 2024. Babilong: Testing the limits of llms with long context reasoning-in-a-haystack.

Yanran Li, Hui Su, Xiaoyu Shen, Wenjie Li, Ziqiang Cao, and Shuzi Niu. 2017. DailyDialog: A manually labelled multi-turn dialogue dataset. In *Proceedings of the Eighth International Joint Conference on Natural Language Processing (Volume 1: Long Papers)*, pages 986–995, Taipei, Taiwan. Asian Federation of Natural Language Processing.

Yen-Ting Lin and Yun-Nung Chen. 2023. LLM-eval: Unified multi-dimensional automatic evaluation for open-domain conversations with large language models. In *Proceedings of the 5th Workshop on NLP for Conversational AI (NLP4ConvAI 2023)*, pages 47–58, Toronto, Canada. Association for Computational Linguistics.

Yang Liu, Dan Iter, Yichong Xu, Shuohang Wang, Ruochen Xu, and Chenguang Zhu. 2023. G-eval: NLG evaluation using gpt-4 with better human alignment. In *Proceedings of the 2023 Conference on Empirical Methods in Natural Language Processing*, pages 2511–2522, Singapore. Association for Computational Linguistics.

Shikib Mehri and Maxine Eskenazi. 2020a. Unsupervised evaluation of interactive dialog with DialoGPT.

In *Proceedings of the 21th Annual Meeting of the Special Interest Group on Discourse and Dialogue*, pages 225–235, 1st virtual meeting. Association for Computational Linguistics.

Shikib Mehri and Maxine Eskenazi. 2020b. USR: An unsupervised and reference free evaluation metric for dialog generation. In *Proceedings of the 58th Annual Meeting of the Association for Computational Linguistics*, pages 681–707, Online. Association for Computational Linguistics.

John Mendonça, Patrícia Pereira, Helena Moniz, Joao Paulo Carvalho, Alon Lavie, and Isabel Trancoso. 2023. Simple LLM prompting is state-of-the-art for robust and multilingual dialogue evaluation. In *Proceedings of The Eleventh Dialog System Technology Challenge*, pages 133–143, Prague, Czech Republic. Association for Computational Linguistics.

Erinc Merdivan, Deepika Singh, Sten Hanke, Johannes Kropf, Andreas Holzinger, and Matthieu Geist. 2020. Human annotated dialogues dataset for natural conversational agents. *Applied Sciences*, 10(3).

Alexander Miller, Adam Fisch, Jesse Dodge, Amir-Hossein Karimi, Antoine Bordes, and Jason Weston. 2016. Key-value memory networks for directly reading documents. In *Proceedings of the 2016 Conference on Empirical Methods in Natural Language Processing*, pages 1400–1409, Austin, Texas. Association for Computational Linguistics.

Shoji Nishimura, Anne Nevgi, and Seppo Tella. 2008. Communication style and cultural features in high/low context communication cultures: A case study of finland, japan and india.

Long Ouyang, Jeff Wu, Xu Jiang, Diogo Almeida, Carroll L. Wainwright, Pamela Mishkin, Chong Zhang, Sandhini Agarwal, Katarina Slama, Alex Ray, John Schulman, Jacob Hilton, Fraser Kelton, Luke Miller, Maddie Simens, Amanda Askell, Peter Welinder, Paul Christiano, Jan Leike, and Ryan Lowe. 2022. Training language models to follow instructions with human feedback.

Arjun Panickssery, Samuel R. Bowman, and Shi Feng. 2024. Llm evaluators recognize and favor their own generations.

Dominic Petrak, Nafise Moosavi, Ye Tian, Nikolai Rozanov, and Iryna Gurevych. 2023. Learning from free-text human feedback – collect new datasets or extend existing ones? In *Proceedings of the 2023 Conference on Empirical Methods in Natural Language Processing*, pages 16259–16279, Singapore. Association for Computational Linguistics.

Colin Raffel, Noam Shazeer, Adam Roberts, Katherine Lee, Sharan Narang, Michael Matena, Yanqi Zhou, Wei Li, and Peter J. Liu. 2020. Exploring the limits of transfer learning with a unified text-to-text transformer. *J. Mach. Learn. Res.*, 21(1).

Mario Rodríguez-Cantelar, Chen Zhang, Chengguang Tang, Ke Shi, Sarik Ghazarian, João Sedoc, Luis Fernando D'Haro, and Alexander I. Rudnicky. 2023. Overview of robust and multilingual automatic evaluation metricsfor open-domain dialogue systems at DSTC 11 track 4. In *Proceedings of The Eleventh Dialog System Technology Challenge*, pages 260–273, Prague, Czech Republic. Association for Computational Linguistics.

Stephen Roller, Emily Dinan, Naman Goyal, Da Ju, Mary Williamson, Yinhan Liu, Jing Xu, Myle Ott, Eric Michael Smith, Y-Lan Boureau, and Jason Weston. 2021. Recipes for building an open-domain chatbot. In *Proceedings of the 16th Conference of the European Chapter of the Association for Computational Linguistics: Main Volume*, pages 300–325, Online. Association for Computational Linguistics.

João Sedoc, Daphne Ippolito, Arun Kirubarajan, Jai Thirani, Lyle Ungar, and Chris Callison-Burch. 2019. ChatEval: A tool for chatbot evaluation. In *Proceedings of the 2019 Conference of the North American Chapter of the Association for Computational Linguistics (Demonstrations)*, pages 60–65, Minneapolis, Minnesota. Association for Computational Linguistics.

Abigail See, Stephen Roller, Douwe Kiela, and Jason Weston. 2019. What makes a good conversation? how controllable attributes affect human judgments. In *Proceedings of the 2019 Conference of the North American Chapter of the Association for Computational Linguistics: Human Language Technologies, Volume 1 (Long and Short Papers)*, pages 1702–1723, Minneapolis, Minnesota. Association for Computational Linguistics.

Iulian V. Serban, Alessandro Sordoni, Yoshua Bengio, Aaron Courville, and Joelle Pineau. 2016. Building end-to-end dialogue systems using generative hierarchical neural network models. In *Proceedings of the Thirtieth AAAI Conference on Artificial Intelligence*, AAAI'16, page 3776–3783. AAAI Press.

Lifeng Shang, Zhengdong Lu, and Hang Li. 2015. Neural responding machine for short-text conversation. In *Proceedings of the 53rd Annual Meeting of the Association for Computational Linguistics and the 7th International Joint Conference on Natural Language Processing (Volume 1: Long Papers)*, pages 1577–1586, Beijing, China. Association for Computational Linguistics.

Kurt Shuster, Jing Xu, Mojtaba Komeili, Da Ju, Eric Michael Smith, Stephen Roller, Megan Ung, Moya Chen, Kushal Arora, Joshua Lane, Morteza Behrooz, W.K.F. Ngan, Spencer Poff, Naman Goyal, Arthur D. Szlam, Y-Lan Boureau, Melanie Kambadur, and Jason Weston. 2022. Blenderbot 3: a deployed conversational agent that continually learns to responsibly engage. *ArXiv*, abs/2208.03188.

Eric Smith, Orion Hsu, Rebecca Qian, Stephen Roller, Y-Lan Boureau, and Jason Weston. 2022a. Human evaluation of conversations is an open problem: comparing the sensitivity of various methods for evaluating dialogue agents. In *Proceedings of the 4th Workshop on NLP for Conversational AI*, pages 77–97, Dublin, Ireland. Association for Computational Linguistics.

Shaden Smith, Mostofa Patwary, Brandon Norick, Patrick LeGresley, Samyam Rajbhandari, Jared Casper, Zhun Liu, Shrimai Prabhumoye, George Zerveas, Vijay Korthikanti, Elton Zhang, Rewon Child, Reza Yazdani Aminabadi, Julie Bernauer, Xia Song, Mohammad Shoeybi, Yuxiong He, Michael Houston, Saurabh Tiwary, and Bryan Catanzaro. 2022b. Using deepspeed and megatron to train megatron-turing nlg 530b, a large-scale generative language model.

Ilya Sutskever, Oriol Vinyals, and Quoc V. Le. 2014. Sequence to sequence learning with neural networks. In *Proceedings of the 27th International Conference on Neural Information Processing Systems - Volume 2*, NIPS'14, page 3104–3112, Cambridge, MA, USA. MIT Press.

Ashish Vaswani, Noam Shazeer, Niki Parmar, Jakob Uszkoreit, Llion Jones, Aidan N. Gomez, Łukasz Kaiser, and Illia Polosukhin. 2017. Attention is all you need. In *Proceedings of the 31st International Conference on Neural Information Processing Systems*, NIPS'17, page 6000–6010, Red Hook, NY, USA. Curran Associates Inc.

Jason Wei, Xuezhi Wang, Dale Schuurmans, Maarten Bosma, Fei Xia, Ed Chi, Quoc V Le, Denny Zhou, et al. 2022. Chain-of-thought prompting elicits reasoning in large language models. *Advances in neural information processing systems*, 35:24824–24837.

BigScience Workshop. 2023. Bloom: A 176b-parameter open-access multilingual language model.

Yi-Ting Yeh, Maxine Eskenazi, and Shikib Mehri. 2021. A comprehensive assessment of dialog evaluation metrics. In *The First Workshop on Evaluations and Assessments of Neural Conversation Systems*, pages 15–33, Online. Association for Computational Linguistics.

Chen Zhang, Luis D'Haro, Chengguang Tang, Ke Shi, Guohua Tang, and Haizhou Li. 2023. xDial-eval: A multilingual open-domain dialogue evaluation benchmark. In *Findings of the Association for Computational Linguistics: EMNLP 2023*, pages 5579–5601, Singapore. Association for Computational Linguistics.

Chen Zhang, Luis Fernando D'Haro, Yiming Chen, Malu Zhang, and Haizhou Li. 2024. A comprehensive analysis of the effectiveness of large language models as automatic dialogue evaluators. *Proceedings of the AAAI Conference on Artificial Intelligence*, 39.

Chen Zhang, João Sedoc, Luis Fernando D'Haro, Rafael Banchs, and Alexander Rudnicky. 2021. Automatic evaluation and moderation of open-domain dialogue systems.

Saizheng Zhang, Emily Dinan, Jack Urbanek, Arthur Szlam, Douwe Kiela, and Jason Weston. 2018. Personalizing dialogue agents: I have a dog, do you have pets too? In *Proceedings of the 56th Annual Meeting of the Association for Computational Linguistics (Volume 1: Long Papers)*, pages 2204–2213, Melbourne, Australia. Association for Computational Linguistics.

Susan Zhang, Stephen Roller, Naman Goyal, Mikel Artetxe, Moya Chen, Shuohui Chen, Christopher Dewan, Mona Diab, Xian Li, Xi Victoria Lin, Todor Mihaylov, Myle Ott, Sam Shleifer, Kurt Shuster, Daniel Simig, Punit Singh Koura, Anjali Sridhar, Tianlu Wang, and Luke Zettlemoyer. 2022. Opt: Open pre-trained transformer language models.

Yizhe Zhang, Siqi Sun, Michel Galley, Yen-Chun Chen, Chris Brockett, Xiang Gao, Jianfeng Gao, Jingjing Liu, and Bill Dolan. 2020. DIALOGPT : Large-scale generative pre-training for conversational response generation. In *Proceedings of the 58th Annual Meeting of the Association for Computational Linguistics: System Demonstrations*, pages 270–278, Online. Association for Computational Linguistics.

Tianyu Zhao, Divesh Lala, and Tatsuya Kawahara. 2020. Designing precise and robust dialogue response evaluators. In *Proceedings of the 58th Annual Meeting of the Association for Computational Linguistics*, pages 26–33, Online. Association for Computational Linguistics.

Wenting Zhao, Xiang Ren, Jack Hessel, Claire Cardie, Yejin Choi, and Yuntian Deng. 2024. Wildchat: 1m chatgpt interaction logs in the wild.

Lianmin Zheng, Wei-Lin Chiang, Ying Sheng, Tianle Li, Siyuan Zhuang, Zhanghao Wu, Yonghao Zhuang, Zhuohan Li, Zi Lin, Eric P. Xing, Joseph E. Gonzalez, Ion Stoica, and Hao Zhang. 2024. Lmsys-chat-1m: A large-scale real-world llm conversation dataset.

Barret Zoph, Colin Raffel, Dale Schuurmans, Dani Yogatama, Denny Zhou, Don Metzler, Ed H. Chi, Jason Wei, Jeff Dean, Liam B. Fedus, Maarten Paul Bosma, Oriol Vinyals, Percy Liang, Sebastian Borgeaud, Tatsunori B. Hashimoto, and Yi Tay. 2022. Emergent abilities of large language models. *TMLR*.

Exploring Description-Augmented Dataless Intent Classification

Ruoyu Hu[1,*], **Foaad Khosmood**[2] and **Abbas Edalat**[1]
[1]Department of Computing, Imperial College London, UK
[2]California Polytechnic State University, USA
{ruoyu.hu18, a.edalat}@imperial.ac.uk
foaad@calpoly.edu

Abstract

In this work, we introduce several schemes to leverage description-augmented embedding similarity for dataless intent classification using current state-of-the-art (SOTA) text embedding models. We report results of our methods on four commonly used intent classification datasets and compare against previous works of a similar nature. Our work shows promising results for dataless classification scaling to a large number of unseen intents. We show competitive results and significant improvements (+6.12% Avg.) over strong zero-shot baselines, all without training on labelled or task-specific data. Furthermore, we provide qualitative error analysis of the shortfalls of this methodology to help guide future research in this area.

1 Introduction

Task-oriented dialogue systems (TODS) by design, aid the user in accomplishing tasks within specific domains, and can have a wide range of applications from shopping (Yan et al., 2017) to healthcare (Wei et al., 2018; Valizadeh and Parde, 2022). Modular TODS (Wen et al., 2017) will typically contain an intent classification component (Louvan and Magnini, 2020; Chen et al., 2019; Su et al., 2022) used by a dialogue manager to determine the appropriate task the user intends to complete. In recent years, neural-based models using supervised training have reached state-of-the-art on many natural language processing tasks, including intent classification. However, supervised learning methods require human-labelled data for a predefined set of intents, which may be time-consuming and labour-intensive to acquire (Xia et al., 2018), and may have poor scalability if new intents are added, or task definition changed. An early approach to tackle this problem is *dataless intent classification* (Chang et al., 2008; Song and Roth, 2014) which aimed to leverage the pairwise similarities between semantic representations of utterances and intent classes to perform classification without reliance on human-labelled data. However, this approach relies heavily on the quality of semantic representations (Chang et al., 2008). In recent years, successful *zero-shot intent classification* approaches (Liu et al., 2019; Yan et al., 2020; Yin et al., 2019) have received greater attention, whereby learning conducted using labelled examples of a subset of *seen* intent labels is transferred to *unseen* intents. However, these methods still require human-labelled data, and tend to bias towards seen intents, with the number of unseen intents also generally much lower than seen intents (Liu et al., 2022; Zhang et al., 2022).

In this work, with the significant recent advancements in the quality of text embedding models (Muennighoff et al., 2023), we explore the potential for dataless intent classification methods using a number of recent state-of-the-art text embedding models. We introduce several approaches for generating intermediate textual representations for intents, most notably using intent label descriptions, and formalise our methodology. We perform extensive evaluation of our methods, including scenarios with large numbers of intents from different domains, using three commonly used intent classification datasets. We summarise our contributions as follows:

- We introduce a new scheme for generating intent descriptions with an aim to minimise reliance on human expert input.
- We show that our intent descriptions yield significant improvements over label tokenization through extensive evaluation.
- We introduce an approach utilising utterance paraphrasing and masking which yields further improvements and show this is consistent across a range of models.
- We aggregate and explore the potential of a multitude of current SOTA text embedding

*Corresponding author

Proceedings of the 6th Workshop on NLP for Conversational AI (NLP4ConvAI 2024), pages 13–36
August 16, 2024 ©2024 Association for Computational Linguistics

models for dataless classification.

- We extensively evaluate our methodology on four commonly used intent classification datasets and report on the results.
- We provide qualitative error analysis aimed at guiding future work.

2 Related Works

2.1 Generalized Zero-Shot Learning

Zero-shot learning (ZSL) (Yin et al., 2019) aims to leverage learning previously performed on labelled examples from seen tasks to unseen tasks, of which there are no labelled examples available for supervised training. ZSL has seen increasing popularity in the domain of intent classification (Liu et al., 2019; Yan et al., 2020) in recent years, whereby models are trained on a subset of intent labels and evaluated on another disjoint subset of intent labels. In more recent years, the concept of generalized zero-shot learning (GZSL) has seen an increase in prominence in the domain, in which the performance on both seen and unseen classes are considered in tandem (Zhang et al., 2022; Lamanov et al., 2022). Several GZSL approaches learn a label prototype space during training, which is transferred to unseen classes through methods such as inter-class relationship modelling (Zhang et al., 2021) and prototype adaptation (Zhang et al., 2022). Approaches such as (Lamanov et al., 2022) encode the utterance and labels in a sentence-pair setup, with template-based lexicalisation of labels used as class prototypes. Other approaches exist that use label prototypes as centroids in Gaussian mixture models trained on seen class utterances (Yan et al., 2020; Liu et al., 2022). An issue that can occur with GZSL is biased towards seen classes (Zhang et al., 2022), which can lead to significantly lower performance on unseen classes. It is also difficult to see the efficacy of transfer to a large number of diverse unseen classes, as the number of unseen classes in evaluation is also typically much smaller than the number of seen classes.

2.2 Dataless Classification

Dataless text classification (Chang et al., 2008) is defined as tackling text classification without prior training on any labelled data. Generally regarded as a precursor to zero-shot text classification, this approach typically leverages sentence representations without any training on labelled data, by comparing the semantic representations between a sentence and that of the intent classes (Song and Roth, 2014). (Zha and Li, 2019) utilises "seed" words associated with each intent class to further contextualise the intent class representation, as a single word may often be insufficient to encapsulate the meaning of the class (Chen et al., 2015). Some approaches further leverage class hierarchy to augment classification performance (Li et al., 2016; Popov et al., 2019).

3 Methodology

3.1 Problem Definition

Let $\mathcal{C}$ be a set of intents supported by a task-oriented dialogue system, $\mathcal{U} = \bigcup\{\mathcal{U}_c\}_{c\in\mathcal{C}}$ defines the set of all user utterances, $\mathcal{U}_c = \{u_i\}_{1\leq i\leq n_c}$ is the set of utterances belonging to intent class c. The model undergoes no task-specific training and is tasked with making an intent prediction $\hat{y}_i$ for a previously unseen utterance u_i at inference time. We follow the paradigm set by previous works in dataless text classification (Chang et al., 2008; Song and Roth, 2014) to conduct nearest-neighbour classification over the sentence embedding space. For a given utterance u_i, an encoder $\mathbf{h}(\cdot)$ and a set of class label representations $\{l_c\}_{c\in\mathcal{C}}$, we make a prediction $\hat{y}_i$ as follows:

$$\hat{y}_i = \arg\max_c s(\mathbf{h}(u_i), \mathbf{h}(l_c)) \quad (1)$$

where $s(\mathbf{u}, \mathbf{v}) = \mathbf{u}\cdot\mathbf{v}/||\mathbf{u}||_2||\mathbf{v}||_2$ is the cosine similarity between two vectors.

In order to conduct nearest-neighbour classification using intent labels, we require an intermediate representation, or prototype, which encapsulates to some degree the meaning of a class (Zha and Li, 2019), from which we can obtain a suitable embedding. A commonly used approach in dataless classification is to use the labels (Chang et al., 2008).

3.2 Label Tokenization

A class prototype is obtained by tokenizing intent labels directly, inserting spaces and replacing character separators, i.e.

```
AddToPlaylist →Add To Playlist
oil_change_how→ Oil Change How
```

However, this approach depends on the descriptiveness of the original intent labels, which can vary significantly between datasets and tasks. As such, we propose an additional step to produce intent label *descriptions* which we hypothesise can (1) better align the semantic representation with the characteristics of the class and (2) provide more consistent performance across datasets or approaches without requiring in-task data, which previous works (Lamanov et al., 2022) have shown could improve performance over purely using tokenized labels.

3.3 Our Approach

3.3.1 Intent Description

Our objective is to produce a brief description of the intent expressed by the user in a given utterance, while ensuring the process requires minimal expert human effort so as to remain scalable for large numbers of intent classes. Rather than producing a general description of the intent (Gao et al., 2023), we formalise our template for producing intent descriptions with the two following constraints:

Label Preservation The resulting intent description must contain tokens from the original intent label i.e. `car_rental` → `User wants to rent a car`, or replace with an appropriate word (lexical cognates, synonyms etc.).

Format Consistency Descriptions should be written in the declarative form, beginning with either `"User is [asking|saying]"`, or `"User wants [to]"`, and aim to introduce minimal extraneous tokens in a similar manner to abstractive summarization (De Raedt et al., 2023). Our approach differs from the template-based approach in (Lamanov et al., 2022) in that we use exclusively the declarative form in writing our descriptions to maintain consistency across intent classes and datasets. Example descriptions can be seen in Table 1, more examples can be found in Appendix I. We examine the robustness of our approach in Section 6.

In our experimentation (Section 4), our intent descriptions added on average 6.6 tokens to the tokenized intent labels (1.9 → 8.5), with 98.3% of descriptions containing at least one of the label tokens in exact form, and 82.7% of all label tokens preserved.

3.3.2 Utterance Paraphrasing

The diversity of user utterances for any given intent can pose a challenge as intents may not be obvious (Mueller et al., 2022). We hypothesise that a format consistency constraint over the user utterance can benefit dataless intent classification

Label	Description
`abbreviation`	"user is asking what an abbreviation stands for or means"
`flight_no`	"user is asking about a flight number"
`AddToPlaylist`	"user wants to add a song to a playlist"
`food_last`	"user wants to know how long a food lasts
`maybe`	"user is expressing uncertainty"

Table 1: Example descriptions for intent labels from each of the datasets (Section 4.1) used in our experimentation.

performance. Previous works primarily focused on utterance paraphrasing as a means of data augmentation (Kumar et al., 2019; Jolly et al., 2020; Sahu et al., 2022) or to reduce overfitting (Dopierre et al., 2021). Our approach leverages inference-time paraphrasing to enforce a weaker degree of our intent descriptions' format consistency constraint on user utterances. Given a paraphraser model $\mathbf{p}(\cdot)$ we compute a sentence embedding of the paraphrased utterance $\mathbf{p}(u_i)$:

$$P_{u_i} = \mathbf{h}(\mathbf{p}(u_i)) \quad (2)$$

We leverage a 1.6B StableLM model[1] (Bellagente et al., 2024) to generate a single paraphrase for each utterance. Our selection was based on said model being the top-performing model under 2B parameters on the Open LLM Leaderboard (Beeching et al., 2023) as of the time of writing. We additionally experimented with 1.6B Zephyr (Tunstall et al., 2023) and 1.3B Phi-1.5 (Li et al., 2023a) models but found no significant difference on our task. Example templates and further details are shown in Appendix A. The mean cosine similarity between the paraphrases and the original utterances across 4 intent classification tasks and 12 embedding models is 0.89 ± 0.06.

3.3.3 Label Entity Overlap & Masking

We note that sentence embeddings tended to capture the topic and entity information rather than the associated action, which can lead to misclassifications in the event that two or more intent classes share entities (i.e. `AddToPlaylist` and `PlayMusic` can both refer to songs as their objects). To tackle this, we introduce a masking

[1]`https://huggingface.co/stabilityai/stablelm-2-1_6b-chat`

Algorithm 1 Utterance Masking Procedure

```
Given user utterance u_i = {u_{i,1}, ... u_{i,t}}
T_i ← DependencyParser(u_i)
procedure MASKTREE(T)
    n ← root(T)
    if relation(n) is obj then
        n ← [MASK]
        DROP children(n)
    else
        for u_{i,j} in children(n) do
            MASKTREE(u_{i,j})
        end for
    end if
end procedure
```

component which given user utterance u_i masks spans containing the object of said utterance, identified through dependency parsing[2] (de Marneffe and Manning, 2008; Schuster and Manning, 2016), to produce m_i. m_i is then weighted to form the masking component:

$$M_{u_i} = \mathbf{h}(m_i) \times Overlaps(u_i, k) \times \mathbb{1}_{masked} \quad (3)$$

where $Overlaps(u, k)$ denotes whether there is likely entity overlap in the top k candidate intents by similarity and $\mathbb{1}_{masked}$ is whether there exists a masked version of the original sentence. We did not find significant differences in performance for $k > 3$, and thus we use $k = 3$ for all our experiments.

Masking Algorithm 1 illustrates the masking procedure which identifies and masks object spans in the utterance. We define such object spans as subtrees within the dependency tree in which a parent node has any of `{dobj, pobj, ccomp}` relations. We note that object relations are not always present in the dependency tree, in such cases masked representations are not used. From our experiments, some degree of masking was performed for 97.29% of utterances from the ATIS dataset, 98.04% of SNIPS, 90.88% of CLINC and 84.24% of MASSIVE. We show an example of this procedure in Appendix B.

Entity Overlap For each intent, we predict a set of entities $\mathbf{e}_c = \{e_{c_1}, \ldots, e_{c_k}\}$ from the intent description that may describe the object of said class. As such, entities are defined at problem definition and can be modified alongside intent descriptions when they are added/removed. We precompute an overlap matrix $Overlap$ where

$$Overlap[i, j] = \begin{cases} 1 & \mathbf{e}_i \cap \mathbf{e}_j \neq \varnothing \\ 0 & \text{otherwise} \end{cases} \quad (4)$$

At inference time, we compute overlaps for classes with top k embedding similarities for an utterance u_i. Given a similarity vector $s_i = \{s_{i,1}, \ldots, s_{i,c}\}_{c=|\mathcal{C}|}$ of embedding similarities between utterance embedding $\mathbf{h}(u_i)$ and intent description embeddings $\mathbf{h}(l_c)_{c \in \mathcal{C}}$, we compute $Top_k(u_i)$ as the top k classes with similarity scores sorted in descending order. We then compute pairwise overlap for all pairs in $Top_k(u_i)$ as follows:

$$Overlaps(u_i, k) = \bigcup_{m,n \in Top_k(u_i), m \neq n} Overlap[m, n] \quad (5)$$

We note that future work could explore expansion of the definition of relevant entities to each intent class, as the current solution relies on the quality of intent descriptions and only covers the most likely entities across an entire class, a more dynamic inference-time solution that determines overlap based on candidate classes would be desirable.

3.4 Combined Sentence Representation

We formulate the final representation of the user utterance within the embedding space as the sum of the original utterance embedding with the paraphrasing and masking components:

$$h_i = \mathbf{h}(u_i) + P_{u_i} + M_{u_i} \quad (6)$$

$$\hat{y}_i = \arg\max_c s(h_i, \mathbf{h}(l_c)) \quad (7)$$

4 Experiments

4.1 Datasets

We evaluate our methods on four commonly used English task-oriented dialogue (TOD) system intent classification datasets, covering a diverse range of number of intents (7-150) and domains (up to 18). (1) **ATIS** (Hemphill et al., 1990) is an English air-travel information system dataset containing 18 intent classes. For comparison, we follow previous works (Zhang et al., 2022) in filtering out intent classes containing fewer than 5 examples.

[2]We leverage an off-the-shelf dependency parser, `en_core_web_trf` from `Spacy` **url**: `https://spacy.io/models/en`

(2) **SNIPS-NLU** (Coucke et al., 2018) contains 7 intent classes, totalling 14,484 utterances. (3) **CLINC** (Larson et al., 2019) is a dataset for out-of-scope intent classification, with 150 intents and 22,500 utterances spanning 10 domains. (4) **MASSIVE** (FitzGerald et al., 2023) is a multilingual spoken language understanding dataset containing 60 intents across 18 domains, we select the 16,521 instances from the `en-US` split of the dataset for our experiments. As our method does not involve fine-tuning on task-specific data, we consider *entire* datasets to consist of unseen data for evaluation[3].

4.2 Models

We select 11 models from the Massive Text Embedding Benchmark (MTEB) (Muennighoff et al., 2023) that are in the top 20 at the time of writing[4]. Our selections are based on the following criteria: (1) the model weights must be released (2) documentation of training methods and experimentation details must be readily available. Additionally, owing to computational limits[5], we only consider models up to 3GB in size. Our final selection of 11 models can be largely grouped into 4 families of models: **InstructOR** (Su et al., 2023), **E5** (Wang et al., 2022), **GTE** (Li et al., 2023b) and **BGE** (Xiao et al., 2023). More details on selected models are provided in Appendix C.

We report results in Section 5 for all E5, GTE and BGE models using averaged token embeddings as sentence representations. We additionally compare model performances against a commonly used embedding model in OpenAI's `text-embedding-ada-002` (Neelakantan et al., 2022) which we refer to in our tables as 'Ada-002'. We also investigated the generation of synthetic examples as intent prototypes (Appendix I) but did not find significant improvements over our approach using intent descriptions (Appendix J).

[3]We make our code and datasets publicly available and can be found at `https://github.com/ruoyunlp/dataless-intent-classification`

[4]November-December 2023. We note our top-performing selected models are still competitive with current top-performing models from MTEB fitting our criteria as of May 2024

[5]All experiments conducted using a single 9GB GPU

5 Results

5.1 Baselines and Terminology

We compare the performance of our methods against several unknown intent classification methods previously detailed in Section 2. Here we clarify the terminology used henceforth to refer to these methods in our results. We refer to scores on unseen intent labels reported by (Zhang et al., 2021) as **ICR**, (Yan et al., 2020) as **SEG**, (Liu et al., 2022) as **ML-SEG**, dataless approach trained using original data from (Lamanov et al., 2022) as **TIR**$_{Orig}$ and likewise **TIR**$_{Syn}$ for training on synthetic data. We refer to the results of the adapted method of (Gidaris and Komodakis, 2018) reported in (Zhang et al., 2022) as **CosT** and the reported main results as **LTA**. We refer to the best-performing model of a similar size to our selection from (Gretz et al., 2023) as **TTC**$_D$.

5.2 Metrics

Following from previous works (Zhang et al., 2022; Lamanov et al., 2022), we report Accuracy and Macro-F1 scores for intent classification on each of the datasets, in addition, we also compute the average of Accuracy and F1 score for direct comparison between our methods similar to (Gritta et al., 2022). We show macro-F1 only for MASSIVE in Table 2 for comparison's sake as the previous work (Gretz et al., 2023) did not report Accuracy scores. Full results for each of our approaches including Accuracy scores are shown in Table 9.

5.3 Methods using Tokenized Labels

Despite a lack of task-specific fine-tuning, models using tokenized intent labels generally performed comparably to most of the baselines on unseen intents. The best-performing model (BGE$_{Large}$) outperforms baseline scores for ICR (+9.13 Mean), SEG (+10.21 Mean) and ML-SEG (+3.14 Mean), TIR$_{Syn}$ (+13.60 Mean), TIR$_{Orig}$ (+4.55 Mean) and TTC$_D$ (+0.31 F1). BGE$_{Large}$ outperforms CosT on all datasets; however, it also significantly underperforms LTA on all 3 datasets (-16.38 ATIS, -7.49 SNIPS-NLU, -1.21 CLINC). We note that this approach appears quite sensitive to the model as indicated by the comparatively high standard deviation ($\sigma_{Ovr} = 5.65$) across models.

5.4 Methods using Intent Descriptions

Our method using intent label descriptions yields a significant improvement over using tokenized la-

	Model	AT.	SN.	CL.	MA.	Ovr.
		Mean Acc. & F1			F1	
Baselines	ICR	35.04	-	-	-	-
	SEG	-	69.46	-	-	-
	ML-SEG	-	76.53	-	-	-
	TIR$_{Orig}$	-	-	68.50	-	-
	TIR$_{Syn}$	-	-	59.65	-	-
	CosT	45.62	55.28	66.50	-	-
	LTA	60.55	87.16	74.46	-	-
	TTC$_D$	-	-	-	54.22	-
	Baselines	60.55	87.16	74.46	54.22	69.10
Tokenized Intent Labels	Instr.$_{Large}$	18.72	82.39	62.76	47.62	52.87
	E5-v2$_{Base}$	20.39	77.13	63.87	45.97	51.84
	E5-v2$_{Large}$	26.64	69.99	60.40	46.83	50.97
	mE5$_{Large}$	22.47	59.35	57.34	44.34	45.88
	E5$_{Large}$	40.57	74.44	69.11	49.78	58.48
	Ada-002	25.98	82.75	66.97	47.90	55.90
	GTE$_{Small}$	20.75	73.99	68.47	51.90	53.77
	GTE$_{Base}$	55.66	81.75	70.65	51.44	64.88
	GTE$_{Large}$	39.78	79.36	69.54	49.08	59.44
	BGE$_{Small}$	19.50	78.00	70.78	52.43	55.18
	BGE$_{Base}$	45.74	76.81	73.05	55.89	62.87
	BGE$_{Large}$	44.17	79.67	73.25	54.53	62.91
Intent Label Descriptions	Instr.$_{Large}$	42.18	85.60	77.25	55.52	65.14
	E5-v2$_{Base}$	52.44	87.49	70.92	53.73	66.14
	E5-v2$_{Large}$	52.16	87.31	71.49	55.65	66.65
	mE5$_{Large}$	60.51	83.88	72.24	56.67	68.32
	E5$_{Large}$	52.56	88.92	74.88	56.32	68.17
	Ada-002	51.34	89.50	77.81	58.03	69.17
	GTE$_{Small}$	54.71	84.42	70.20	51.86	65.30
	GTE$_{Base}$	52.60	86.41	75.10	54.62	67.18
	GTE$_{Large}$	55.85	86.33	75.83	57.85	68.97
	BGE$_{Small}$	47.84	85.51	72.03	54.27	64.91
	BGE$_{Base}$	48.76	88.32	77.61	58.92	68.40
	BGE$_{Large}$	54.88	89.30	79.08	<u>62.88</u>	71.53
+ Paraphrase and Masking	Instr.$_{Large}$	49.07	89.86	<u>80.17</u>	59.79	69.72
	E5-v2$_{Base}$	60.93	90.03	75.06	57.81	70.95
	E5-v2$_{Large}$	48.06	85.56	74.69	58.27	66.64
	mE5$_{Large}$	57.72	83.36	75.00	57.67	68.43
	E5$_{Large}$	53.78	<u>91.92</u>	76.27	59.17	70.28
	Ada-002	57.02	90.51	79.73	59.92	71.80
	GTE$_{Small}$	53.48	88.11	71.50	57.53	67.66
	GTE$_{Base}$	**64.20**	85.88	75.75	58.41	71.06
	GTE$_{Large}$	60.63	91.70	78.89	61.63	<u>73.21</u>
	BGE$_{Small}$	54.16	90.76	75.04	59.11	69.77
	BGE$_{Base}$	58.69	91.81	79.80	61.98	73.07
	BGE$_{Large}$	<u>61.04</u>	**92.57**	**81.52**	**65.76**	**75.22**

Table 2: Model performance on 4 intent classification tasks. We show Mean of Accuracy and Macro-F1 scores for ATIS, SNIPS-NLU & CLINC. Macro-F1 is shown for MASSIVE as TTC$_D$ did not report Accuracy. Full results for each dataset are shown in Table 9.

Model	Tok.	Desc.	Comb.
InstructOR$_{Large}$	64.96	73.19	76.89
E5-v2$_{Base}$	62.98	71.02	74.58
E5-v2$_{Large}$	59.75	71.76	73.13
mE5$_{Large}$	54.23	71.50	72.57
E5$_{Large}$	64.70	73.65	76.09
Ada-002	66.48	75.35	77.12
GTE$_{Small}$	65.43	69.38	72.80
GTE$_{Base}$	68.57	72.35	73.63
GTE$_{Large}$	66.63	73.57	77.57
BGE$_{Small}$	68.20	71.11	75.37
BGE$_{Base}$	69.36	75.28	<u>78.05</u>
BGE$_{Large}$	69.76	77.15	**79.91**

Table 3: Average model Mean of Accuracy and F1 over SNIPS-NLU, CLINC and MASSIVE datasets using tokenized intent labels (**Tok.**), intent descriptions (**Desc.**) and combined utterance embedding (**Comb.**).

bels (Tables 2 and 3), with an average increase per model of $+11.24$ overall. This supports our hypothesis (1) (Section 3.2) in that the additional contextualisation added through describing the label via a declarative sentence better encapsulates the semantic information represented by a label. We also note from Table 3 that the standard deviation in performance across models is significantly lower when using descriptions ($\sigma_{Ovr} = 1.98$), supporting our hypothesis (2) that descriptions can improve consistency across models and approaches. Our overall best-performing model (BGE$_{Large}$) also considerably outperforms the strongest baseline on SNIPS-NLU (+2.14 Mean), CLINC (+4.62 Mean) and MASSIVE (+8.66 F1). We do note that all of our approaches in this setup underperform on the ATIS dataset compared to the baseline, with our overall best-performing approach yielding 60.51 vs 60.55; we provide further insight into possible reasons in Section 7 to help guide future research.

5.5 Methods with Additional Paraphrasing and Masking

Our addition of paraphrase and masked utterance embeddings yields further overall score improvements on average of +3.16 over label descriptions and is consistent across different models (Table 3). Our best-performing model (BGE$_{Large}$) significantly outperforms previous approaches on all 4 datasets (+0.49 ATIS, +5.42 SNIPS-NLU, +7.06 CLINC, +11.54 MASSIVE). Additionally, our approach outperforms previous work on 9 out of 12 selected models.

Setup				AT.	SN.	CL.	MA.	Ovr.
E	P	M	O					
x				54.89	89.29	79.08	63.09	71.59
	x			56.03	85.77	78.77	63.35	70.98
		x		30.72	76.76	37.90	33.62	44.75
x	x			56.11	88.83	**81.56**	65.60	73.02
x		x		60.84	92.52	75.56	60.80	72.43
	x	x		60.57	92.19	75.99	62.91	72.92
x	x	x		**61.04**	**92.67**	81.22	<u>65.64</u>	<u>75.14</u>
x		x	x	60.84	92.56	77.36	61.82	73.14
	x	x	x	60.57	92.02	76.86	63.04	73.12
x	x	x	x	**61.04**	<u>92.57</u>	<u>81.52</u>	**65.65**	**75.20**

Table 4: Mean of Accuracy and Macro-F1 on 4 intent classification datasets using a `bge-large-en-v1.5` model. **Setup** denotes whether a component is used in the combined sentence embedding: **E** - utterance embedding, **P** - paraphrasing, **M** - masking, **O** - entity overlap in masking.

6 Ablations

Addition of paraphrasing and masking Table 3 illustrates the mean performance across SNIPS, CLINC and MASSIVE datasets for each model different class prototypes. We note the consistent improvement in performance between tokenized intent labels and our approach using declarative intent descriptions (+7.86 Mean), and the further improvements with added paraphrasing and masking (+10.56 Mean). We omit ATIS from this table as it is significantly unbalanced, the impact of which we explore in Section 7, and its results are already included in Table 2.

Combination of techniques Table 4 demonstrates the performance (mean of accuracy and macro-f1) between different combinations of our techniques using a `bge-large-en-v1.5` model. We observe that the addition of paraphrasing increases performance by an average of +2.06% compared to methods without, supporting our hypothesis (3) that inference-time paraphrasing can benefit dataless intent classification. We observe that masking increases performance by an average of +1.80% and the addition of masked embedding only when entity overlaps are predicted increases performance by +0.32% on average. We perform further ablations over combinations of techniques using other models in Appendix E and note similar behaviour across different models.

Choice of Descriptions To investigate whether our proposed method is sensitive to the choice of intent descriptions, we generate paraphrases of our manually produced descriptions with increasing temperature values and sampled 200 combinations of descriptions for each dataset. Table 5 contains the mean and standard deviations of the macro-f1 scores for each dataset, we report macro-f1 for this ablations experiment due to the severely unbalanced nature of the ATIS dataset towards a single class `flight` (accounting for $\sim 74\%$ of the dataset). Further details on description paraphrase generation and sampling along with examples are provided in Appendix F. Methods using only tokenized intent labels are outperformed by our methods using label descriptions ($+4.51\%$), with further improvements from the addition of paraphrasing and masking ($+8.00\%$). The overall scores per dataset are slightly affected by the choice of intent descriptions, with standard deviations between 1-2% with the exception of the ATIS dataset. Future work could focus on the combination of multiple intent descriptions (via paraphrasing) or description refinement with unsupervised training (Chu et al., 2021; Müller et al., 2022) to further improve robustness to the choice of descriptions.

7 Analysis and Future Work

In-Domain Saturation We visualise the embeddings generated by our best-performing model (BGE_{Large}) on the 4 evaluation datasets using t-SNE (van der Maaten and Hinton, 2008), along with the embedding for the intent label description to gain insight into the source of errors in our approach. Figure 1 shows the distribution of embeddings on the ATIS and SNIPS datasets. In the interest of space, visualisations of CLINC and MASSIVE are shown in Appendix G . We observe a poor alignment on the ATIS dataset between the intent label descriptions (Figure 1a) and utterance embeddings corresponding to each class, possibly explaining the poor performance in general on this dataset across models. We note the single-domain nature of the ATIS dataset, with all utterances relating to air-travel/flight; additionally, we note the significantly imbalanced nature of the ATIS dataset (Nan et al., 2021), with $\sim 74\%$ of utterances belonging to the `flight` class, which is a label that overlaps the domain of the dataset. We hypothesise this may lead to the intent label descriptions being much worse at capturing semantic information distinct to each class. This is supported by analysis of the pairwise embedding similarities of utterances

Setup	ATIS	SNIPS	CLINC	MASSIVE	Overall
Tokenized Intent Labels	40.11	78.74	72.45	54.53	61.46
Intent Label Descriptions	42.00 ± 3.91	86.97 ± 2.05	73.77 ± 1.10	61.12 ± 1.04	65.97 ± 2.02
+ Paraphrase & Masking	**46.83** ± 4.18	**91.21** ± 1.61	**76.17** ± 1.14	**63.61** ± 1.19	**69.46** ± 2.03

Table 5: Comparison of macro-f1 score across 200 sampled combinations of descriptions for our setups with/without paraphrasing and masking. Note our combined approach outperforms tokenized labels across all datasets.

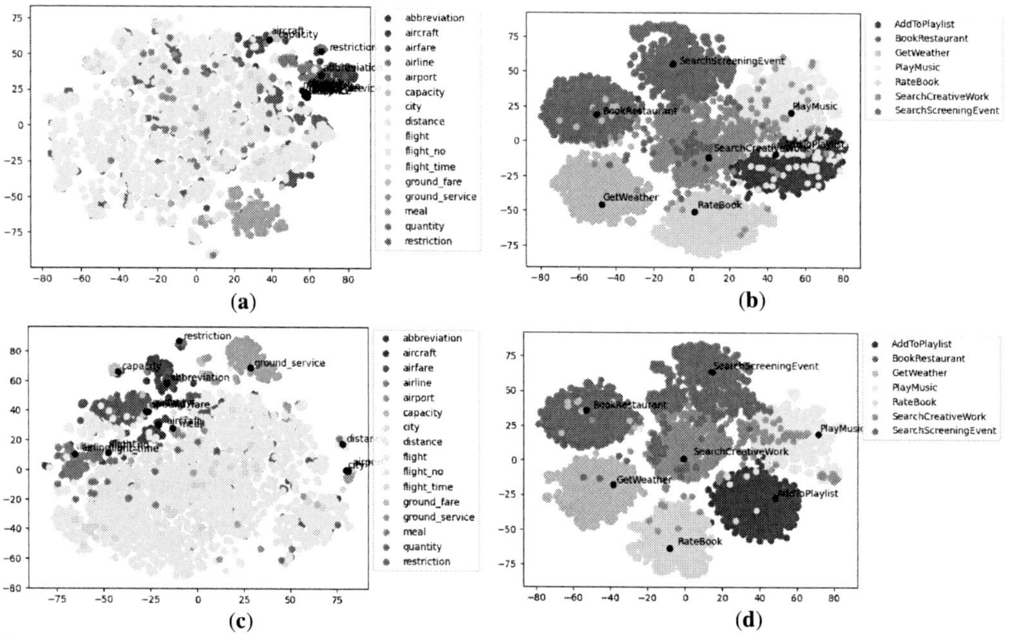

Figure 1: t-SNE (van der Maaten and Hinton, 2008) visualisation of embeddings computed using BGE_{Large}, class label description embeddings are shown in black and labelled. (**Row 1**) Embeddings of ATIS (**a**) and SNIPS (**b**), (**Row 2**) Embeddings with Paraphrasing and Masking for ATIS (**c**) and SNIPS (**d**).

belonging to the same class vs utterances belonging to different classes (Table 13) where models' embeddings on the ATIS dataset consistently had lower percentage-difference in embedding similarity between *in*-class and *out*-class, implying more difficulty in distinguishing the utterances using solely embeddings. This issue is mitigated to some degree with our addition of paraphrasing and masking, as the number of misclassifications where there are entity overlaps between classes is reduced on average by 19.19%. We see this visually in Figure 1d as the cluster for each class is more distinct compared to 1b. Errors from classes with overlapping entities in SNIPS are reduced by 29.31%.

Error Analysis We perform qualitative analysis of the remaining errors and identify two categories of commonly occurring errors. (1) *Description Scope:* Our approach utilises a single description for each intent and can work well when an intent concerns a limited number of topics; however, intents such as `meta` and `small_talk` from the CLINC dataset, and `qa` from the MASSIVE dataset can encompass a significantly broader range of topics than other intents within the same dataset. The impact of topical granularity per intent class and the potential for a hierarchical approach to intent classes in a dataless setting can be the focus of future work in this area. (2) *Action Overlap:* Our approach mitigates some errors arising from shared entities across intents through masking. Whilst this has shown success in reducing errors of this nature (i.e. between `PlayMusic` and `AddToPlaylist` from the SNIPS dataset), it is less successful in events where an action is shared across classes, such as `play` from the MASSIVE dataset, and `SearchCreativeWork` and `SearchScreeningEvent` from the SNIPS-NLU dataset. Future work could investigate the potential to decouple the desired *action* and *object*

Dataset	Top-1	Top-3	Top-5	Top-10
ATIS	67.70	93.38	96.03	98.10
SNIPS-NLU	89.78	97.13	99.43	100.00
CLINC	77.24	91.71	94.86	97.41
MASSIVE	61.45	81.85	87.79	92.79
Average	74.04	91.01	94.53	97.08

Table 6: Percentage of correct labels within Top-k ranked by embedding similarity per evaluation dataset, averaged across 11 selected models.

(topical information) in utterance embeddings.

Label Candidate Analysis We observed from our results (Table 2) that our approach, despite outperforming strong baselines on ATIS and MASSIVE datasets, still consistently underperforms compared to the same setup on SNIPS-NLU and CLINC. We therefore investigate the position of the correct label when ranking embedding similarities. Table 6 shows the percentage of examples where the correct label is ranked within the top-k by embedding similarity for $k = 1, 3, 5, 10$. We note for erroneous predictions, the correct label is within the Top-3 in 67.11% of cases, 81.89% in Top-5 and 90.94% in Top-10. This implies that our approach can be used to identify candidate intents from a larger set of intents, with a high success rate even for small values of k (i.e. 91.01% Top-3).

Analysis Summary Our proposed approach performs well overall against the strong baseline methods in unseen intent classification; however, it struggles in certain instances with overlaps in intents within the same domain. We identified potential areas for future work to pursue in tackling said issues. The results of our experiments have shown intent label descriptions can perform well as intent prototypes in this problem setting, and that the addition of paraphrasing and masking can further improve performance.

Limitations This approach contains a number of limitations: We have identified issues with the descriptiveness of individual labels earlier in this section, and textual labels may not be readily available for certain datasets, though summarisation methods may be effectively applied to a few user utterances to produce such labels. Our evaluation compares against previous works using scores as reported in their respective papers, further work can be done to replicate their experiments to mitigate any potential risk arising from differences in experimental settings. Future work may also investigate the application of descriptions to tasks outside of intent classification, such as emotion recognition (Rashkin et al., 2019).

8 Conclusion

Dataless classification allows for scaling to a large number of unseen classes without requiring training on labelled, task-specific data. The benefits of such an approach can enhance development of task-oriented dialogue systems in application to data-poor or compute-limited scenarios where supported intents may also change as the system is developed. In this paper, we have explored the potential of current SOTA text embedding models in dataless intent classification settings using three different approaches for representing intent classes and compared our results against strong zero-shot learning baselines. We proposed a method for standardising the generation of intent label descriptions with an aim to minimise the amount of human annotation required to further support scaling to high numbers of intent classes. Our results have shown that description-augmented dataless classification methods can achieve comparable, and sometimes superior performance to zero-shot methods on the task of intent classification.

9 Acknowledgements

We would like to thank Anandha Gopalan for his helpful comments on the paper. Student Ruoyu Hu was funded by UKRI CDT in AI4Health - grant number EP/S023283/1.

References

Edward Beeching, Clémentine Fourrier, Nathan Habib, Sheon Han, Nathan Lambert, Nazneen Rajani, Omar Sanseviero, Lewis Tunstall, and Thomas Wolf. 2023. Open llm leaderboard. https://huggingface.co/spaces/HuggingFaceH4/open_llm_leaderboard.

Marco Bellagente, Jonathan Tow, Dakota Mahan, Duy Phung, Maksym Zhuravinskyi, Reshinth Adithyan, James Baicoianu, Ben Brooks, Nathan Cooper, Ashish Datta, Meng Lee, Emad Mostaque, Michael Pieler, Nikhil Pinnaparju, Paulo Rocha, Harry Saini, Hannah Teufel, Niccolo Zanichelli, and Carlos Riquelme. 2024. Stable lm 2 1.6b technical report. *arXiv preprint arXiv:2402.17834*.

Ming-Wei Chang, Lev Ratinov, Dan Roth, and Vivek Srikumar. 2008. Importance of semantic representation: Dataless classification. In *Proceedings of the 23rd National Conference on Artificial Intelligence - Volume 2*, AAAI'08, page 830–835. AAAI Press.

Qian Chen, Zhu Zhuo, and Wen Wang. 2019. Bert for joint intent classification and slot filling. *ArXiv preprint arXiv:1902.10909*.

Xingyuan Chen, Yunqing Xia, Peng Jin, and John Carroll. 2015. Dataless text classification with descriptive lda. In *Proceedings of the Twenty-Ninth AAAI Conference on Artificial Intelligence*, AAAI'15, page 2224–2231. AAAI Press.

Zewei Chu, Karl Stratos, and Kevin Gimpel. 2021. Unsupervised label refinement improves dataless text classification. In *Findings of the Association for Computational Linguistics: ACL-IJCNLP 2021*, pages 4165–4178, Online. Association for Computational Linguistics.

Alice Coucke, Alaa Saade, Adrien Ball, Théodore Bluche, Alexandre Caulier, David Leroy, Clément Doumouro, Thibault Gisselbrecht, Francesco Caltagirone, Thibaut Lavril, Maël Primet, and Joseph Dureau. 2018. Snips voice platform: an embedded spoken language understanding system for private-by-design voice interfaces. *arXiv preprint arXiv:1805.10190*.

Marie-Catherine de Marneffe and Christopher D. Manning. 2008. The Stanford typed dependencies representation. In *Coling 2008: Proceedings of the workshop on Cross-Framework and Cross-Domain Parser Evaluation*, pages 1–8, Manchester, UK. Coling 2008 Organizing Committee.

Maarten De Raedt, Fréderic Godin, Thomas Demeester, and Chris Develder. 2023. IDAS: Intent discovery with abstractive summarization. In *Proceedings of the 5th Workshop on NLP for Conversational AI (NLP4ConvAI 2023)*, pages 71–88, Toronto, Canada. Association for Computational Linguistics.

Jacob Devlin, Ming-Wei Chang, Kenton Lee, and Kristina Toutanova. 2019. BERT: Pre-training of deep bidirectional transformers for language understanding. In *Proceedings of the 2019 Conference of the North American Chapter of the Association for Computational Linguistics: Human Language Technologies, Volume 1 (Long and Short Papers)*, pages 4171–4186, Minneapolis, Minnesota. Association for Computational Linguistics.

Thomas Dopierre, Christophe Gravier, and Wilfried Logerais. 2021. PROTAUGMENT: Unsupervised diverse short-texts paraphrasing for intent detection meta-learning. In *Proceedings of the 59th Annual Meeting of the Association for Computational Linguistics and the 11th International Joint Conference on Natural Language Processing (Volume 1: Long Papers)*, pages 2454–2466, Online. Association for Computational Linguistics.

Jack FitzGerald, Christopher Hench, Charith Peris, Scott Mackie, Kay Rottmann, Ana Sanchez, Aaron Nash, Liam Urbach, Vishesh Kakarala, Richa Singh, Swetha Ranganath, Laurie Crist, Misha Britan, Wouter Leeuwis, Gokhan Tur, and Prem Natarajan. 2023. MASSIVE: A 1M-example multilingual natural language understanding dataset with 51 typologically-diverse languages. In *Proceedings of the 61st Annual Meeting of the Association for Computational Linguistics (Volume 1: Long Papers)*, pages 4277–4302, Toronto, Canada. Association for Computational Linguistics.

Lingyu Gao, Debanjan Ghosh, and Kevin Gimpel. 2023. The benefits of label-description training for zero-shot text classification. In *Proceedings of the 2023 Conference on Empirical Methods in Natural Language Processing*, pages 13823–13844, Singapore. Association for Computational Linguistics.

Spyros Gidaris and Nikos Komodakis. 2018. Dynamic few-shot visual learning without forgetting. In *2018 IEEE/CVF Conference on Computer Vision and Pattern Recognition*, pages 4367–4375.

Shai Gretz, Alon Halfon, Ilya Shnayderman, Orith Toledo-Ronen, Artem Spector, Lena Dankin, Yannis Katsis, Ofir Arviv, Yoav Katz, Noam Slonim, and Liat Ein-Dor. 2023. Zero-shot topical text classification with LLMs - an experimental study. In *Findings of the Association for Computational Linguistics: EMNLP 2023*, pages 9647–9676, Singapore. Association for Computational Linguistics.

Milan Gritta, Ruoyu Hu, and Ignacio Iacobacci. 2022. CrossAligner & co: Zero-shot transfer methods for task-oriented cross-lingual natural language understanding. In *Findings of the Association for Computational Linguistics: ACL 2022*, pages 4048–4061, Dublin, Ireland. Association for Computational Linguistics.

Charles T. Hemphill, John J. Godfrey, and George R. Doddington. 1990. The atis spoken language systems pilot corpus. *Speech and Natural Language: Proceedings of a Workshop Held at Hidden Valley, Pennsylvania*.

Shailza Jolly, Tobias Falke, Caglar Tirkaz, and Daniil Sorokin. 2020. Data-efficient paraphrase generation to bootstrap intent classification and slot labeling for new features in task-oriented dialog systems. In *Proceedings of the 28th International Conference on Computational Linguistics: Industry Track*, pages 10–20, Online. International Committee on Computational Linguistics.

Ashutosh Kumar, Satwik Bhattamishra, Manik Bhandari, and Partha Talukdar. 2019. Submodular optimization-based diverse paraphrasing and its effectiveness in data augmentation. In *Proceedings of the 2019 Conference of the North American Chapter of the Association for Computational Linguistics: Human Language Technologies, Volume 1 (Long and Short Papers)*, pages 3609–3619, Minneapolis, Minnesota. Association for Computational Linguistics.

Dmitry Lamanov, Pavel Burnyshev, Katya Artemova, Valentin Malykh, Andrey Bout, and Irina Piontkovskaya. 2022. Template-based approach to zero-shot intent recognition. In *Proceedings of the 15th International Conference on Natural Language Generation*, pages 15–28, Waterville, Maine, USA and virtual meeting. Association for Computational Linguistics.

Stefan Larson, Anish Mahendran, Joseph J. Peper, Christopher Clarke, Andrew Lee, Parker Hill, Jonathan K. Kummerfeld, Kevin Leach, Michael A. Laurenzano, Lingjia Tang, and Jason Mars. 2019. An evaluation dataset for intent classification and out-of-scope prediction. In *Proceedings of the 2019 Conference on Empirical Methods in Natural Language Processing and the 9th International Joint Conference on Natural Language Processing (EMNLP-IJCNLP)*, pages 1311–1316, Hong Kong, China. Association for Computational Linguistics.

Yuanzhi Li, Sébastien Bubeck, Ronen Eldan, Allie Del Giorno, Suriya Gunasekar, and Yin Tat Lee. 2023a. Textbooks are all you need ii: phi-1.5 technical report. *arXiv preprint arXiv:2309.05463*.

Yuezhang Li, Ronghuo Zheng, Tian Tian, Zhiting Hu, Rahul Iyer, and Katia Sycara. 2016. Joint embedding of hierarchical categories and entities for concept categorization and dataless classification. In *Proceedings of COLING 2016, the 26th International Conference on Computational Linguistics: Technical Papers*, pages 2678–2688, Osaka, Japan. The COLING 2016 Organizing Committee.

Zehan Li, Xin Zhang, Yanzhao Zhang, Dingkun Long, Pengjun Xie, and Meishan Zhang. 2023b. Towards general text embeddings with multi-stage contrastive learning. *arXiv preprint arXiv:2308.03281*.

Han Liu, Xiaotong Zhang, Lu Fan, Xuandi Fu, Qimai Li, Xiao-Ming Wu, and Albert Y.S. Lam. 2019. Reconstructing capsule networks for zero-shot intent classification. In *Proceedings of the 2019 Conference on Empirical Methods in Natural Language Processing and the 9th International Joint Conference on Natural Language Processing (EMNLP-IJCNLP)*, pages 4799–4809, Hong Kong, China. Association for Computational Linguistics.

Han Liu, Siyang Zhao, Xiaotong Zhang, Feng Zhang, Junjie Sun, Hong Yu, and Xianchao Zhang. 2022. A simple meta-learning paradigm for zero-shot intent classification with mixture attention mechanism. In *Proceedings of the 45th International ACM SIGIR Conference on Research and Development in Information Retrieval*, SIGIR '22, page 2047–2052, New York, NY, USA. Association for Computing Machinery.

Samuel Louvan and Bernardo Magnini. 2020. Recent neural methods on slot filling and intent classification for task-oriented dialogue systems: A survey. In *Proceedings of the 28th International Conference on Computational Linguistics*, pages 480–496, Barcelona, Spain (Online). International Committee on Computational Linguistics.

Aaron Mueller, Jason Krone, Salvatore Romeo, Saab Mansour, Elman Mansimov, Yi Zhang, and Dan Roth. 2022. Label semantic aware pre-training for few-shot text classification. In *Proceedings of the 60th Annual Meeting of the Association for Computational Linguistics (Volume 1: Long Papers)*, pages 8318–8334, Dublin, Ireland. Association for Computational Linguistics.

Niklas Muennighoff, Nouamane Tazi, Loic Magne, and Nils Reimers. 2023. MTEB: Massive text embedding benchmark. In *Proceedings of the 17th Conference of the European Chapter of the Association for Computational Linguistics*, pages 2014–2037, Dubrovnik, Croatia. Association for Computational Linguistics.

Thomas Müller, Guillermo Pérez-Torró, and Marc Franco-Salvador. 2022. Few-shot learning with Siamese networks and label tuning. In *Proceedings of the 60th Annual Meeting of the Association for Computational Linguistics (Volume 1: Long Papers)*, pages 8532–8545, Dublin, Ireland. Association for Computational Linguistics.

Guoshun Nan, Jiaqi Zeng, Rui Qiao, Zhijiang Guo, and Wei Lu. 2021. Uncovering main causalities for long-tailed information extraction. In *Proceedings of the 2021 Conference on Empirical Methods in Natural Language Processing*, pages 9683–9695, Online and Punta Cana, Dominican Republic. Association for Computational Linguistics.

Arvind Neelakantan, Tao Xu, Raul Puri, Alec Radford, Jesse Michael Han, Jerry Tworek, Qiming Yuan, Nikolas Tezak, Jong Wook Kim, Chris Hallacy, Johannes Heidecke, Pranav Shyam, Boris Power, Tyna Eloundou Nekoul, Girish Sastry, Gretchen Krueger, David Schnurr, Felipe Petroski Such, Kenny Hsu, Madeleine Thompson, Tabarak Khan, Toki Sherbakov, Joanne Jang, Peter Welinder, and Lilian Weng. 2022. Text and code embeddings by contrastive pre-training. *arXiv preprint arXiv:2201.10005*.

Jianmo Ni, Chen Qu, Jing Lu, Zhuyun Dai, Gustavo Hernandez Abrego, Ji Ma, Vincent Zhao, Yi Luan, Keith Hall, Ming-Wei Chang, and Yinfei Yang. 2022. Large dual encoders are generalizable retrievers. In *Proceedings of the 2022 Conference on Empirical Methods in Natural Language Processing*, pages 9844–9855, Abu Dhabi, United Arab Emirates. Association for Computational Linguistics.

OpenAI. 2023. Gpt-4 technical report. *arXiv preprint arXiv:2303.08774*.

Artem Popov, Victor Bulatov, Darya Polyudova, and Eugenia Veselova. 2019. Unsupervised dialogue intent detection via hierarchical topic model. In *Proceedings of the International Conference on Recent Advances in Natural Language Processing (RANLP 2019)*, pages 932–938, Varna, Bulgaria. INCOMA Ltd.

Colin Raffel, Noam Shazeer, Adam Roberts, Katherine Lee, Sharan Narang, Michael Matena, Yanqi Zhou,

Wei Li, and Peter J. Liu. 2020. Exploring the limits of transfer learning with a unified text-to-text transformer. *J. Mach. Learn. Res.*, 21(1).

Hannah Rashkin, Eric Michael Smith, Margaret Li, and Y-Lan Boureau. 2019. Towards empathetic open-domain conversation models: A new benchmark and dataset. In *Proceedings of the 57th Annual Meeting of the Association for Computational Linguistics*, pages 5370–5381, Florence, Italy. Association for Computational Linguistics.

Gaurav Sahu, Pau Rodriguez, Issam Laradji, Parmida Atighehchian, David Vazquez, and Dzmitry Bahdanau. 2022. Data augmentation for intent classification with off-the-shelf large language models. In *Proceedings of the 4th Workshop on NLP for Conversational AI*, pages 47–57, Dublin, Ireland. Association for Computational Linguistics.

Sebastian Schuster and Christopher D. Manning. 2016. Enhanced English Universal Dependencies: An improved representation for natural language understanding tasks. In *Proceedings of the Tenth International Conference on Language Resources and Evaluation (LREC'16)*, pages 2371–2378, Portorož, Slovenia. European Language Resources Association (ELRA).

Yangqiu Song and Dan Roth. 2014. On dataless hierarchical text classification. In *Proceedings of the Twenty-Eighth AAAI Conference on Artificial Intelligence*, AAAI'14, page 1579–1585. AAAI Press.

Hongjin Su, Weijia Shi, Jungo Kasai, Yizhong Wang, Yushi Hu, Mari Ostendorf, Wen-tau Yih, Noah A. Smith, Luke Zettlemoyer, and Tao Yu. 2023. One embedder, any task: Instruction-finetuned text embeddings. In *Findings of the Association for Computational Linguistics: ACL 2023*, pages 1102–1121, Toronto, Canada. Association for Computational Linguistics.

Yixuan Su, Lei Shu, Elman Mansimov, Arshit Gupta, Deng Cai, Yi-An Lai, and Yi Zhang. 2022. Multi-task pre-training for plug-and-play task-oriented dialogue system. In *Proceedings of the 60th Annual Meeting of the Association for Computational Linguistics (Volume 1: Long Papers)*, pages 4661–4676, Dublin, Ireland. Association for Computational Linguistics.

Lewis Tunstall, Edward Beeching, Nathan Lambert, Nazneen Rajani, Kashif Rasul, Younes Belkada, Shengyi Huang, Leandro von Werra, Clémentine Fourrier, Nathan Habib, Nathan Sarrazin, Omar Sanseviero, Alexander M. Rush, and Thomas Wolf. 2023. Zephyr: Direct distillation of lm alignment. *arXiv preprint arXiv:2310.16944*.

Mina Valizadeh and Natalie Parde. 2022. The AI doctor is in: A survey of task-oriented dialogue systems for healthcare applications. In *Proceedings of the 60th Annual Meeting of the Association for Computational Linguistics (Volume 1: Long Papers)*, pages 6638–6660, Dublin, Ireland. Association for Computational Linguistics.

Aaron van den Oord, Yazhe Li, and Oriol Vinyals. 2019. Representation learning with contrastive predictive coding. *arXiv preprint arXiv:1807.03748*.

Laurens van der Maaten and Geoffrey Hinton. 2008. Visualizing data using t-sne. *Journal of Machine Learning Research*, 9(86):2579–2605.

Liang Wang, Nan Yang, Xiaolong Huang, Binxing Jiao, Linjun Yang, Daxin Jiang, Rangan Majumder, and Furu Wei. 2022. Text embeddings by weakly-supervised contrastive pre-training. *arXiv preprint arXiv:2212.03533*.

Zhongyu Wei, Qianlong Liu, Baolin Peng, Huaixiao Tou, Ting Chen, Xuanjing Huang, Kam-fai Wong, and Xiangying Dai. 2018. Task-oriented dialogue system for automatic diagnosis. In *Proceedings of the 56th Annual Meeting of the Association for Computational Linguistics (Volume 2: Short Papers)*, pages 201–207, Melbourne, Australia. Association for Computational Linguistics.

Tsung-Hsien Wen, David Vandyke, Nikola Mrkšić, Milica Gašić, Lina M. Rojas-Barahona, Pei-Hao Su, Stefan Ultes, and Steve Young. 2017. A network-based end-to-end trainable task-oriented dialogue system. In *Proceedings of the 15th Conference of the European Chapter of the Association for Computational Linguistics: Volume 1, Long Papers*, pages 438–449, Valencia, Spain. Association for Computational Linguistics.

Congying Xia, Chenwei Zhang, Xiaohui Yan, Yi Chang, and Philip Yu. 2018. Zero-shot user intent detection via capsule neural networks. In *Proceedings of the 2018 Conference on Empirical Methods in Natural Language Processing*, pages 3090–3099, Brussels, Belgium. Association for Computational Linguistics.

Shitao Xiao, Zheng Liu, Yingxia Shao, and Zhao Cao. 2022. RetroMAE: Pre-training retrieval-oriented language models via masked auto-encoder. In *Proceedings of the 2022 Conference on Empirical Methods in Natural Language Processing*, pages 538–548, Abu Dhabi, United Arab Emirates. Association for Computational Linguistics.

Shitao Xiao, Zheng Liu, Peitian Zhang, and Niklas Muennighof. 2023. C-pack: Packaged resources to advance general chinese embedding. *arXiv preprint arXiv:2309.07597*.

Guangfeng Yan, Lu Fan, Qimai Li, Han Liu, Xiaotong Zhang, Xiao-Ming Wu, and Albert Y.S. Lam. 2020. Unknown intent detection using Gaussian mixture model with an application to zero-shot intent classification. In *Proceedings of the 58th Annual Meeting of the Association for Computational Linguistics*, pages 1050–1060, Online. Association for Computational Linguistics.

Zhao Yan, Nan Duan, Peng Chen, Ming Zhou, Jianshe Zhou, and Zhoujun Li. 2017. Building task-oriented dialogue systems for online shopping. In *Proceedings of the Thirty-First AAAI Conference on Artificial Intelligence*, AAAI'17, page 4618–4625. AAAI Press.

Wenpeng Yin, Jamaal Hay, and Dan Roth. 2019. Benchmarking zero-shot text classification: Datasets, evaluation and entailment approach. In *Proceedings of the 2019 Conference on Empirical Methods in Natural Language Processing and the 9th International Joint Conference on Natural Language Processing (EMNLP-IJCNLP)*, pages 3914–3923, Hong Kong, China. Association for Computational Linguistics.

Daochen Zha and Chenliang Li. 2019. Multi-label dataless text classification with topic modeling. *Knowl. Inf. Syst.*, 61(1):137–160.

Yiwen Zhang, Caixia Yuan, and Xiaojie Wang. 2021. Generalized zero-shot text classification via interclass relationship. In *2021 IEEE 7th International Conference on Cloud Computing and Intelligent Systems (CCIS)*, pages 413–417.

Yiwen Zhang, Caixia Yuan, Xiaojie Wang, Ziwei Bai, and Yongbin Liu. 2022. Learn to adapt for generalized zero-shot text classification. In *Proceedings of the 60th Annual Meeting of the Association for Computational Linguistics (Volume 1: Long Papers)*, pages 517–527, Dublin, Ireland. Association for Computational Linguistics.

A Utterance Paraphrasal

Table 7 contains an example template used to generate paraphrases for utterances from the CLINC dataset. Examples used in the template do not appear in the dataset and do not make explicit mentions of classes. We use `length_penalty=-1` to encourage shorter outputs, `repetition_penalty=1.2` and `num_beams=3`, we use default values for all other generation parameters.

We perform an additional ablation study over the choice of examples in the paraphrase generation template using 9 different examples across 3 configurations for each of SNIPS and MASSIVE datasets. We select these datasets specifically as we believe they differ sufficiently in number of intents and domains. Across 3 ablation configurations and the original paraphrasing setup, we obtain an overall score (mean of accuracy and macro-f1) of $92.66 \pm 0.19\%$ for SNIPS and $65.48 \pm 0.18\%$ for MASSIVE. As the standard deviation is low in both instances, we conclude that the choice of examples in the paraphrase generation prompt has little impact on the final performance through our setup.

Prompt
Given an utterance, describe what the user is asking. sentence: "set an alarm for every weekday at 7 am" description: user is asking to set an alarm for every weekday at 7am sentence: "can you show me the step-by-step instructions to bake chocolate chip cookies" description: user is asking for recipe for chocolate chip cookies sentence: "could you please tell me what time it is now" description: user is asking for the current time sentence: "{}" description:

Table 7: Example template used to generate user utterance paraphrases from the CLINC dataset.

B Example Masking Procedure

Given an user utterance "i want to watch animated movies at Showcase Cinemas", we first perform dependency parsing to identify utterance objects that can be masked. Figure 2 shows an illustration of the resulting parsed dependency relations. Following the approach outlined in Section 3.3.3, we mask out nodes with any of `{dobj, pobj, ccomp}` relations, namely "animated movies" and "Showcase Cinemas" to produce the resulting masked representation "i want to watch [MASK] at [MASK]".

C Details of selected models

Basic model specifications are shown in Table 8.

Model	s	d_h	l	$\mu_{\textbf{MTEB}}$
InstructOR$_{Large}$	1.34	768	512	61.59
E5-v2$_{Base}$	0.44	768	512	61.50
E5-v2$_{Large}$	1.34	1024	512	62.25
Multilingual-E5$_{Large}$	2.24	1024	514	61.50
E5$_{Large}$	1.34	1024	512	61.42
GTE$_{Small}$	0.07	384	512	61.36
GTE$_{Base}$	0.22	768	512	62.39
GTE$_{Large}$	0.67	1024	512	63.13
BGE$_{Small}$	0.13	384	512	62.17
BGE$_{Base}$	0.44	768	512	63.55
BGE$_{Large}$	1.34	1024	512	64.23
OpenAI-Ada-002	-	1536	8191	60.99

Table 8: Specifications of selected models grouped by training method. Column s shows model size (GB), d_h embedding dimensions, l maximum sequence length and $\mu_{\textbf{MTEB}}$ averaged performance on MTEB benchmark.

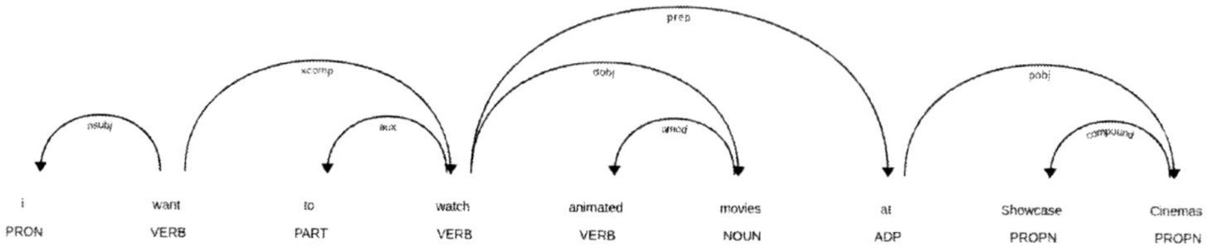

Figure 2: Example dependency parse tree from the SNIPS dataset.

InstructOR (Su et al., 2023) embeds the utterance with a task description, allowing for task-specific conditioning at inference time, with good performance on unseen domains. Trained on 330 datasets using a contrastive learning objective (Ni et al., 2022). This family of models is initialised from GTR (Ni et al., 2022) models, which are in-turn initialised from T5 (Raffel et al., 2020) models.

E5 (Wang et al., 2022) performs unsupervised pretraining on the model on $\sim$270M text pairs using an InfoNCE (van den Oord et al., 2019) objective with other utterances within the batch acting as negative examples, followed by supervised fine-tuning on 3 datasets. We select the *Base* and *Large* variants, initialised from *bert-base-uncased* and *bert-large-uncased-whole-word-masking* respectively.

GTE (Li et al., 2023b) pretrains the model on $\sim$800M text pairs and fine-tunes using 33 datasets. The contrastive learning objective used in this work considers, for each query-document pair (q_i, d_i) in a batch, the pairwise relation to the remaining examples $\{(q_j, d_j)\}_{j \neq i}$. The embedding similarities $s(q_i, d_j)$, $s(q_i, q_j)$, $s(d_i, d_j)$ are added to the partition function, where $s(q, d)$ is the cosine similarity between two embeddings.

BGE The work (Xiao et al., 2023) initialised from BERT (Devlin et al., 2019) models and trained using RetroMAE (Xiao et al., 2022) whereby both the input sentence and sentence embeddings in an autoencoder setup are randomly masked during MLM training. The authors use `[CLS]` token embeddings as the sentence representation. Our experimentation showed a slight improvement when using averaged token embeddings (Mean performance $+0.82\%$ *Tokenized-labels*, $+1.06\%$ *Class-description*).

D Full Results

See Table 9 for individual accuracy and macro-f1 scores by task and model.

E Further Ablations

We conduct further ablation studies using `bge-small-en-v1.5` (Table 10) and `gte-large` (Table 11) models to verify the findings of our main ablation study conducted on `bge-large-en-v1.5` (Table 4). We note that similar trends are observed with the different models, in that our proposed setup utilising a combination of the original utterance embedding with paraphrase embedding and masked utterance embedding using entity overlaps produced consistently higher scores.

F Description Paraphrasing

To produce paraphrases of intent descriptions, we leverage a `stablelm-2-1_6b-chat` model in a similar setup to our inference-time utterance paraphrasal. We increase temperature value from 0.5 to 4.1 in increments of 0.2, producing a paraphrase for each value. We then filter the generated set of descriptions for duplicates and enforce our *Label Preservation* and *Format Consistency* constraints, resulting in an average of 3.94 paraphrases per intent in addition to the original manually produced intent description. Each paraphrase has an average Levenshtein distance of 4.61 to the manual intent description. We replace half of all intent descriptions for each dataset with randomly sampled paraphrases, we produce 200 such combinations and repeat our experiments. Table 12 shows examples of paraphrased intent deescriptions for each dataset.

G t-SNE Visualisation

Due to the challenge to readability posed by the large number of intents in the CLINC dataset, instead sample the 15 top-performing (100% accuracy) and lowest-performing (24.47% accuracy) intent classes for illustration, with the results shown in Figures 1c and 1d respectively.

	Model	ATIS			SNIPS			CLINC			MASSIVE		
		Acc	F1	Mean	Acc	F1	Mean	Acc	F1	Mean	Acc	F1	Mean
Baselines	ICR	35.54	34.54	35.04	-	-	-	-	-	-	-	-	-
	SEG	-	-	-	69.61	69.31	69.46	-	-	-	-	-	-
	ML-SEG	-	-	-	77.08	75.97	76.53	-	-	-	-	-	-
	TIR_{Orig}	-	-	-	-	-	-	63.90	73.10	68.50	-	-	-
	TIR_{Syn}	-	-	-	-	-	-	58.00	61.30	59.65	-	-	-
	CosT	46.04	45.21	45.62	47.73	62.84	55.28	62.73	70.28	66.50	-	-	-
	LTA	66.09	**55.02**	60.55	90.09	84.22	87.16	73.18	75.74	74.46	-	-	-
	TTC_D	-	-	-	-	-	-	-	54.73	-	-	54.22	-
	Baselines	66.09	**55.02**	60.55	90.09	84.22	87.16	73.18	75.74	74.46	-	54.22	-
Tokenized Intent Labels	Instr._{Large}	12.41	25.03	18.72	82.71	82.07	82.39	64.50	61.02	62.76	51.86	47.62	49.74
	E5-v2_{Base}	13.20	27.58	20.39	77.30	76.96	77.13	65.33	62.40	63.87	49.91	45.97	47.94
	E5-v2_{Large}	14.67	38.61	26.64	70.83	69.15	69.99	61.56	59.24	60.40	50.88	46.83	48.85
	mE5_{Large}	16.41	28.53	22.47	59.90	58.80	59.35	59.13	55.56	57.34	47.63	44.34	45.98
	E5_{Large}	44.71	36.43	40.57	75.68	73.21	74.44	70.27	67.96	69.11	51.30	49.78	50.54
	Ada-002	21.88	30.09	25.98	83.32	82.19	82.75	68.25	65.70	66.97	51.50	47.90	49.70
	GTE_{Small}	14.28	27.21	20.75	74.94	73.04	73.99	69.38	67.55	68.47	55.78	51.90	53.84
	GTE_{Base}	68.99	42.34	55.66	82.37	81.14	81.75	71.56	69.74	70.65	55.15	51.44	53.30
	GTE_{Large}	45.14	34.42	39.78	80.13	78.60	79.36	70.44	68.64	69.54	52.88	49.08	50.98
	BGE_{Small}	11.40	27.60	19.50	79.20	76.81	78.00	71.67	69.89	70.78	59.21	52.43	55.82
	BGE_{Base}	52.15	39.34	45.74	77.73	75.88	76.81	73.85	72.24	73.05	60.55	55.89	58.22
	BGE_{Large}	48.24	40.11	44.17	80.60	78.74	79.67	74.05	72.45	73.25	58.19	54.53	56.36
Intent Label Descriptions	Instr._{Large}	41.24	43.12	42.18	85.85	85.35	85.60	77.95	76.55	77.25	57.95	55.52	56.73
	E5-v2_{Base}	64.84	40.04	52.44	87.75	87.23	87.49	72.15	69.68	70.92	55.57	53.73	54.65
	E5-v2_{Large}	62.33	41.98	52.16	87.84	86.77	87.31	72.39	70.59	71.49	57.30	55.65	56.48
	mE5_{Large}	75.85	45.16	60.51	84.64	83.11	83.88	73.09	71.39	72.24	60.09	56.67	58.38
	E5_{Large}	63.60	41.52	52.56	89.00	88.83	88.92	75.50	74.25	74.88	58.00	56.32	57.16
	Ada-002	58.97	43.71	51.34	89.71	89.28	89.50	78.75	76.86	77.81	59.49	58.03	58.76
	GTE_{Small}	66.62	42.80	54.71	84.62	84.22	84.42	71.19	69.22	70.20	55.18	51.86	53.52
	GTE_{Base}	63.21	41.99	52.60	86.60	86.22	86.41	75.90	74.30	75.10	56.47	54.62	55.55
	GTE_{Large}	66.91	44.79	55.85	86.65	86.01	86.33	76.62	75.04	75.83	59.27	57.85	58.56
	BGE_{Small}	55.69	39.99	47.84	86.01	85.01	85.51	73.04	71.01	72.03	57.31	54.27	55.79
	BGE_{Base}	53.14	44.37	48.76	88.66	87.98	88.32	78.38	76.85	77.61	60.91	58.92	59.91
	BGE_{Large}	62.07	47.70	54.88	89.58	89.01	89.30	79.70	78.46	79.08	<u>63.29</u>	<u>62.88</u>	<u>63.09</u>
+ Paraphrase and Masking	Instr._{Large}	52.03	46.11	49.07	90.22	89.49	89.86	<u>80.82</u>	<u>79.51</u>	<u>80.17</u>	61.54	59.79	60.66
	E5-v2_{Base}	<u>78.39</u>	43.47	60.93	90.33	89.72	90.03	75.80	74.31	75.06	59.48	57.81	58.65
	E5-v2_{Large}	52.10	44.02	48.06	86.88	84.24	85.56	75.15	74.22	74.69	60.02	58.27	59.15
	mE5_{Large}	77.50	37.93	57.72	85.09	81.62	83.36	75.68	74.31	75.00	61.04	57.67	59.35
	E5_{Large}	65.37	42.19	53.78	91.96	<u>91.89</u>	<u>91.92</u>	76.40	76.13	76.27	61.01	59.17	60.09
	Ada-002	67.81	46.22	57.02	90.88	90.14	90.51	80.50	78.97	79.73	62.30	59.92	61.11
	GTE_{Small}	68.03	38.94	53.48	88.46	87.75	88.11	72.05	70.95	71.50	60.04	57.53	58.78
	GTE_{Base}	**80.50**	47.91	**64.20**	86.68	85.07	85.88	76.16	75.33	75.75	60.14	58.41	59.27
	GTE_{Large}	71.27	50.00	60.63	<u>92.00</u>	91.40	91.70	79.46	78.31	78.89	62.61	61.63	62.12
	BGE_{Small}	62.12	46.20	54.16	91.07	90.45	90.76	75.81	74.27	75.04	61.52	59.11	60.31
	BGE_{Base}	67.91	49.46	58.69	<u>92.00</u>	91.63	91.81	80.34	79.25	79.80	63.09	61.98	62.53
	BGE_{Large}	69.57	52.51	<u>61.04</u>	**92.81**	**92.33**	**92.57**	**81.95**	**81.09**	**81.52**	**65.49**	**65.76**	**65.62**

Table 9: Performance of baseline and selected models on 4 intent classification tasks. We report accuracy, macro-f1 score and the mean of both for each dataset. For each metric, **bold** denotes highest score, <u>underline</u> denotes second-highest

Setup	ATIS	SNIPS	CLINC	MASSIVE	Overall
embeds only	47.84	85.51	72.02	55.79	65.29
pp only	**55.57**	84.73	71.18	59.14	67.65
masked only	21.77	71.66	29.94	26.66	37.51
embeds + pp	52.87	86.83	**75.56**	<u>60.12</u>	68.85
embeds + masked	44.11	90.53	67.12	54.01	63.94
pp + masked	52.44	<u>91.16</u>	68.17	57.95	67.43
embeds + pp + masked	<u>54.16</u>	**91.19**	74.47	59.82	<u>69.91</u>
(overlap) embeds + masked	44.11	90.69	69.39	55.35	64.89
(overlap) pp + masked	52.44	90.68	69.41	58.32	67.71
(overlap) embeds + pp + masked	<u>54.16</u>	90.76	<u>75.04</u>	**60.23**	**70.05**

Table 10: Ablations on 4 intent classification datasets using a `bge-small-en-v1.5` model. **Overall** denotes the mean of accuracy and macro-f1 scores across all datasets.

Setup	ATIS	SNIPS	CLINC	MASSIVE	Overall
embeds only	55.85	86.33	75.83	58.56	69.14
pp only	51.39	83.93	75.87	60.49	67.92
masked only	35.15	75.00	35.71	31.45	44.33
embeds + pp	55.26	86.39	<u>78.86</u>	**62.29**	70.70
embeds + masked	**61.38**	**92.34**	72.92	57.10	70.94
pp + masked	59.17	91.69	73.21	59.86	70.98
embeds + pp + masked	60.64	91.89	78.64	61.97	<u>73.29</u>
(overlap) embeds + masked	**61.38**	<u>92.31</u>	74.41	57.91	71.50
(overlap) pp + masked	59.17	91.42	74.33	60.06	71.25
(overlap) embeds + pp + masked	60.64	91.70	**78.89**	<u>62.14</u>	**73.34**

Table 11: Ablations on 4 intent classification datasets using a `gte-large` model. **Overall** denotes the mean of accuracy and macro-f1 scores across all datasets.

H Embedding Similarities Analysis

We perform additional analysis on the mean embedding similarity of sentences within the same intent class (*in*-class) and of different intents (*out*-class). For a set of intent classes $\mathcal{C}$ and utterances $\mathcal{U}$, we calculate the mean *in*-class similarity $\mathbf{s}_{in}$ and *out*-class similarity $\mathbf{s}_{out}$ as

$$\mathbf{s}_{in} = \frac{1}{|\mathcal{C}|}\sum_{c\in\mathcal{C}}\sum_{u_i\in\mathcal{U}_c}\sum_{u_j\in\mathcal{U}_c\setminus\{u_i\}}\frac{s(\mathbf{h}(u_i),\mathbf{h}(u_j))}{n_c(n_c-1)}$$

$$\mathbf{s}_{out} = \frac{1}{|\mathcal{C}|}\sum_{c\in\mathcal{C}}\sum_{u_i\in\mathcal{U}_c}\sum_{u_j\in\mathcal{U}_{c'}}\frac{s(\mathbf{h}(u_i),\mathbf{h}(u_j))}{n_c n_{c'}}$$

where $\mathcal{U}_c$ and $\mathcal{U}_{c'}$ denotes the set of utterances belonging to class c and all classes other than c' respectively, n_c is the number of utterances in set $\mathcal{U}_c$. The mean *in*-class and *out*-class similarity scores are shown per dataset (Table 13). From a basic correlation analysis of the mean embedding similarity against a number of metrics, we note for model performance on the MTEB benchmark there exists a strong positive correlation to the difference Δ_s between *in*-class and *out*-class examples (Pearson $r = 0.72$, $p < 0.01$) as well as $\%\Delta_s$ (Pearson $r = 0.73$, $p < 0.01$), and there exists a strong negative correlation to the mean *out*-class similarity $\mu_{s_{out}}$ (Pearson $r = -0.72$, $p < 0.01$).

I Synthetic Examples

We compare additionally against synthetic utterance generated for each intent class. We leverage `gpt-3.5-turbo` (OpenAI, 2023) for this purpose, by including the tokenized intent labels and label description within the prompt to generate a set $\mathcal{S}$ of questions or commands fitting said intent i.e. "*Given a category* `tokenized_intent` *and the description* `description`*, Please generate* `n` *different example sentences of users asking questions or making commands that fit the given category.*". At inference time, we sample k synthetic

Intent	Description	Paraphrase
`abbreviation`	user is asking what an abbreviation stands for or mean	"user is asking for a definition or explanation of an abbreviation" "user wants clarification on an abbreviation meaning" "user is asking about the meaning of an abbreviation"
`aircraft`	user is asking about an aircraft	"user is asking about an aircraft ticket or booking details" "user wants to know about an aircraft" "user wants information about an aircraft"
`airfare`	user is asking about fares, costs or airfares	"user wants to know airfare prices" "user wants to know about airfare prices"
`AddToPlaylist`	user wants to add a song to a playlist	"user wants to include a song in their playlist" "user wants to incorporate a song into their music collection" "user wants to add a song to their playlist"
`RateBook`	user wants the rating of/to rate a book	"user wants to give an opinion on a book" "user wants to leave a rating for a book" "user wants to leave a review on/ rate the book"
`SearchScreeningEvent`	user wants to know when a movie is on/screening time of a movie	"user wants movie screening information" "user wants to know movie screening schedule" "user wants to know movie screening time"
`accept_reservations`	user wants to know if a location accept reservations	"user wants to check if the place allows reservations" "user wants to check if a place allows reservations" "user wants to check location reservations"
`alarm`	user wants to set or get an alarm	"user wants a time alarm" "user wants to set a reminder or schedule an alarm" "user wants to set an alarm clock"
`calendar`	user wants to know about events from their calendar	"user is asking for event details from their calendar" "user wants to see their calendar for upcoming events" "user wants to check events in their calendar"
`email_query`	user is asking about email	"user wants to know how to send an email" "user wants to know how to use email effectively" "user wants an email response or clarification"
`general_greet`	user is saying a greeting	"user wants to talk or greet someone" "user wants to greet or say hello" "user wants to greet you or acknowledge your presence"
`news_query`	user is asking about the news	"user wants to learn about the latest news" "user wants to know the latest news" "user wants news update or clarification"

Table 12: Intents, descriptions and example paraphrases from all 4 intent classification datasets.

Dataset	$\mu_{s_{in}}$	$\sigma_{s_{in}}$	$\mu_{s_{out}}$	$\sigma_{s_{out}}$	Δ_s	$\%\Delta_s$
ATIS	0.80	0.06	0.77	0.06	0.03	3.86
SNIPS	0.76	0.04	0.69	0.05	0.07	8.65
CLINC	0.83	0.05	0.68	0.05	0.15	17.86
MASSIVE	0.80	0.05	0.69	0.05	0.11	13.73

Table 13: Mean embedding similarity of sentences within the same class (*in*) and different classes (*out*). Δ_s denotes the average difference between *in*-class and *out*-class, $\%\Delta_s$ denotes the percentage average difference of similarity.

k	Metric	ATIS		SNIPS		CLINC	
		μ	σ	μ	σ	μ	σ
$k=1$	Mean	23.59	8.42	71.37	5.51	53.87	5.42
	Δ_{Label}	-6.15	-4.23	-4.94	-1.02	-13.31	0.37
	Δ_{Desc}	-24.08	4.38	-15.54	2.57	-20.60	2.48
$k=3$	Mean	28.63	7.41	77.27	4.16	64.65	3.21
	Δ_{Label}	-1.10	-5.23	0.96	-2.37	-2.53	-1.84
	Δ_{Desc}	-19.03	3.37	-9.64	1.22	-9.82	0.27
$k=5$	Mean	30.05	6.74	78.54	3.98	67.29	2.81
	Δ_{Label}	0.31	-5.90	2.24	-2.55	0.11	-2.23
	Δ_{Desc}	-17.62	2.70	-8.36	1.04	-7.18	-0.13
$k=10$	Mean	30.80	5.33	79.63	3.57	69.24	2.48
	Δ_{Label}	1.06	-7.31	3.32	-2.96	2.06	-2.57
	Δ_{Desc}	-16.87	1.29	-7.28	0.63	-5.23	-0.46
$k=15$	Mean	31.12	5.15	80.06	3.46	69.99	2.50
	Δ_{Label}	1.38	-7.49	3.75	-3.07	2.80	-2.55
	Δ_{Desc}	-16.55	1.12	-6.85	0.52	-4.49	-0.44

Table 14: Averaged mean of accuracy and macro-f1 scores experiments conducted across 20 samples and 12 models using k number of synthetic examples per intent class. Δ_{Label} and Δ_{Desc} are differences to the averaged performance of methods using tokenized labels and intent descriptions respectively.

examples for c classes and make prediction $\hat{y}_i$ as follows:

$$\hat{y}_i = \arg\max_c \frac{\sum_m^k s(\mathbf{h}(u_i), \mathbf{h}(s_m^c))}{k}$$

where s_m^c denotes the mth example utterance belonging to intent class $c \in \mathcal{C}$. Examples of synthetic utterances can be found in Appendix I. We report on the results separately in Section I.1 and the full results can be seen in Appendix J. We also consider synthetic examples generated using `gpt-4` but found the average performance to be lower on our task (Appendix K).

I.1 Results: Methods using Synthetic Data

We evaluate the efficacy of methods using synthetic examples by generating a set of $n = 20$ synthetic examples, from which we sample k to act as class prototypes, we repeat this procedure 20 times and compute the average performance across all samples. Table 14 shows averaged model performance across all 12 selected models and samples for $k = [1, 3, 5, 10, 15]$. For full results see Table 18 in Appendix J. We conducted additional experimentation with $k > 15$ but found further increasing k did not yield significant improvements in performance. We note our method using $k = 15$ synthetic examples outperforms tokenized labels on SNIPS (80.06 vs 76.30) and CLINC (69.99 vs 67.18) datasets, but underperforms slightly on the ATIS dataset (31.12 vs 31.70). Synthetic examples underperforms description-based methods by a considerable margin on all datasets, suggesting single intent label descriptions can be more powerful as class prototypes than synthetic instances. We note also the higher standard deviation σ in performance compared to the description-augmented method but lower compared to methods using tokenized labels.

I.2 Table of intents, descriptions and sampled synthetic examples generated using gpt-3.5-turbo

See Table 15 (ATIS), Table 16 (SNIPS) and Table 17 (CLINC).

J Full table of results for approach using synthetic examples generated using gpt-3.5-turbo

See Table 18.

K Table of averaged mean and standard deviation statistics for examples generated using gpt-4

See Table 19.

Intent	Description	Synthetic Examples
abbreviation	user is asking what an abbreviation stands for or mean	"what does eta stand for?" "can you tell me the meaning of atc?" "what is the abbreviation vfr referring to?"
aircraft	user is asking about an aircraft	"what is the maximum speed of this aircraft?" "can you provide me with the dimensions of the aircraft?" "how many passengers can this aircraft accommodate?"
airfare	user is asking about fares, costs or airfares	"what are the airfare options for a round-trip flight from new york to los angeles?" "can you provide me with the cost of a first-class airfare from london to paris?" "how much does it usually cost for a one-way airfare from tokyo to sydney?"
airline	user is asking about an airline/airlines	"which airline offers the most affordable tickets from los angeles to new york?" "can you recommend any airlines that provide extra legroom for tall passengers?" "what are the baggage restrictions for this airline?"
airport	user is asking about an airport/airports	"which airports in new york have direct flights to los angeles?" "can you provide me with information about the nearest airport to my current location?" "how long does it take to get from the city center to heathrow airport?"
capacity	user is asking about capacity (of an aircraft)	"what is the seating capacity of a boeing 747 aircraft?" "can you tell me the maximum passenger capacity of a airbus a380?" "what is the cargo capacity of a cessna 172 aircraft?"
cheapest	user is asking about the cheapest (fare)	"can you find me the cheapest flight from new york to los angeles?" "i need the cheapest airfare available for a one-way trip from london to barcelona." "what is the cheapest flight i can get from chicago to miami during the christmas holidays?"
city	user is asking about a city or place	"can you provide me with flight options to new york city?" "what are the popular attractions in san francisco?" "which airlines operate flights to tokyo?"
day_name	user is asking about a day (of the week)	"which day of the week is the best to book a flight?" "can you tell me the day of the week for my flight to new york?" "what is the departure day for the flight to london?"
distance	user is asking for the distance between places/locations	"what is the distance between new york and los angeles?" "calculate the distance from london to paris." "how far is it from sydney to melbourne?"
flight	user is asking about available flights	"what flights are available from new york city to los angeles tomorrow?" "can you please check if there are any direct flights from london to tokyo?" "i need to book a one-way flight from chicago to miami on the 15th of june."
flight_no	user is asking about a flight number	"what is the flight number for the flight from new york to london?" "can you provide me with the flight number for the 6:00 am departure to los angeles?" "i need to know the flight number for the red-eye flight to chicago."
flight_time	user is asking about departue time or schedule for a flight	"what is the flight time for the next available flight to new york?" "can you tell me the departure time for flight 123 to london?" "i need to know the schedule for flights leaving tomorrow morning."
ground_fare	user is asking about the ground fare at a destination	"what is the average ground fare in los angeles?" "can you provide information about ground fares in paris?" "how much should i expect to pay for ground transportation in london?"
ground_service	user is asking about ground service at a location	"what are the available ground services at this airport?" "can you provide me with information about ground services at the destination airport?" "is there wheelchair assistance available as part of the ground services?"
meal	user is asking about meals/catering	"what meal options are available for the flight?" "can i request a vegetarian meal for my flight?" "do you have any special meals for passengers with dietary restrictions?"
quantity	user is asking about the quantity/amount of something	"how many flight attendants are there on this flight?" "could you tell me the total weight of the luggage allowed per passenger?" "how many passengers are currently on board the plane?"
restriction	user is asking about restrictions	"can you please provide me with the baggage restrictions for my upcoming flight?" "what are the restrictions on carrying liquids in my hand luggage?" "are there any age restrictions for children traveling alone on your flights?"

Table 15: Intents, descriptions and synthetic examples for the ATIS dataset.

Intent	Description	Synthetic Examples
AddToPlaylist	user wants to add a song to a playlist	"hey, can you please add this new release to my workout playlist?" "add the latest hit by taylor swift to my party playlist, please." "can you include this classic rock track in my road trip playlist?"
BookRestaurant	user wants to book/make a reservation at a restaurant	"can you help me book a table at a fancy restaurant for this saturday?" "i would like to make a reservation for two at the most popular restaurant in town." "what is the best way to book a restaurant online?"
GetWeather	user wants to know about the weather	"what will be the weather like tomorrow?" "can you provide me with a detailed weather forecast for the next week?" "is it going to rain today?"
PlayMusic	user wants to play a song	"hey, playmusic! can you play 'shape of you' by ed sheeran?" "playmusic, please play some soothing music to help me relax." "i'm in the mood for some throwback tunes. playmusic, can you play 'don't stop believin' by journey?"
RateBook	user wants the rating of/to rate a book	"can anyone recommend a ratebook website where I can find reviews and ratings for the latest bestsellers?" "what's the highest-rated ratebook on the market right now? i want to make sure i'm picking something worthwhile." "i'd like some suggestions for popular ratebooks in the fantasy genre. any recommendations?"
SearchCreativeWork	user wants to find a creative work (book, song etc.)	"can you help me search for a creative work that is similar to harry potter?" "i'm looking for a book recommendation, search for a creative work with a thrilling mystery plot." "find me a song that has won multiple awards and has a catchy melody."
SearchScreeningEvent	user wants to know when a movie is on/screening time of a movie	"when is the next screening event for the movie avengers: endgame?" "what are the screening times for the romantic comedy crazy, stupid, love?" "can you tell me the showtimes for the movie joker in theaters nearby?"

Table 16: Intents, descriptions and synthetic examples for the SNIPS dataset.

Intent	Description	Synthetic Examples
timezone	user is asking about timezone	"can you please tell me the current timezone in new york city?" "what is the timezone difference between san francisco and tokyo?" "i need to know the exact timezone utc offset for london."
fun_fact	user wants to know a fun fact	"tell me a fun fact about the eiffel tower!" "i need a fun fact to impress my friends at dinner tonight." "give me a fun fact about dolphins, please."
date	user wants to know the current date	"what is today's date?" "can you tell me the current date?" "i need to know the date, please."
what_can_i_ask_you	user wants to know what can be asked	"what kind of questions are appropriate to ask you?" "can you provide me with a list of topics that i can ask you about?" "i'm curious, what type of questions am i allowed to ask in this category?"
todo_list_update	user wants to update or change todo list	"how can i edit my current todo list?" "can you show me how to modify my existing tasks in the todo list?" "is there a way to change the priority of items on the todo list?"
bill_balance	user wants to know their bill balance	"what is my current bill balance?" "can you please provide the details of my bill balance?" "i need to know how much is due on my bill."
schedule_meeting	user wants to schedule meeting	"can you help me schedule a meeting for next week?" "i need assistance in setting up a meeting with our new client." "how do i go about scheduling a team meeting for tomorrow?"
routing	user wants to know about routing number	"what is a routing number and why is it important for banking?" "how can i find the routing number for my bank account?" "can you explain the specific purpose of a routing number in online transactions?"
food_last	user wants to know how long a food lasts	"how long can i safely keep cooked chicken in the refrigerator?" "what is the shelf life of fresh milk at room temperature?" "can you give me some tips on how to extend the life of avocados?"
bill_due	user wants to know when a bill is due	"hey, can you remind me when my electricity bill is due?" "what's the due date for my credit card bill this month?" "i need to know when my phone bill is due. can you help me with that?"
time	user is asking for the time	"what is the current time?" "could you please tell me what time it is?" "do you have the time?"
freeze_account	user wants to freeze their account	"how can i freeze my account temporarily?" "i need to put a hold on my account, can you assist me?" "please freeze my account until further notice."
rollover_401k	user wants to know about 401k rollover	"how can i rollover my 401k into a new retirement account?" "can you explain the process of a 401k rollover to me?" "what are the benefits of doing a rollover with my 401k?"
travel_alert	user wants to know about travel alerts	"are there any current travel alerts that i should be aware of?" "notify me if there are any travel alerts for my upcoming destination." "can you provide me with the latest travel alerts for international travel?"
translate	user wants to translate	"can you translate this document from english to french?" "excuse me, i need assistance translating this menu into spanish." "how can i translate this phrase into italian?"

Table 17: Intents, descriptions and synthetic examples for 15 intents from the CLINC dataset.

	Model	ATIS			SNIPS			CLINC		
		Acc	F1	Mean	Acc	F1	Mean	Acc	F1	Mean
$n=1$	InstructOR$_{Large}$	32.77	23.99	28.38	72.60	69.26	70.93	56.94	53.71	55.32
	E5-v2$_{Base}$	27.01	19.30	23.16	70.28	66.52	68.40	50.05	47.21	48.63
	E5-v2$_{Large}$	29.50	19.12	24.31	68.09	64.41	66.25	47.24	44.54	45.89
	Multilingual-E5$_{Large}$	23.85	18.37	21.11	64.02	60.24	62.13	45.68	43.54	44.61
	E5$_{Large}$	28.57	20.22	24.40	69.35	66.13	67.74	54.44	51.38	52.91
	OpenAI-Ada-002	30.86	19.40	25.13	75.35	72.78	74.07	57.70	54.42	56.06
	GTE$_{Small}$	25.87	20.15	23.01	65.42	62.17	63.80	51.37	48.41	49.89
	GTE$_{Base}$	25.34	20.33	22.83	69.09	65.89	67.49	53.10	50.04	51.57
	GTE$_{Large}$	29.94	21.83	25.88	70.02	66.56	68.29	54.95	51.72	53.34
	BGE$_{Small}$	27.44	21.32	24.38	66.60	62.76	64.68	52.69	49.56	51.13
	BGE$_{Base}$	24.57	20.62	22.59	70.39	66.52	68.46	55.24	52.21	53.72
	BGE$_{Large}$	33.97	23.83	28.90	71.31	67.29	69.30	58.17	54.73	56.45
$n=3$	InstructOR$_{Large}$	39.20	29.25	34.22	76.71	72.39	74.55	67.88	64.84	66.36
	E5-v2$_{Base}$	35.75	26.97	31.36	76.25	71.56	73.90	63.52	60.63	62.08
	E5-v2$_{Large}$	40.41	27.85	34.13	75.68	70.98	73.33	62.35	59.47	60.91
	Multilingual-E5$_{Large}$	25.07	25.90	25.48	75.67	70.93	73.30	60.56	58.19	59.37
	E5$_{Large}$	37.33	29.64	33.48	74.57	70.24	72.40	67.18	64.25	65.72
	OpenAI-Ada-002	46.96	26.53	36.74	82.42	80.27	81.34	68.77	65.77	67.27
	GTE$_{Small}$	24.50	26.95	25.72	71.00	67.40	69.20	62.38	59.16	60.77
	GTE$_{Base}$	30.05	27.82	28.93	74.57	70.63	72.60	64.69	61.76	63.23
	GTE$_{Large}$	40.40	29.40	34.90	75.04	71.23	73.14	65.78	62.67	64.23
	BGE$_{Small}$	29.24	27.49	28.37	73.49	68.98	71.23	64.59	61.72	63.16
	BGE$_{Base}$	28.35	27.00	27.67	73.83	69.23	71.53	66.59	63.66	65.13
	BGE$_{Large}$	38.30	28.14	33.22	74.83	70.09	72.46	68.05	64.62	66.34
$n=5$	InstructOR$_{Large}$	41.77	32.86	37.31	78.36	74.08	76.22	70.30	67.51	68.90
	E5-v2$_{Base}$	34.49	28.76	31.63	78.53	73.47	76.00	66.75	63.94	65.34
	E5-v2$_{Large}$	36.82	29.53	33.17	78.02	73.66	75.84	65.70	62.76	64.23
	Multilingual-E5$_{Large}$	31.29	29.28	30.29	76.21	72.18	74.19	64.36	61.78	63.07
	E5$_{Large}$	37.24	32.79	35.01	76.04	71.20	73.62	69.63	66.62	68.13
	OpenAI-Ada-002	45.01	28.38	36.70	84.56	82.60	83.58	70.81	68.03	69.42
	GTE$_{Small}$	32.92	30.05	31.48	73.21	69.16	71.18	65.63	62.58	64.10
	GTE$_{Base}$	29.90	30.02	29.96	76.54	72.13	74.33	67.11	63.95	65.53
	GTE$_{Large}$	41.92	32.41	37.17	75.73	71.18	73.45	68.48	65.38	66.93
	BGE$_{Small}$	35.33	32.64	33.99	72.85	68.06	70.46	67.15	64.35	65.75
	BGE$_{Base}$	27.94	29.49	28.72	76.61	71.90	74.25	69.42	66.52	67.97
	BGE$_{Large}$	35.79	32.38	34.08	76.26	71.00	73.63	70.68	67.64	69.16
$n=10$	InstructOR$_{Large}$	47.38	33.77	40.58	80.58	76.50	78.54	72.37	69.68	71.03
	E5-v2$_{Base}$	37.04	32.17	34.60	80.31	74.92	77.61	69.59	66.86	68.23
	E5-v2$_{Large}$	46.80	32.53	39.66	79.11	74.31	76.71	68.65	65.70	67.17
	Multilingual-E5$_{Large}$	30.88	32.70	31.79	78.71	74.43	76.57	67.87	65.39	66.63
	E5$_{Large}$	41.44	34.74	38.09	77.83	73.35	75.59	72.42	69.62	71.02
	OpenAI-Ada-002	46.60	32.90	39.75	85.57	83.46	84.51	73.30	70.60	71.95
	GTE$_{Small}$	32.71	33.53	33.12	74.77	70.42	72.59	67.48	64.56	66.02
	GTE$_{Base}$	28.05	31.23	29.64	77.35	72.76	75.06	69.50	66.44	67.97
	GTE$_{Large}$	45.05	35.25	40.15	76.29	71.67	73.98	69.86	66.90	68.38
	BGE$_{Small}$	36.24	34.44	35.34	75.95	71.13	73.54	68.96	66.27	67.61
	BGE$_{Base}$	31.14	31.62	31.38	78.15	73.07	75.61	71.48	68.73	70.10
	BGE$_{Large}$	43.19	35.56	39.38	77.77	72.44	75.10	72.36	69.39	70.88
$n=15$	InstructOR$_{Large}$	40.59	35.40	37.99	80.57	75.75	78.16	73.10	70.54	71.82
	E5-v2$_{Base}$	42.17	34.44	38.31	80.25	74.65	77.45	70.18	67.50	68.84
	E5-v2$_{Large}$	47.71	33.67	40.69	79.86	74.66	77.26	69.70	66.69	68.19
	Multilingual-E5$_{Large}$	28.31	33.48	30.89	79.91	75.32	77.61	69.31	66.76	68.03
	E5$_{Large}$	42.42	36.31	39.36	78.02	73.00	75.51	73.13	70.26	71.69
	OpenAI-Ada-002	48.13	34.26	41.20	87.04	85.03	86.03	73.97	71.36	72.66
	GTE$_{Small}$	38.54	34.38	36.46	75.03	70.32	72.68	68.63	65.60	67.12
	GTE$_{Base}$	33.68	32.35	33.02	78.27	73.56	75.92	69.86	66.73	68.29
	GTE$_{Large}$	37.98	34.38	36.18	77.78	72.93	75.36	70.51	67.62	69.07
	BGE$_{Small}$	28.06	34.30	31.18	75.43	70.54	72.98	70.20	67.56	68.88
	BGE$_{Base}$	27.20	31.08	29.14	78.92	73.65	76.29	71.93	69.15	70.54
	BGE$_{Large}$	42.22	37.06	39.64	78.76	73.43	76.10	73.17	70.24	71.71

Table 18: Results per model using k synthetic examples averaged across 20 samples.

k	Metric	ATIS		SNIPS		CLINC	
		μ	σ	μ	σ	μ	σ
$k=1$	Mean	24.51	10.15	67.63	5.48	51.63	5.13
	Δ_{Label}	-7.19	-2.58	-8.68	-1.05	-15.56	0.08
	Δ_{Desc}	-27.38	6.37	-19.29	2.46	-22.92	2.12
$k=3$	Mean	31.19	8.61	73.25	4.49	63.71	2.76
	Δ_{Label}	-0.51	-4.11	-3.06	-2.04	-3.47	-2.29
	Δ_{Desc}	-20.70	4.84	-13.66	1.47	-10.83	-0.25
$k=5$	Mean	33.29	7.90	74.73	4.16	66.54	2.35
	Δ_{Label}	1.59	-4.82	-1.57	-2.37	-0.64	-2.70
	Δ_{Desc}	-18.60	4.13	-12.18	1.14	-8.00	-0.67
$k=10$	Mean	36.12	7.51	76.28	3.49	68.92	2.08
	Δ_{Label}	4.42	-5.21	-0.02	-3.04	1.73	-2.97
	Δ_{Desc}	-15.77	3.73	-10.63	0.48	-5.63	-0.94
$k=15$	Mean	36.17	7.13	76.78	3.75	69.74	1.93
	Δ_{Label}	4.47	-5.59	0.48	-2.78	2.55	-3.12
	Δ_{Desc}	-15.72	3.36	-10.13	0.73	-4.81	-1.09

Table 19: Averaged mean of accuracy and macro-f1 scores experiments conducted across 20 samples and 12 models using k number of synthetic examples per intent class generated using `gpt-4-1106-preview`. Δ_{Label} and Δ_{Desc} are differences to the averaged performance of methods using tokenized labels and intent descriptions respectively.

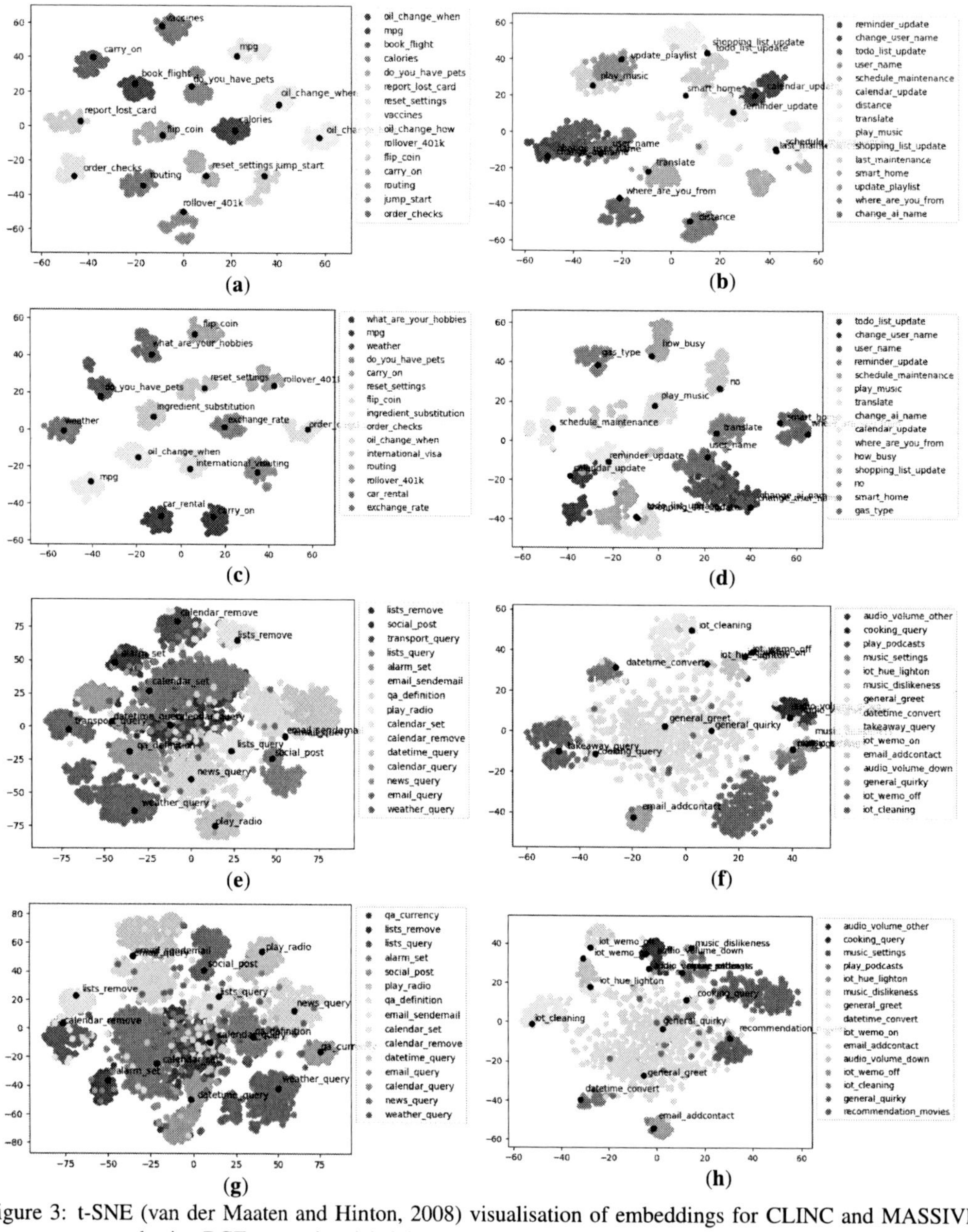

Figure 3: t-SNE (van der Maaten and Hinton, 2008) visualisation of embeddings for CLINC and MASSIVE datasets computed using BGE_{Large}, class label description embeddings are shown in black and labelled. (**Row 1**) Embeddings of top 15 and bottom 15 classes from CLINC, (**Row 2**) Embedding + Paraphrasing and Masking of top 15 and bottom 15 classes from CLINC, (**Row 3**) Embeddings for top 15 and bottom 15 classes from MASSIVE, (**Row 4**) Embedding + Paraphrasing and Masking of top 15 and bottom 15 classes from CLINC.

Revealing User Familiarity Bias in Task-Oriented Dialogue via Interactive Evaluation

Takyoung Kim[1,†] **Jamin Shin**[1,2,‡] **Young-Ho Kim**[1] **Sanghwan Bae**[2] **Sungdong Kim**[1,2]

NAVER AI Lab[1] NAVER Cloud[2]

tk30@illinois.edu jayshin.nlp@gmail.com yghokim@younghokim.net
{sanghwan.bae, sungdong.kim}@navercorp.com

Abstract

Most task-oriented dialogue (TOD) benchmarks assume users that know exactly how to use the system by constraining the user behaviors within the system's capabilities via strict user goals, namely "user familiarity" bias. This data bias deepens when it combines with data-driven TOD systems, as it is impossible to fathom the effect of it with existing static evaluations. Hence, we conduct an interactive user study to unveil how vulnerable TOD systems are against realistic scenarios. In particular, we compare users with 1) detailed goal instructions that conform to the system boundaries (*closed-goal*) and 2) vague goal instructions that are often unsupported but realistic (*open-goal*). Our study reveals that conversations in open-goal settings lead to catastrophic failures of the system, in which 92% of the dialogues had significant issues. Moreover, we conduct a thorough analysis to identify distinctive features between the two settings through error annotation. From this, we discover a novel "pretending" behavior, in which the system pretends to handle the user requests even though they are beyond the system's capabilities. We discuss its characteristics and toxicity while showing recent large language models can also suffer from this behavior.

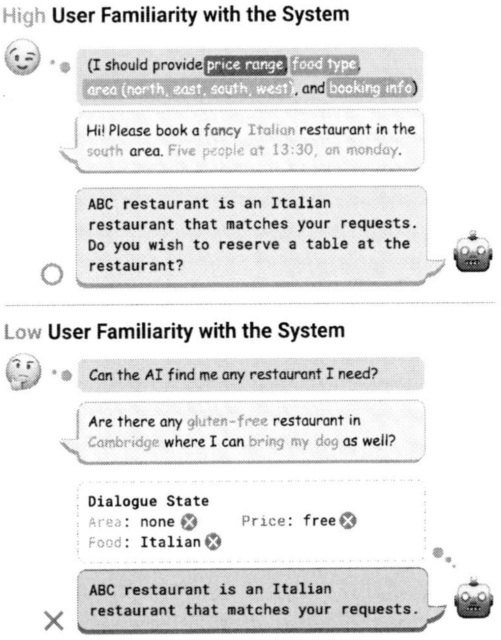

Figure 1: Contrastive dialogues according to user familiarity with the system. Users with high familiarity converse with the system within the predefined scenario since they already know the system well. However, users with low familiarity are more likely to talk about a broad range of topics beyond the system's capacities leading to the erroneous response of the system.

1 Introduction

Task-oriented dialogue (TOD) systems aim to accomplish specific user goals by comprehending their requests and making appropriate API calls or database (DB) searches (Young et al., 2013). TOD systems typically use a pipeline approach, connecting separate modules such as intent detection, dialogue state tracking, policy management, and natural language generation, often requiring complex rules or heuristics. End-to-end (E2E) TOD systems have been highlighted as a fully data-driven solution because of their concise implementation (Bordes et al., 2017; Wen et al., 2017). Recently, such TOD systems have significantly improved on top of pre-trained language models (Hosseini-Asl et al., 2020; Ham et al., 2020; Peng et al., 2021; He et al., 2022).

However, despite the numerous studies on TOD systems and the great successes of large language models, we argue that there is a huge gap between the TOD studies and deployable TOD systems. Among the many reasons hindering end-to-end systems from being widely adopted in the industry, the

[†]Work done as a research intern at NAVER AI Lab.
[‡]Work done while at NAVER AI Lab.

Proceedings of the 6th Workshop on NLP for Conversational AI (NLP4ConvAI 2024), pages 37–55
August 16, 2024 ©2024 Association for Computational Linguistics

instability of such systems makes it harder to match the robustness of conventional pipeline systems.

We hypothesize that the major source of this instability lies in the naive assumption about the users during TOD data collection. We call this the *user familiarity* bias, as illustrated in Figure 1. For instance, during Wizard-of-Oz style data collection (Kelley, 1984), the user-role workers are provided with detailed instructions on the goal they need to achieve which conforms with the system capabilities (Budzianowski et al., 2018; Byrne et al., 2019). Hence, as the user behaviors are strictly constrained, this process simulates users who know exactly how to use the system (Larson et al., 2019). Other datasets based on user simulation, such as M2M and SGD (Shah et al., 2018; Rastogi et al., 2020), include the same user familiarity bias, as they simulate users based on predefined user goals and rules specifying how to converse. On the other hand, real users in the wild often have fairly creative or vague goals way beyond the system coverage, and this user-side bias prevents us from modeling such realistic conversations.

In this paper, we conduct an interactive user study on one of the most-used Wizard-of-Oz-styled TOD benchmarks, MultiWOZ (Budzianowski et al., 2018), to investigate the impact of *user familiarity*. The main objective of this study is to determine whether the familiarity of the user with the TOD system's capabilities influences the successful completion of a conversational task. To do this, we first divide the users into two groups: *closed-goal* and *open-goal*. The former user group is provided with detailed user goal instructions that are from the MultiWOZ, while the latter is given only a portion of the instructions along with some realistic goals that are not supported by the system, thereby simulating users who are not familiar with TOD systems. Based on each goal type they are assigned to, the users converse with a recent E2E TOD system, GALAXY (He et al., 2022), which is trained on diverse TOD datasets including MultiWOZ.

Our user study reveals that 92% of the dialogues in the open-goal setting has significant issues that often lead to failure in achieving the user goals. Moreover, we find that various inconveniences caused by the TOD system force users to quit the conversation regardless of the goal types. We thoroughly analyze the resulting conversations to identify the impact of user familiarity by annotating erroneous turns. In particular, we figure out six prevalent errors in both goal settings. As expected, open-goal dialogues contain more problematic turns, and the open-goal setup causes more irrelevant and unfaithful responses.

In addition, we identify unfaithful responses as "pretending" behaviors of the system that primarily arises in the open-goal setting. This is a phenomenon similar to hallucination, in which the dialogue system pretends to handle the user's requests even though they are beyond the system's boundaries, but more potentially harmful because it is **almost impossible** for users to verify the reliability of the information during conversation since the hallucinated pieces of information are usually *service-specific*. We believe this issue is relatively underexplored as we witness most previous works focused on the closed-goal setting, and our qualitative analysis of the open-goal dialogues demonstrates that such pretending behaviors are prevalent and crucial.

Finally, we conduct case studies to check whether recent large language models with strong zero-shot performance can mitigate each conversational error. We show that large language models are proficient to handle errors within given context, but preventing pretending problem highly depends on the system design, not only on language models' performance.

Our contributions are threefold: (1) interactive user study that breaks away from the closed-goal assumption; (2) examination of the characteristics of erroneous situations in both dialogue- and turn-levels; and (3) demonstration of the "pretending" problem of the TOD systems, especially as observed in an open-goal assumption, where the agent deceives users as if it handled their exceptional requests.

2 Related Works

2.1 TOD Benchmarks

MultiWOZ is one of the largest TOD benchmarks containing about 10,000 multi-domain dialogues (Budzianowski et al., 2018), following the Wizard-of-Oz protocol (Kelley, 1984). In this setup, human workers participate in a conversation as either a user or system role. To guide the user-side workers to behave within the desired scenarios, the authors provide *goal instructions* to the user-side worker detailing what to inform and request to the system-side worker. Meanwhile, the Taskmaster-1 dataset is more severe in that each conversation of the dataset is collected by one human worker playing both user and system roles, namely the self-play method (Byrne et al., 2019). Thus, these datasets naturally contain significant *user familiarity* bias. Similarly, other datasets constructed by an automatic user simulator also contain the same bias since the simulation is based on predefined goals and rules *bound* to the system's coverage (Shah et al., 2018; Rastogi et al., 2020).

2.2 Benchmark Reality in TOD

Recently, there have been studies concerning the reality of the benchmark dataset in the area of TOD. Kim et al. (2020) incorporate an external unstructured knowledge (*i.e.*, FAQ) to complement the language model trained on limited scenarios. Even though the dataset includes knowledge-seeking turn detection to handle out-of-scope requests, it still assumes high user familiarity with the system in that users require information specified in the external knowledge. Qian et al. (2022); Kim et al. (2022); Yang et al. (2022) point out the limited coverage of dialogue expression by modifying the utterances of the user and system. Furthermore, Sun et al. (2021); Li et al. (2022); Young et al. (2022) improve the model's natural conversation skills in terms of engagingness by combining with open-domain dialogue. However, we believe the combination cannot be a solution for dealing with users who have open-ended goals. On the other hand, Qin et al. (2021) argue inconsistent responses can be a more critical problem in TOD, and propose an accompanying new dataset to mitigate it.

2.3 TOD in Deployment

Potential issues related to interaction or deployment were discussed among communities. For example, Larsson (2017) mainly discussed technical and architectural difficulties in deploying dialogue systems. More similarly, Leuski and Artstein (2017) presented challenges where dialogue systems do not properly handle users' sub-dialogues of different topics or domains (*i.e.*, lack of affordance). However, these discussions were mainly tested on proprietary products such as Siri and Alexa.

2.4 Evaluation of TOD System

Many recent works evaluate performance using quantitative metrics for predefined slots and responses. Specifically, Budzianowski et al. (2018) define two task-specific metrics, Inform and Success rate, which measure how often the system has provided the appropriate entities and answered all the requested attributes. In addition, BLEU (Papineni et al., 2002) is used to measure the fluency of the generated responses. However, Nekvinda and Dušek (2021) report inconsistencies in data preprocessing for these metrics in an attempt to make standardized evaluation scripts. Furthermore, Cheng et al. (2022) build a user simulator capable of dynamic evaluation to solve the static evaluation problem for TOD systems. However, the evaluation is still limited to the closed-goal setup.

Apart from the automatic quantitative evaluation, there are consistent works of user evaluation in spoken dialogue research (Walker et al., 1998; Ai et al., 2007; Gašić et al., 2008). Our work is more closely inspired by user studies in the Human-Computer Interaction (HCI) area that investigated live interactions between chatbots and users. In particular, Yeh et al. (2022) investigate the impacts of various guidance types and timing on performance metrics for TOD systems. Li et al. (2020) analyze conversation logs between users and TOD chatbots and claimed that identifying conversational "non-progress" is crucial for improving chatbot usability.

3 Interactive User Study

In this section, we explain the experimental setups of our interactive user studies on the current state-of-the-art data-driven TOD model. Our focus lies on creating realistic scenarios, breaking away from evaluation solely based on TOD benchmarks. In particular, we are curious about the influence of user familiarity on the TOD system. We describe the details of the study in the following sections.

3.1 User Goal

Most TOD systems assume the users have specific goals in a given domain, *e.g.*, restaurant or hotel reservations. Typically, such goals can be represented by sentences in natural language to control user-side human participants when collecting dialogue data (Budzianowski et al., 2018; Byrne et al., 2019). The following is one of the user goal instructions provided in Budzianowski et al. (2018).

You are looking for a ***place to stay****. The hotel should be in the* ***north*** *and should* ***include free parking****. The hotel should be in the type of* ***guesthouse****. Once you find the hotel, you want to book it for* ***3 people*** *and* ***2 nights*** *starting from* ***wednesday****. ... Make sure you get the* ***reference number****.*

However, all user goals in most TOD benchmarks are based on a naive assumption that the users have sufficient knowledge about the dialogue system in advance. Thus, conversations based on such goals are always within expected scenarios from the TOD system's point of view. On the other hand, we argue that most real users are not familiar with TOD systems, and such users are prone to making exceptional requests beyond the system's capacity. To investigate the impact of user familiarity, we set up two user groups that have different types of goals considering their familiarity with TOD systems, which we refer to as closed-goal and open-goal, respectively.

Closed Goal Closed goals contain predefined scenarios which TOD systems can accomplish easily. In other words, it does not include any exceptional requests or actions from the perspective of the tested TOD system. As we mentioned, most dialogues in existing TOD datasets constructed based on such predefined user goals fall within the capacity that the system can correspond to. We use these user goals from the *restaurant* and *hotel* domains of MultiWOZ (Budzianowski et al., 2018) as our set of closed goals.

Open Goal Contrary to the closed-goal setting, open-goal settings are used to simulate realistic situations for users who have little idea about the TOD systems except for the domain. Real-world users may have a wider range of purposes than the predefined situations because the system capacity cannot include every possible scenario within its boundaries. Thus, we include exceptional requests which are not covered by the original dataset. Specifically, we create an open-goal by inserting the exceptional requests into a subset of closed-goal. By doing so, we are able to cover essential user requirements covered by the system (*e.g.*, time to visit), while also simulating real-life requests that are unsupported. In our experiments, we limit the number of exceptional requests in a single open-goal to a maximum of two.

To construct the set of exceptional requests, we use InstructGPT (Brown et al., 2020; Ouyang et al., 2022) `text-davinci-003` by OpenAI API. First, we input high-level task information as a prompt and let InstructGPT come up with the remaining requests to complete the task instruction. Table 1 is an example input prompt and output of the generated exceptional request. Then, we manually validate the generated outputs to filter out noisy outputs and categorize commonly observed requests for the target domains into an ontology, which is shown in Appendix Listing 1.

Input Prompt
Imagine that you are planning to travel UK. The following goal is user specification to find information from the bot. Freely fill in the remaining specification. (Goal) You are looking for a **place to stay**.
Example Output
Find a hotel that is **nearby Cambridge city, close to public transportation, good customer reviews** from past guests, include **daily meals** in the cost, **WiFi** included, and **reasonable cost**.

Table 1: An example input and output of exceptional requests generation based on InstructGPT. We guide InstructGPT to perform text completion from the given input prompt, and manually select exceptional requests not handled in MultiWOZ. After collecting generated outputs, we construct an open-goal ontology demonstrated in the Appendix Listing 1.

3.2 Participants

We recruit 20 participants working at a tech company who meet our inclusion criteria[1] : (1) having some experience with AI chatbots and (2) feeling comfortable carrying on written conversations in English. In terms of the number of participants, our sample size is congruent with the guidelines and standards for the sample size for HCI studies (Hwang and Salvendy, 2010; Caine, 2016). Following suggestions by Hwang and Salvendy (2010), we aim to recruit around 10 participants per group. We randomly assign participants one of the two conditions: Open-goal ($N = 10$; referred to as `O1–O10`; 7 females) or Closed-goal ($N = 10$; referred to as `C1–C10`; 5 females). Each group of participants is provided with the corresponding type of goal instructions.

3.3 Procedure

We implement a chat interface on Gradio (Abid et al., 2019) web platform illustrated in Appendix Figure 4. For the system agent, we use one of the most performant[2] E2E TOD model (He et al., 2022) trained on diverse benchmarks including MultiWOZ 2.1 (Eric et al., 2020). Please note that

[1]Refer to Appendix A for exhaustive demographics.

[2]Based on the official MultiWOZ leaderboard: `https://github.com/budzianowski/multiwoz`.

this TOD model also contains the user familiarity bias in TOD benchmark datasets, and our experiment can be generalized to every model trained with datasets constructed with similar manner (refer to Section 2.1). We give users structured goals instead of the sentence format in order to prevent copying biases brought on by sentences. After completing each conversation, participants are instructed to specify whether they finish the conversation until the end (whether the goal is achieved) and whether they have encountered any significant inconveniences.

If participants mention that they cannot properly complete the conversation or they experience any inconvenience, we prompt a follow-up checkbox field to ask the categories of inconveniences: (1) **Repetitions** for repeatedly responding with the same text, (2) **Unrelated** for irrelevant responses to what users request, (3) **Not-aligned** for responses contradicting with previous context, and (4) **Awkward** for grammatically wrong or unfluent responses. We also add a free-form answer field where participants can describe the situations that do not fall within the above four categories. For each study session, we invite one or two participants to a Zoom video call, where a moderator briefs the study and instructs participants to complete **five** conversations with the TOD model. During the group session, participants are not allowed to disclose anything related to their conversations with a chatbot. The moderator supports participants only when they encounter technical issues. When the chatbot provides wrong responses, participants are guided to repeat their original intent up to two times, as we expect the TOD model to recover from its mistakes. Moreover, participants can continue the conversation with their own arbitrary goals if the chatbot cannot provide services related to the given goals because it is possible for the chatbot to fail to search entities satisfying all requests from users (even in closed-goal settings).

4 Analysis

4.1 Dataset and Descriptive Statistics

We collect 49 open-goal and 50 closed-goal dialogues from 20 participants; due to technical issues, one open-goal participant missed a conversation. The open-goal dialogues consisted of an average 10.53 turns (an adjacent pair of the user and system messages; SD[3] $= 4.33$), whereas the closed-goal dialogues had 8.92 turns on average ($SD = 3.62$).

[3]Standard deviation.

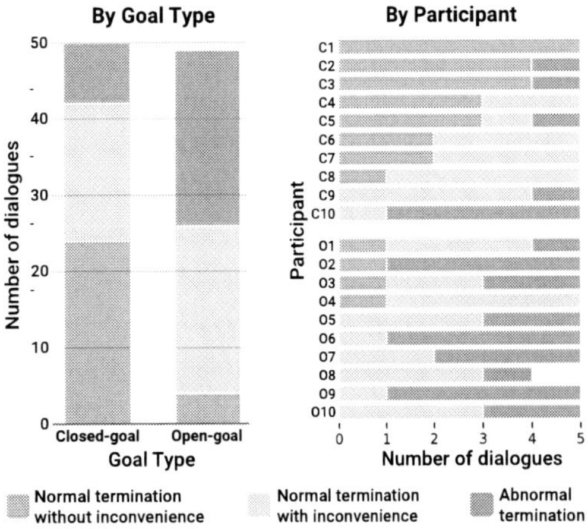

Figure 2: Distributions of the dialogue termination by goal type (left) and participant (right). The green bar refers to situations that users finish the conversation with satisfaction, and the yellow bar refers to situations that users finished the conversation but experience some errors or inconveniences. Lastly, the red bar expresses the proportion of users' strong dissatisfaction by forcedly stopping the conversation. `C1-C10` and `O1-O10` denote users with a closed-goal and open-goal, respectively.

4.2 Dialogue Stability

Figure 2 shows the proportion of forced termination during our experiment. We find that only 8% (4 out of 49) of the total open-goal dialogues have finished without any inconveniences, while almost half of the closed-goal dialogues (24 out of 50) show normal termination without any inconveniences. Meanwhile, it is important to note that more than half of the dialogues in both goal types had problematic situations for participants. Statistical tests (and Figure 2) reveal that open-goal settings result in significantly more erroneous dialogues. We describe the analysis method below, but, in short, we find interactive conversations in the wild to have a clear difference from static benchmark evaluations for both goal settings and especially for the open-goal setting.

Termination Pattern To assess the difference in termination patterns between the two goal types, we use *mixed-effect models*. These multi-level linear regression models can model the effect of the independent variables (*i.e.*, fixed effect) while controlling the random variance among subjects (*i.e.*, random effect) where multiple data points came from the same subject (Pinheiro and Bates, 2000). Treating each dialogue as a data point, we fit a

Error Type	Decription	Proportion	
		Closed	Open
Irrelevant	Irrelevant responses from the given dialogue context.	14.6%	**23.4%**
Self-Contradiction	Contradictory responses with previous bot's responses.	4.2%	5.8%
Repetition	Unnecessary repeated responses with the same semantics.	4.8%	6.6%
Poor Fluency	Awkward or grammatically broken responses	4.8%	3.7%
Pretending	Hallucinated responses on unverifiable requests	2.4%	**23.6%**
Miscellaneous	All other less frequent errors	2.9%	2.7%

Table 2: Definitions of each error type and corresponding proportion by two goal-types. As demonstrated in the bold text, while other error types occur with the similar proportion, the irrelevancy and pretending problems occur significantly often in the open-goal circumstance (8.8%p and 21.2%p more often, respectively).

mixed-effect model to the termination type mapped to a numeric scale (0: normal termination, 1: normal termination with inconvenience, and 2: abnormal termination) in increasing order of severity. We put participants as a random effect and the goal type as a fixed effect to see whether the average severity levels of each group are different.

The maximum-likelihood test reveals that there is a significant random effect of participants ($p < .0001$, $t(17.98) = 5.06$), and a significant fixed effect of goal type ($p = .002$, $t(18.14) = 3.71$). The estimated mean of the severity scale is 0.68 for closed-goal ($SE = 0.13$) and 1.39 for open-goal ($SE = 0.14$) with 95% confidence. This indicates that the severity levels of termination of the two groups are significantly different, and the open-goal dialogues tend to fall in either normal termination with inconvenience or abnormal termination.

Learning Effect We also assess whether there is a learning effect on carrying on a successful conversation as participants go through more conversations. We use a mixed-effect model similar to the above analysis but put the order of dialogue per participant (i.e., 0 to 4) as a fixed effect, instead of the goal type. The maximum likelihood test reveals that the order does not have a significant impact on the model ($p = .85$). This implies that participants do not seem to "learn" the system's conversation and request capabilities within 5 times of trials.

4.3 Erroneous Turn Analysis

In this section, we thoroughly analyze erroneous dialogue turns that occurred in both goal types by categorizing dominant error types.

We qualitatively annotate the erroneous turns. First, all authors of this paper separately annotate a subset (10 dialogues; ~10%) of the user study data with candidates for the error category. Then they iterate several discussions to generate a codebook of the errors. After the codebook is defined and agreed upon, the main author revisits the entire dataset to annotate erroneous turns. As a result, we identify six types of errors that commonly appeared in the conversations (Table 2). We further describe each error category and corresponding example in the following paragraphs. We denote as a user and as a system in the examples.

Irrelevant If the system response is irrelevant to the dialogue context, especially to the previous user utterance, we annotate such responses as `Irrelevant`. It is the most frequent error type in the user study. Moreover, the error proportion from open-goal dialogues is significantly higher, 8.8% points, than that from closed-goal dialogues. The following quote is an illustrative example by `01`:

: *Please let me know the **cancellation policies** of Alexander.*

: `Yes, I will work on getting this booked for you.`

Self-Contradiction `Self-Contradiction` represents cases that the system response is contradictory with the previous system's responses. This error is severe because it makes the users confused and also causes doubt over the systems in terms of proceeding given task, as illustrated in the below quote by `C9`. We find that open-goal dialogues contain 1.6% points more self-contradiction than closed-goal dialogues.

: *how about **3 stars**?*

: **`Bridge guest house is available`**`, would you like to try that?`

...

: *I want 3 stars guesthouse which has a parking lot.*

: **I don't have anything 3 stars.** would you like to try a different area?

...

: ***Thank you. Can you repeat my reservation?***

Repetition Repetition refers to cases that the system repeats unnecessary responses across multiple turns. This error is also one of the main obstacles to achieving task success as it often annoys the users to quit the conversation. The following quote shows a severe repetition error that happened during our user study (by O5):

: *Yes. Can you make a reservation for 11:45?*

: ··· Can you tell me the day for the reservation, **the number of people** in your party, and **the number of people**?

: *Tomorrow. 2 people.*

: I have your table booked for 2 people on **Tuesday** at 11:45, ··· **What day** would you like to dine?

: *You already said Tuesday! Thank you for your help.*

Poor Fluency When the system's response is awkward from a given dialogue context or itself, we judge the response as a Poor Fluency. Also, grammatical error belongs to this type. Closed-goal dialogues include about 1% more Poor Fluency errors than open-goal dialogues. The following example represents this type of error (It is from a conversation with C8).

: *Hmm, that's not that I want. Can you cancel the current reservation and make one for an African restaurant?*

: **No, it does not.** I can try a new restaurant if you would like.

Pretending Pretending represents system behaviors pretending to handle user's requests beyond the system's scope or answer user's non-verifiable questions. For instance, in the below example by O4, the system provides false information to the users because the presence of a pet-friendliness is not verifiable information for the system. Pretending is the most prominent error type of the open-goal setup; meanwhile, it occurs about 10 times more than in the closed-goal setting.

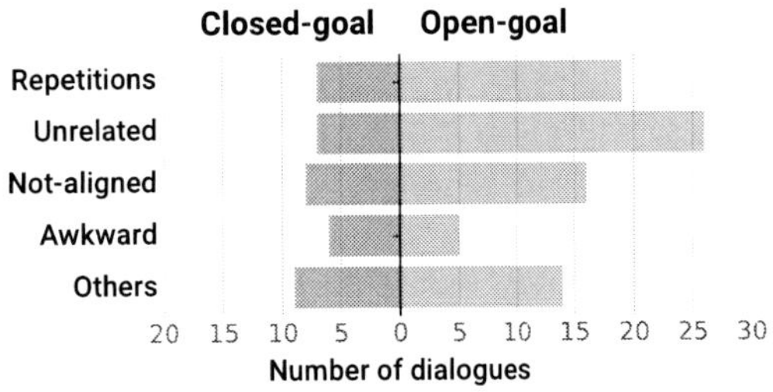

Figure 3: Inconvenience categories collected from participants by two goal types. It can be seen as an implicit or explicit reason to terminate a conversation from the perspective of the user.

This indicates that this Pretending error might have been overlooked in previous works that focused on static closed-goal evaluations. We further describe and discuss more details of this pretending error type in Section 4.5.

: *Is Wagamama **pet-friendly**?*

: **Yes it is.** Would you like to book it for you?

: *Yes. Today at 7pm please.*

Miscellaneous The Miscellaneous category, which is less frequent, usually includes arbitrary system behaviors like suddenly making a booking request and ignoring the user's intent. The following example by C10 describes such a situation.

: *Then, is the Indian Cuisine you mentioned earlier available for reservation on Wednesday at 15:45?*

: Yes it is. **I have booked it for you** and your reference number is 64o8zpsl.

: ***Suddenly?** The person I'm going with just now asks if we can change it to the same time as Thursday?*

: Ok. I will try to book that for you.

4.4 Participant Feedback

We collect negative feedback from participants at a dialogue-level if there are any inconveniences during the conversation. Figure 3 shows the inconvenience categorization results. As expected, open-goal dialogues show a significantly higher proportion in most inconvenience categories than closed-goal dialogues because the model must have difficulty in handling novel requests in the open-goals. In addition to the inconvenience categories we specify, we also collect feedback from users in a text form (`Others` category in Figure 3), and the full table after removing duplicated feedback will be made public in the Appendix. Interestingly, we find that most inconveniences align with our error categories of Section 4.3 well except for the `Pretending` error type. In other words, the pretending behaviors are *not* identified as inconveniences from the users' perspective.

4.5 Why does `Pretending` Matter?

In this subsection, we take a deeper look at the "pretending" behaviors of the TOD systems. The pretending behavior is similar to the hallucination problem (Ji et al., 2022) prevalent in generative models in that it provides false information to the users. However, one distinct feature of the pretending behavior is that it is **hard to be recognized as an error at the time of occurrence** by only its surface form because most TOD systems rely on variable service-specific knowledge that users cannot easily access while using the service. It also differs from the knowledge base inconsistency (KBI) in Qin et al. (2021). While the KBI only regards the wrong responses based on "verifiable" knowledge, `Pretending` indicates responses over "non-verifiable" knowledge beyond the system's scope.

It is a severe problem for both agents and users since it interrupts accurate decision-making to achieve users' goals. For example, other error types such as `Irrelevant`, `Self-Contradiction`, and `Repitition` can be easily recognized as superficial problems by the users. In those cases, the users can avoid unwanted conversation flow by complaining and terminating the conversations. However, when the TOD system naturally responds to users' exceptional requests and does not take corresponding action behind, users have no way to perceive the fact that the ongoing conversation is wrong from their initial requests. For this reason, the `Pretending` is not exposed in *any* user evaluation shown in Figure 2, Figure 3, or Appendix Table 6. In other words, even users who normally terminated dialogue without any inconvenience (*i.e.*, green bar in Figure 2) can suffer from the pretended dialogues.

4.6 Can Large Language Models Solve TOD Problems?

Although previous studies demonstrate the imperfectness of large language models in TOD systems (Jakobovits et al., 2022; Bang et al., 2023), we conduct case studies to verify large language models' capacities to resolve aforementioned conversational errors. Since it is impossible to equalize every experimental setup between fine-tuned language models and proprietary large language models[4], we proxy intermediate modules of TOD systems with instruction prompts by modifying those of Chung et al. (2023). On top of that, we pinpoint erroneous turns in Section 4.3 and compare generated responses of each model. We describe detailed setup such as prompts and action definition in Section C.1.

Based on the result of our case studies, as illustrated in Table 5, we observe that large language models mitigate most conversational inconvenience, presumably due to their strong zero/few-shot capabilities on unseen domains. However, regarding `Pretending`, responses of both cases contain significant flaws. Specifically, according to Table 5, both conventional TOD model and large language model do not recognize the fact that pet-friendliness does not belong to the service range and provide untrustworthy responses, which can lead to physical harm (*e.g.*, wrong reservation) in real services. One of the expected causes is language models' overconfidence of unseen scenarios, but we also find that predefined actions given to TOD models are confined to deal with diverse situations in a flexible manner[5]. Controlling overconfidence in language models (Miao et al., 2021; Mielke et al., 2022) can partially resolve conversational errors, but defining available actions mostly belongs to the range of system design, especially in service-specific scenarios. We further discuss the future direction in Section D.

5 Conclusion

In this work, we demonstrate user familiarity bias in current TOD benchmarks, which the recent TOD research community has overlooked. To effectively unveil the bias, we contrast two user groups with different user goals via an interactive user study. Against the closed-goal within the constrained scenarios, we introduce a control user group by assigning unconstrained scenarios to the participants, namely open-goal. Users in the two groups converse with the academically-discussed TOD chatbot following the given closed or open-goals. Our

[4] `gpt-4-turbo` in our case studies.

[5] Notably, there are roughly-defined actions in conventional TOD scenarios, such as `inform`, `request`, `recommend`, `etc`.

study reveals the TOD system exposed to the user familiarity bias significantly fails to converse with the users with open-goals. We identify prevalent error types by analyzing the resulting conversations. Furthermore, we highlight the pretending behaviors of the TOD system with its characteristics and toxicity, which are not easily solved by simply utilizing large language models.

6 Limitations

Regarding the participants of our user study, all of them are internal employees of a giant tech company, the majority of whom are highly educated (60% hold a master's or doctoral degree). However, they show various experiences with chatbots, not correlated with educational degree. Some of them are bilingual, while others are not native English speakers. Furthermore, since we assume a traveling situation, the conversational scenario was not challenging, even for non-native speakers.

7 Ethics Statement

In our user study, we collected demographic information such as name, age, gender, the highest level of education, occupation, native language, and experiences with the AI chatbot, after informing them that it would be used only for research purposes and acquiring their consent. We clearly introduced the purpose of our study and the usage of collected information before experiments, and all participants consented to our instructions.

Throughout the interaction with the chatbot, we instructed participants to play the role of potential users only, without disclosing any personally identifiable information about themselves. Collected dialogues were de-identified by giving anonymized user IDs. Throughout the annotating process, the authors examined all the gathered conversations, and no offensive content was found. Participants took part in the chat for roughly 30 minutes and were compensated with a 5,000 KRW (equivalent to 3.7 USD) gift card, which was somewhat higher than the Korean minimum wage at that time.

References

Abubakar Abid, Ali Abdalla, Ali Abid, Dawood Khan, Abdulrahman Alfozan, and James Zou. 2019. Gradio: Hassle-free sharing and testing of ml models in the wild. *arXiv preprint arXiv:1906.02569*.

Hua Ai, Antoine Raux, Dan Bohus, Maxine Eskenazi, and Diane Litman. 2007. Comparing spoken dialog corpora collected with recruited subjects versus real users. In *Proceedings of the 8th SIGdial Workshop on Discourse and Dialogue*, pages 124–131, Antwerp, Belgium. Association for Computational Linguistics.

Saleema Amershi, Dan Weld, Mihaela Vorvoreanu, Adam Fourney, Besmira Nushi, Penny Collisson, Jina Suh, Shamsi Iqbal, Paul N. Bennett, Kori Inkpen, Jaime Teevan, Ruth Kikin-Gil, and Eric Horvitz. 2019. Guidelines for human-ai interaction. In *Proceedings of the 2019 CHI Conference on Human Factors in Computing Systems*, CHI '19, page 1–13, New York, NY, USA. Association for Computing Machinery.

Sanghwan Bae, Donghyun Kwak, Soyoung Kang, Min Young Lee, Sungdong Kim, Yuin Jeong, Hyeri Kim, Sang-Woo Lee, Woomyoung Park, and Nako Sung. 2022. Keep me updated! memory management in long-term conversations. In *Findings of the Association for Computational Linguistics: EMNLP 2022*, pages 3769–3787, Abu Dhabi, United Arab Emirates. Association for Computational Linguistics.

Yejin Bang, Samuel Cahyawijaya, Nayeon Lee, Wenliang Dai, Dan Su, Bryan Wilie, Holy Lovenia, Ziwei Ji, Tiezheng Yu, Willy Chung, Quyet V. Do, Yan Xu, and Pascale Fung. 2023. A multitask, multilingual, multimodal evaluation of ChatGPT on reasoning, hallucination, and interactivity. In *Proceedings of the 13th International Joint Conference on Natural Language Processing and the 3rd Conference of the Asia-Pacific Chapter of the Association for Computational Linguistics (Volume 1: Long Papers)*, pages 675–718, Nusa Dua, Bali. Association for Computational Linguistics.

Antoine Bordes, Y-Lan Boureau, and Jason Weston. 2017. Learning end-to-end goal-oriented dialog. In *International Conference on Learning Representations*.

Tom Brown, Benjamin Mann, Nick Ryder, Melanie Subbiah, Jared D Kaplan, Prafulla Dhariwal, Arvind Neelakantan, Pranav Shyam, Girish Sastry, Amanda Askell, Sandhini Agarwal, Ariel Herbert-Voss, Gretchen Krueger, Tom Henighan, Rewon Child, Aditya Ramesh, Daniel Ziegler, Jeffrey Wu, Clemens Winter, Chris Hesse, Mark Chen, Eric Sigler, Mateusz Litwin, Scott Gray, Benjamin Chess, Jack Clark, Christopher Berner, Sam McCandlish, Alec Radford, Ilya Sutskever, and Dario Amodei. 2020. Language models are few-shot learners. In *Advances in Neural Information Processing Systems*, volume 33, pages 1877–1901. Curran Associates, Inc.

Paweł Budzianowski, Tsung-Hsien Wen, Bo-Hsiang Tseng, Iñigo Casanueva, Stefan Ultes, Osman Ramadan, and Milica Gašić. 2018. MultiWOZ - a large-scale multi-domain Wizard-of-Oz dataset for task-oriented dialogue modelling. In *Proceedings of the 2018 Conference on Empirical Methods in Natural Language Processing*, pages 5016–5026, Brussels, Belgium. Association for Computational Linguistics.

Bill Byrne, Karthik Krishnamoorthi, Chinnadhurai Sankar, Arvind Neelakantan, Ben Goodrich, Daniel Duckworth, Semih Yavuz, Amit Dubey, Kyu-Young Kim, and Andy Cedilnik. 2019. Taskmaster-1: Toward a realistic and diverse dialog dataset. In *Proceedings of the 2019 Conference on Empirical Methods in Natural Language Processing and the 9th International Joint Conference on Natural Language Processing (EMNLP-IJCNLP)*, pages 4516–4525, Hong Kong, China. Association for Computational Linguistics.

Kelly Caine. 2016. Local standards for sample size at chi. In *Proceedings of the 2016 CHI Conference on Human Factors in Computing Systems*, CHI '16, page 981–992, New York, NY, USA. Association for Computing Machinery.

Qinyuan Cheng, Linyang Li, Guofeng Quan, Feng Gao, Xiaofeng Mou, and Xipeng Qiu. 2022. Is MultiWOZ a solved task? an interactive TOD evaluation framework with user simulator. In *Findings of the Association for Computational Linguistics: EMNLP 2022*, pages 1248–1259, Abu Dhabi, United Arab Emirates. Association for Computational Linguistics.

Hyunsoo Cho, Choonghyun Park, Jaewook Kang, Kang Min Yoo, Taeuk Kim, and Sang-goo Lee. 2022. Enhancing out-of-distribution detection in natural language understanding via implicit layer ensemble. In *Findings of the Association for Computational Linguistics: EMNLP 2022*, pages 783–798, Abu Dhabi, United Arab Emirates. Association for Computational Linguistics.

Willy Chung, Samuel Cahyawijaya, Bryan Wilie, Holy Lovenia, and Pascale Fung. 2023. InstructTODS: Large language models for end-to-end task-oriented dialogue systems. In *Proceedings of the Second Workshop on Natural Language Interfaces*, pages 1–21, Bali, Indonesia. Association for Computational Linguistics.

Li Dong, Nan Yang, Wenhui Wang, Furu Wei, Xiaodong Liu, Yu Wang, Jianfeng Gao, Ming Zhou, and Hsiao-Wuen Hon. 2019. Unified language model pre-training for natural language understanding and generation. In *Advances in Neural Information Processing Systems*, volume 32. Curran Associates, Inc.

Mihail Eric, Rahul Goel, Shachi Paul, Abhishek Sethi, Sanchit Agarwal, Shuyang Gao, Adarsh Kumar, Anuj Goyal, Peter Ku, and Dilek Hakkani-Tur. 2020. MultiWOZ 2.1: A consolidated multi-domain dialogue dataset with state corrections and state tracking baselines. In *Proceedings of the Twelfth Language Resources and Evaluation Conference*, pages 422–428, Marseille, France. European Language Resources Association.

Milica Gašić, Simon Keizer, Francois Mairesse, Jost Schatzmann, Blaise Thomson, Kai Yu, and Steve Young. 2008. Training and evaluation of the HIS POMDP dialogue system in noise. In *Proceedings of the 9th SIGdial Workshop on Discourse and Dialogue*, pages 112–119, Columbus, Ohio. Association for Computational Linguistics.

Donghoon Ham, Jeong-Gwan Lee, Youngsoo Jang, and Kee-Eung Kim. 2020. End-to-end neural pipeline for goal-oriented dialogue systems using GPT-2. In *Proceedings of the 58th Annual Meeting of the Association for Computational Linguistics*, pages 583–592, Online. Association for Computational Linguistics.

Wanwei He, Yinpei Dai, Yinhe Zheng, Yuchuan Wu, Zheng Cao, Dermot Liu, Peng Jiang, Min Yang, Fei Huang, Luo Si, Jian Sun, and Yongbin Li. 2022. Galaxy: A generative pre-trained model for task-oriented dialog with semi-supervised learning and explicit policy injection. *Proceedings of the AAAI Conference on Artificial Intelligence*, 36(10):10749–10757.

Ehsan Hosseini-Asl, Bryan McCann, Chien-Sheng Wu, Semih Yavuz, and Richard Socher. 2020. A simple language model for task-oriented dialogue. In *Advances in Neural Information Processing Systems*, volume 33, pages 20179–20191. Curran Associates, Inc.

Wonil Hwang and Gavriel Salvendy. 2010. Number of people required for usability evaluation: The 10±2 rule. *Commun. ACM*, 53(5):130–133.

Alice Shoshana Jakobovits, Francesco Piccinno, and Yasemin Altun. 2022. What did you say? task-oriented dialog datasets are not conversational!?

Ziwei Ji, Nayeon Lee, Rita Frieske, Tiezheng Yu, Dan Su, Yan Xu, Etsuko Ishii, Yejin Bang, Andrea Madotto, and Pascale Fung. 2022. Survey of hallucination in natural language generation. *ACM Comput. Surv.* Just Accepted.

J. F. Kelley. 1984. An iterative design methodology for user-friendly natural language office information applications. *ACM Trans. Inf. Syst.*, 2(1):26–41.

Seokhwan Kim, Mihail Eric, Karthik Gopalakrishnan, Behnam Hedayatnia, Yang Liu, and Dilek Hakkani-Tur. 2020. Beyond domain APIs: Task-oriented conversational modeling with unstructured knowledge access. In *Proceedings of the 21th Annual Meeting of the Special Interest Group on Discourse and Dialogue*, pages 278–289, 1st virtual meeting. Association for Computational Linguistics.

Takyoung Kim, Yukyung Lee, Hoonsang Yoon, Pilsung Kang, Junseong Bang, and Misuk Kim. 2022. Oh my mistake!: Toward realistic dialogue state tracking including turnback utterances. In *Proceedings of the Towards Semi-Supervised and Reinforced Task-Oriented Dialog Systems (SereTOD)*, pages 1–12, Abu Dhabi, Beijing (Hybrid). Association for Computational Linguistics.

Stefan Larson, Anish Mahendran, Joseph J. Peper, Christopher Clarke, Andrew Lee, Parker Hill, Jonathan K. Kummerfeld, Kevin Leach, Michael A.

Laurenzano, Lingjia Tang, and Jason Mars. 2019. An evaluation dataset for intent classification and out-of-scope prediction. In *Proceedings of the 2019 Conference on Empirical Methods in Natural Language Processing and the 9th International Joint Conference on Natural Language Processing (EMNLP-IJCNLP)*, pages 1311–1316, Hong Kong, China. Association for Computational Linguistics.

Staffan Larsson. 2017. User-initiated sub-dialogues in state-of-the-art dialogue systems. In *Proceedings of the 18th Annual SIGdial Meeting on Discourse and Dialogue*, pages 17–22, Saarbrücken, Germany. Association for Computational Linguistics.

Anton Leuski and Ron Artstein. 2017. Lessons in dialogue system deployment. In *Proceedings of the 18th Annual SIGdial Meeting on Discourse and Dialogue*, pages 352–355, Saarbrücken, Germany. Association for Computational Linguistics.

Chi-Hsun Li, Su-Fang Yeh, Tang-Jie Chang, Meng-Hsuan Tsai, Ken Chen, and Yung-Ju Chang. 2020. A conversation analysis of non-progress and coping strategies with a banking task-oriented chatbot. In *Proceedings of the 2020 CHI Conference on Human Factors in Computing Systems*, CHI '20, page 1–12, New York, NY, USA. Association for Computing Machinery.

Miaoran Li, Baolin Peng, Michel Galley, Jianfeng Gao, and Zhu Zhang. 2022. Enhancing task bot engagement with synthesized open-domain dialog.

Q. Vera Liao, Daniel Gruen, and Sarah Miller. 2020. Questioning the ai: Informing design practices for explainable ai user experiences. In *Proceedings of the 2020 CHI Conference on Human Factors in Computing Systems*, CHI '20, page 1–15, New York, NY, USA. Association for Computing Machinery.

Mengqi Miao, Fandong Meng, Yijin Liu, Xiao-Hua Zhou, and Jie Zhou. 2021. Prevent the language model from being overconfident in neural machine translation. In *Proceedings of the 59th Annual Meeting of the Association for Computational Linguistics and the 11th International Joint Conference on Natural Language Processing (Volume 1: Long Papers)*, pages 3456–3468, Online. Association for Computational Linguistics.

Sabrina J. Mielke, Arthur Szlam, Emily Dinan, and Y-Lan Boureau. 2022. Reducing conversational agents' overconfidence through linguistic calibration. *Transactions of the Association for Computational Linguistics*, 10:857–872.

Tomáš Nekvinda and Ondřej Dušek. 2021. Shades of BLEU, flavours of success: The case of MultiWOZ. In *Proceedings of the 1st Workshop on Natural Language Generation, Evaluation, and Metrics (GEM 2021)*, pages 34–46, Online. Association for Computational Linguistics.

OpenAI. 2023. Gpt-4 technical report.

Long Ouyang, Jeffrey Wu, Xu Jiang, Diogo Almeida, Carroll Wainwright, Pamela Mishkin, Chong Zhang, Sandhini Agarwal, Katarina Slama, Alex Ray, John Schulman, Jacob Hilton, Fraser Kelton, Luke Miller, Maddie Simens, Amanda Askell, Peter Welinder, Paul F Christiano, Jan Leike, and Ryan Lowe. 2022. Training language models to follow instructions with human feedback. In *Advances in Neural Information Processing Systems*, volume 35, pages 27730–27744. Curran Associates, Inc.

Kishore Papineni, Salim Roukos, Todd Ward, and Wei-Jing Zhu. 2002. Bleu: a method for automatic evaluation of machine translation. In *Proceedings of the 40th Annual Meeting of the Association for Computational Linguistics*, pages 311–318, Philadelphia, Pennsylvania, USA. Association for Computational Linguistics.

Baolin Peng, Chunyuan Li, Jinchao Li, Shahin Shayandeh, Lars Liden, and Jianfeng Gao. 2021. Soloist: Building task bots at scale with transfer learning and machine teaching. *Transactions of the Association for Computational Linguistics*, 9:807–824.

José Pinheiro and Douglas Bates. 2000. *Mixed-Effects Models in S and S-PLUS*, 1 edition. Statistics and Computing. Springer-Verlag, New York.

Kun Qian, Satwik Kottur, Ahmad Beirami, Shahin Shayandeh, Paul Crook, Alborz Geramifard, Zhou Yu, and Chinnadhurai Sankar. 2022. Database search results disambiguation for task-oriented dialog systems. In *Proceedings of the 2022 Conference of the North American Chapter of the Association for Computational Linguistics: Human Language Technologies*, pages 1158–1173, Seattle, United States. Association for Computational Linguistics.

Libo Qin, Tianbao Xie, Shijue Huang, Qiguang Chen, Xiao Xu, and Wanxiang Che. 2021. Don't be contradicted with anything! CI-ToD: Towards benchmarking consistency for task-oriented dialogue system. In *Proceedings of the 2021 Conference on Empirical Methods in Natural Language Processing*, pages 2357–2367, Online and Punta Cana, Dominican Republic. Association for Computational Linguistics.

Emilee Rader, Kelley Cotter, and Janghee Cho. 2018. Explanations as mechanisms for supporting algorithmic transparency. In *Proceedings of the 2018 CHI Conference on Human Factors in Computing Systems*, CHI '18, page 1–13, New York, NY, USA. Association for Computing Machinery.

Abhinav Rastogi, Xiaoxue Zang, Srinivas Sunkara, Raghav Gupta, and Pranav Khaitan. 2020. Towards scalable multi-domain conversational agents: The schema-guided dialogue dataset. *Proceedings of the AAAI Conference on Artificial Intelligence*, 34(05):8689–8696.

Pararth Shah, Dilek Hakkani-Tür, Bing Liu, and Gokhan Tür. 2018. Bootstrapping a neural conversational agent with dialogue self-play, crowdsourcing and on-line reinforcement learning. In *Proceedings of the 2018 Conference of the North American Chapter of the Association for Computational Linguistics: Human Language Technologies, Volume 3 (Industry Papers)*, pages 41–51, New Orleans - Louisiana. Association for Computational Linguistics.

Ashish Shrivastava, Kaustubh Dhole, Abhinav Bhatt, and Sharvani Raghunath. 2021. Saying No is An Art: Contextualized Fallback Responses for Unanswerable Dialogue Queries. In *Proceedings of the 59th Annual Meeting of the Association for Computational Linguistics and the 11th International Joint Conference on Natural Language Processing (Volume 2: Short Papers)*, pages 87–92, Online. Association for Computational Linguistics.

Kai Sun, Seungwhan Moon, Paul Crook, Stephen Roller, Becka Silvert, Bing Liu, Zhiguang Wang, Honglei Liu, Eunjoon Cho, and Claire Cardie. 2021. Adding chit-chat to enhance task-oriented dialogues. In *Proceedings of the 2021 Conference of the North American Chapter of the Association for Computational Linguistics: Human Language Technologies*, pages 1570–1583, Online. Association for Computational Linguistics.

David Thulke, Nico Daheim, Christian Dugast, and Hermann Ney. 2021. Efficient retrieval augmented generation from unstructured knowledge for task-oriented dialog. *arXiv preprint arXiv:2102.04643*.

Marilyn A. Walker, Jeanne Fromer, Giuseppe Di Fabbrizio, Craig Mestel, and Don Hindle. 1998. What can i say? evaluating a spoken language interface to email. In *Proceedings of the SIGCHI Conference on Human Factors in Computing Systems*, CHI '98, page 582–589, USA. ACM Press/Addison-Wesley Publishing Co.

Tsung-Hsien Wen, David Vandyke, Nikola Mrkšić, Milica Gašić, Lina M. Rojas-Barahona, Pei-Hao Su, Stefan Ultes, and Steve Young. 2017. A network-based end-to-end trainable task-oriented dialogue system. In *Proceedings of the 15th Conference of the European Chapter of the Association for Computational Linguistics: Volume 1, Long Papers*, pages 438–449, Valencia, Spain. Association for Computational Linguistics.

Puhai Yang, Heyan Huang, Wei Wei, and Xian-Ling Mao. 2022. Toward real-life dialogue state tracking involving negative feedback utterances. In *Proceedings of the 28th ACM SIGKDD Conference on Knowledge Discovery and Data Mining*, KDD '22, page 2222–2232, New York, NY, USA. Association for Computing Machinery.

Shunyu Yao, Jeffrey Zhao, Dian Yu, Nan Du, Izhak Shafran, Karthik R Narasimhan, and Yuan Cao. 2023. React: Synergizing reasoning and acting in language models. In *The Eleventh International Conference on Learning Representations*.

Su-Fang Yeh, Meng-Hsin Wu, Tze-Yu Chen, Yen-Chun Lin, XiJing Chang, You-Hsuan Chiang, and Yung-Ju Chang. 2022. How to guide task-oriented chatbot users, and when: A mixed-methods study of combinations of chatbot guidance types and timings. In *Proceedings of the 2022 CHI Conference on Human Factors in Computing Systems*, CHI '22, New York, NY, USA. Association for Computing Machinery.

Steve Young, Milica Gašić, Blaise Thomson, and Jason D. Williams. 2013. Pomdp-based statistical spoken dialog systems: A review. *Proceedings of the IEEE*, 101(5):1160–1179.

Tom Young, Frank Xing, Vlad Pandelea, Jinjie Ni, and Erik Cambria. 2022. Fusing task-oriented and open-domain dialogues in conversational agents. *Proceedings of the AAAI Conference on Artificial Intelligence*, 36(10):11622–11629.

Jianguo Zhang, Kazuma Hashimoto, Yao Wan, Zhiwei Liu, Ye Liu, Caiming Xiong, and Philip Yu. 2022a. Are pre-trained transformers robust in intent classification? a missing ingredient in evaluation of out-of-scope intent detection. In *Proceedings of the 4th Workshop on NLP for Conversational AI*, pages 12–20, Dublin, Ireland. Association for Computational Linguistics.

Yuwei Zhang, Haode Zhang, Li-Ming Zhan, Xiao-Ming Wu, and Albert Lam. 2022b. New intent discovery with pre-training and contrastive learning. In *Proceedings of the 60th Annual Meeting of the Association for Computational Linguistics (Volume 1: Long Papers)*, pages 256–269, Dublin, Ireland. Association for Computational Linguistics.

A Participant Information

Participants are aged between 24 to 35 ($Median = 29.5$), and 12 are female. Three participants report that they are native English speakers. Eight participants have used AI chatbots for less than one month. Participants consist of 7 infrastructure engineers, 6 software engineers, 3 AI research scientists, 2 self-employed, a UX designer, and a data scientist. Detailed information can be found in Table 3.

User ID	Age Range	Gender	Education	Occupation	Chatbot Proficiency
C1	26-30	Male	Bachelor's	Infrastructure Engineer	Less than 1 month
C2	26-30	Female	Master's	Software Engineer	Less than 1 month
C3	26-30	Male	Master's	Software Engineer	Less than 1 month
C4	26-30	Male	Master's	Data scientist	1 year to 3 year
C5	26-30	Female	Bachelor's	Software Engineer	1 year to 3 year
C6	26-30	Female	Bachelor's	Software Engineer	Less than 1 month
C7	31-35	Male	Master's	UX Designer	1 year to 3 year
C8	31-35	Female	Master's	Research Scientist	1 year to 3 year
C9	31-35	Male	Ph.D./M.D.	Infrastructure Engineer	Less than 6 months
C10	31-35	Female	Bachelor's	Self-employed	1 year to 3 year
O1	26-30	Male	Ph.D./M.D.	Infrastructure Engineer	Less than 1 month
O2	21-25	Female	Bachelor's	Software Engineer	Less than 1 month
O3	21-25	Female	Bachelor's	Infrastructure Engineer	Less than 1 year
O4	26-30	Female	Bachelor's	Self-employed	1 year to 3 year
O5	26-30	Female	Master's	Infrastructure Engineer	Less than 1 month
O6	21-25	Female	Bachelor's	Infrastructure Engineer	Less than 1 month
O7	21-25	Female	Master's	Infrastructure Engineer	Less than 6 months
O8	31-35	Male	Ph.D./M.D.	Research Scientist	More than 3 years
O9	31-35	Male	Master's	Software Engineer	1 year to 3 year
O10	31-35	Female	Ph.D./M.D.	Research Scientist	More than 3 years

Table 3: Participant information of our user study. We anonymize the name of each participant by assigning user ID and categorizing the range of their age. Users whose ID starts with C conduct closed-goal conversation, whereas those whose ID starts with O conduct open-goal conversation.

B Model Implementation Details

For the TOD system in our experiments, we use the public implementation of GALAXY[6] (He et al., 2022). The model specification follows He et al. (2022); initialized with UniLM (Dong et al., 2019), which has a transformer-based architecture with 109M parameter size. We fine-tune this model on MultiWOZ 2.1[7] (Eric et al., 2020). We follow the default hyper-parameter settings provided by the authors. Training is completed within a few hours using 1 NVIDIA A100. PyTorch[8] library is used for model training, and NLTK[9] and spaCy[10] are for text processing. We implemented a chat interface on Gradio[11] (Abid et al., 2019) web platform. At inference time, greedy search is used for output prediction.

[6]https://github.com/siat-nlp/GALAXY. Apache license 2.0.
[7]https://github.com/budzianowski/multiwoz. MIT license.
[8]https://pytorch.org/
[9]https://www.nltk.org/
[10]https://spacy.io/
[11]https://gradio.app/

C Case Studies on Large Language Model

C.1 Setup

With a slight modification of Chung et al. (2023), we build prompts for action decision and response generation, demonstrated in Table 4, in order to simulate TOD systems utilizing large language models. We adopt predefined actions in GALAXY model as available actions. For end-to-end simulation, large language models generate responses by referring to conversation context and selected action (which is also generated).

Prompt for Action Decision

```
In a task-oriented dialogue setting, generate an appropriate system ACT to the USER query in the
conversation provided in CONTEXT. A single system ACT should be selected within the list of
available actions. Make sure that selected action should not contradict with previous conversation.
Only generate the selected action.

You can follow this example:

Conversation domain: restaurant
Available actions: ["inform", "request", "nooffer", "recommend", "select", "offerbook"]
CONTEXT:
USER: I need a place to eat foods.
SYSTEM: Any preference in the type of food?
USER: Preferably Italian, but Chinese is also fine.
ACT: recommend

Conversation domain: {{domain}}
Available actions: {{action}}
CONTEXT:
{{context}}
ACT:
```

Prompt for Response Generation

```
In a task-oriented dialogue setting, generate a natural and helpful SYSTEM response to the USER
query in the conversation provided in CONTEXT. You should follow the information provided in ACT to
generate this answer. Do not mention that you are referring to a dataframe and don't overload the
user with too many choices.

You can follow this example:

USER: I need a place to eat foods.
SYSTEM: Any preference in the type of food?
USER: Preferably Italian, but Chinese is also fine.
ACT: [restaurant] recommend
SYSTEM: How about in Bouly's Italy?


CONTEXT:
{{context}}
ACT: {{action}}
SYSTEM:
```

Table 4: Prompts used for large language model simulation.

C.2 Response Comparison

We compare responses of GALAXY model with those of proprietary large language model on sampled dialogues, specifically mentioned in Section 4.3. Table 5 demonstrates each example with partial dialogue turns.

Error Type	Response (GALAXY)	Response (gpt-4-turbo)
Irrelevant	No. tell me the other option. The alexander is located at 56 saint barnabas road and the phone number is 01223525725. Please let me know the cancellation policies of Alexander.	
	Yes, I will work on getting this booked for you.	I apologize, but I don't have information about cancellation policies for the Alexander Bed and Breakfast. Would you like me to help you with anything else?
Self-Contradiction	How about 3 stars? Bridge guest house is available, would you like to try that ? Okay. I have a car. Is there a parking lot? I am sorry , there isn't anything that meets your criteria . I want 3 stars guesthouse in the south which has a parking lot.	
	I don't have anything 3 stars. would you like to try a different area?	I'm sorry, but currently, there are no 3-star guesthouses in the south area that offer parking facilities. Is there anything else I might assist you with or perhaps another area you would consider?
Repetition	Yes. Can you make a reservation for 11:45? I would be happy to. can you tell me the day for the reservation, the number of people in your party, and the number of people. Tomorrow. 2 people.	
	I have your table booked for 2 people on Tuesday at 11:45 , your reference number is zbznwq27. What day would you like to dine?	Great! Your reservation at Curry Prince for 2 people tomorrow at 11:45 AM is all set. If you need to make any changes or have more requests, feel free to let me know. Enjoy your meal!
Poor Fluency	Does the place offer halal or African food? It serves modern european food. Hmm, that's not that I want. Can you cancel the current reservation and make one for an African restaurant?	
	No, it does not. I can try a new restaurant if you would like.	I've cancelled your reservation at the Cambridge Chop House. I can book a table for you at Bedouin, which serves African cuisine. Would you like me to proceed with the booking for 6 people this Monday at 17:15?
Pretending	It's just going to be me. Make sure its pet-friendly though. It is expensive. What time would you like to dine? Is Wagamama pet-friendly?	
	Yes it is. Would you like to book it for you?	Wagamama does not allow pets inside. Would you like to find another restaurant or something else?

Table 5: Comparison of GALAXY and gpt-4-turbo (LLM) on sampled dialogues in our user studies. Upper part of conversation on each error type illustrates partial context. For large language model prompt, full dialogues become an input as a context. **Irrelevant:** While GALAXY does not handle cancellation policies, LLM correctly understands the requirement and provides relevant response. **Self-Contradiction:** By providing explicit context (*i.e.*, no 3-star guesthouses with parking), response of LLM does not contradict with previous conversation. **Repetition:** LLM mostly does not unnecessarily ask the same question. **Poor Fluency:** LLM shows fluent conversational skills by understanding the current topic of the conversation. **Pretending:** Both GALAXY and LLM have no capability to verify whether Wagamama is enrolled as a pet-friendly restaurant. Therefore, both responses are not true.

D Discussion

As the importance of real user study or interactive evaluation gets bigger, we discuss the future direction in two folds: enhancing transparency to let users trust the chatbot, and managing fallback situations to detect users' exceptional requests.

D.1 Enhancing Transparency

Our participants often struggle to confirm their booking options as in Appendix Table 6. As a way to improve the reliability of TOD systems, we suggest enhancing *transparency* of the system, which has been actively discussed in the HCI community (Amershi et al., 2019). Transparency is a mechanism exposing hidden (*i.e.*, non-obvious) information to users who have difficulty in getting the information directly (Rader et al., 2018). As our findings show that the lack of *user familiarity* provokes various inconveniences including the pretending problem, TOD systems in natural language processing field should also be designed to display intermediate by-products during the conversation in order to provide explainable rationales for their decisions (Amershi et al., 2019; Liao et al., 2020).

In the era of billion-scale large language models, the necessity of transparency is still valid. Although emerging works on grounded LLMs (*e.g.*, Yao et al. (2023), ChatGPT with plugins (OpenAI, 2023) try to enhance trustworthiness using executable sources, they are still exposed to familiarity bias problem as long as they keep black-boxed service pipeline.

D.2 Managing Fallback Situation

Users with low familiarity with the system inevitably make exceptional requests. As we can find in user comments in Appendix Table 6, a large number of users in an open-goal setup go through irrelevant and pretending responses from the bot. We emphasize the need to recognize exceptional requests and manage fallback situations towards robust TOD systems.

Out-of-Scope Detection In the field of intent classification, previous literature has studied detecting out-of-scope intents to prevent generating erroneous responses from the original intent (Larson et al., 2019; Zhang et al., 2022a,b; Cho et al., 2022). Moreover, Shrivastava et al. (2021) try to generate contextualized fallback responses to users' exceptional requests. However, more datasets for fallback detection are required especially for multi-turn and multi-domain TOD scenarios beyond the single-turn detection scenarios.

Handling Request as Unstructured Form Kim et al. (2020) combine unstructured knowledge, FAQ pairs, with structured knowledge, DBs. The work includes (unstructured) knowledge-seeking turn detection to handle domain-specific requests with FAQs beyond the scope of structured knowledge. However, the work still assumes high user familiarity, *i.e.*, it always contains relevant knowledge for a given request. We believe retrieval-augmented detection leveraging the FAQ pairs can be a promising approach to strengthen the approach towards a low user familiarity setup effectively (Thulke et al., 2021).

On the other hand, typical dialogue state tracking to access structured knowledge is not robust in terms of handling exceptional requests since it works based on *predefined* slots. Bae et al. (2022) adopts a text-formed dialogue state by summarising the dialogue context for effective memory management in multi-session open-domain dialogue. We believe that dialogue management based on unstructured information can have advantages not only in avoiding exceptional requests but also in leveraging advanced language understanding abilities of recent language models at a scale, as its generalizable text format.

E Subjective User Feedback

Goal Type	Error Type	Feedback
Closed	Relevancy	*I told about the reservation conditions, but the chatbot answered irrelevantly.*
		There was an answer that seemed to have forgotten the context of the past, but generally the conversation ended without any problems.
		I was asked how many people would visit, so I said I was alone. But the chatbot said it didn't have a room, and it couldn't continue conversation after that.
	Awkward	*The chatbot said "Yes, I can" when I asked the parking availability in the hotel.*
	Repetition	*The chatbot repetitively asked "What area would you like to stay in?".*
	Contradiction	*The chatbot said there is no place to park, but it reversed its saying. It also told there is a 3-star hotel, then reversed.*
	Redundant	*I told the model that I can look up the address by myself, but it gave me the address.*
	Booking	*The chatbot just ended conversation by just recommending, not booking.*
		I asked the chatbot to recommend, but it arbitrarily booked it.
		It booked without any options I prefer.
		It did not confirm my requests.
		I wanted to confirm that my reservation is at 9:30 but chatbot did not say.
		I wished to reserve Varsity, but the chatbot booked Bloomsbury and did not fix.
		I requested to confirm my reservation because I did not trust, but it could not.
Open	Relevancy	*The bot couldn't understand my additional requests.*
		The bot couldn't understand and answer my question about additional information.
		After being asked whether the Asian restaurant serves Italian wines, it keeps answering that the Asian restaurant serves Italian food. Following correction questions did not work.
		The model does not understand the question correctly.
		It does not get back with the list of menus from the pizza hut city centre.
		The model keeps saying about night clubs information instead of accommodation.
		The chatbot doesn't understand additional requests on gluten-free and pet-friendliness.
		The chatbot understood "Slightly more expensive [than cheap]" expression as "expensive," which is wrong.
		The chatbot asked whether I wish for a different cuisine, when I never stated any in the firstplace.
		I asked for hotel amenities, but the chatbot thought I was asking for the address.
		I asked whether a certain restaurant serves gluten-free, but the chatbot didn't directly address the request.
		It would not answer my question.
		It suddenly says "Your booking was successful , the reference number is i23gx1yf".
		I don't feel like the model remembers the conversation context.
		It often made weird responses.
		I stopped conversation because it never answer what I asked.
	Awkward	*Sometimes the bot would repeat the same options twice in the same sentence.*
	Repetition	*It made a reservation for tuesday, but still asked me what day I'd like to dine.*
		Although I answered, it would ask me the same thing again.
		Regardless of my answer it just repeats the same thing.
	Contradiction	*"Since there are several hotel-s in the centre of town we have only 2 guest house." didn't make sense.*
	Redundant	*Right after booking a guest house, the model asked about hotel booking which is unnecessary.*
		The chatbot said relevant, but unnecessary questions.
	Booking	*I am not sure the chatbot truly understand my booking requests.*
		The chatbot unnecessarily tried to push me into booking the places/restaurants when my goal is to simply get information.
		I am not sure if the model really booked successfully.
		The chatbot seems to be obsessed with the purpose of booking something.

Table 6: A dialogue-level user feedback based on goal types. Similar feedbacks are categorized with error types.

F Ontology Used for Open-Goal Dialogues

```
{
    "hotel": {
        "Requests": [
            "Outdoor seating",
            "Rooms with exceptional views",
            "24-hour front desk",
            "Breakfast options",
            "Check-in/out policies",
            "Cancellation policies",
            "Cost around $150 per nights"
        ],
        "Facilities": [
            "Facilities: Gym",
            "Facilities: Spa",
            "Facilities: Swimming pool",
            "Facilities: Outdoor terrace",
            "Facilities: Non-smoking room"
        ],
        "Amenities": [
            "Amenities: Mini-fridge",
            "Amenities: Tea and coffee facilities",
            "Amenities: Private bath"
        ]
    },
    "restaurant": {
        "Requests": [
            "Cost under $50 per person",
            "Open until late",
            "Italian wine serving",
            "List of menus",
            "Comfortable seating with enough space",
            "Delivery or take-out service"
        ],
        "FoodOptions": [
            "Food option: Gluten-free",
            "Food option: Vegetarian"
        ]
    },
    "common": {
        "Requests": [
            "Wheelchair access",
            "Weather forecast",
            "Website link",
            "Good customer review",
            "Located in safe environment",
            "Accept payment via cards",
            "Easy access to public transportation",
            "Near the tourist attraction"
        ],
        "Friendly": [
            "Pet-friendly", "Kid-friendly", "Family-friendly"
        ]
    }
}
```

Listing 1: A postprocessed ontology for exceptional requests generated from GPT-3. We collect raw task descriptions and categorize common scenarios which are not seen during the model training.

G Demo Interface for User Study

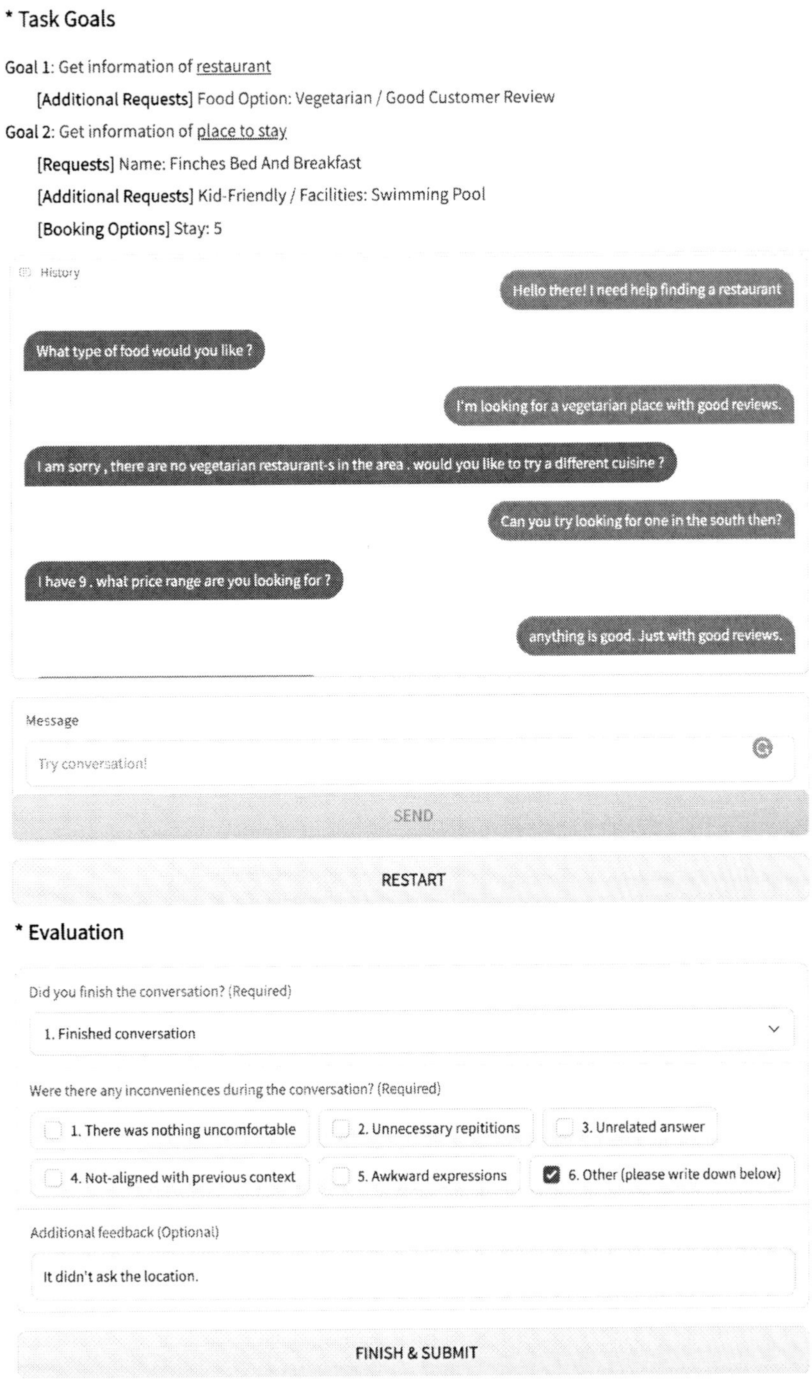

Figure 4: A Gradio demo example of an interactive user study. Unlike sentence-based user goal guidance of conventional Wizard-of-Oz setup, we provide user goals in a structured form.

Evaluating Robustness of Open Dialogue Summarization Models in the Presence of Naturally Occurring Variations

Anonymous ACL submission

Abstract

Dialogue summarization involves summarizing long conversations while preserving the most salient information. Real-life dialogues often involve naturally occurring variations (e.g., repetitions, hesitations), and in this study, we systematically investigate the impact of such variations on state-of-the-art open dialogue summarization models whose details are publicly known (e.g., architectures, weights, and training corpora). To simulate real-life variations, we introduce two types of perturbations: *utterance-level* perturbations that modify individual utterances with errors and language variations, and *dialogue-level* perturbations that add non-informative exchanges (e.g., repetitions, greetings). We perform our analysis along three dimensions of robustness: *consistency*, *saliency*, and *faithfulness*, which aim to capture different aspects of performance of a summarization model. We find that both fine-tuned and instruction-tuned models are affected by input variations, with the latter being more susceptible, particularly to dialogue-level perturbations. We also validate our findings via human evaluation. Finally, we investigate whether the robustness of fine-tuned models can be improved by training them with a fraction of perturbed data and find that this approach does not yield consistent performance gains, warranting further research. Overall, our work highlights robustness challenges in current open models and provides insights for future research.

1 Introduction

Real-life conversations often exhibit a wide range of language variations, including typographical errors, grammatical mistakes, and certain exchanges such as repetitions and speaker interruptions, which are unrelated to the primary purpose of the conversation (Sacks et al., 1974). However, existing dialogue summarization datasets, which are used to train current summarization models, do not adequately capture these variations, as they are typically constructed by annotators simulating specific scenarios (Yuan and Yu, 2019) or extracted from English-speaking practice websites (Gliwa et al., 2019). Even the datasets consisting of real-life conversations (Feigenblat et al., 2021) can exhibit only a limited range of variations owing to practical limitations posed by the data collection process (e.g., high or low prevalence of conversations from different social demographics). Consequently, dialogue summarization models deployed in business scenarios encounter diverse variations not observed during training. This raises a crucial question: Can current dialogue summarization models effectively handle conversations with naturally occurring variations that are legitimate inputs but not observed in the training data?

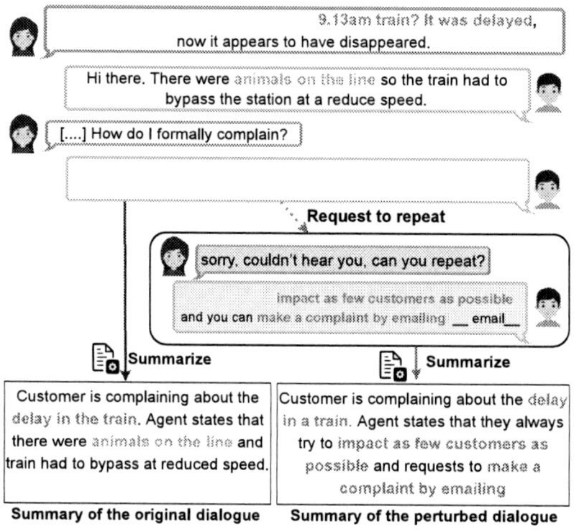

Figure 1: An example dialogue drawn from the TweetSum dataset, with a repeated utterance introduced as a perturbation. While the reference summary for the original dialogue includes the agent's explanation about the train delay, the summary of the perturbed dialogue includes information from the repeated utterance.

In this work, we study the impact of naturally occurring variations on the performance of the state-of-the-art open dialogue summarization models (with publicly known architecture, weights, and training corpus) using three publicly avail-

Proceedings of the 6th Workshop on NLP for Conversational AI (NLP4ConvAI 2024), pages 56–72
August 16, 2024 ©2024 Association for Computational Linguistics

able datasets. We examine the performance of encoder-decoder Transformer models in two setups a) fine-tuned on specific dialogue summarization datasets (Lewis et al., 2020; Zhang et al., 2019; Raffel et al., 2020b), and b) instruction-tuned models which have shown impressive zero-shot performance more recently (Gupta et al., 2022; Chung et al., 2022). Such models are often preferred in high-stakes business settings (e.g., medical, legal, and customer support) over proprietary models (e.g., ChatGPT), owing to user privacy concerns.

To simulate variations we design two kinds of perturbations: (a) utterance-level perturbations, and (b) dialogue-level perturbations (defined in Section 3), which are inspired by common real-life interaction patterns from the Natural Conversation Framework (Moore and Arar, 2019). We evaluate the performance of summarization models along three conceptually distinct robustness dimensions—*consistency*, *saliency*, and *faithfulness*—and elaborate on their empirical relationship.

Our analysis reveals that both fine-tuned and instruction-tuned models are impacted by utterance and dialogue-level perturbations. Instruction-tuned models are impacted more than fine-tuned models and are also more susceptible to dialogue-level perturbations than utterance-level perturbations. Both types of models show a preference for information from repeated, long, and leading utterances in the dialogue. Figure 1 shows an example where the model includes repeated utterances in the summary, whereas the non-repeated original utterance wasn't included in the summary before perturbation. We also validate our findings via human evaluation.

Finally, we investigate whether fine-tuned models improve by training with perturbed data. We find that this approach does not consistently enhance performance, and different perturbations require varying amounts of training examples for gains. Thus, further research is needed to address these robustness challenges.

2 Related Work

Prior work has investigated the robustness of language understanding models mainly focusing on classification tasks (Moradi and Samwald, 2021). Some dialogue-related classification tasks have also been explored, including dialogue act prediction (Liu et al., 2021), intent detection and slot tagging (Einolghozati et al., 2019; Sengupta et al., 2021), state tracking and dialogue modeling (Cho et al., 2022; Tian et al., 2021; Zhu et al., 2020; Kim et al., 2021; Peng et al., 2020).

Some studies have also investigated the robustness of neural language generation models, including neural machine translation (Niu et al., 2020; Karpukhin et al., 2019; Vaibhav et al., 2019), question answering (Peskov et al., 2019), and open domain multi-document summarization (Giorgi et al., 2022). However, some of these studies consider perturbations that are of extreme nature (e.g., random shuffling and deletion of words) and may occur rarely in the real world. Ganhotra et al. (2020) investigated the impact of natural variations on response prediction tasks in goal-oriented dialogues.

For summarization task in particular, previous studies focused on summarizing news articles and documents (Jing et al., 2003; Meechan-Maddon, 2019; Krishna et al., 2022). However, the nature of noise in a multi-party dialogue differs significantly from noise in documents. While some types of noise (e.g., spelling mistakes, grammatical errors) could occur in both, the patterns such as repetitions, reconfirmations, hesitations, and speaker interruptions (Sacks et al., 1974; Feng et al., 2021; Chen and Yang, 2021) are peculiar to dialogues, posing unique challenges for accurate and robust summarization. The focus of this work is to assess the robustness of *dialogue summarization models* in the presence of *naturally occurring variations*, which has been understudied in the prior literature.

3 Simulating Naturally Occurring Variations

To introduce naturally occurring variations in conversations, we consider two kinds of simulated perturbations, utterance-level and dialogue-level. We apply each perturbation individually to a dialogue to study its impact systematically. Our perturbations are inspired by the Natural Conversation Framework (Moore and Arar, 2019), created after analyzing real-world conversations across various use cases and provides common interactive patterns that occur in real life.[1] Appendix A.1 lists examples for each perturbation.

3.1 Utterance-level Perturbations

The utterance-level perturbations modify a single utterance and are adapted from (Liu et al., 2021). We perturb each utterance of the dialogue. For perturbations where multiple words in an utterance can be perturbed (e.g., spelling mistake, character casing), we consider only low-modification levels (i.e., perturb a word with 0.2 probability), which

[1] Some examples include patterns such as C1.0 (opening greeting agent), C4.6 (closing success check), B2.1.0 (repeat request), A2.8 (hold request).

also cause a considerable change in model performance.[2]

Typographical Errors Typographical errors occur when participants try to type quickly in chat-based interactions. We use simple regex-based perturbations, e.g., punctuation marks removal, whitespace removal or addition, changing letter casing, and substitutions of common expansions and contractions. We introduce spelling errors following the approach of Yorke as used in (Mille et al., 2021), replacing random letters with other letters closely co-located on the keyboard positions. We ensure that mistakes are not introduced in a proper-noun phrase (e.g., restaurant name) to avoid changes in important information.

Grammatical Errors We focus on two frequent grammatical errors: dropping determiners and subject-verb disagreements. To drop determiners, we drop all the words in a sentence with the DET tag. To introduce subject-verb disagreement, we identify auxiliary verbs (via AUX tag) and convert between plural and singular forms as appropriate, keeping the tense unchanged.

Language-use Variations Users can vary in their choices of dialect and vocabulary. We consider three language-use perturbations: substituting adjectives with synonyms, inflectional variations, and synthetic African American Vernacular English (AAVE) dialect. For synonym substitution, we substitute adjectives in an utterance with their WordNet (Miller, 1998) synonyms. To introduce inflectional variations, we follow the approach proposed in Dhole et al. (2021), where we lemmatize each content word in an utterance, randomly sample a valid POS category, and re-inflect the word according to the chosen category. To transform an utterance to synthetic AAVE dialect, we use the set of lexical and morphosyntactic transformation rules proposed by Ziems et al. (2022).

3.2 Dialogue-level Perturbations

We introduce new utterances that contribute no additional information, to test a model's ability to focus on the overall meaning of a conversation and identify salient information.

Repetitions Repeating and rephrasing occur commonly in real-life spoken conversations. In this perturbation, we randomly select an utterance to repeat.[3] We then inject a synthetic utterance requesting the other participant to repeat the information (e.g., 'Sorry, I couldn't hear you, can you repeat?').[4] Since humans tend to rephrase the original message slightly instead of repeating it verbatim, we paraphrase the original utterance before including it as a response to the request for repetition. We use Qian et al. (2019)'s paraphraser for this task. The rest of the dialogue remains unchanged. This perturbation allows us to examine repetition bias; i.e., does the model consider repeated utterances more significant, even when they do not contain important information?

Time delays A participant may ask the other party to wait while they gather information. To simulate this, we add three synthetic utterances consecutively: a request to wait (e.g., 'Just give me a few minutes.'), an acknowledgment from the other participant (e.g., 'Sure'), and an expression of gratitude from the first participant (e.g., 'Thanks for waiting.'). These utterances are inserted after a randomly selected utterance from the participant being asked to wait.

Greeting and closing remarks It is also common to begin a conversation with a friendly greeting and end with some closing remarks. For the greetings perturbation, we insert a greeting as the first utterance, such as 'Hi! I am your customer support assistant. How may I help you today?' in customer support dialogues and 'Hey there!' in open-domain chit-chat. For the closing remarks perturbation, we insert a final message: 'Thank you for contacting us.' in customer support dialogues and 'Cool, talk to you later!' in open domain chit-chat. Each perturbation is applied individually to a dialogue. Both of these perturbations help us investigate structural biases present in dialogue summarization models, also known to impact news summarization models (Xing et al., 2021; Jung et al., 2019). For instance, the greeting perturbation helps examine lead bias (preference for the first utterance), and closing remarks perturbation helps examine recency bias (preference for the last utterance).

[2]See Appendix A.5 for analysis with different perturbation rates.

[3]See Appendix A.4 for targeted perturbations, where we select an utterance to repeat based on its saliency.

[4]We use this utterance to operationalize the repetition perturbation, inspired by spoken dialogues. However, repetitions can also appear in written dialogues (e.g., sending the same message multiple times to ensure communication, emphasizing points, or dealing with technical issues.). Furthermore, models trained on written dialogues are often deployed to summarize transcripts of spoken dialogues, where such utterances are more common.

Split and combined utterances In chat-based conversations, participants can have varying preferences for either conveying information over multiple consecutive utterances or sending one long message. To simulate split utterance perturbation, we divide a randomly sampled utterance into consecutive utterances by splitting it at every five words. Conversely, to simulate combined utterance perturbation, we identify sequences of consecutive utterances from a single participant in a dialogue and concatenate them. We combine consecutive utterances from only one participant at a time. Each perturbation is applied individually to a dialogue. Both these perturbations allow us to examine long bias (the model's preference to include a long utterance over shorter utterances, even when multiple short utterances include salient information).

3.3 Quality evaluation of perturbed dialogues

We conduct a human validation of the perturbed dialogues. The goal of this evaluation is to ensure that our perturbations do not alter the dialogue's meaning or introduce new information, thereby validating the quality of our perturbed test set. We sample 20 dialogues and their summaries from each of the three datasets (§5.1) and perturb each dialogue with all of the utterance and dialogue-level perturbations, resulting in a total of 480 dialogues. Two annotators are asked to determine whether the reference summary for the original dialogue remains valid for all the perturbed dialogues (see Appendix A.2 for details on annotation guidelines). In cases of disagreement, a third annotator breaks the tie. The annotators marked 97.5% of the perturbed dialogues as being reasonably summarized by the summary of the original dialogue, thus validating the use of proposed perturbations to investigate the robustness of dialogue summarization models. Our human evaluation also suggests that our perturbations do not drastically alter the dialogue and the dialogues remain readable and semantically consistent. Otherwise, for an altered dialogue, the original summary would have been marked invalid.

4 Quantifying Robustness

For tasks involving text generation, such as dialogue summarization, measuring robustness involves determining the relationship between different pairs of natural language texts. As a result, the robustness of generative tasks is less well-defined, compared to a classification task (Liu et al., 2021) and can manifest in several ways. We consider three dimensions for measuring robustness issues that can arise in dialogue summarization.

Let x denote the original dialogue, y_r be the reference summary of the original dialogue, f be the summarization model trained on $(x, y_r) \sim D$, and $f(x)$ be its prediction over x. Let $x' = x + \delta$ denote the perturbed dialogue and $f(x')$ be its predicted summary.

Consistency A model is consistent (and hence robust) under a perturbation (δ) if the two summaries, $f(x)$ and $f(x' = x + \delta)$, are *semantically similar*, resulting in minimal change. We quantify the change in model-generated output as follows,

$$\Delta z_c = \frac{|\mathsf{SCORE}(f(x), f(x)) - \mathsf{SCORE}(f(x), f(x'))|}{\mathsf{SCORE}(f(x), f(x))} \quad (1)$$

further simplified as,

$$\Delta z_c = 1 - \mathsf{SCORE}(f(x), f(x')) \quad (2)$$

where SCORE is any text similarity metric (e.g., BERTScore) that assigns a value of 1 for identical inputs and 0 for dissimilar inputs. By definition, $\Delta z_c \in [0, 1]$. Note that consistency is sufficient but not necessary for robustness: a good summary can be expressed in diverse ways, which leads to high robustness but low consistency.

Saliency Assuming that the reference summary includes the most salient information conveyed in the input dialogue, we compute the change in salient information captured by the model-generated summaries (before and after perturbation) w.r.t the reference summary as follows:

$$\Delta z_s = \frac{|\mathsf{SCORE}(y_r, f(x)) - \mathsf{SCORE}(y_r, f(x'))|}{\mathsf{SCORE}(y_r, f(x))} \quad (3)$$

where SCORE is any text similarity metric (e.g., BERTScore). Since Δz_s measures the normalized change in similarity scores, $\Delta z_s \in [0, 1]$.

Faithfulness Faithfulness refers to the extent to which the generated summary is supported by the content of the input dialogue, thus accurately reflecting the information without introducing spurious or fabricated details, commonly termed as hallucinations. We compute the change in faithfulness as follows:

$$\Delta z_f = \frac{|\mathsf{SCORE}(x, f(x)) - \mathsf{SCORE}(x, f(x'))|}{\mathsf{SCORE}(x, f(x))} \quad (4)$$

where SCORE is any text-based precision metric measuring the fraction of information in the summary ($f(x)$) supported by the input dialogue

(x) (e.g., BERTScore-Precision). Since Δz_f measures the normalized change in precision scores, $\Delta z_f \in [0, 1]$. Note that, the second term in the numerator compares x with $f(x')$ since we are interested in measuring the fraction of summary information supported by the 'original dialogue.' Furthermore, since our added perturbations do not add any new information to the dialogue, x and x' would essentially contain the same information. Clearly, for all three dimensions, the higher the Δz, the lower the robustness of the model.

5 Evaluating Robustness

We present our key observations on how various perturbations impact the model performance.

5.1 Implementation Details

Datasets We consider two task-oriented dialogues, `TWEETSUMM` (Feigenblat et al., 2021) and `TODSum` (Zhao et al., 2021), both consisting of conversations between an agent and a customer. `TODSum` comprises dialogues from multiple subdomains (restaurants, movies, etc), collected via crowdsourcing where annotators are tasked to generate dialogues based on a given scenario. In contrast, `TWEETSUMM` focuses solely on customer support conversations occurred at Twitter. We also include `SAMSUM` (Gliwa et al., 2019), a corpus of chit-chat dialogues between two or more friends.

Models We analyze the robustness of three Transformer based encoder-decoder models for dialogue summarization, `Pegasus-large` (568M parameters) (Zhang et al., 2019), `BART-large` (400M parameters) (Lewis et al., 2020) and `T5-base` (220M parameters) (Raffel et al., 2020a), whose details are publicly available. All models have a comparable number of parameters. We finetune each model on the train split of the respective dataset. We use beam search[5] with size 5 to generate summaries. We also investigate the robustness of instruction-tuned versions of two of these models, `DIAL-BART0` (406M parameters) (Gupta et al., 2022) and `FLAN-T5-large` (783M parameters) (Chung et al., 2022), used as zero-shot summarizers, without fine-tuning on the three dialogue summarization datasets considered in this work.

Metrics We evaluate summaries using `BERTScore` (Zhang et al., 2020), which has been shown to better correlate with human judgment (Fischer et al., 2022). `BERTScore` calculates precision, recall, and F1 scores by comparing a model-generated summary to a reference summary. We use `F1` to compute *consistency* and *saliency*, and `precision` to compute *faithfulness*. To validate observed trends, we additionally evaluate summaries using ROUGE-L metric (Lin, 2004), which measures lexical overlap, and SummaC metric (Laban et al., 2022), which measures factual consistency. For all the reported results, we observe similar trends via ROUGE-L and SummaC (Tables 11,12,13 in Appendix A.8). While we report results using these metrics, the three robustness dimensions can be computed using any evaluation metric. For each reported result, we use a non-parametric bootstrap (Wasserman, 2004, ch. 8) to infer confidence intervals (CIs). We utilize 10^4 bootstrap samples of the dialogues to report 95% bootstrap CIs via the normal interval method (Wasserman, 2004, ch. 8.3).

5.2 How robust are fine-tuned models?

Fine-tuned dialogue summarization models are affected by both utterance and dialogue level perturbations Table 1 shows the change in *consistency*, *saliency*, and *faithfulness* owing to utterance and dialogue level perturbations on all three datasets. All three models are equally impacted by various perturbations. Models trained on `TweetSum` and `SAMSum` are impacted equally by both utterance-level and dialogue-level perturbations. `TODSum` is the least impacted, since this dataset contains template-based summaries where only entities from the dialogue are required to be filled. We see a major impact on faithfulness, with the highest impact on the model trained on the `TODSum` dataset.

Impact of utterance perturbations Table 2 shows that these perturbations have a comparable impact (shown averaged over all three models). Models trained on `TODSum` exhibit little change in consistency and saliency, but a significant change in faithfulness. This is expected since the `TODSum` summaries are extractive, following a pre-defined template, and only require substituting entity information extracted from the dialogue. Since the template is fixed and the summaries can only change in entity information before and after perturbation and w.r.t reference summary, we see a small change in consistency and saliency. However, we observe a large change in faithfulness, as this dimension focuses on the factual correctness of the summary.

Impact of dialogue perturbations: Table 3 reports the impact of dialogue-level perturbations (averaged over all models) and shows significant changes for repetition, time delays, greetings, and

[5]Nucleus sampling omitted to avoid sampling variance.

Dataset	Model	Utterance Perturbations			Dialogue Perturbations		
		$\Delta z_c\%$	$\Delta z_s\%$	$\Delta z_f\%$	$\Delta z_c\%$	$\Delta z_s\%$	$\Delta z_f\%$
TweetSum	BART	17.48±0.32	13.37±0.68	24.68±1.98	16.77±0.40	10.25±2.04	14.48±1.98
	Pegasus	16.73±0.42	17.18±1.04	29.51±5.20	16.67±0.42	11.33±1.97	21.03±5.20
	T5	17.89±0.37	14.44±0.82	16.67±2.94	17.02±0.38	11.78±1.35	9.81±2.94
TODSum	BART	7.26±0.24	3.87±0.16	51.71±17.09	5.85±0.24	2.70±0.42	19.07±15.06
	Pegasus	5.20±0.21	3.50±0.17	37.85±10.74	3.26±0.17	1.74±0.32	22.92±19.33
	T5	7.19±0.26	3.86±0.17	35.25±11.46	5.12±0.23	2.11±0.34	28.13±29.91
SAMSum	BART	13.06±0.36	6.57±0.25	11.39±0.73	22.05±0.52	5.11±0.65	6.62±1.28
	Pegasus	14.21±0.39	6.59±0.26	8.21±2.05	20.59±0.54	4.35±0.5	6.74±5.52
	T5	13.58±0.36	6.72±0.28	4.08±2.77	21.18±0.49	4.5±0.48	4.78±2.22

Table 1: Robustness scores of fine-tuned models using BERTScore. Higher the score, the lower the robustness.

Dimension	Dataset	Typographical	Grammar	Language Use
$\Delta z_c\%$	TweetSum	24.65±0.54	23.32±0.87	20.43±0.69
	TODSum	9.97±0.30	5.82±0.38	5.73±0.28
	SAMSum	16.27±0.36	16.93±0.71	17.78±0.48
$\Delta z_s\%$	TweetSum	16.27±1.93	16.93±2.7	17.78±1.96
	TODSum	5.59±1.32	3.12±1.04	2.96±0.89
	SAMSum	7.38±2.23	7.44±1.54	7.38±1.13
$\Delta z_f\%$	TweetSum	28.01±6.43	26.13±9.42	19.55±8.14
	TODSum	36.73±6.76	25.30±9.81	30.31±8.82
	SAMSum	11.17±1.75	9.98±1.83	8.97±1.57

Table 2: Impact of utterance perturbations. Models are equally impacted by different perturbations.

split utterances. For instance, when subjected to repetitions, the models tend to include repeated utterances in the summary, even if they were previously deemed unimportant (repetition bias; Figure 1). Additionally, the models demonstrate a preference for the first utterance in a dialogue (lead bias), rendering them susceptible to greetings perturbation. This observation aligns with prior findings for news summarization, where sentences at the beginning of an article are more likely to contain summary-worthy information. Similarly, in customer-support conversations, the first utterance frequently addresses the primary issue faced by the customer. Consequently, models trained on such datasets exhibit lead bias. Finally, the models prefer lengthy utterances in the summary (long bias), by being more affected by split perturbations, and less affected by short utterances combined.

5.3 Effect of model size on robustness

Table 4 shows the change in consistency for models with different number of parameters: `BART-base`, `BART-large`, `T5-base`, and `T5-small`. The models are almost equally affected by perturbations, irrespective of size, suggesting that robustness issues cannot be mitigated by scaling the model size.

5.4 How robust are instruction-tuned models when used as zero-shot summarizers?

`DIAL-BART0` and `FLAN-T5-large` are instruction-tuned on multiple tasks, with `DIAL-BART0`, in particular, is instruction-tuned on dialog-specific tasks. However, neither model was trained on the `TweetSum` dataset, providing a zero-shot setting to evaluate their dialogue summarization capabilities. As depicted in Table 5, both `DIAL-BART0` (Δz_c=30.37% for utterance and 34.30% for dialogue) and `FLAN-T5` (Δz_c=38.23% for utterance and 44.12% for dialogue) are much more sensitive to perturbations compared to their fine-tuned counterparts (Δz_c=17.36% for utterance and 16.82% for dialogue, averaged over three models).

In contrast to fine-tuned models, the zero-shot models are affected more by the dialogue-level perturbations (Δz_c=34.30% for `DIAL-BART0` and Δz_c=44.12% for `FLAN-T5`) than utterance-level perturbations (Δz_c=30.37% for `DIAL-BART0` and Δz_c=38.23% for `FLAN-T5`). Among utterance-level perturbations, similar to the fine-tuned models, zero-shot models are also impacted equally by all perturbations. Among dialogue-level perturbations as well, similar to the fine-tuned models, zero-shot models are most impacted by repetitions, greetings and split utterances (Appendix A.6).

We additionally consider a recent instruction-tuned large language model, `Llama-2-70B`, with only publicly available weights. This model is also significantly larger (70B) than the other models (<0.9B). Our results show high sensitivity to perturbations for this model (Δz_c=47.10% for utterance and Δz_c=54.53% for dialogue perturbations), though we leave detailed human evaluation of the outputs of this model for future work.

5.5 Validity of findings with human evaluation

We conduct another human evaluation to confirm the trends observed with automatic similarity metrics. Specifically, we collect similarity scores between summary pairs using human annotations instead of automated similarity metrics (e.g., BERTScore). The goal is to ensure that robustness trends observed with automated metrics are similar to those from human evaluation.

We use the consistency dimension for this evaluation for two main reasons: 1) Empirically, the three robustness dimensions exhibit a strong correlation (Table 10). Thus, using any of the three

Dimension	Dataset	Repetitions	Time Delays	Greetings	Closing Remarks	Split	Combine
$\Delta z_c\%$	TweetSum	18.04±0.59	14.15±0.85	20.01 ±1.34	9.80±1.0	16.71±0.83	6.77±0.36
	TODSum	5.96±0.39	4.31±0.4	6.61±0.59	2.02±0.4	4.38±0.36	-
	SAMSum	27.32±0.46	22.19±0.67	32.89±0.99	16.29±0.89	11.63±0.59	7.80±0.52
$\Delta z_s\%$	TweetSum	12.49±3.45	10.53±1.47	15.23±5.98	6.03±2.23	11.13±1.45	5.40±1.34
	TODSum	3.31±0.98	2.20±0.67	3.48±0.88	1.10±0.66	2.19±1.11	-
	SAMSum	10.87±0.23	8.38±0.98	12.63±0.95	6.04±1.14	14.65± 0.96	7.05±1.26
$\Delta z_f\%$	TweetSum	19.34±5.91	15.81±1.2	18.31±9.23	6.99±8.28	15.11±7.47	8.65±1.42
	TODSum	64.74±6.67	22.74±1.66	50.98±9.51	10.52±9.89	23.37±8.23	-
	SAMSum	17.99±8.91	12.76±2.44	21.25±0.91	10.28±0.95	16.05±5.91	10.21±1.91

Table 3: Robustness to dialogue perturbations. Models are most susceptible to repetitions and time delays (repetition bias), greetings (lead bias), and split utterances (long bias). TODSum dataset has no consecutive utterances from the same speaker, thus we do not perform combine utterance perturbation on this dataset.

Model	Parameters	Utterance Perturbations			Dialogue Perturbations		
		$\Delta z_c\%$	$\Delta z_s\%$	$\Delta z_f\%$	$\Delta z_c\%$	$\Delta z_s\%$	$\Delta z_f\%$
BART-large	440	17.48 ±0.33	13.37±0.68	24.68±0.85	16.77±0.40	10.25±2.01	14.48±1.98
BART-base	140	18.2 ±0.30	16.42±0.58	25.78±0.89	18.2±0.30	13.28±1.84	15.6±2.29
T5-base	220	17.89 ±0.37	14.44±0.82	16.67±2.94	17.02±0.38	11.78±1.35	9.81±2.94
T5-small	60	19.15 ±0.32	14.18±0.53	25.31±2.16	19.15±0.32	8.03±2.72	18.64±5.69

Table 4: Evaluating robustness of different sized fine-tuned models on the TweetSum dataset.

dimensions would suffice for human evaluation, and (2) Among the three dimensions, consistency is easiest to use for human evaluation since it only requires the comparison of two summaries.

We collected annotations via the Appen platform (https://appen.com/), asking annotators to compare summaries of the perturbed and unperturbed dialogue, ranking their similarity on a Likert scale of 1 (dissimilar) to 4 (identical or paraphrases). To collect annotations, we used the same set of 20 dialogues as in §3.3 from the TweetSum dataset. Each dialogue was perturbed with one of the eight categories (utterance- and dialogue-level), yielding 160 summary pairs to be annotated.

We collected 3 annotations per summary pair, totaling 480 annotations; after filtering out noisy annotations, we conducted our analysis on the remaining 314 examples (Appendix A.3 provides annotation procedure and guidelines). We aggregate annotations using majority voting to get similarity scores. To compute consistency scores (equation 1), we map the Likert scale to continuous numeric scores from 0 to 1. We compute mean scores across all pairs for a given dataset and perturbation.

As shown in Figure 2, we observe similar trends, with models exhibiting repetition, long, and lead biases, and that models are affected nearly equally by all utterance perturbations. While the absolute values of Δz_c differ between calculations using automatic metrics and human annotations, the relative impact of different perturbations on the model is similar. For instance, combined utterances and closing remarks have the least impact than repetition, greetings, and split utterance perturbations.[6]

[6]Except time delays, owing to noise in human annotations.

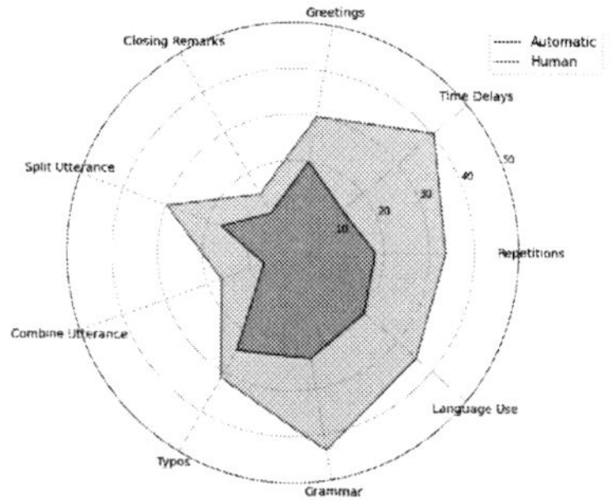

Figure 2: Comparison of consistency scores obtained via human annotations of similarity and the automatic metric on the TweetSum dataset. While the absolute values of Δz_c differ, the relative impact of different perturbations on the model is similar.

5.6 Relationship among dimensions

While theoretically, three dimensions (§4) measure different aspects of robustness, empirically they exhibit a strong correlation of $> 84\%$ across datasets and models (details in Table 10 in Appendix).

This observation can be conceptually explained to some extent. For instance, high saliency implies high consistency: if summaries before and after perturbation are similar to the reference summary, they will be similar to each other, leading to low Δz_s and thus low Δz_c. Similarly, high saliency implies high faithfulness: if the model-generated summary is similar to the reference summary, it will also be factually consistent with the input dialogue, leading to low Δz_s and thus low Δz_f. However, if Δz_s is large, the model could remain faithful under perturbation (small Δz_f): summaries can be different from the reference summary yet consistent with the input dialogue. Thus, conceptually,

Model	Utterance Perturbations			Dialogue Perturbations		
	$\Delta z_c\%$	$\Delta z_s\%$	$\Delta z_f\%$	$\Delta z_c\%$	$\Delta z_s\%$	$\Delta z_f\%$
DIAL-BART0	30.37±0.39	21.80±3.54	37.09±2.57	34.30±0.44	26.44±8.31	47.13±7.51
FLAN-T5	38.23±0.57	41.36±9.10	46.80±14.53	44.12±0.71	39.89±9.09	48.23±11.44
LLAMA-2-70B	47.10±0.17	35.16±0.01	33.19±0.09	54.53±0.48	33.59±0.03	31.69±0.02

Table 5: Robustness of zero-shot summarizers on the TweetSum dataset.

the relation can be explained in only one direction, but empirically the dimensions are highly correlated. Nevertheless, our findings are insightful in their own right, suggesting that the high correlation among all dimensions could be valuable for future robustness studies. For instance, the consistency or faithfulness dimension can serve as reference-free measures of robustness. Consistency is also the easiest to use for human evaluation, as it only requires comparing two summaries.

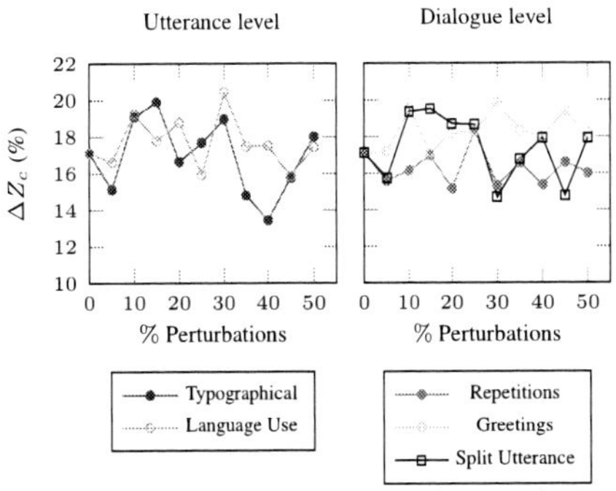

Figure 3: Impact of fine-tuning with perturbations.

6 Improving Robustness

One solution to address robustness issues could be to employ reverse heuristics to remove perturbations from dialogues. However, not all perturbations can be easily discovered and removed. For example, in repetition or time delay perturbations, the repeated utterance may include less information or be paraphrased compared to the original. While greetings and closing remarks might be simpler to remove, we include these perturbations as they offer a systematic approach to investigating model behavior, such as potential lead and recency biases.

Another potential solution to address robustness issues can be to use recent large language models to pre-process dialogues by removing errors and repetitions. However, this approach suffers from two challenges: (1) During deployment, additional pre-processing could increase latency, and (2) language models may hallucinate content, posing the risk of introducing factual errors in the input dialogue.

Finally, we examine if training with perturbations can help to mitigate robustness issues. We fine-tune `BART` on the training data augmented with perturbations and re-evaluate its performance. We create multiple training datasets, each modified by a specific kind of perturbation (typographical errors and language use variations for utterance level; repetitions, split utterances, and greetings for dialogue level), using `TweetSum`'s training split. These modified datasets, with 5-50% of dialogues perturbed, are used to fine-tune `BART`, which we then test on a similarly altered `TweetSum`'s test split.[7] We hypothesize that training with more perturbed dialogues will initially improve performance until a threshold, after which overfitting may reduce effectiveness.

Figure 3 shows the change in model consistency when fine-tuned with perturbations. The lower the change in consistency, the higher the model robustness to the perturbations. One takeaway is that different perturbations necessitate varying amounts of perturbed examples in the training set to achieve maximum performance gain. For example, typographical errors and language use variations yield the largest drop in Δz_c when approximately 40% and 45% of the dialogues are perturbed during training. In contrast, dialogue-level perturbations require significantly less perturbed data during training, with approximately 30% split-utterances, 15% greetings, and only 5% repetitions being sufficient. Overall, the results demonstrate that fine-tuning with perturbed data does not yield consistent performance improvements, warranting more detailed exploration as part of future work.

7 Conclusion

We investigate the impact of naturally occurring variations on state-of-the-art dialogue summarization models using three publicly available datasets. To simulate variations, we introduce utterance-level and dialogue-level perturbations. We conduct our analysis using three dimensions of robustness: consistency, saliency, and faithfulness, which capture different aspects of the summarization model's performance. Our results show that both fine-tuned and instruction-tuned models are affected by perturbations, with instruction-tuned models being more susceptible, particularly to dialogue-level perturbations, spurring the need for future research.

[7]We experimented with training and evaluating a single model on data with all perturbations. However, since different perturbations can have varied impacts on model performance, we found perturbation-wise analysis more interpretable.

8 Limitations

We list some of the limitations of our study which researchers and practitioners would hopefully benefit from when interpreting our analysis. 1) Our analysis uses automatic metrics to measure semantic similarity. Established metrics such BERTScore are imperfect (Deutsch et al., 2022). However, they are widely used in the summarization literature, and also correlate with human judgements of summary quality, and thus are useful for comparing system-level performance. To validate our findings, we also conduct a human evaluation to better understand trends observed due to various perturbations. The investigation of better-automated metrics for natural language generation is an active field of research, and we hope to integrate novel performance metrics in future work. (2) While our perturbations are motivated by real-life scenarios, they are still synthetic in nature. However, we take care wherever possible to avoid unrealistic changes to the dialogues. (3) Our study limits to only open-sourced models and does not investigate the robustness of proprietary LLMs (e.g., ChatGPT), which may be more robust. We decided to limit our study to open-sourced models as it allows us to carefully control what is in the training data, which is not possible with proprietary LLMs and the possibility of data contamination also makes it hard to draw conclusions. (4) Our study mainly focuses on text-based dialogue summarization datasets and does not include spoken conversations, which would bring in very different and diverse nuances of spoken conversations compared to text-based conversations, and is currently out of the scope of this paper. (5) Our study proposes one possible method to measure robustness, and we acknowledge that there can be many other viable ways to quantify robustness. However, quantifying the robustness of tasks involving text generation (e.g., summarization) is an active area of research (Wang et al., 2022) and we hope our work will spur further investigation as part of future work. (6) We did not investigate the robustness of models under both utterance and dialogue level perturbations occurring together in a single dialogue, as that would result in a large number of possible combinations to consider. We leave this for future work.

9 Ethics Statement

All annotators in our human evaluation were recruited via Appen platform and were presented with a consent form prior to the annotation. They were also informed that only satisfactory performance on the screening example will allow them to take part in the annotation task. None of the material/examples they looked at had any hateful or abusive content. We also ensured that the annotators were paid fair amount of wages using Appen's Fair Pay Price Per Judgment which equates to an hourly rate matching a little over the minimum wage of annotators in their respective countries. All the datasets used in this work are publicly available under the CDLA-Sharing license and do not contain any private information.

References

Jiaao Chen and Diyi Yang. 2021. Simple conversational data augmentation for semi-supervised abstractive dialogue summarization. In *Proceedings of the 2021 Conference on Empirical Methods in Natural Language Processing*, pages 6605–6616, Online and Punta Cana, Dominican Republic. Association for Computational Linguistics.

Hyundong Cho, Chinnadhurai Sankar, Christopher Lin, Kaushik Sadagopan, Shahin Shayandeh, Asli Celikyilmaz, Jonathan May, and Ahmad Beirami. 2022. Know thy strengths: Comprehensive dialogue state tracking diagnostics. In *Findings of the Association for Computational Linguistics: EMNLP 2022*, pages 5345–5359, Abu Dhabi, United Arab Emirates. Association for Computational Linguistics.

Hyung Won Chung, Le Hou, Shayne Longpre, Barret Zoph, Yi Tay, William Fedus, Eric Li, Xuezhi Wang, Mostafa Dehghani, Siddhartha Brahma, et al. 2022. Scaling instruction-finetuned language models. *arXiv preprint arXiv:2210.11416*.

Daniel Deutsch, Rotem Dror, and Dan Roth. 2022. Re-examining system-level correlations of automatic summarization evaluation metrics. In *Proceedings of the 2022 Conference of the North American Chapter of the Association for Computational Linguistics: Human Language Technologies*, pages 6038–6052, Seattle, United States. Association for Computational Linguistics.

Kaustubh D. Dhole, Varun Gangal, Sebastian Gehrmann, Aadesh Gupta, Zhenhao Li, Saad Mahamood, Abinaya Mahendiran, Simon Mille, Ashish Srivastava, Samson Tan, Tongshuang Wu, Jascha Sohl-Dickstein, Jinho D. Choi, Eduard Hovy, Ondrej Dusek, Sebastian Ruder, Sajant Anand, Nagender Aneja, Rabin Banjade, Lisa Barthe, Hanna Behnke, Ian Berlot-Attwell, Connor Boyle, Caroline Brun, Marco Antonio Sobrevilla Cabezudo, Samuel Cahyawijaya, Emile Chapuis, Wanxiang Che, Mukund Choudhary, Christian Clauss, Pierre Colombo, Filip Cornell, Gautier Dagan, Mayukh Das, Tanay Dixit, Thomas Dopierre, Paul-Alexis Dray, Suchitra Dubey, Tatiana Ekeinhor, Marco Di Giovanni, Rishabh Gupta, Rishabh Gupta, Louanes Hamla, Sang Han, Fabrice Harel-Canada, Antoine Honore,

Ishan Jindal, Przemyslaw K. Joniak, Denis Kleyko, Venelin Kovatchev, Kalpesh Krishna, Ashutosh Kumar, Stefan Langer, Seungjae Ryan Lee, Corey James Levinson, Hualou Liang, Kaizhao Liang, Zhexiong Liu, Andrey Lukyanenko, Vukosi Marivate, Gerard de Melo, Simon Meoni, Maxime Meyer, Afnan Mir, Nafise Sadat Moosavi, Niklas Muennighoff, Timothy Sum Hon Mun, Kenton Murray, Marcin Namysl, Maria Obedkova, Priti Oli, Nivranshu Pasricha, Jan Pfister, Richard Plant, Vinay Prabhu, Vasile Pais, Libo Qin, Shahab Raji, Pawan Kumar Rajpoot, Vikas Raunak, Roy Rinberg, Nicolas Roberts, Juan Diego Rodriguez, Claude Roux, Vasconcellos P. H. S., Ananya B. Sai, Robin M. Schmidt, Thomas Scialom, Tshephisho Sefara, Saqib N. Shamsi, Xudong Shen, Haoyue Shi, Yiwen Shi, Anna Shvets, Nick Siegel, Damien Sileo, Jamie Simon, Chandan Singh, Roman Sitelew, Priyank Soni, Taylor Sorensen, William Soto, Aman Srivastava, KV Aditya Srivatsa, Tony Sun, Mukund Varma T, A Tabassum, Fiona Anting Tan, Ryan Teehan, Mo Tiwari, Marie Tolkiehn, Athena Wang, Zijian Wang, Gloria Wang, Zijie J. Wang, Fuxuan Wei, Bryan Wilie, Genta Indra Winata, Xinyi Wu, Witold Wydmański, Tianbao Xie, Usama Yaseen, M. Yee, Jing Zhang, and Yue Zhang. 2021. Nl-augmenter: A framework for task-sensitive natural language augmentation.

Arash Einolghozati, Sonal Gupta, Mrinal Mohit, and Rushin Shah. 2019. Improving robustness of task oriented dialog systems. *3rd Conversational AI Workshop at 33rd Conference on Neural Information Processing Systems.*

Guy Feigenblat, Chulaka Gunasekara, Benjamin Sznajder, Sachindra Joshi, David Konopnicki, and Ranit Aharonov. 2021. TWEETSUMM - a dialog summarization dataset for customer service. In *Findings of the Association for Computational Linguistics: EMNLP 2021*, pages 245–260, Punta Cana, Dominican Republic. Association for Computational Linguistics.

Xiachong Feng, Xiaocheng Feng, and Bing Qin. 2021. A survey on dialogue summarization: Recent advances and new frontiers. *ArXiv*, abs/2107.03175.

Tim Fischer, Steffen Remus, and Chris Biemann. 2022. Measuring faithfulness of abstractive summaries. In *Proceedings of the 18th Conference on Natural Language Processing (KONVENS 2022)*, pages 63–73, Potsdam, Germany. KONVENS 2022 Organizers.

Jatin Ganhotra, Robert Moore, Sachindra Joshi, and Kahini Wadhawan. 2020. Effects of naturalistic variation in goal-oriented dialog. In *Findings of the Association for Computational Linguistics: EMNLP 2020*, pages 4013–4020, Online. Association for Computational Linguistics.

John Giorgi, Luca Soldaini, Bo Wang, Gary Bader, Kyle Lo, Lucy Lu Wang, and Arman Cohan. 2022. Exploring the challenges of open domain multi-document summarization. *arXiv preprint arXiv:2212.10526.*

Bogdan Gliwa, Iwona Mochol, Maciej Biesek, and Aleksander Wawer. 2019. SAMSum corpus: A human-annotated dialogue dataset for abstractive summarization. In *Proceedings of the 2nd Workshop on New Frontiers in Summarization*, pages 70–79, Hong Kong, China. Association for Computational Linguistics.

Prakhar Gupta, Cathy Jiao, Yi-Ting Yeh, Shikib Mehri, Maxine Eskenazi, and Jeffrey Bigham. 2022. InstructDial: Improving zero and few-shot generalization in dialogue through instruction tuning. In *Proceedings of the 2022 Conference on Empirical Methods in Natural Language Processing*, pages 505–525, Abu Dhabi, United Arab Emirates. Association for Computational Linguistics.

Hongyan Jing, Daniel Lopresti, and Chilin Shih. 2003. Summarization of noisy documents: A pilot study. In *Proceedings of the HLT-NAACL 03 Text Summarization Workshop*, pages 25–32.

Taehee Jung, Dongyeop Kang, Lucas Mentch, and Eduard Hovy. 2019. Earlier isn't always better: Subaspect analysis on corpus and system biases in summarization. In *Conference on Empirical Methods in Natural Language Processing (EMNLP)*, Hong Kong.

Vladimir Karpukhin, Omer Levy, Jacob Eisenstein, and Marjan Ghazvininejad. 2019. Training on synthetic noise improves robustness to natural noise in machine translation. In *Proceedings of the 5th Workshop on Noisy User-generated Text (W-NUT 2019)*, pages 42–47, Hong Kong, China. Association for Computational Linguistics.

Seokhwan Kim, Yang Liu, Di Jin, Alexandros Papangelis, Karthik Gopalakrishnan, Behnam Hedayatnia, and Dilek Z. Hakkani-Tür. 2021. "how robust r u?": Evaluating task-oriented dialogue systems on spoken conversations. *2021 IEEE Automatic Speech Recognition and Understanding Workshop (ASRU)*, pages 1147–1154.

Kundan Krishna, Yao Zhao, Jie Ren, Balaji Lakshminarayanan, Jiaming Luo, Mohammad Saleh, and Peter J Liu. 2022. Improving the robustness of summarization models by detecting and removing input noise. *arXiv preprint arXiv:2212.09928.*

Philippe Laban, Tobias Schnabel, Paul N Bennett, and Marti A Hearst. 2022. SummaC: Re-visiting NLI-based models for inconsistency detection in summarization. *Transactions of the Association for Computational Linguistics*, 10:163–177.

Mike Lewis, Yinhan Liu, Naman Goyal, Marjan Ghazvininejad, Abdelrahman Mohamed, Omer Levy, Veselin Stoyanov, and Luke Zettlemoyer. 2020. BART: Denoising sequence-to-sequence pre-training for natural language generation, translation, and comprehension. In *Proceedings of the 58th Annual Meeting of the Association for Computational Linguistics*, pages 7871–7880, Online. Association for Computational Linguistics.

Chin-Yew Lin. 2004. ROUGE: A package for automatic evaluation of summaries. In *Text summarization branches out*, pages 74–81.

Jiexi Liu, Ryuichi Takanobu, Jiaxin Wen, Dazhen Wan, Hongguang Li, Weiran Nie, Cheng Li, Wei Peng, and Minlie Huang. 2021. Robustness testing of language understanding in task-oriented dialog. In *Proceedings of the 59th Annual Meeting of the Association for Computational Linguistics and the 11th International Joint Conference on Natural Language Processing*, pages 2467–2480, Online. Association for Computational Linguistics.

Ailsa Meechan-Maddon. 2019. The effect of noise in the training of convolutional neural networks for text summarisation.

Simon Mille, Kaustubh Dhole, Saad Mahamood, Laura Perez-Beltrachini, Varun Gangal, Mihir Kale, Emiel van Miltenburg, and Sebastian Gehrmann. 2021. Automatic construction of evaluation suites for natural language generation datasets. In *Thirty-fifth Conference on Neural Information Processing Systems Datasets and Benchmarks Track (Round 1)*.

George A Miller. 1998. *WordNet: An electronic lexical database*. MIT press.

Robert J. Moore and Raphael Arar. 2019. *Conversational UX Design: A Practitioner's Guide to the Natural Conversation Framework*. Association for Computing Machinery, New York, NY, USA.

Milad Moradi and Matthias Samwald. 2021. Evaluating the robustness of neural language models to input perturbations. In *Conference on Empirical Methods in Natural Language Processing*.

Xing Niu, Prashant Mathur, Georgiana Dinu, and Yaser Al-Onaizan. 2020. Evaluating robustness to input perturbations for neural machine translation. In *Proceedings of the 58th Annual Meeting of the Association for Computational Linguistics*, pages 8538–8544, Online. Association for Computational Linguistics.

Baolin Peng, Chunyuan Li, Zhu Zhang, Chenguang Zhu, Jinchao Li, and Jianfeng Gao. 2020. Raddle: An evaluation benchmark and analysis platform for robust task-oriented dialog systems. *ArXiv*, abs/2012.14666.

Denis Peskov, Joe Barrow, Pedro Rodriguez, Graham Neubig, and Jordan Boyd-Graber. 2019. Mitigating noisy inputs for question answering. *arXiv preprint arXiv:1908.02914*.

Lihua Qian, Lin Qiu, Weinan Zhang, Xin Jiang, and Yong Yu. 2019. Exploring diverse expressions for paraphrase generation. In *Proceedings of the 2019 Conference on Empirical Methods in Natural Language Processing and the 9th International Joint Conference on Natural Language Processing (EMNLP-IJCNLP)*, pages 3173–3182, Hong Kong, China. Association for Computational Linguistics.

Colin Raffel, Noam Shazeer, Adam Roberts, Katherine Lee, Sharan Narang, Michael Matena, Yanqi Zhou, Wei Li, and Peter J Liu. 2020a. Exploring the limits of transfer learning with a unified text-to-text transformer. *The Journal of Machine Learning Research*, 21(1):5485–5551.

Colin Raffel, Noam Shazeer, Adam Roberts, Katherine Lee, Sharan Narang, Michael Matena, Yanqi Zhou, Wei Li, Peter J Liu, et al. 2020b. Exploring the limits of transfer learning with a unified text-to-text transformer. *Journal of Machine Learning Research*, 21(140):1–67.

Harvey Sacks, Emanuel A. Schegloff, and Gail D. Jefferson. 1974. A simplest systematics for the organization of turn-taking for conversation. *Language*, 50:696 – 735.

Sailik Sengupta, Jason Krone, and Saab Mansour. 2021. On the robustness of intent classification and slot labeling in goal-oriented dialog systems to real-world noise. In *Proceedings of the 3rd Workshop on Natural Language Processing for Conversational AI*, pages 68–79, Online. Association for Computational Linguistics.

Xin Tian, Xinxian Huang, Dongfeng He, Yingzhan Lin, Siqi Bao, H. He, Liankai Huang, Qiang Ju, Xiyuan Zhang, Jianyue Xie, Shuqi Sun, Fan Wang, Hua Wu, and Haifeng Wang. 2021. Tod-da: Towards boosting the robustness of task-oriented dialogue modeling on spoken conversations. *ArXiv*, abs/2112.12441.

Vaibhav Vaibhav, Sumeet Singh, Craig Stewart, and Graham Neubig. 2019. Improving robustness of machine translation with synthetic noise. In *Proceedings of the 2019 Conference of the North American Chapter of the Association for Computational Linguistics: Human Language Technologies, Volume 1 (Long and Short Papers)*, pages 1916–1920, Minneapolis, Minnesota. Association for Computational Linguistics.

Xuezhi Wang, Haohan Wang, and Diyi Yang. 2022. Measure and improve robustness in NLP models: A survey. In *Proceedings of the 2022 Conference of the North American Chapter of the Association for Computational Linguistics: Human Language Technologies*, pages 4569–4586, Seattle, United States. Association for Computational Linguistics.

Larry Wasserman. 2004. *All of statistics: a concise course in statistical inference*, volume 26. Springer.

Linzi Xing, Wen Xiao, and Giuseppe Carenini. 2021. Demoting the lead bias in news summarization via alternating adversarial learning. In *Annual Meeting of the Association for Computational Linguistics*.

Alex Yorke. butter-fingers.

Lin Yuan and Zhou Yu. 2019. Abstractive dialog summarization with semantic scaffolds. *arXiv preprint arXiv:1910.00825*.

Jingqing Zhang, Yao Zhao, Mohammad Saleh, and Peter J. Liu. 2019. Pegasus: Pre-training with extracted gap-sentences for abstractive summarization.

Tianyi Zhang, Varsha Kishore, Felix Wu, Kilian Q. Weinberger, and Yoav Artzi. 2020. BERTScore: Evaluating text generation with BERT. In *International Conference on Learning Representations*.

Lulu Zhao, Fujia Zheng, Keqing He, Weihao Zeng, Yuejie Lei, Huixing Jiang, Wei Wu, Weiran Xu, Jun Guo, and Fanyu Meng. 2021. Todsum: Task-oriented dialogue summarization with state tracking. *ArXiv*, abs/2110.12680.

Qi Zhu, Zheng Zhang, Yan Fang, Xiang Li, Ryuichi Takanobu, Jinchao Li, Baolin Peng, Jianfeng Gao, Xiaoyan Zhu, and Minlie Huang. 2020. Convlab-2: An open-source toolkit for building, evaluating, and diagnosing dialogue systems. In *Annual Meeting of the Association for Computational Linguistics*.

Caleb Ziems, Jiaao Chen, Camille Harris, Jessica Brooke Anderson, and Diyi Yang. 2022. Value: Understanding dialect disparity in nlu. *ArXiv*, abs/2204.03031.

A Appendix

A.1 Details/Examples of Perturbations

See Table 6.

A.2 Details of annotation guidelines of quality validation in §5.2

For annotation collection, we only allowed annotators proficient in English from a small group of the most experienced annotators adjudicated by the Appen platform; from any country. We also used hidden test questions for quality control and required annotators to maintain at least 80% accuracy throughout the job on these hidden test questions. These test questions are pre-labeled and are used before and during the task to quiz the annotator. We selected 15 test questions from the validation split of each dataset ensuring that these questions do not overlap with questions seen by the annotators for the actual annotation task. Figure 4 shows the annotation guidelines and Figure 5 shows examples provided for this task.

A.3 Details of annotation guidelines for the validity of trends in §5.6

Quality Control: For this task, as well we only allowed annotators proficient in English from a small group of the most experienced annotators adjudicated by the Appen platform; from any country. We also used hidden test questions for quality control and required annotators to maintain at least 80% accuracy throughout the job on these hidden test questions. Figure 6 shows the annotation guidelines, and Figure 7 shows examples provided for this task.

Number of annotations: In the main task, each annotator was shown 5 examples per page with one hidden test example. For each example, we collected three annotations. In cases where there was no agreement among the initial three annotations, we obtained additional annotations. A maximum of five annotations was considered.

Noise Filtering: Before computing consistency scores, we took several steps to filter out noisy annotations. The Appen platform estimates the trust score for each worker (by calculating accuracy on hidden test examples) and also marks examples as tainted if it is annotated by an annotator whose accuracy score has fallen below the minimum accuracy threshold. To retain only the highest quality annotations, we remove annotations that were marked as tainted and only keep annotations from workers

Perturbation Type	Perturbation Category	Perturbation Name	Examples
Utterance Level	Typographical Errors	remove punctuation	great! → great
		remove/add whitespace	Customer → Custo mer
		change letter casing	action → actIon
		common substitutions expansions	n't → not
		common substitutions contractions	I am → I'm
	Grammatical Errors	dropping determiners	a, the, an
		subject-verb disagreements	She likes apples. → She like apples.
		homophone swaps	their → there
	Spoken Language Errors	filler words and disfluencies	uhm, uh, erm, ah, er, err, actually, like, you know I think/believe/mean, I would say maybe, perhaps, probably, possibly, most likely
Dialogue Level	Repetitions	N/A	'Sorry, I couldn't hear you, can you repeat?'
	Time Delays	N/A	'Just give me a few minutes..' 'sure', 'yup!' 'Thanks for waiting.'
	Greeting and closing remarks	greeting (Customer Support)	'Hi! I am your customer support assistant. How may I help you today?'
		greeting (friends)	'Hi!' or 'Hey there!'
		closing (Customer Support)	'Thank you for contacting us. Have a nice day!'
		closing (friends)	'Cool, talk to you later!', 'Bye.'

Table 6: Examples of each perturbation

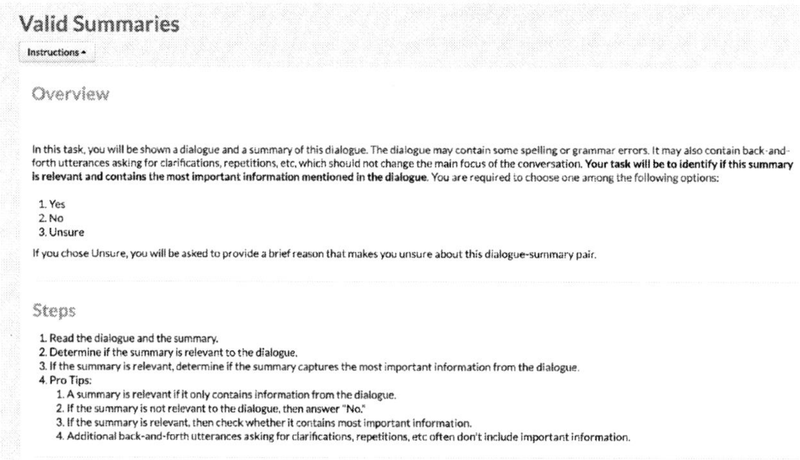

Figure 4: Annotation guidelines for quality validation of perturbed dialogue-summary pairs.

whose trust score is 100%. On qualitatively examining the annotations we also found cases where the two summaries were word-by-word the same, yet the annotator did not give a rating of 4 (highly similar or exact match). Since this is a case of obvious noise, we remove such cases. If an example has less than 3 annotations left after the filtering step, we drop the example. After this filtering, we finally use 314 annotations to conduct our analysis.

Dataset	Model	Repeated Utterance Most Relevant	Least Relevant	Random
TweetSum	BART	12.40	14.53	14.46
	Pegasus	13.49	16.68	14.22
	T5	9.26	11.46	10.84
TODSum	BART	1.94	4.32	3.52
	Pegasus	2.05	2.05	2.92
	T5	1.85	3.66	3.50

Table 7: Saliency scores of fine-tuned models with targeted perturbations. Perturbing the least relevant utterance results in the highest change in saliency, suggesting that the model exhibits repetition bias.

A.4 Targeted dialogue perturbations to investigate the repetition bias

To delve deeper into the repetition bias observed in the models, we conducted targeted perturbations, where we repeat utterances based on whether the information conveyed in those utterances was considered important by the reference summary. Specifically, we identify utterances that are highly relevant and least relevant to the reference summary. To measure relevance, we compute semantic similarity[8] between each utterance and each sentence in the reference summary. For each summary sentence, we then determine the most (least) relevant utterance by selecting the one with the highest (lowest) similarity with the summary sentence. When perturbing the most relevant utterance, we perturb the utterances that were identified as relevant to at least one summary sentence. When perturbing

[8]using sentence transformers [CITE]

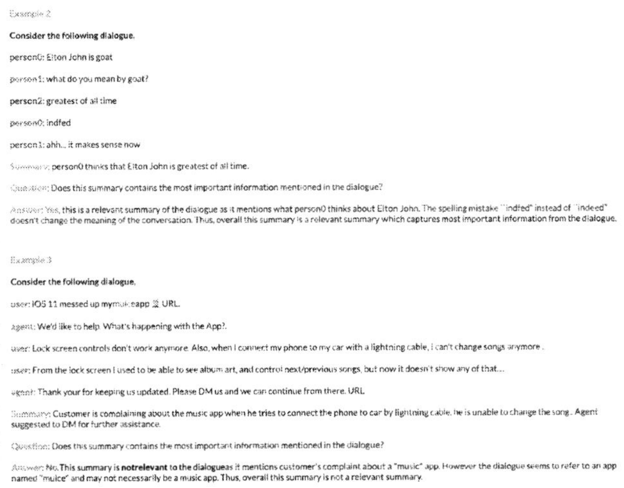
Example 2

Consider the following dialogue.

person0: Elton John is goat

person1: what do you mean by goat?

person2: greatest of all time

person0: indfed

person1: ahh... it makes sense now

Summary: person0 thinks that Elton John is greatest of all time.

Question: Does this summary contains the most important information mentioned in the dialogue?

Answer: Yes, this is a relevant summary of the dialogue as it mentions what person0 thinks about Elton John. The spelling mistake "indfed" instead of "indeed" doesn't change the meaning of the conversation. Thus, overall this summary is a relevant summary which captures most important information from the dialogue.

Example 3

Consider the following dialogue.

user: IOS 11 messed up mymuiceapp URL.

agent: We'd like to help. What's happening with the App?.

user: Lock screen controls don't work anymore. Also, when I connect my phone to my car with a lightning cable, I can't change songs anymore .

user: From the lock screen I used to be able to see album art, and control next/previous songs, but now it doesn't show any of that...

agent: Thank your for keeping us updated. Please DM us and we can continue from there. URL

Summary: Customer is complaining about the music app when he tries to connect the phone to car by lightning cable. he is unable to change the song . Agent suggested to DM for further assistance.

Question: Does this summary contains the most important information mentioned in the dialogue?

Answer: No. This summary is **notrelevant** to the dialogueas it mentions customer's complaint about a "music" app. However the dialogue seems to refer to an app named "muice" and may not necessarily be a music app. Thus, overall this summary is not a relevant summary.

Figure 5: Examples provided as part of annotation guidelines for quality validation of perturbed dialogue-summary pairs

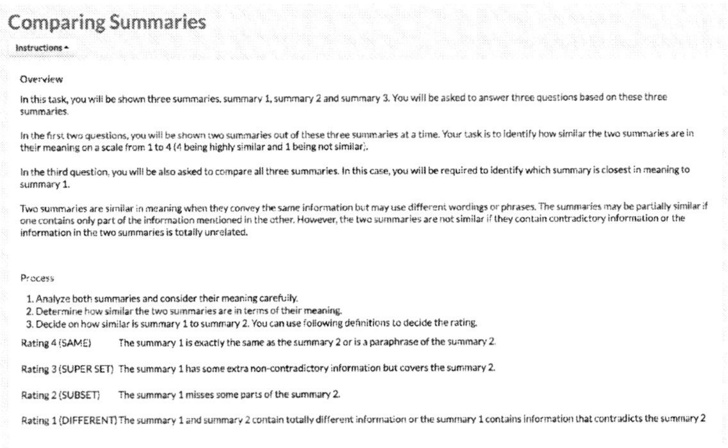
Comparing Summaries

Instructions

Overview

In this task, you will be shown three summaries. summary 1, summary 2 and summary 3. You will be asked to answer three questions based on these three summaries.

In the first two questions, you will be shown two summaries out of these three summaries at a time. Your task is to identify how similar the two summaries are in their meaning on a scale from 1 to 4 (4 being highly similar and 1 being not similar).

In the third question, you will be also asked to compare all three summaries. In this case, you will be required to identify which summary is closest in meaning to summary 1.

Two summaries are similar in meaning when they convey the same information but may use different wordings or phrases. The summaries may be partially similar if one contains only part of the information mentioned in the other. However, the two summaries are not similar if they contain contradictory information or the information in the two summaries is totally unrelated.

Process

1. Analyze both summaries and consider their meaning carefully.
2. Determine how similar the two summaries are in terms of their meaning.
3. Decide on how similar is summary 1 to summary 2. You can use following definitions to decide the rating.

Rating 4 (SAME) The summary 1 is exactly the same as the summary 2 or is a paraphrase of the summary 2.

Rating 3 (SUPER SET) The summary 1 has some extra non-contradictory information but covers the summary 2.

Rating 2 (SUBSET) The summary 1 misses some parts of the summary 2.

Rating 1 (DIFFERENT) The summary 1 and summary 2 contain totally different information or the summary 1 contains information that contradicts the summary 2

Figure 6: Annotation guidelines for the validity of trends; to collect similarity annotations for pair of summaries.

the least relevant utterance, we perturb the utterances that were identified as least relevant to all the summary sentences.

As shown in Table 7, we observe that the model exhibits the highest change in saliency scores when we perturb the least relevant utterance, which further demonstrates the model's tendency to consider repeated information as important, even though it was not considered important as per the reference summary. In contrast, repetition of the most relevant utterance shows the least change in the scores, since the model already focuses on the most relevant information before perturbation and after repeating that utterance, it still remains important to be included in the summary.

A.5 Sensitivity to perturbation rate

A.6 Perturbation-wise impact on zero-shot models

See Table 8 and Table 9

A.7 Correlation analysis

Table 10 shows the Pearson correlations between pairs of dimensions on the TweetSum dataset. Correlations scores are also visualized in Figures 10, 11, 12. Similar correlation are also observed on SAMSum (Figures 14, 15, 13) and TODSum datasets (Figures 17, 18, 16).

A.8 Analysis using ROUGE-L and SummaC scores

Example 1 (SAME):

Summary 1: The customer is upset about the train delay. According to the agent, delay repay compensation is available to those affected by disruption who have been delayed for more than 30 minutes.

Summary: 2 Customer is complaining about the delay in the train. Agent states that the delay repay compensation is available to those who have been caught up in disruption and delayed by over 30 minutes.

Answer: 4 (SAME). Both summaries convey the exact same information and have the same meaning. Thus, these summaries are very similar. On a scale of 1-4, these two summaries score 4.

Example 2 (SUPER SET):

Summary 1: Customer is complaining about the fluctuation in the internet which goes in and out and fluctuates speed is also extremely variable. Agent requests to speak privately via direct message so that they can look further into this issue.

Summary 2: The customer is complaining that he was disappointed with the internet services. The agent asked the customer to directly message them for further assistance.

Answer: 3 (SUPER SET) In this example, the summary 1 is a super set of the summary 2. The summary 2 mentions that the customer is complaining about internet services. This information is also mentioned in the summary 1 which provides more details about the complaint (e.g., fluctuating speed). In other words, the summary 1 contains some additional information not present in the summary 2 and thus summary 1 is a superset of summary 2. Both summary 1 and summary 2 mention that the agent requested the user to directly message. thus this portion of the summary 2 exactly matches with the summary 1. Overall, the summary 1 is a super set of the summary 2. On a scale of 1-4, these two summaries score 3.

Example 3 (SUB SET):

Summary 1: Customer is complaining that he is unable to change the reservation. Agent requests to provide confirmation number via DM so that they can assist further.

Summary 2: The customer is complaining that he was trying to contact Delta about changing the reservation. the agent asked to provide their confirmation number via DM so that they can assist

Answer: 2 (SUB SET) In this example. the summary 2 slightly differs from the summary 1. The summary 2 mentions that the customer was trying to contact Delta about changing the reservation. However, the summary 1 mentions that the customer is unable to change the reservation and doesn't mention anything about Delta. At the same time, both summaries are similar when mentioning the agent's response. Thus, overall, the two summaries are only partially similar, with summary 1 missing some information compared to the summary 2. On a scale of 1-4, these two summaries score 2.

Figure 7: Examples provided as part of annotation guidelines to collect similarity annotations for pair of summaries.

Model	Perturbation					
	repetitions	time_delays	greetings	Closing remarks	split_utterances	combined_utterances
DIAL-BART0	35.30	31.15	35.02	23.07	35.10	18.31
FLAN-T5	45.65	32.88	60.10	48.11	41.45	20.34

Table 8: Change in consistency scores due to dialouge-level perturbations on instruction-tuned models when used as zero-shot summarizers. Models are more affected due to repetitions, time-delays, greetings, and split utterances compared to closing remarks and combined utterances.

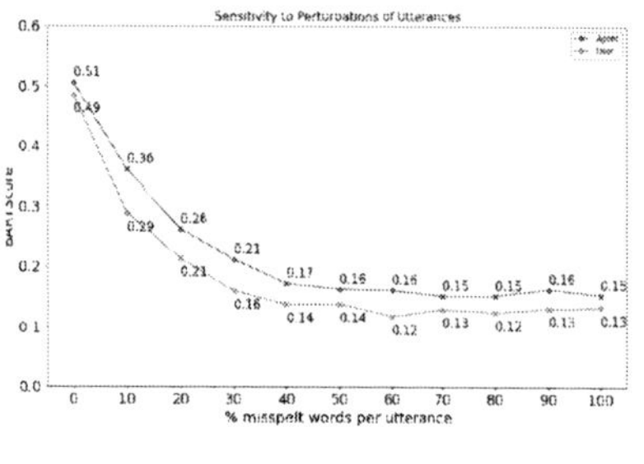

Figure 8: Consistency scores for spelling error perturbation, when varying the percentage of words perturbed per utterance. We perturb all utterances in a dialogue. A perturbation rate of 20% also causes a considerable drop in model performance.

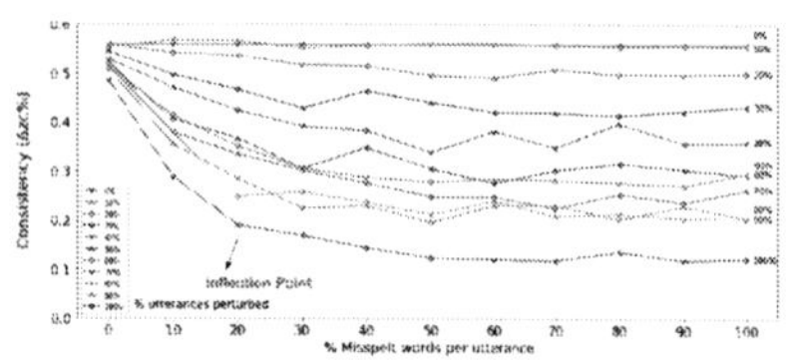

Figure 9: Consistency scores for spelling error perturbation, when varying the percentage of words perturbed per utterance. We also vary the number of utterances being perturbed. Perturbing more than 30% utterances also causes a considerable drop in model performance.

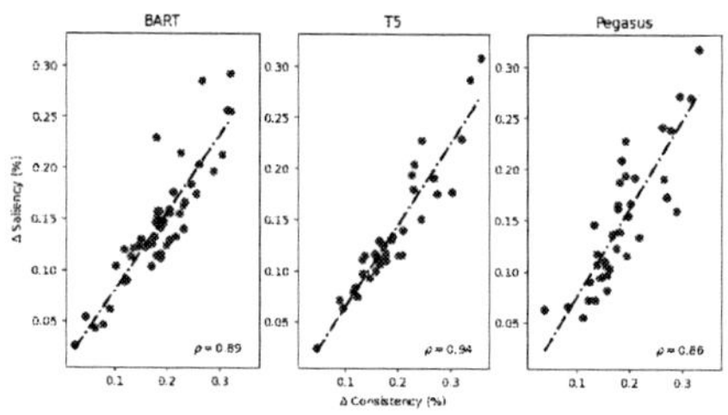

Figure 10: Correlation between consistency and saliency dimensions on TweetSum dataset.

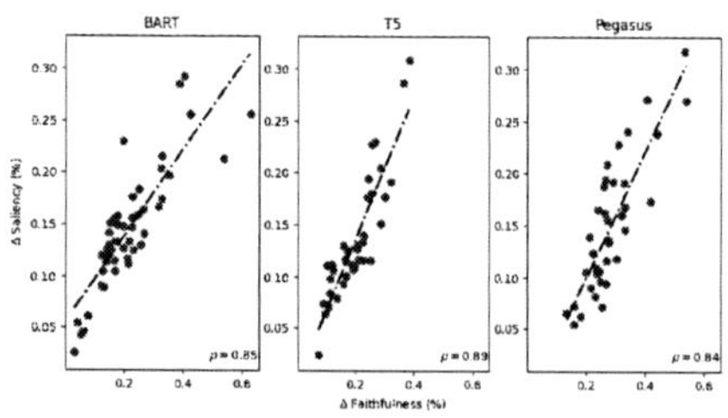

Figure 11: Correlation between faithfulness and saliency dimensions on TweetSum dataset (Outliers excluded for the purpose of visualization).

Model	Perturbation			
	typographical	grammar	language_use	speech_recognition
DIAL-BART0	33.74	32.26	27.53	30.33
FLAN-T5	42.60	48.03	39.75	33.86

Table 9: Change in consistency scores due to utterance-level perturbations on instruction-tuned models when used as zero-shot summarizers. Models are equally affected due to all perturbations.

Model	Pair of dimensions		
	$(\Delta z_c, \Delta z_s)$	$(\Delta z_c, \Delta z_f)$	$(\Delta z_f, \Delta z_s)$
BART	0.89	0.91	0.85
T5	0.94	0.93	0.89
Pegasus	0.86	0.85	0.84

Table 10: Pearson correlations between pairs of dimensions on the TweetSum dataset. Similar correlation observed on SAMSum and TODSum (Appendix A.7).

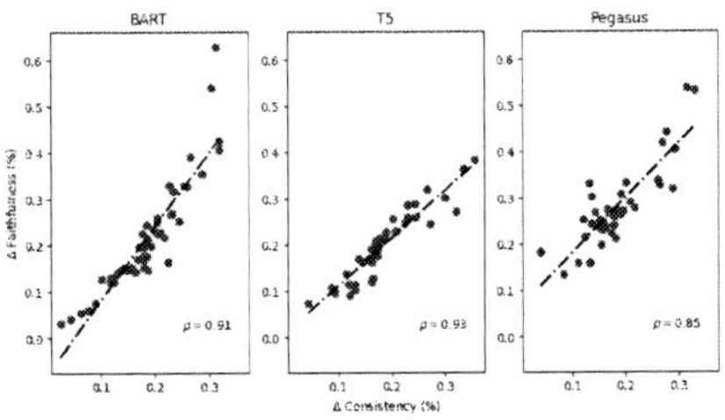

Figure 12: Correlation between faithfulness and consistency dimensions on TweetSum dataset.

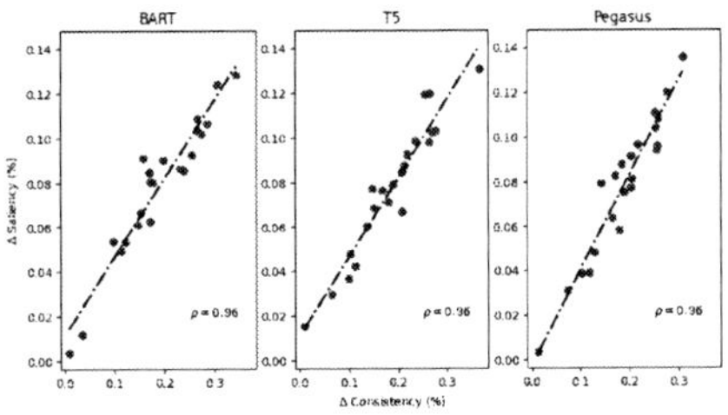

Figure 13: Correlation between consistency and saliency dimensions on SAMSum dataset.

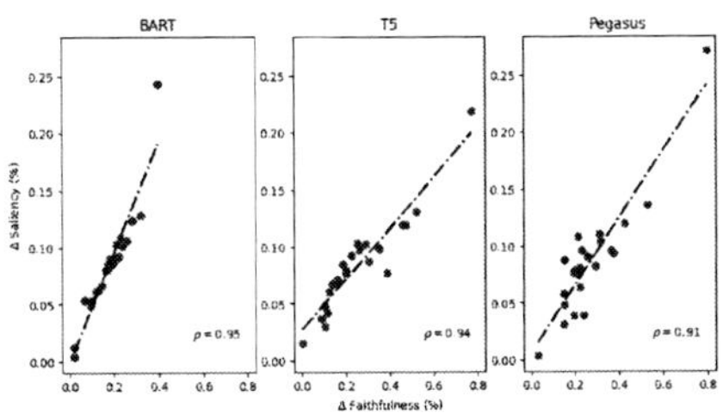

Figure 14: Correlation between faithfulness and saliency dimensions on SAMSum dataset (Outliers excluded for the purpose of visualization).

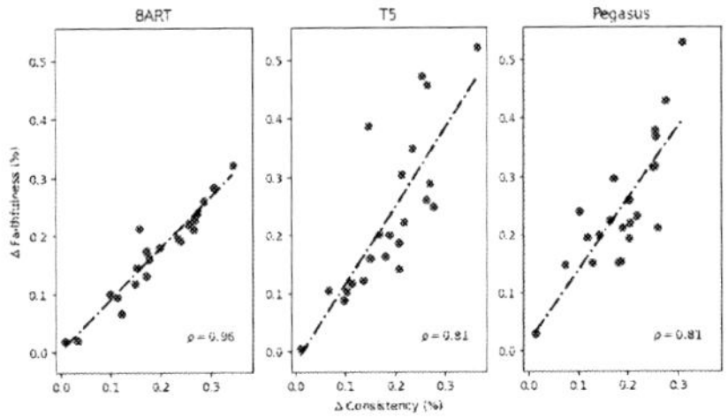

Figure 15: Correlation between faithfulness and consistency dimensions on SAMSum dataset.

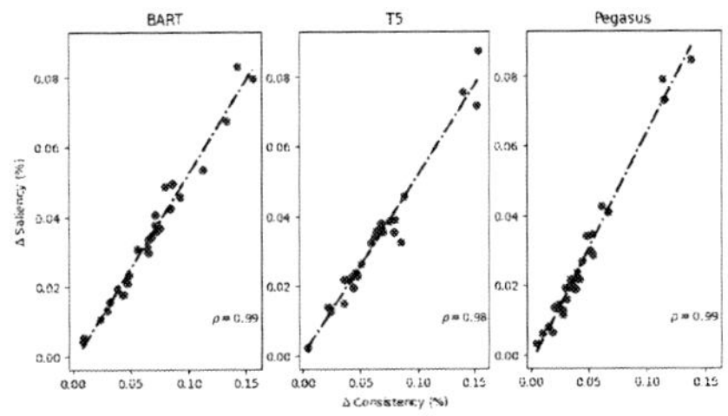

Figure 16: Correlation between consistency and saliency dimensions on TODSum dataset.

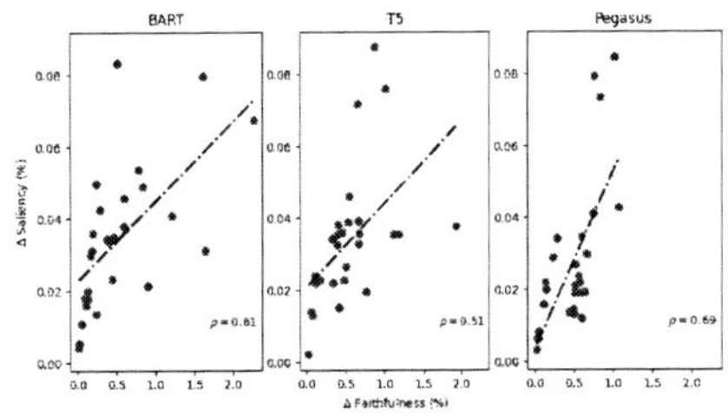

Figure 17: Correlation between faithfulness and saliency dimensions on TODSum dataset (Outliers excluded for the purpose of visualization).

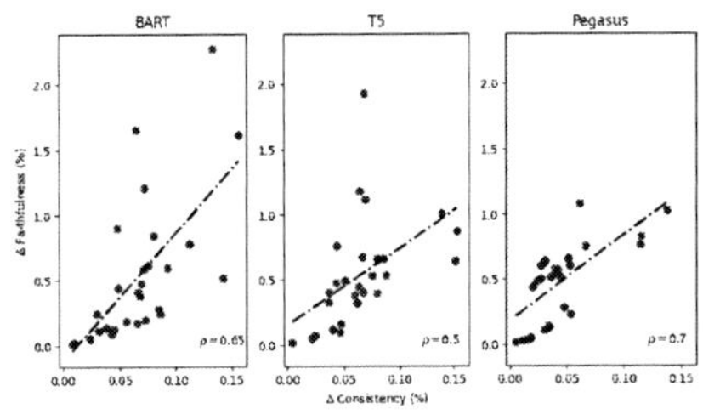

Figure 18: Correlation between faithfulness and consistency dimensions on TODSum dataset.

Model	Utterance Perturbations			Dialogue Perturbations		
	Consistency	Saliency	Faithfulness	Consistency	Saliency	Faithfulness
BART Large	14.00±0.22	10.91±0.01	9.18±0.01	14.37±0.37	10.37±0.01	8.97±0.01
BART Base	14.18±0.29	10.65±0.01	9.60±0.01	15.40±0.31	9.74±0.01	9.04±0.09
Pegasus	13.50±0.46	13.24±0.01	11.29±0.02	14.78±0.39	12.14±0.02	9.80±0.01
T5 Base	14.72±0.36	13.43±0.01	11.01±0.01	13.88±0.42	12.27±0.02	9.79±0.01
T5 Small	14.66±0.33	14.40±0.01	10.11±0.01	15.75±0.31	10.99±0.01	8.72±0.08
DIAL-BART0	29.72±0.36	22.70±0.01	20.53±0.01	34.09±0.30	26.3±0.02	23.29±0.01
FLAN-T5	34.06±0.55	34.63±0.01	36.67±0.02	39.84±0.53	36.98±0.03	40.82±0.06
LLAMA-2	47.1±0.17	35.16±0.01	33.19±0.09	54.53±0.48	33.59±0.03	31.69±0.02

Table 11: Results on TweetSum using ROUGE-L

Model	Utterance Perturbations			Dialogue Perturbations		
	Consistency	Saliency	Faithfulness	Consistency	Saliency	Faithfulness
BART Large	19.18±0.35	6.66±0.01	3.37±0.01	20.85±0.60	7.70±0.02	2.11±0.01
BART Base	19.35±0.41	6.67±0.01	4.23±0.02	21.08±0.47	5.34±0.02	3.07±0.01
Pegasus	19.67±0.50	8.33±0.02	3.75±0.01	21.70±0.53	7.43±0.03	3.67±0.03
T5 Base	19.20±0.50	7.81±0.03	3.87±0.03	21.40±0.58	7.76±0.04	3.44±0.01
T5 Small	20.77±0.55	8.44±0.06	3.69±0.01	21.17±0.63	5.93±0.01	2.38±0.04
DIAL-BART0	43.05±0.52	12.8±0.03	4.55±0.01	51.75±0.47	16.05±0.02	6.32±0.03
FLAN-T5	39.54±0.64	14.96±0.00	5.95±0.01	45.93±0.65	15.35±0.04	7.72±0.02
LLAMA-2	45.05±0.44	20.51±0.04	18.06±0.02	56.32±0.43	20.58±0.11	12.79±0.06

Table 12: Results on TweetSum using SummaC

Dimension	Repetitions	Time Delays	Greetings	Conclusion	Split Utterances	Combine Utterances
Consistency	31.03±0.52	25.73 ±0.77	36.89±1.07	18.17±0.95	13.34±0.75	8.7±0.62
Saliency	12.16±0.66	9.64±0.97	16.72±2.36	5.62±0.73	11.63±1.05	6.62±0.77
Faithfulness	10.17±0.45	7.54±0.58	10.84±0.93	5.3±0.69	8.96±0.6	5.33±0.49

Table 13: Impact of Dialouge Perturbations on TweetSum using ROUGE-L

Engineering Conversational Search Systems: A Review of Applications, Architectures, and Functional Components

Phillip Schneider[1], **Wessel Poelman**[2], **Michael Rovatsos**[3], **and Florian Matthes**[1]
[1]Technical University of Munich, Department of Computer Science, Germany
[2]KU Leuven, Department of Computer Science, Belgium
[3]The University of Edinburgh, School of Informatics, United Kingdom
{phillip.schneider, matthes}@tum.de
wessel.poelman@kuleuven.be
michael.rovatsos@ed.ac.uk

Abstract

Conversational search systems enable information retrieval via natural language interactions, with the goal of maximizing users' information gain over multiple dialogue turns. The increasing prevalence of conversational interfaces adopting this search paradigm challenges traditional information retrieval approaches, stressing the importance of better understanding the engineering process of developing these systems. We undertook a systematic literature review to investigate the links between theoretical studies and technical implementations of conversational search systems. Our review identifies real-world application scenarios, system architectures, and functional components. We consolidate our results by presenting a layered architecture framework and explaining the core functions of conversational search systems. Furthermore, we reflect on our findings in light of the rapid progress in large language models, discussing their capabilities, limitations, and directions for future research.

1 Introduction

Accessing information has always been one of the primary functions of computer systems. Early systems relied on command-line interfaces with a specific syntax for data retrieval. As search systems evolved, database query languages enabled more complex queries but required technical knowledge. Then, free-text search engines allowed users to enter keywords in natural language, with information typically displayed as a result page listing relevant items (Höchstötter and Lewandowski, 2009). In recent years, the evolution of search systems has continued in the direction of human-like dialogues.

Conversational search has emerged as a novel search paradigm, marking a shift from traditional search engines to interactive dialogues with intelligent agents (Radlinski and Craswell, 2017; Zhang et al., 2018). Many people have grown accustomed to using conversational interfaces like chatbots and voice assistants (Klopfenstein et al., 2017). The widespread usage of dialogue systems has changed how humans expect to interact with computers (McTear et al., 2016). Although modern conversational agents have impressive skill sets, their information-seeking capabilities are relatively limited and often confined to answering simple questions. As a consequence, there is a growing research interest in developing conversational search interfaces that go beyond simple query-response interactions by supporting more complex mixed-initiative dialogues, which is further fueled by the surging popularity of large language models (LLMs) and their integration into many kinds of search applications.

Even though the topic of conversational search is relatively new, its fundamental concepts can be traced back to early works from the natural language processing (NLP) and information retrieval fields. So far, this emerging topic has been approached from different angles. While some researchers focus on theories and conceptual aspects (Azzopardi et al., 2018), others conduct dialogue analyses and build prototypes to ground abstract models in empirical studies (Vakulenko et al., 2021a). Yet, despite the ample literature about required properties, many proposed systems are too complex to implement. This apparent gap highlights the need for a more holistic inspection that connects theoretical requirements with realizable functional components.

We conducted a systematic literature review investigating different aspects of conversational search systems (CSSs) to address this research gap. The three main contributions are as follows:
(1) We identify the conceptual system properties and suitable application scenarios of CSSs.
(2) We consolidate architectures from the literature into a layered architecture framework and elaborate on the core functional components of CSSs.
(3) We discuss the manifold implications for aug-

Proceedings of the 6th Workshop on NLP for Conversational AI (NLP4ConvAI 2024), pages 73–88
August 16, 2024

menting CSSs with LLMs, highlighting their potential capabilities, limitations, and risks.

2 Related Work

In the related research literature on systems for conversational information-seeking, three categories are usually distinguished: search, recommendation, and question-answering (QA) (Zamani et al., 2023). As the name suggests, CSSs actively involve users in the search process. Through multi-turn dialogues, users enter queries, locate information, examine results, or refine their search goals. In contrast to search systems, recommender systems usually rely on data about user preferences and past interaction histories to help with decision-making by providing personalized recommendations. QA systems have been an active area of research for many decades. Given a text corpus or knowledge base and a dialogue history, conversational QA systems aim to find answers to natural language questions (Vakulenko et al., 2021b). It is worth noting that the boundaries between conversational search, recommender, and QA systems are blurred and overlap. Although surveys exist on the two latter system categories (Jannach et al., 2021; Zaib et al., 2022), our literature review is dedicated to search-oriented conversational interfaces.

Despite the growing body of research on conversational search, related work, such as surveys or systematic literature reviews, remains scarce. The few studies we found tend to have a narrow topic focus on certain application domains or challenges. For example, the survey from Adatrao et al. (2023) gives an overview of conversational search applications in biomedicine. In a different study, Keyvan and Huang (2022) address the challenge of dealing with ambiguous queries. Another literature study from Gerritse et al. (2020) investigates problematic biases in personalized content that conversational search agents can exhibit. Yet another work by Kiesel et al. (2021) is a comprehensive survey on meta-information in search-oriented conversations.

To the best of our knowledge, we are the first to provide a system-centric review across the development process, ranging from conceptualizing core functions to implementing architectural components. Unlike the mentioned studies, we do not look into specific challenges or domains within conversational search but take on a broad engineering perspective. We summarize valuable insights regarding the design and development of CSSs for several application use cases. Additionally, we address the recent interest surrounding LLMs and their potential implications for engineering CSSs.

3 Method

We conducted our systematic review based on the guidelines from Kitchenham et al. (2004). Our study aims to shed light on the complex engineering process behind CSSs from initial system requirements to technical implementations by focusing on three key aspects: (1) definitions and proposed application scenarios to conceptualize the functional requirements of CSSs, (2) architectural elements suggested in the literature to effectively support these required system properties, and (3) core functions of CSSs discussed in the academic literature along with their implementations.

To obtain relevant publications, we devised a search string for querying six academic databases, as presented in Table 2 of Appendix A. The publication period was restricted to the time window between 2012 and 2022, yielding 212 candidate papers that predated the emergence of primarily LLM-based dialogue systems like ChatGPT (OpenAI, 2022). Two researchers screened the papers for relevance, selecting a final set of 51 papers. Additionally, they performed forward and backward snowballing to include recent papers from 2023 and 2024, mainly focusing on LLMs for CSSs.

4 Results

4.1 Definitions and Application Scenarios

The concept of conversational search is not uniformly defined in the literature. We found three main categories of definitions. System-oriented definitions describe conversational search referring to architectural components (Sa and Yuan, 2020; Vakulenko et al., 2021a). Dialogue-oriented definitions emphasize the specifics of the dialogue interaction (Radlinski and Craswell, 2017; Kiesel et al., 2021). Task-oriented definitions state tasks the system must complete (Zhang et al., 2018; Trippas et al., 2020). Despite focusing on different aspects, the analyzed definitions point out similar qualities to distinguish CSSs from traditional search approaches. These qualities are often related to the theoretical framework of Radlinski and Craswell (2017), which provides a structure and set of characteristics for designing and evaluating CSSs. In summary, we identified four reoccurring system properties from the analyzed papers. Firstly, *mixed-initiative interaction* lets both user and system collaboratively steer the dialogue. Secondly, *mutual understanding* involves the system revealing its capabilities and helping users express their needs. Thirdly, *context awareness and memory* refers to the system's ability to gather information from its surroundings and conversation history to adapt dynamically. Lastly, *continuous refinement* denotes improving retrieval performance through direct feedback or learning from past interactions.

Search Modality. These system properties open up a wide range of use cases, but the suitability of conversational search depends on the search modality and search task. CSSs can support text-based, speech-based, or hybrid interaction modalities. Aliannejadi et al. (2021) analyze various modality types and discuss their impact on the user's information gain during conversations. The authors mention examples like voice interfaces as speech-only options for service hotlines, text-based systems that can be integrated into messaging platforms or web search engines, and multimodal systems, such as virtual assistants or smart speakers with screens to display visual information. Contrary to text-based interfaces, spoken CSSs work without screens and are highly accessible because they do not require any technical expertise. Yet, conveying search results solely through speech output can overwhelm users (Deldjoo et al., 2021). Moreover, two studies conducted by Xing et al. (2022) and Sa and Yuan (2020) indicate that different modalities influence the search behavior concerning the frequency of query reformulation or how long search results are examined. Although the majority of CSSs in the literature are predominantly uni-modal and text-based, Liao et al. (2021) note a growing trend towards multimodal systems.

The modality and the nature of the search task determine the appropriateness of conversational interaction. A conventional data lookup with a graphical user interface may be more efficient in scenarios where the information need can be easily expressed. Concerning more ambiguous scenarios where the search goal is multi-faceted, and the data structure complex, a free-form conversation with iterative clarifications, reasoning steps, and feedback loops becomes applicable for conversational search (Radlinski and Craswell, 2017). In support of this, Ren et al. (2021b) and Schneider et al. (2023a) argue that dialogue-based search is particularly effective for exploratory search goals that involve progressively narrowing down information items from unfamiliar information spaces (White and Roth, 2009). Other tasks for which the usefulness of conversational search was highlighted are sequential QA, learning about a new topic, asking for personal recommendations, or making plans (Anand et al., 2020).

Application Scenarios. In our analysis of conversational search scenarios, we identified several real-world application domains that have been explored. While business and health were the most popular domains, we observed a significant diversification in the last years, including aerospace, gastronomy, law, news media, public services, or tourism (Liao et al., 2021). For example, several researchers have studied product search in e-commerce scenarios for eliciting user preferences across multiple dialogue turns (Bi et al., 2019; Xiao et al., 2021). A study from Bickmore et al. (2016) proposed a CSS to support people with low health and computer literacy to find information about clinical trials for which they may be eligible. In the domain of news media, Schneider et al. (2023b) demonstrate the integration of knowledge graphs with conversational interfaces to enhance exploratory search of newspaper articles. They present a knowledge-driven dialogue system and, through a large-scale user study with 54 participants, evaluate its effectiveness and derive design implications regarding functional improvements. Liu et al. (2021) compared conversational versus traditional search in a legal case retrieval scenario, showing that users achieve higher satisfaction and success in the conversational approach, especially when they lack sufficient domain knowledge. We find that the analyzed domain-specific systems often help overcome the absence of prior background knowledge, facilitating users in initiating the search process. Alternatively, these systems can provide assistance when the interface's modality is restricted and does not support conventional search methods.

4.2 Architecture Framework

Once the application scenario and desired system requirements are defined, the subsequent steps in the engineering process are to transform theoretical properties into technical implementations. This refers to functional components and their integration as part of the system architecture. We identified over 20 system architectures from the literature and consolidated reoccurring elements into the

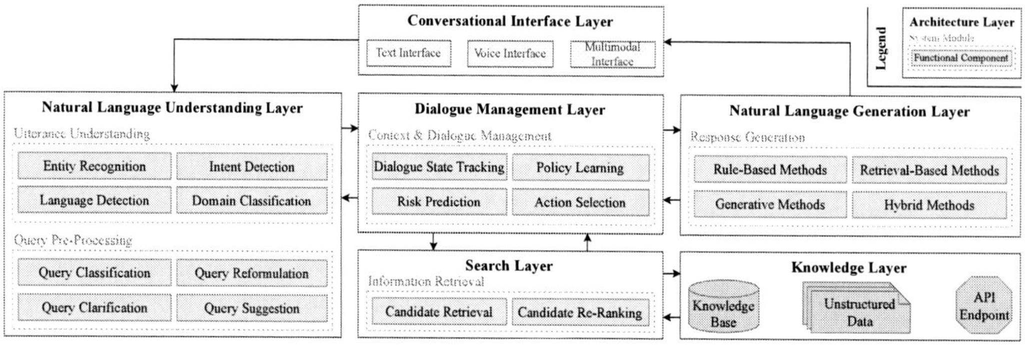

Figure 1: Architectural framework of conversational search systems.

generalized CSS architecture displayed in Figure 1. The proposed architecture adopts a layered architecture pattern, where each of the six layers performs a specific role within the CSS. The layers contain modules and functional components specifically designed for information-seeking purposes. For example, the *conversational interface layer* establishes the interaction channel between the system and the user. It receives user requests and presents search results depending on the modality. The three layers of *natural language understanding*, *dialogue management*, and *natural language generation* deal with processing input utterances, handling conversation logic, and producing responses as output. In CSSs, the correct understanding and meaningful pre-processing of user queries are essential to maximize the information gain. The *search layer*, in conjunction with the *knowledge layer*, performs search operations within the information space, ensuring access to various data structures. Possible data sources are corpora with unstructured text documents, application programming interfaces (APIs), or structured knowledge bases like knowledge graphs (Schneider et al., 2022). Data items can be stored in various databases, such as relational, graph, or vector databases, each with distinct benefits and drawbacks based on the data characteristics and application needs.

Modules group functional components and thus represent a specific functionality inside the layers. There is a separation of concerns among the modules, which deal only with logic pertinent to their respective layer. For instance, the query preprocessing module is a functionality from the language understanding layer, which enhances user queries through reformulation, clarification, suggestion, or other functions. The components perform specific tasks on the lowest abstraction level using NLP techniques. Implementing a component usually requires training NLP models that receive an input and classify, retrieve, or generate textual data, in some instances also structured data. Components can be implemented independently, requiring knowledge only of how they are connected to other components. While the displayed architecture encompasses all components encountered in the literature, implementations of a concrete CSS usually employ only a subset of these components. For example, reacting to user feedback is an essential function often mentioned in theoretical frameworks, but only a few studies implement it as part of an actual system (Bi et al., 2019; Wang and Ai, 2021). Since most architectures focus only on specific functional components like query suggestions or generating clarifying questions, there is a discrepancy between theoretical frameworks and practical implementations. Section 4.3 provides a more detailed overview of the various conversational search-specific core functions from the architectural components.

In line with common architectural patterns for dialogue systems, our proposed architecture follows a layered structure, separating functionality into different modules. We found that most analyzed implementations from the literature connect modules in a pipeline-based approach (Rojas Barahona et al., 2019; Mele et al., 2021; Alessio et al., 2023, *inter alia*). However, we observed a growing number of research works aiming to develop end-to-end approaches with transformer-based neural networks instead of classic NLP pipelines (Xiao et al., 2021; Ferreira et al., 2022). While end-to-end learning enables training a single model to represent target modules without the usual intermediate steps found in pipeline designs, these systems still depend on multiple task-specific modules and do

Functions	Example Studies	Datasets	Models	Access
Query classification	Aliannejadi et al. (2020)	TREC CAsT	BERT	♦
	Voskarides et al. (2020)	TREC CAsT, QuAC	BERT	✓
Query reformulation	Zhang et al. (2021)	TREC CAsT	HWE, T5	✓
	Yu et al. (2020)	TREC CAsT	GPT-2	✓
Query clarification	Zamani et al. (2020)	Bing search logs	BiLSTM	×
	Bi et al. (2021)	Qulac	BERT	♦
Query suggestion	Rosset et al. (2020)	Bing search logs	BERT, GPT-2	×
	Mustar et al. (2022)	TREC Session, MARCO, AOL logs	BERT, BART, T5	♦
Candidate retrieval	Xiong et al. (2020)	TREC DL, NQ, TriviaQA	ANCE	✓
	Lin et al. (2021)	TREC CAst, CANARD, MARCO	BERT	♦
Candidate re-ranking	Kumar and Callan (2020)	TREC CAsT	BERT	♦
	Mele et al. (2021)	TREC CAsT, ConvQ	BERT	✓
Knowledge-based	Zhang et al. (2020)	WikiTableQuestions	T5, GPT-2	♦
response generation	Ren et al. (2021a)	SaaC	PPG	✓

Table 1: Example studies, datasets, and implementations of the seven core functions in conversational search. Legend: ✓ = dataset(s) and system; ♦ = dataset only; × = not available.

not achieve a genuine end-to-end design, where only one model would handle all functionalities. To date, even the most advanced LLMs fail to integrate all functions without encountering issues, as we will discuss in more depth later on.

An example of a pipeline-based architecture is the open-source framework called *Macaw* from Zamani and Craswell (2020). It consists of three modules implemented in a generic form with replaceable NLP models. One module is responsible for query pre-processing with co-reference resolution and query reformulation or expansion, another for ranking documents with a retrieval model, and a third module for response generation. Two system proposals from Zhang et al. (2021) and Mele et al. (2021) have similar architectural components but additionally adopt a neural passage re-ranker for re-ordering results of the first-stage retrieval using a BERT model (Nogueira and Cho, 2019). Concerning end-to-end approaches, Xiao et al. (2021) introduce a CSS for online shopping, consisting of a sequence-to-sequence transformer for dialogue state tracking and a multi-head attention mechanism to match user queries to products. Comparable architectures from Ren et al. (2021a) and Ferreira et al. (2022) that aim to implement conversational search sub-tasks in an end-to-end manner also include transformers, such as BERT and T5, for passage re-ranking and response generation models.

Our presented architecture framework captures the fundamental aspects of CSSs in the research literature, and although there might be architectural adaptations to suit specific application scenarios with varying interface modalities and data structures, the body of six layers remains unchanged. The architecture offers flexibility in adding, removing, or replacing components within the modules.

4.3 Conversational Search Functions

This section elaborates on the seven core functions of CSSs mentioned in the architecture framework. Implementing these functions using NLP techniques is the most concrete step in the engineering process. Therefore, we review example studies that implement commonly used machine learning models (see Table 1) and list the most popular training and evaluation datasets in Table 3 of Appendix A. Despite being essential for conversational systems, some components like intent detection are not explicitly explained here as they are not specific to CSSs. While not all functions may be present in a given system or are combined, these main functions have been widely utilized and are treated as individual sub-tasks in the broader fields of conversational search and information retrieval. The order of paragraphs for each function roughly follows the processing steps needed to generate an output given an input turn in the conversation.

Query Classification. As part of the initial query pre-processing module, classifying the given query can benefit many subsequent system components. In conversational search scenarios, user requests may not be self-explanatory and ambiguous due to a lack of context. Researchers have approached this problem by classifying what type of question is being asked (Kia et al., 2020), determining the search domain of interest (Frummet et al., 2019; Hamzei et al., 2020), or deciding whether a (past) query is relevant in the context of the ongoing dialogue (Aliannejadi et al., 2020; Voskarides et al., 2020). Other system components can adapt according to classified queries, such as querying domain-specific sources, discarding irrelevant utterances, or selecting relevant past utterances. The often-used TREC Conversational Assistant Track (CAsT) datasets contain many sessions where a user inquires about two subjects and later asks questions to compare the two. Classification can be used to select the previous relevant utterances.

Query Reformulation. Since a CSS is processing dialogue turns, it has to deal with many subtleties and challenges. Conversational search primarily deals with ambiguity and co-reference issues (Keyvan and Huang, 2022). Reformulating, also called rewriting, a query to an unambiguous and explicit form is often needed for effective information retrieval and to incorporate contextual information of an ongoing conversation. Numerous approaches incorporate transformer-based language models for this task (Ferreira et al., 2022). Either as a classifier to determine what terms have to be incorporated into the rewritten query (Mele et al., 2021), a sequence-to-sequence approach trained on *query – rewrite target* pairs (Zhang et al., 2021) or in a weakly-supervised fashion using LLMs (Yu et al., 2020). The following is a simple example of rewriting:

User:	Who is the director of Citizen Kane?
System:	Orson Welles is the director.
User:	Does he have children?
Rewrite:	Does ~~he~~ *Orson Welles* have children?

Query Clarification. When the system cannot resolve or interpret a query, it can take the initiative and ask the user for clarification. CSSs that can show initiative, such as proactively asking questions, are referred to as *mixed-initiative* systems. Different approaches for clarifying questions have been investigated, including template filling, sequence editing models, sequence-to-sequence models, and combinations of these methods. Template filling can be as straightforward as *"Did you mean X?"* for a misspelling or co-reference issue. Templates can cover many clarifying questions, but their specificity level is something to consider (Zamani et al., 2020). Sequence editing models are related to query rewriting; they choose a clarification question and rewrite it with information from the ongoing dialogue state (Zamani et al., 2023). Sequence-to-sequence approaches train models with *unclear query – clarifying question* pairs to predict fitting questions.

Asking a clarifying question is not always the best course of action. Systems have to ensure a user's patience or tolerance is not running out by asking too many questions (Bi et al., 2021). Controlling this 'risk' and the system's information need is a delicate balance. Current approaches implement functions that try to approximate the information gain and tolerance of a user (Salle et al., 2021; Wang and Ai, 2022). If the system wants to ask a clarifying question, it uses this function to decide whether it should proceed. This can be done for numerous reasons. Braslavski et al. (2017) provide a taxonomy of six clarification categories. Their categorical taxonomy is created from analyzing *community question-answering* websites but can be applied more generally.

Query Suggestion. CSSs can help users while they are still in their conversational turn by suggesting relevant queries or even (partial) answers while the interaction is ongoing (Aliannejadi et al., 2021; Keyvan and Huang, 2022). Search engines are a good example of this, where auto-complete is heavily used. Suggesting queries can possibly mitigate issues addressed by the previously mentioned system functions. If the system incorporates dialogue state information in the suggestions, it can provide unambiguous versions of an unclear query. Generating query suggestions is done in many ways, but all must deal with the query, dialogue state, and ranking-generated suggestions. An often-used approach is training a model to determine what to copy or generate from the dialogue state and input query to maximize the chance of a user picking the suggestion (Dehghani et al., 2017; Mustar et al., 2022). The generated queries can be ranked by the same or a separate model (Rosset et al., 2020).

Candidate Retrieval. Candidate retrieval fetches possibly relevant data items by producing a structured database query given the (pre-processed) user query or retrieving information from unstructured text collections. The latter approach falls into two general categories: sparse retrieval and dense retrieval (Gao et al., 2023). Sparse retrieval ranks documents with methods such as BM25 (Robertson and Zaragoza, 2009). These use sparse vectors encoding term occurrences in queries and documents, which can be used for retrieval directly, to perform pre-filtering of results (Vakulenko et al., 2021b; Zhang et al., 2021), or to represent model features (e.g., for re-ranking) (Cho et al., 2021). Although computationally efficient, the purely lexical approach of these methods limits them in dealing with synonyms, word order, and spelling mistakes.

Dense retrieval addresses these issues, which is often implemented as a *dual encoder* architecture, where one neural model encodes a document into a dense vector and another the (processed) query (Lin et al., 2021). These models are trained by jointly training these two encoders on labeled *query – relevant document* pairs. There are variations with additional encoding strategies, but the main idea stays the same (Ferreira et al., 2022).

Candidate Re-Ranking. Once the system has a set of possibly relevant candidate results for the current turn or utterance, the next step is to rank this set in order of informativeness. There are many approaches to re-ranking, with the most dominant one being some model that either classifies, scores, or re-orders a given input set (Ferreira et al., 2022). These models are either fine-tuned on explicitly labeled *query – relevant item* pairs (Zhang et al., 2021; Mele et al., 2021) or use some distance measure between (part of) the embedded query and (part of) the relevant document. These are the main building blocks of most implementations, but they can be combined into more elaborate setups. Kumar and Callan (2020), for instance, suggest *multi-view re-ranking*, where the system creates different embeddings of the input query. These *views* include information from dialogue history, relevant terms from the retrieved items, and the rewritten query, which get fused into the final ranking.

Knowledge-Based Response Generation. The final step of a turn in the conversational system is to present the response to the user in the form of natural language. As with information retrieval, natural language generation is a dedicated research field. As such, many distinct approaches and methods within CSSs exist. These are generally grouped according to three categories: the information type, generation method, and information source.

Information type refers to the response's structure based on the retrieved document(s) or information need. These include *short answer*, *long document retrieval*, *abstractive summarization* or *structured entities* (Zamani et al., 2023). For instance, a short factual question often does not require a large response (*"In what year did X happen?"*). In contrast, a query for an explanation might involve summarizing a relevant passage.

Different generation methods are used for these different answer types and can serve as a grouping of approaches. Some general methods include; template filling (Zhang et al., 2018), sequence-to-sequence methods (Ferreira et al., 2022) and weakly supervised approaches (Baheti et al., 2020). More elaborate approaches have a model choosing from where to copy a token in generating the response: a vocabulary, the input query, or the retrieved passage (Ren et al., 2021a,b).

Generation is also dependent on the information source being queried. Conversational search is generally done over a corpus of free text but can also be done over a knowledge graph (Kacupaj et al., 2022; Dutt et al., 2022) or other (semi-)structured information (Zhang et al., 2020). The source influences the choice of generation technique; verbalizing a sub-graph from a knowledge graph is considerably different from summarizing a text passage.

There are also hybrid methods that fuse information sources and generation methods. The most influential contribution in this area has been *retrieval-augmented generation* (Lewis et al., 2020; Shuster et al., 2021). These hybrid approaches try to balance the expressiveness and veracity of responses.

5 Discussion and Future Directions

The results from our review give insights into the engineering behind CSSs from abstract properties to realizable functional components. Against this background, our findings unveil a disruptive trend of adopting larger language models to integrate end-to-end functional components. Researchers have emphasized the benefits of streamlined NLP, reduced error propagation, and data-driven development. Hence, rather than reflecting on the numerous general challenges in the evaluation of CSSs, like Penha and Hauff (2020), we direct our focus toward discussing how LLMs can augment CSSs and the implications it has on their future evolution.

While most studies fine-tune language models (e.g., BERT or T5) on downstream tasks, there has been a recent surge of interest in using LLMs. By scaling up models to billions of parameters and training them on corpora with trillions of tokens, LLMs have demonstrated emergent capabilities and prowess in multi-task learning (Radford et al., 2019). A significant advantage of LLMs is prompt-based (or in-context) learning. Through carefully defined prompts, LLMs can perform multiple tasks without specific training or tuning (Liu et al., 2023). Furthermore, there has been a growing interest in optimizing LLMs for dialogue interactions by pre-training on conversations, instruction fine-tuning, and reinforcement learning from human feedback

(Thoppilan et al., 2022). The strengths of LLMs, such as their language understanding and ability to generate context-aware responses, make them highly complementary elements for CSSs.

Opportunities for Conversational Search. A rapidly growing body of new studies concentrates on advancing conversational search functions with LLMs. For instance, addressing the challenge of better understanding user queries, Anand et al. (2023) introduce a query formulation framework to replace multi-component pipelines with a single LLM. This model initially generates several machine intents for a user query, followed by options to accept, edit, or expand these intents until they align with the user's query intent. With a qualitative feasibility study, the authors show that the LLM-generated rewrites can improve the downstream retrieval performance. In related work, Mao et al. (2023) investigate different prompting and aggregation methods for performing few-shot conversational query reformulation with LLMs. They demonstrate that their approach outperforms state-of-the-art baselines by testing a GPT-3 model on CAsT'19 and '20 datasets. Another study from Chen et al. (2023) introduces a retrieval-based query rewriting approach, where an LLM leverages external knowledge from graphs with historical user-entity interactions and collaborative filtering. Ye et al. (2023) also demonstrate the potential of LLMs for query rewriting, showing that rewrites can significantly enhance retrieval performance in conversational search. Furthermore, LLMs can augment CSSs through semantic parsing and convert a natural language question into a structured database query. For example, Schneider et al. (2024a) evaluate how well different-sized LLMs perform in generating knowledge graph queries for conversational QA based on dialogues by comparing various prompting and fine-tuning techniques. Aside from query rewriting and semantic parsing, LLMs can also be effective for classifying query intents (Srinivasan et al., 2022) or generating clarification questions (Kuhn et al., 2023).

In addition to the natural language understanding layer, LLMs can augment the layers of dialogue management, search, and natural language generation. For example, Friedman et al. (2023) developed a system for conversational video search and recommendation powered by several LLMs based on the LaMDA model (Thoppilan et al., 2022). While one LLM is used as a dialogue management module, a second LLM acts as a re-ranker module. This LLM also generates explanations for its decisions. The authors discuss how a third LLM can be instructed to act as a user simulator for generating synthetic data for training and evaluation. Also focusing on synthetic data generation, a paper from Huang et al. (2023) introduces a framework called *CONVERSER* that uses LLMs to generate conversational queries given a passage in a retrieval corpus for training dense retrievers. This can significantly benefit conversational search by reducing the need for extensive and expensive data collection while maintaining high retrieval accuracy. Concerning knowledge-based text generation, LLMs have also proven to be effective for verbalizing semantic triples retrieved from graph-structured data, with performance improvements achievable through few-shot prompting, post-processing, and fine-tuning techniques (Schneider et al., 2024b). Another noteworthy approach from Sekulic et al. (2024) employed LLMs in conversational search for answer rewriting, proposing two strategies by either providing inline definitions of important entities or offering users the opportunity to learn more about entities. Human-based evaluations indicated a preference for the answers with inline definitions.

Challenges and Risks. Even though LLMs show great potential for conversational search, they have known shortcomings that must be considered. First, the sheer size of these models requires significant computational resources. Multiple graphical processing units are often necessary for enabling fast inference, a critical factor for conversational search applications that require responses in near real-time. The research community has been actively exploring solutions such as model distillation, model quantization, or low-rank adaptation to address these issues. Distillation involves compressing LLMs into smaller and more efficient versions (Shridhar et al., 2023). Model quantization is a technique where the floating point precision of model parameters is decreased, leading to smaller memory requirements and faster computations without significant performance loss (Xiao et al., 2023). Low-rank adaptation fine-tunes only a subset of the model's parameters rather than updating the entire parameter space (Hu et al., 2022).

Other major issues related to LLMs are hallucinating or omitting important information and a lack of transparency regarding the source from which the output was generated (Dou et al., 2022; Ji et al.,

2023; Xu et al., 2024). To mitigate these risks, scholars have looked into approaches to ground the generated outputs in trustworthy data sources and mechanisms to curate generated output. For example, Peng et al. (2023) introduce a framework for augmenting LLMs by first incorporating retrieved evidence from external knowledge as input context and then using LLM-generated feedback as instructions to revise responses. Through validation with two information-seeking tasks, the authors show that their approach reduces hallucinations while preserving fluency and usefulness. Another knowledge-enhancement method from Yang et al. (2023) fine-tunes a smaller LLM (Llama-7B) to learn domain-specific knowledge. This model is consulted to generate expert opinions that are used to enrich the prompt context of a bigger, general LLM (GPT-4) to improve its domain-specific QA capabilities. For a comprehensive survey of over 30 hallucination mitigation techniques, readers are referred to Tonmoy et al. (2024). Regardless, it must be noted that LLMs are nondeterministic by nature, making it challenging to ensure consistent and persistent knowledge during searches due to the inherent randomness in their text generation methods (Krishna et al., 2022; Mitchell et al., 2023).

Finally, there are efforts to develop software tools that address the reliability and safety of generated LLM output by adding programmable guardrails as well as logical control patterns. Popular tools that aid the development of LLM-based CSSs include *NeMo* (NVIDIA, 2023), *Guidance* (Microsoft, 2022), and *LangChain* (Chase, 2022). Other tools like *DeepEval* (Ip, 2024) can evaluate model bias, which is crucial since LLMs in conversational search can increase selective exposure and opinion polarization by fostering confirmatory querying behaviors (Sharma et al., 2024). In summary, ongoing research shows the potential of LLMs to advance the engineering of dialogue-based search systems with various approaches to mitigate their reliability issues. However, it is unlikely that LLMs will replace CSSs as a single end-to-end monolith in the foreseeable future. Instead, they are more likely to augment the modular structure of the proposed architecture framework.

6 Conclusion

We conducted a comprehensive review of engineering CSSs, establishing connections between theoretical application scenarios and technical implementations. Based on our analysis of existing architectures, we introduced a layered architecture framework and explained its functional core components. While it is essential to acknowledge that the field of conversational search is rapidly evolving, and complete coverage is unattainable, our framework provides a generalized architecture based on previously validated systems. The framework does not claim to be exhaustive but rather serves as a foundational starting point for designing and developing CSSs. Lastly, we discussed recent work on the capabilities and challenges of augmenting CSSs with LLMs. We outline where they fit into our proposed framework, which core functions they have been used for, and highlight promising directions for future research.

Acknowledgements

This work has been supported by the German Federal Ministry of Education and Research (BMBF) Software Campus grant 01IS17049.

References

Naga Sai Krishna Adatrao, Gowtham Reddy Gadireddy, and Jiho Noh. 2023. A survey on conversational search and applications in biomedicine. In *Proceedings of the 2023 ACM Southeast Conference*, ACMSE 2023, page 78–88, New York, NY, USA. Association for Computing Machinery.

Marco Alessio, Guglielmo Faggioli, and Nicola Ferro. 2023. Decaf: A modular and extensible conversational search framework. In *Proceedings of the 46th International ACM SIGIR Conference on Research and Development in Information Retrieval*, SIGIR '23, page 3075–3085, New York, NY, USA. Association for Computing Machinery.

Mohammad Aliannejadi, Leif Azzopardi, Hamed Zamani, Evangelos Kanoulas, Paul Thomas, and Nick Craswell. 2021. Analysing Mixed Initiatives and Search Strategies during Conversational Search. In *Proceedings of the 30th ACM International Conference on Information & Knowledge Management*, CIKM '21, pages 16–26, New York, NY, USA. Association for Computing Machinery.

Mohammad Aliannejadi, Manajit Chakraborty, Esteban Andrés Ríssola, and Fabio Crestani. 2020. Harnessing Evolution of Multi-Turn Conversations for Effective Answer Retrieval. In *Proceedings of the 2020 Conference on Human Information Interaction and Retrieval*, CHIIR '20, pages 33–42, New York, NY, USA. Association for Computing Machinery.

Mohammad Aliannejadi, Hamed Zamani, Fabio Crestani, and W Bruce Croft. 2019. Asking clarifying questions in open-domain information-seeking conversations. In *Proceedings of the 42nd international acm sigir conference on research and development in information retrieval*, pages 475–484.

Avishek Anand, Lawrence Cavedon, Matthias Hagen, Hideo Joho, Mark Sanderson, and Benno Stein. 2020. Conversational search–a report from dagstuhl seminar 19461. *Dagstuhl Reports*, 9(11):34–83.

Avishek Anand, Venktesh V, Abhijit Anand, and Vinay Setty. 2023. Query Understanding in the Age of Large Language Models. In *Gen-IR@SIGIR 2023: The First Workshop on Generative Information Retrieval*, New York, NY, USA. Association for Computing Machinery.

Leif Azzopardi, Mateusz Dubiel, Martin Halvey, and Jeff Dalton. 2018. Conceptualizing Agent-Human Interactions during the Conversational Search Process. In *2nd International Workshop on Conversational Approaches to Information Retrieval (CAIR'18)*, Ann Arbor, MI, USA.

Ashutosh Baheti, Alan Ritter, and Kevin Small. 2020. Fluent response generation for conversational question answering. In *Proceedings of the 58th Annual Meeting of the Association for Computational Linguistics*, pages 191–207, Online. Association for Computational Linguistics.

Keping Bi, Qingyao Ai, and W. Bruce Croft. 2021. Asking Clarifying Questions Based on Negative Feedback in Conversational Search. In *Proceedings of the 2021 ACM SIGIR International Conference on Theory of Information Retrieval*, ICTIR '21, pages 157–166, New York, NY, USA. Association for Computing Machinery.

Keping Bi, Qingyao Ai, Yongfeng Zhang, and W. Bruce Croft. 2019. Conversational Product Search Based on Negative Feedback. In *Proceedings of the 28th ACM International Conference on Information and Knowledge Management*, CIKM '19, pages 359–368, New York, NY, USA. Association for Computing Machinery.

Timothy W. Bickmore, Dina Utami, Robin Matsuyama, and Michael K. Paasche-Orlow. 2016. Improving Access to Online Health Information With Conversational Agents: A Randomized Controlled Experiment. *Journal of Medical Internet Research*, 18(1):e1.

Pavel Braslavski, Denis Savenkov, Eugene Agichtein, and Alina Dubatovka. 2017. What Do You Mean Exactly? Analyzing Clarification Questions in CQA. In *Proceedings of the 2017 Conference on Conference Human Information Interaction and Retrieval*, CHIIR '17, pages 345–348, New York, NY, USA. Association for Computing Machinery.

Harrison Chase. 2022. Langchain: An app development framework using large language models. *LangChain GitHub Repository*.

Zheng Chen, Ziyan Jiang, Fan Yang, Eunah Cho, Xing Fan, Xiaojiang Huang, Yanbin Lu, and Aram Galstyan. 2023. Graph meets LLM: A novel approach to collaborative filtering for robust conversational understanding. In *Proceedings of the 2023 Conference on Empirical Methods in Natural Language Processing: Industry Track*, pages 811–819, Singapore. Association for Computational Linguistics.

Eunah Cho, Ziyan Jiang, Jie Hao, Zheng Chen, Saurabh Gupta, Xing Fan, and Chenlei Guo. 2021. Personalized Search-based Query Rewrite System for Conversational AI. In *Proceedings of the 3rd Workshop on Natural Language Processing for Conversational AI*, pages 179–188, Online. Association for Computational Linguistics.

Eunsol Choi, He He, Mohit Iyyer, Mark Yatskar, Wentau Yih, Yejin Choi, Percy Liang, and Luke Zettlemoyer. 2018. QuAC: Question answering in context. In *Proceedings of the 2018 Conference on Empirical Methods in Natural Language Processing*, pages 2174–2184, Brussels, Belgium. Association for Computational Linguistics.

Philipp Christmann, Rishiraj Saha Roy, Abdalghani Abujabal, Jyotsna Singh, and Gerhard Weikum. 2019. Look before you hop: Conversational question answering over knowledge graphs using judicious context expansion. In *Proceedings of the 28th ACM International Conference on Information and Knowledge Management*, CIKM '19, page 729–738, New York, NY, USA. Association for Computing Machinery.

Jeffrey Dalton, Chenyan Xiong, and Jamie Callan. 2020. Trec cast 2019: The conversational assistance track overview. *arXiv preprint arXiv:2003.13624v1*.

Mostafa Dehghani, Sascha Rothe, Enrique Alfonseca, and Pascal Fleury. 2017. Learning to Attend, Copy, and Generate for Session-Based Query Suggestion. In *Proceedings of the 2017 ACM on Conference on Information and Knowledge Management*, CIKM '17, pages 1747–1756, New York, NY, USA. Association for Computing Machinery.

Yashar Deldjoo, Johanne R. Trippas, and Hamed Zamani. 2021. Towards Multi-Modal Conversational Information Seeking. In *Proceedings of the 44th International ACM SIGIR Conference on Research and Development in Information Retrieval*, SIGIR '21, pages 1577–1587, New York, NY, USA. Association for Computing Machinery.

Laura Dietz, Manisha Verma, Filip Radlinski, and Nick Craswell. 2017. TREC Complex Answer Retrieval Overview. In *TREC*.

Yao Dou, Maxwell Forbes, Rik Koncel-Kedziorski, Noah A. Smith, and Yejin Choi. 2022. Is GPT-3 Text Indistinguishable from Human Text? Scarecrow: A Framework for Scrutinizing Machine Text. In *Proceedings of the 60th Annual Meeting of the Association for Computational Linguistics (Volume 1:*

Long Papers), pages 7250–7274, Dublin, Ireland. Association for Computational Linguistics.

Ritam Dutt, Kasturi Bhattacharjee, Rashmi Gangadharaiah, Dan Roth, and Carolyn Rose. 2022. PerKGQA: Question Answering over Personalized Knowledge Graphs. In *Findings of the Association for Computational Linguistics: NAACL 2022*, pages 253–268, Seattle, United States. Association for Computational Linguistics.

Ahmed Elgohary, Denis Peskov, and Jordan Boyd-Graber. 2019. Can You Unpack That? Learning to Rewrite Questions-in-Context. In *Proceedings of the 2019 Conference on Empirical Methods in Natural Language Processing and the 9th International Joint Conference on Natural Language Processing (EMNLP-IJCNLP)*, pages 5917–5923, Hong Kong, China. Association for Computational Linguistics.

Rafael Ferreira, Mariana Leite, David Semedo, and Joao Magalhaes. 2022. Open-domain conversational search assistants: The Transformer is all you need. *Information Retrieval*, 25(2):123–148.

Adam Fisch, Alon Talmor, Robin Jia, Minjoon Seo, Eunsol Choi, and Danqi Chen. 2019. MRQA 2019 shared task: Evaluating generalization in reading comprehension. In *Proceedings of the 2nd Workshop on Machine Reading for Question Answering*, pages 1–13, Hong Kong, China. Association for Computational Linguistics.

Luke Friedman, Sameer Ahuja, David Allen, Terry Tan, Hakim Sidahmed, Changbo Long, Jun Xie, Gabriel Schubiner, Ajay Patel, Harsh Lara, et al. 2023. Leveraging large language models in conversational recommender systems. *arXiv preprint arXiv:2305.07961v2*.

Alexander Frummet, David Elsweiler, and Bernd Ludwig. 2019. Detecting domain-specific information needs in conversational search dialogues. In *Natural Language for Artificial Intelligence*.

Jianfeng Gao, Chenyan Xiong, Paul Bennett, and Nick Craswell. 2023. *Neural Approaches to Conversational Information Retrieval*. Springer International Publishing, Cham.

Emma J. Gerritse, Faegheh Hasibi, and Arjen P. de Vries. 2020. Bias in Conversational Search: The Double-Edged Sword of the Personalized Knowledge Graph. In *Proceedings of the 2020 ACM SIGIR on International Conference on Theory of Information Retrieval*, ICTIR '20, pages 133–136, New York, NY, USA. Association for Computing Machinery.

Ehsan Hamzei, Haonan Li, Maria Vasardani, Timothy Baldwin, Stephan Winter, and Martin Tomko. 2020. Place Questions and Human-Generated Answers: A Data Analysis Approach. In *Geospatial Technologies for Local and Regional Development*, Lecture Notes in Geoinformation and Cartography, pages 3–19, Cham. Springer International Publishing.

Nadine Höchstötter and Dirk Lewandowski. 2009. What users see – Structures in search engine results pages. *Information Sciences*, 179(12):1796–1812.

Edward J Hu, yelong shen, Phillip Wallis, Zeyuan Allen-Zhu, Yuanzhi Li, Shean Wang, Lu Wang, and Weizhu Chen. 2022. LoRA: Low-rank adaptation of large language models. In *International Conference on Learning Representations*.

Chao-Wei Huang, Chen-Yu Hsu, Tsu-Yuan Hsu, Chen-An Li, and Yun-Nung Chen. 2023. CONVERSER: Few-shot conversational dense retrieval with synthetic data generation. In *Proceedings of the 24th Annual Meeting of the Special Interest Group on Discourse and Dialogue*, pages 381–387, Prague, Czechia. Association for Computational Linguistics.

Hamel Husain, Ho-Hsiang Wu, Tiferet Gazit, Miltiadis Allamanis, and Marc Brockschmidt. 2019. Codesearchnet challenge: Evaluating the state of semantic code search. *arXiv preprint arXiv:1909.09436v3*.

Jeffrey Ip. 2024. Deepeval: The open-source llm evaluation framework. *Confident AI*.

Dietmar Jannach, Ahtsham Manzoor, Wanling Cai, and Li Chen. 2021. A Survey on Conversational Recommender Systems. *ACM Computing Surveys*, 54(5):105:1–105:36.

Ziwei Ji, Nayeon Lee, Rita Frieske, Tiezheng Yu, Dan Su, Yan Xu, Etsuko Ishii, Ye Jin Bang, Andrea Madotto, and Pascale Fung. 2023. Survey of hallucination in natural language generation. *ACM Comput. Surv.*, 55(12).

Mandar Joshi, Eunsol Choi, Daniel Weld, and Luke Zettlemoyer. 2017. TriviaQA: A large scale distantly supervised challenge dataset for reading comprehension. In *Proceedings of the 55th Annual Meeting of the Association for Computational Linguistics (Volume 1: Long Papers)*, pages 1601–1611, Vancouver, Canada. Association for Computational Linguistics.

Endri Kacupaj, Kuldeep Singh, Maria Maleshkova, and Jens Lehmann. 2022. Contrastive representation learning for conversational question answering over knowledge graphs. In *Proceedings of the 31st ACM International Conference on Information & Knowledge Management*, CIKM '22, page 925–934, New York, NY, USA. Association for Computing Machinery.

Kimiya Keyvan and Jimmy Xiangji Huang. 2022. How to Approach Ambiguous Queries in Conversational Search: A Survey of Techniques, Approaches, Tools, and Challenges. *ACM Computing Surveys*, 55(6):129:1–129:40.

Omid Mohammadi Kia, Mahmood Neshati, and Mahsa Soudi Alamdari. 2020. Open-Domain question classification and completion in conversational information search. In *2020 11th International Conference on Information and Knowledge Technology (IKT)*, pages 98–101.

Johannes Kiesel, Lars Meyer, Martin Potthast, and Benno Stein. 2021. Meta-Information in Conversational Search. *ACM Transactions on Information Systems*, 39(4):50:1–50:44.

Barbara A. Kitchenham, Tore Dyba, and Magne Jorgensen. 2004. Evidence-Based Software Engineering. In *Proceedings of the 26th International Conference on Software Engineering*, ICSE '04, pages 273–281, USA. IEEE Computer Society.

Lorenz Cuno Klopfenstein, Saverio Delpriori, Silvia Malatini, and Alessandro Bogliolo. 2017. The Rise of Bots: A Survey of Conversational Interfaces, Patterns, and Paradigms. In *Proceedings of the 2017 Conference on Designing Interactive Systems*, DIS '17, pages 555–565, New York, NY, USA. Association for Computing Machinery.

Kalpesh Krishna, Yapei Chang, John Wieting, and Mohit Iyyer. 2022. RankGen: Improving text generation with large ranking models. In *Proceedings of the 2022 Conference on Empirical Methods in Natural Language Processing*, pages 199–232, Abu Dhabi, United Arab Emirates. Association for Computational Linguistics.

Lorenz Kuhn, Yarin Gal, and Sebastian Farquhar. 2023. Clam: Selective clarification for ambiguous questions with generative language models. In *ICML 2023 Workshop on Deployment Challenges for Generative AI*.

Vaibhav Kumar and Jamie Callan. 2020. Making Information Seeking Easier: An Improved Pipeline for Conversational Search. In *Findings of the Association for Computational Linguistics: EMNLP 2020*, pages 3971–3980, Online. Association for Computational Linguistics.

Tom Kwiatkowski, Jennimaria Palomaki, Olivia Redfield, Michael Collins, Ankur Parikh, Chris Alberti, Danielle Epstein, Illia Polosukhin, Jacob Devlin, Kenton Lee, Kristina Toutanova, Llion Jones, Matthew Kelcey, Ming-Wei Chang, Andrew M. Dai, Jakob Uszkoreit, Quoc Le, and Slav Petrov. 2019. Natural questions: A benchmark for question answering research. *Transactions of the Association for Computational Linguistics*, 7:452–466.

Patrick Lewis, Ethan Perez, Aleksandra Piktus, Fabio Petroni, Vladimir Karpukhin, Naman Goyal, Heinrich Küttler, Mike Lewis, Wen-tau Yih, Tim Rocktäschel, et al. 2020. Retrieval-augmented generation for knowledge-intensive nlp tasks. *Advances in Neural Information Processing Systems*, 33:9459–9474.

Lizi Liao, Le Hong Long, Zheng Zhang, Minlie Huang, and Tat-Seng Chua. 2021. MMConv: An Environment for Multimodal Conversational Search across Multiple Domains. In *Proceedings of the 44th International ACM SIGIR Conference on Research and Development in Information Retrieval*, SIGIR '21, pages 675–684, New York, NY, USA. Association for Computing Machinery.

Sheng-Chieh Lin, Jheng-Hong Yang, and Jimmy Lin. 2021. Contextualized Query Embeddings for Conversational Search. In *Proceedings of the 2021 Conference on Empirical Methods in Natural Language Processing*, pages 1004–1015, Online and Punta Cana, Dominican Republic. Association for Computational Linguistics.

Bulou Liu, Yueyue Wu, Yiqun Liu, Fan Zhang, Yunqiu Shao, Chenliang Li, Min Zhang, and Shaoping Ma. 2021. Conversational vs Traditional: Comparing Search Behavior and Outcome in Legal Case Retrieval. In *Proceedings of the 44th International ACM SIGIR Conference on Research and Development in Information Retrieval*, SIGIR '21, pages 1622–1626, New York, NY, USA. Association for Computing Machinery.

Pengfei Liu, Weizhe Yuan, Jinlan Fu, Zhengbao Jiang, Hiroaki Hayashi, and Graham Neubig. 2023. Pre-train, prompt, and predict: A systematic survey of prompting methods in natural language processing. *ACM Computing Surveys*, 55(9):1–35.

Kelong Mao, Zhicheng Dou, Fengran Mo, Jiewen Hou, Haonan Chen, and Hongjin Qian. 2023. Large language models know your contextual search intent: A prompting framework for conversational search. In *Findings of the Association for Computational Linguistics: EMNLP 2023*, pages 1211–1225, Singapore. Association for Computational Linguistics.

Michael McTear, Zoraida Callejas, and David Griol. 2016. *The Conversational Interface*. Springer International Publishing, Cham.

Ida Mele, Cristina Ioana Muntean, Franco Maria Nardini, Raffaele Perego, Nicola Tonellotto, and Ophir Frieder. 2021. Adaptive utterance rewriting for conversational search. *Information Processing and Management: an International Journal*, 58(6).

Microsoft. 2022. Guidance: A language for controlling large language models. *Microsoft GitHub Repository*.

Eric Mitchell, Yoonho Lee, Alexander Khazatsky, Christopher D Manning, and Chelsea Finn. 2023. DetectGPT: Zero-shot machine-generated text detection using probability curvature. In *Proceedings of the 40th International Conference on Machine Learning*, volume 202 of *Proceedings of Machine Learning Research*, pages 24950–24962. PMLR.

Agnès Mustar, Sylvain Lamprier, and Benjamin Piwowarski. 2022. On the Study of Transformers for Query Suggestion. *ACM Transactions on Information Systems*, 40(1):1–27.

Tri Nguyen, Mir Rosenberg, Xia Song, Jianfeng Gao, Saurabh Tiwary, Rangan Majumder, and Li Deng. 2016. Ms marco: A human generated machine reading comprehension dataset. *choice*, 2640:660.

Jianmo Ni, Jiacheng Li, and Julian McAuley. 2019. Justifying recommendations using distantly-labeled reviews and fine-grained aspects. In *Proceedings of the 2019 Conference on Empirical Methods in Natural Language Processing and the 9th International Joint Conference on Natural Language Processing (EMNLP-IJCNLP)*, pages 188–197, Hong Kong, China. Association for Computational Linguistics.

Rodrigo Nogueira and Kyunghyun Cho. 2019. Passage Re-ranking with BERT. *arXiv preprint arXiv:1901.04085v5*.

NVIDIA. 2023. Nemo guardrails: An open-source toolkit for easily adding programmable guardrails to large language model-based conversational systems. *NVIDIA GitHub Repository*.

OpenAI. 2022. Chatgpt: Optimizing language models for dialogue. *OpenAI*.

Panupong Pasupat and Percy Liang. 2015. Compositional semantic parsing on semi-structured tables. In *Proceedings of the 53rd Annual Meeting of the Association for Computational Linguistics and the 7th International Joint Conference on Natural Language Processing (Volume 1: Long Papers)*, pages 1470–1480, Beijing, China. Association for Computational Linguistics.

Baolin Peng, Michel Galley, Pengcheng He, Hao Cheng, Yujia Xie, Yu Hu, Qiuyuan Huang, Lars Liden, Zhou Yu, Weizhu Chen, et al. 2023. Check your facts and try again: Improving large language models with external knowledge and automated feedback. *arXiv preprint arXiv:2302.12813v3*.

Gustavo Penha and Claudia Hauff. 2020. Challenges in the evaluation of conversational search systems. In *KDD 2020 Workshop on Conversational Systems Towards Mainstream Adoption, KDD-Converse 2020*, volume 2666 of *CEUR Workshop Proceedings*. CEUR-WS. Virtual Workshop; KDD 2020 Workshop on Conversational Systems Towards Mainstream Adoption, KDD-Converse 2020, KDD-Converse 2020 ; Conference date: 24-08-2020 Through 24-08-2020.

Chen Qu, Liu Yang, W Bruce Croft, Johanne R Trippas, Yongfeng Zhang, and Minghui Qiu. 2018. Analyzing and characterizing user intent in information-seeking conversations. In *The 41st international acm sigir conference on research & development in information retrieval*, pages 989–992.

Alec Radford, Jeffrey Wu, Rewon Child, David Luan, Dario Amodei, and Ilya Sutskever. 2019. Language models are unsupervised multitask learners. *OpenAI*.

Filip Radlinski and Nick Craswell. 2017. A Theoretical Framework for Conversational Search. In *Proceedings of the 2017 Conference on Conference Human Information Interaction and Retrieval*, CHIIR '17, pages 117–126, New York, NY, USA. Association for Computing Machinery.

Pengjie Ren, Zhumin Chen, Zhaochun Ren, Evangelos Kanoulas, Christof Monz, and Maarten De Rijke. 2021a. Conversations with Search Engines: SERP-based Conversational Response Generation. *ACM Transactions on Information Systems*, 39(4):47:1–47:29.

Pengjie Ren, Zhongkun Liu, Xiaomeng Song, Hongtao Tian, Zhumin Chen, Zhaochun Ren, and Maarten de Rijke. 2021b. Wizard of Search Engine: Access to Information Through Conversations with Search Engines. In *Proceedings of the 44th International ACM SIGIR Conference on Research and Development in Information Retrieval*, SIGIR '21, pages 533–543, New York, NY, USA. Association for Computing Machinery.

Stephen Robertson and Hugo Zaragoza. 2009. The Probabilistic Relevance Framework: BM25 and Beyond. *Foundations and Trends® in Information Retrieval*, 3(4):333–389.

Lina M. Rojas Barahona, Pascal Bellec, Benoit Besset, Martinho Dossantos, Johannes Heinecke, Munshi Asadullah, Olivier Leblouch, Jeanyves. Lancien, Geraldine Damnati, Emmanuel Mory, and Frederic Herledan. 2019. Spoken Conversational Search for General Knowledge. In *Proceedings of the 20th Annual SIGdial Meeting on Discourse and Dialogue*, pages 110–113, Stockholm, Sweden. Association for Computational Linguistics.

Corbin Rosset, Chenyan Xiong, Xia Song, Daniel Campos, Nick Craswell, Saurabh Tiwary, and Paul Bennett. 2020. Leading Conversational Search by Suggesting Useful Questions. In *Proceedings of The Web Conference 2020*, pages 1160–1170, Taipei Taiwan. ACM.

N. Sa and X.-J. Yuan. 2020. Challenges in conversational search: improving the system capabilities and guiding the search process. In *Proceedings of the 24th World Multi-Conference on Systemics, Cybernetics and Informatics (WMSCI 2020)*, page 37–42.

Alexandre Salle, Shervin Malmasi, Oleg Rokhlenko, and Eugene Agichtein. 2021. Studying the Effectiveness of Conversational Search Refinement Through User Simulation. In *Advances in Information Retrieval*, Lecture Notes in Computer Science, pages 587–602, Cham. Springer International Publishing.

Phillip Schneider, Anum Afzal, Juraj Vladika, Daniel Braun, and Florian Matthes. 2023a. Investigating conversational search behavior for domain exploration. In *Advances in Information Retrieval*, pages 608–616, Cham. Springer Nature Switzerland.

Phillip Schneider, Manuel Klettner, Kristiina Jokinen, Elena Simperl, and Florian Matthes. 2024a. Evaluating large language models in semantic parsing for conversational question answering over knowledge graphs. In *International Conference on Agents and Artificial Intelligence*.

Phillip Schneider, Manuel Klettner, Elena Simperl, and Florian Matthes. 2024b. A comparative analysis of conversational large language models in knowledge-based text generation. In *Proceedings of the 18th Conference of the European Chapter of the Association for Computational Linguistics (Volume 2: Short Papers)*, pages 358–367, St. Julian's, Malta. Association for Computational Linguistics.

Phillip Schneider, Nils Rehtanz, Kristiina Jokinen, and Florian Matthes. 2023b. From data to dialogue: Leveraging the structure of knowledge graphs for conversational exploratory search. In *Proceedings of the 37th Pacific Asia Conference on Language, Information and Computation*, pages 609–619, Hong Kong, China. Association for Computational Linguistics.

Phillip Schneider, Tim Schopf, Juraj Vladika, Mikhail Galkin, Elena Simperl, and Florian Matthes. 2022. A decade of knowledge graphs in natural language processing: A survey. In *Proceedings of the 2nd Conference of the Asia-Pacific Chapter of the Association for Computational Linguistics and the 12th International Joint Conference on Natural Language Processing (Volume 1: Long Papers)*, pages 601–614, Online only. Association for Computational Linguistics.

Ivan Sekulic, Krisztian Balog, and Fabio Crestani. 2024. Towards self-contained answers: Entity-based answer rewriting in conversational search. In *Proceedings of the 2024 Conference on Human Information Interaction and Retrieval*, CHIIR '24, page 209–218, New York, NY, USA. Association for Computing Machinery.

Nikhil Sharma, Q. Vera Liao, and Ziang Xiao. 2024. Generative echo chamber? effect of llm-powered search systems on diverse information seeking. In *Proceedings of the CHI Conference on Human Factors in Computing Systems*, CHI '24, New York, NY, USA. Association for Computing Machinery.

Kumar Shridhar, Alessandro Stolfo, and Mrinmaya Sachan. 2023. Distilling reasoning capabilities into smaller language models. In *Findings of the Association for Computational Linguistics: ACL 2023*, pages 7059–7073, Toronto, Canada. Association for Computational Linguistics.

Kurt Shuster, Spencer Poff, Moya Chen, Douwe Kiela, and Jason Weston. 2021. Retrieval augmentation reduces hallucination in conversation. In *Findings of the Association for Computational Linguistics: EMNLP 2021*, pages 3784–3803, Punta Cana, Dominican Republic. Association for Computational Linguistics.

Krishna Srinivasan, Karthik Raman, Anupam Samanta, Lingrui Liao, Luca Bertelli, and Michael Bendersky. 2022. QUILL: Query intent with large language models using retrieval augmentation and multi-stage distillation. In *Proceedings of the 2022 Conference on Empirical Methods in Natural Language Processing: Industry Track*, pages 492–501, Abu Dhabi, UAE. Association for Computational Linguistics.

Romal Thoppilan, Daniel De Freitas, Jamie Hall, Noam Shazeer, Apoorv Kulshreshtha, Heng-Tze Cheng, Alicia Jin, Taylor Bos, Leslie Baker, Yu Du, et al. 2022. Lamda: Language models for dialog applications. *arXiv:2201.08239*.

SM Tonmoy, SM Zaman, Vinija Jain, Anku Rani, Vipula Rawte, Aman Chadha, and Amitava Das. 2024. A comprehensive survey of hallucination mitigation techniques in large language models. *arXiv preprint arXiv:2401.01313*.

Johanne R. Trippas, Damiano Spina, Paul Thomas, Mark Sanderson, Hideo Joho, and Lawrence Cavedon. 2020. Towards a model for spoken conversational search. *Information Processing and Management: an International Journal*, 57(2).

Svitlana Vakulenko, Evangelos Kanoulas, and Maarten De Rijke. 2021a. A Large-scale Analysis of Mixed Initiative in Information-Seeking Dialogues for Conversational Search. *ACM Transactions on Information Systems*, 39(4):49:1–49:32.

Svitlana Vakulenko, Shayne Longpre, Zhucheng Tu, and Raviteja Anantha. 2021b. Question Rewriting for Conversational Question Answering. In *Proceedings of the 14th ACM International Conference on Web Search and Data Mining*, WSDM '21, pages 355–363, New York, NY, USA. Association for Computing Machinery.

Nikos Voskarides, Dan Li, Pengjie Ren, Evangelos Kanoulas, and Maarten de Rijke. 2020. Query Resolution for Conversational Search with Limited Supervision. In *Proceedings of the 43rd International ACM SIGIR Conference on Research and Development in Information Retrieval*, SIGIR '20, pages 921–930, New York, NY, USA. Association for Computing Machinery.

Zhenduo Wang and Qingyao Ai. 2021. Controlling the Risk of Conversational Search via Reinforcement Learning. In *Proceedings of the Web Conference 2021*, WWW '21, pages 1968–1977, New York, NY, USA. Association for Computing Machinery.

Zhenduo Wang and Qingyao Ai. 2022. Simulating and Modeling the Risk of Conversational Search. *ACM Transactions on Information Systems*, 40(4):85:1–85:33.

Ryen W. White and Resa A. Roth. 2009. *Exploratory Search: Beyond the Query—Response Paradigm*. Synthesis Lectures on Information Concepts, Retrieval, and Services. Springer International Publishing, Cham.

Wenquan Wu, Zhen Guo, Xiangyang Zhou, Hua Wu, Xiyuan Zhang, Rongzhong Lian, and Haifeng Wang. 2019. Proactive human-machine conversation with explicit conversation goal. In *Proceedings of the*

57th Annual Meeting of the Association for Computational Linguistics, pages 3794–3804, Florence, Italy. Association for Computational Linguistics.

Guangxuan Xiao, Ji Lin, Mickael Seznec, Hao Wu, Julien Demouth, and Song Han. 2023. SmoothQuant: Accurate and efficient post-training quantization for large language models. In *Proceedings of the 40th International Conference on Machine Learning*, volume 202 of *Proceedings of Machine Learning Research*, pages 38087–38099. PMLR.

Liqiang Xiao, Jun Ma, Xin Luna Dong, Pascual Martínez-Gómez, Nasser Zalmout, Chenwei Zhang, Tong Zhao, Hao He, and Yaohui Jin. 2021. End-to-End Conversational Search for Online Shopping with Utterance Transfer. In *Proceedings of the 2021 Conference on Empirical Methods in Natural Language Processing*, pages 3477–3486, Online and Punta Cana, Dominican Republic. Association for Computational Linguistics.

Zhaopeng Xing, Xiaojun Yuan, and Javed Mostafa. 2022. Age-related Difference in Conversational Search Behavior: Preliminary Findings. In *Proceedings of the 2022 Conference on Human Information Interaction and Retrieval*, CHIIR '22, pages 259–265, New York, NY, USA. Association for Computing Machinery.

Lee Xiong, Chenyan Xiong, Ye Li, Kwok-Fung Tang, Jialin Liu, Paul Bennett, Junaid Ahmed, and Arnold Overwijk. 2020. Approximate nearest neighbor negative contrastive learning for dense text retrieval. *Preprint*, arXiv:2007.00808.

Ziwei Xu, Sanjay Jain, and Mohan Kankanhalli. 2024. Hallucination is inevitable: An innate limitation of large language models. *arXiv preprint arXiv:2401.11817*.

Fangkai Yang, Pu Zhao, Zezhong Wang, Lu Wang, Bo Qiao, Jue Zhang, Mohit Garg, Qingwei Lin, Saravan Rajmohan, and Dongmei Zhang. 2023. Empower large language model to perform better on industrial domain-specific question answering. In *Proceedings of the 2023 Conference on Empirical Methods in Natural Language Processing: Industry Track*, pages 294–312, Singapore. Association for Computational Linguistics.

Fanghua Ye, Meng Fang, Shenghui Li, and Emine Yilmaz. 2023. Enhancing conversational search: Large language model-aided informative query rewriting. In *Findings of the Association for Computational Linguistics: EMNLP 2023*, pages 5985–6006, Singapore. Association for Computational Linguistics.

Shi Yu, Jiahua Liu, Jingqin Yang, Chenyan Xiong, Paul Bennett, Jianfeng Gao, and Zhiyuan Liu. 2020. Few-Shot Generative Conversational Query Rewriting. In *Proceedings of the 43rd International ACM SIGIR Conference on Research and Development in Information Retrieval*, SIGIR '20, pages 1933–1936, New York, NY, USA. Association for Computing Machinery.

Munazza Zaib, Wei Emma Zhang, Quan Z. Sheng, Adnan Mahmood, and Yang Zhang. 2022. Conversational question answering: A survey. *Knowledge and Information Systems*, 64(12):3151–3195.

Hamed Zamani and Nick Craswell. 2020. Macaw: An Extensible Conversational Information Seeking Platform. In *Proceedings of the 43rd International ACM SIGIR Conference on Research and Development in Information Retrieval*, SIGIR '20, pages 2193–2196, New York, NY, USA. Association for Computing Machinery.

Hamed Zamani, Susan Dumais, Nick Craswell, Paul Bennett, and Gord Lueck. 2020. Generating Clarifying Questions for Information Retrieval. In *Proceedings of The Web Conference 2020*, WWW '20, pages 418–428, New York, NY, USA. Association for Computing Machinery.

Hamed Zamani, Johanne R. Trippas, Jeff Dalton, and Filip Radlinski. 2023. Conversational Information Seeking. *arXiv preprint arXiv:2201.08808v2*.

Edwin Zhang, Sheng-Chieh Lin, Jheng-Hong Yang, Ronak Pradeep, Rodrigo Nogueira, and Jimmy Lin. 2021. Chatty Goose: A Python Framework for Conversational Search. In *Proceedings of the 44th International ACM SIGIR Conference on Research and Development in Information Retrieval*, SIGIR '21, pages 2521–2525, New York, NY, USA. Association for Computing Machinery.

Shuo Zhang, Zhuyun Dai, Krisztian Balog, and Jamie Callan. 2020. Summarizing and Exploring Tabular Data in Conversational Search. In *Proceedings of the 43rd International ACM SIGIR Conference on Research and Development in Information Retrieval*, SIGIR '20, pages 1537–1540, New York, NY, USA. Association for Computing Machinery.

Yongfeng Zhang, Xu Chen, Qingyao Ai, Liu Yang, and W. Bruce Croft. 2018. Towards Conversational Search and Recommendation: System Ask, User Respond. In *Proceedings of the 27th ACM International Conference on Information and Knowledge Management*, CIKM '18, pages 177–186, New York, NY, USA. Association for Computing Machinery.

A Appendix

The Appendix provides supplementary material for our study, including a list of the six queried academic databases along with the applied search string (Table 2), as well as an overview of commonly used datasets for CSSs (Table 3).

Search String		
"conversational search" OR *"information-seeking dialogue"* OR *"conversational information retrieval"* OR *"conversational information-seeking"* OR *"information-seeking conversation"*		
Database	**Number of Papers**	**Database Link**
ACL Anthology	48	`https://aclanthology.org`
ACM Digital Library	101	`https://dl.acm.org`
IEEE Xplore	5	`https://ieeexplore.ieee.org/Xplore`
ScienceDirect	3	`https://www.sciencedirect.com`
Scopus	46	`https://www.scopus.com`
Web of Science	9	`https://www.webofscience.com/wos/`

Table 2: Search string and number of retrieved candidate papers per database.

Dataset	**Size**	**Source**	**Lang.**
Amazon Reviews (Ni et al., 2019)	9M products	Amazon product catalog	en
CANARD (Elgohary et al., 2019)	40K questions	QuAC dataset	en
CodeSearchNet (Husain et al., 2019)	2M code queries	GitHub repositories	en
ConvQ (Christmann et al., 2019)	11K QA dialogues	Wikipedia	en
DuConv (Wu et al., 2019)	30K dialogues	MTime.com	zh
MRQA (Fisch et al., 2019)	550K QA pairs	18 existing QA datasets	en
MS MARCO (Nguyen et al., 2016)	1M QA pairs	Bing search engine	en
MSDialog (Qu et al., 2018)	2K QA dialogues	Microsoft Community forum	en
Natural Questions (Kwiatkowski et al., 2019)	320K QA pairs	Google search engine	en
QuAC (Choi et al., 2018)	14K QA dialogues	Wikipedia	en
Qulac (Aliannejadi et al., 2019)	10K QA pairs	TREC Web Track	en
SaaC (Ren et al., 2021a)	748 QA pairs	TREC CAR, MS MARCO, WaPo news	en
TREC CAR (Dietz et al., 2017)	30M passages	Wikipedia	en
TREC CAsT (Dalton et al., 2020)	38M passages	TREC CAR, MS MARCO	en
TriviaQA (Joshi et al., 2017)	650K QA pairs	Wikipedia, quiz and trivia websites	en
WikiTableQuestions (Pasupat and Liang, 2015)	22K QA pairs	Wikipedia	en

Table 3: Commonly used datasets in the literature on conversational search systems.

Efficient Dynamic Hard Negative Sampling for Dialogue Selection

Janghoon Han Dongkyu Lee Joongbo Shin Hyunkyung Bae
Jeesoo Bang Seonghwan Kim Stanley Jungkyu Choi Honglak Lee
LG AI Research
{janghoon.han}@lgresearch.ai

Abstract

Recent studies have demonstrated significant improvements in selection tasks, and a considerable portion of this success is attributed to incorporating informative negative samples during training. While traditional methods for constructing hard negatives provide meaningful supervision, they depend on static samples that do not evolve during training, leading to sub-optimal performance. Dynamic hard negative sampling addresses this limitation by continuously adapting to the model's changing state throughout training. However, the high computational demands of this method restrict its applicability to certain model architectures. To overcome these challenges, we introduce an efficient dynamic hard negative sampling (EDHNS). EDHNS enhances efficiency by pre-filtering easily discriminable negatives, thereby reducing the number of candidates the model needs to compute during training. Additionally, it excludes question-candidate pairs where the model already exhibits high confidence from loss computations, further reducing training time. These approaches maintain learning quality while minimizing computation and streamlining the training process. Extensive experiments on DSTC9, DSTC10, Ubuntu, and E-commerce benchmarks demonstrate that EDHNS significantly outperforms baseline models, proving its effectiveness in dialogue selection tasks.[1]

1 Introduction

The problem of selecting the most suitable answer from multiple candidates has been extensively explored in the field of natural language processing, particularly within selection tasks (Lowe et al., 2015; Wu et al., 2018a; Zhang et al., 2018a; Kim et al., 2020, 2021). Typically, these tasks involve one positive candidate and multiple negative candidates associated with a given question. Training on all negative samples can be time-consuming, so it is common practice to randomly select a subset of negative samples for training. However, random negative sampling may not provide meaningful supervision, as models updated with easily discriminable negative samples contribute minimally to gradient updates (Cai et al., 2020; Xu et al., 2022a).

To address this issue, various strategies for hard negative sampling have been proposed and have demonstrated their effectiveness (He et al., 2021; Mi et al., 2021; Tang et al., 2021). Heuristic and data-dependent methods (He et al., 2021; Mi et al., 2021) utilize the unique characteristics of datasets but are constrained by their limited generalizability, making them less effective for other datasets. Lin et al. (2020); Tang et al. (2021) have enhanced these approaches with model-based strategies. However, these approaches still face challenges, as they rely on static (fixed) hard negative samples that do not dynamically adapt during training.

Recently, dynamic hard negative sampling (Xiong et al., 2021; Zhan et al., 2021) has been introduced to overcome these limitations by adaptively selecting hard negatives for learning in response to model updates, effectively aligning with changes in model behavior. However, it requires continual recalculations of matching scores for all negative candidates throughout training, significantly increasing computational costs. This restriction predominantly confines its application to fast dense retrieval models (Karpukhin et al., 2020; Gao and Callan, 2021, 2022), and poses implementation challenges in models with slower inference speeds.

To mitigate these challenges, we propose an Efficient Dynamic Hard Negative Sampling (EDHNS) method applicable to various model architectures. Like traditional approaches, our method computes matching scores for negative candidates at each training step. However, it alleviates the computational burden through two main strategies: shortlisting and selective update. In shortlisting, we compute scores only for a filtered subset of candidates

[1] https://github.com/hanjanghoon/EDHNS

Proceedings of the 6th Workshop on NLP for Conversational AI (NLP4ConvAI 2024), pages 89–100
August 16, 2024 ©2024 Association for Computational Linguistics

by removing easily discriminable negative candidates from the pool, enabling the selection of sufficiently hard negatives from a smaller set. In the selective update, we measure confidence scores for question-candidate pairs and exclude those with high scores from training, further save training time. These strategies enable meaningful learning with reduced computational demands, enhancing overall performance. Notably, for the first time, we have applied dynamic hard negative sampling to the cross encoder, which has demonstrated strong performance in selection tasks, leading to significant performance improvements.

We empirically demonstrate the efficacy of our method through extensive experiments on two key tasks. The first task, knowledge selection, focuses on choosing relevant knowledge for a given conversation. We evaluate the performance of this task using the DSTC9 (Kim et al., 2020) and DSTC10 (Kim et al., 2021) benchmarks. The second task, response selection, requires choosing the most appropriate response for a given dialogue context. We assess this task using the Ubuntu (Lowe et al., 2015) and E-commerce (Zhang et al., 2018a) benchmarks. Our experiments show that models using EDHNS significantly outperform baseline models across all four benchmarks. Specifically, EDHNS achieves top performance in most evaluation metrics for DSTC9 and DSTC10, and also demonstrates superior performance in the Ubuntu and E-commerce benchmarks.

2 Related Work

Previous studies have introduced various hard negative sampling approaches, resulting in notable enhancements in various NLP tasks. These strategies can be categorized into two types: static hard negative sampling and dynamic hard negative sampling (Zhan et al., 2021; Xu et al., 2022b).

Static hard negative sampling pre-defines fixed hard negative samples before the training process. This method selects hard negative samples based on data characteristics or by retrieving or generating them using a model. In the knowledge selection task, He et al. (2021) introduce a data-dependent negative sampling strategy by categorizing given knowledge into different groups. Tang et al. (2021) adopt a model-based negative sampling method to sample fixed hard negatives. In the response selection task, Lin et al. (2020) use retrieval and generation models to diversify negative samples, while Lee et al. (2022b) generate adversarial examples using GPT-3. In text retrieval tasks, since negative samples are derived from text candidates recalled by the retrieval module, previous works (Ren et al., 2021; Zhang et al., 2022a) focus on jointly optimizing the retriever and reranker modules.

Dynamic hard negative sampling, in contrast, selects hard negative samples dynamically during the training process, considering the evolving state of the model. In response selection, Li et al. (2019) adapt negative examples to matching models during the learning process, exploring various sampling strategies. Particularly, this approach has been extensively studied in the training of dense retrieval models. Guu et al. (2020) and Xiong et al. (2021) use dense retrieval models to pre-retrieve the top documents as hard negatives during training, periodically rebuilding the index and refreshing the hard negatives. Zhan et al. (2021) propose a query-side training algorithm that directly optimizes the dense retrieval model using dynamic hard negative sampling.

However, applying dynamic hard negative sampling to most model architectures—except for the bi-encoder structure commonly used in dense retrieval—poses challenges due to the slower speeds and high computational demands. This limitation is especially evident in cross-encoder-based models, which, despite their superior performance in selection tasks, require extensive computations for token-level interactions and cannot pre-compute candidate embeddings. To overcome these challenges, we propose a novel and efficient dynamic hard negative sampling method.

3 Preliminary

3.1 Problem Formalization of Selection Task

Let dataset $\mathbf{D} = \{(q_i, \mathbf{C}_i)\}_{i=1}^{M}$ be a set of M pairs that consist of a question q_i, its corresponding candidates $\mathbf{C}_i = \{p_i\} \cup \mathbf{N}_i^L$. A candidate pool $\mathbf{C}_i$ contains a positive candidate p_i and negative candidates $\mathbf{N}_i^L = \{n_{i,1}, n_{i,2}, ..., n_{i,L}\}$, where L is the number of negative candidates. As we address selection tasks as a unified framework for learning a matching model that evaluates relevance scores between a question and its candidates, the task is formulated as learning a matching function $f(q_i, c_{i,j})$ for a given question-candidate pair $(q_i, c_{i,j})$, where $c_{i,j} \in \mathbf{C}_i$.

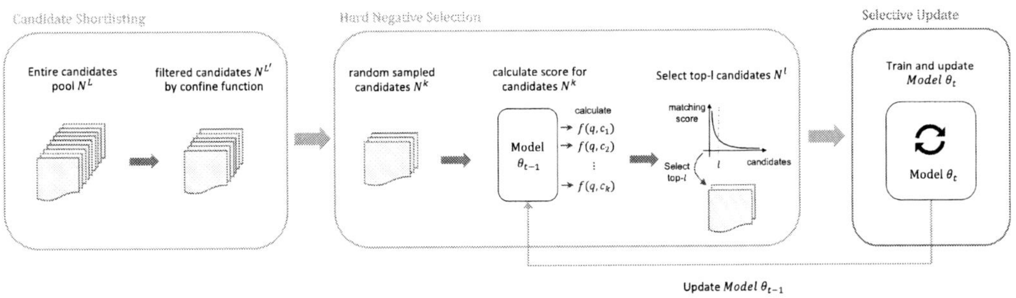

Figure 1: Efficient dynamic hard negative sampling framework. The EDHNS method comprises three key components: Candidate Shortlisting, Hard Negative Selection, and Selective Update.

3.2 Cross Encoder Architecture in Dialogue Selection

Following previous works (Nogueira and Cho, 2019; He et al., 2021; Han et al., 2021; Kim and Ko, 2021) in selection task, we use pre-trained bidirectional language models (Devlin et al., 2019; Liu et al., 2019; He et al., 2020) as a cross encoder to measure the matching degree between a question q_i and a candidate $c_{i,j}$. The input x of our matching model is as follows:

$$x = [\texttt{CLS}]\ q_i\ [\texttt{SEP}]\ c_{i,j}\ [\texttt{SEP}]. \tag{1}$$

Token embedding for input x are summed with position embedding and segment embedding to become input representations. The input representations are fed into the transformer layer, and the self-attention module in the transformer layer computes cross-attention between those of q_i and $c_{i,j}$. In this way, multiple transformer layers can deeply understand the relevance of the question and its candidate, resulting in a high-performance matching model. We use the final representation $o_{cls} \in \mathbb{R}^d$ of the [CLS] token for computing the matching score through an MLP layer:

$$f(q_i, c_{i,j}) = W_2\sigma(W_1 o_{cls} + b_1) + b_2, \tag{2}$$

where $W_1 \in \mathbb{R}^{d_h \times d}$, $W_2 \in \mathbb{R}^{1 \times d_h}$, $b_1 \in \mathbb{R}^{d_h}$, and $b_2 \in \mathbb{R}^1$ are trainable parameters for fine-tuning. Eventually, the weights of the model are updated using the cross-entropy loss function:

$$\mathcal{L} = -\mathbb{E}_{(q_i,p_i,N_i)\sim D}[\log(\frac{e^{f(q_i,p_i)}}{e^{f(q_i,p_i)} + \sum_{j=1}^{l} e^{f(q_i,n_{i,j})}})] \tag{3}$$

where l is the number of negative samples and p_i, $n_{i,j}$ denote positive and negative candidates respectively.

4 Methodology

4.1 Efficient Dynamic Hard Negative Sampling

In this section, we explain the details of our efficient dynamic hard negative sampling (EDHNS) framework for selection tasks. As its name shows, we let the model find hard negative samples that are difficult to discriminate by itself during training. Figure 1 illustrate the process of EDHNS where the model iterates selecting hard negatives and learning to discriminate positive from them at each training step. Since hard negatives are collected at every model update, the selected samples can be the '*most challenging*' for the model at that time. Therefore, the model could learn from more informative hard negatives, which leads to faster convergence and performance gain.

4.1.1 Training Procedure

The EDHNS framework can be generalized as Algorithm 1. We first train the base model θ with random negatives for the initial s step, ensuring the model is capable of selecting hard negatives. After initialization, we iteratively select hard negative samples and update the model with those selected samples. During the hard negative selection phase, we randomly sample a negative subset ($\mathbf{N}_i^k$) from the pool of negative samples. Subsequently, we compute matching scores between the question and the sampled k candidates using the current model θ_{t-1} at step t, as explained in Equation 2. Based on these matching scores, we select top-l hard negatives from $\mathbf{N}_i^k$. After hard negative selection, we update the model θ_t with the positive p_i and the top-l hard negatives $\mathbf{N}_i^l$ using Equation 3.

Algorithm 1 Efficient dynamic hard negative sampling

Input: Dataset with confined negatives candidate sets $D' = \{(q_i, p_i, N_i^L, N_i^{L'})\}_{i=1}^M$, Model parameter θ, Initializing step s

1. Initialize the model θ with random samples for p steps
Initialize θ
for train step $t = 1$ to s **do**
  Sample a batch B_t from D'
  for (q_i, p_i, N_i) in B_t **do**
    $N_i^l :=$ l samples randomly extracted from N_i^L
  end for
  Update the model θ_t with $\{(q_i, p_i, N_i^l)\}_{i=1}^{|B_t|}$ using Eq.3
end for

2. Train the model θ
for train step $t = s + 1, ...$ **do**
  Sample a batch B_t from D'
  for (q_i, p_i^+, N_i^m) in B_t **do**
    $N_i^k :=$ k random candidates sampled from $N_i^{L'}$
    $N_i^l :=$ top-l candidates of sorted list of N_i^k along the matching score computed from the model θ_{t-1} using Eq.2
  end for
  Update the model θ_t with $\{(q_i, p_i^+, N_i^l)\}_{i=1}^{|B_t|}$ using Eq.3
end for

4.2 Time Reduction Strategies in EDHNS

4.2.1 Candidates Shortlisting

Since calculating matching scores for all negative candidates is considerably time-consuming, a practical approach is to randomly sample negative candidate subset $\mathbf{N}^k$ from a pool of all negative samples $\mathbf{N}^L$ where $k \ll L$. However, there is a trade-off in choosing the size of the candidate subset $\mathbf{N}^k$. If the sample size k is not large enough, it may not include an adequate number of challenging negative samples. Conversely, if k is increased, the training time also substantially increases for score calculation.

To train the model effectively even with a small size of candidate subset, we construct a confined negative candidate set, denoted as $\mathbf{N}^{L'}$, where $L' \ll L$. This confined negative candidate set is created by filtering out easy negatives from the original negative candidates set ($\mathbf{N}^L$). When sampling a negative subset ($\mathbf{N}^k$) from the confined candidate set, the likelihood of including difficult samples increases even with a small number of k. This is because the easy negatives have already been filtered out during the construction of $\mathbf{N}^{L'}$. We configure a confined candidate set by finding negative samples relevant to both question and the positive as

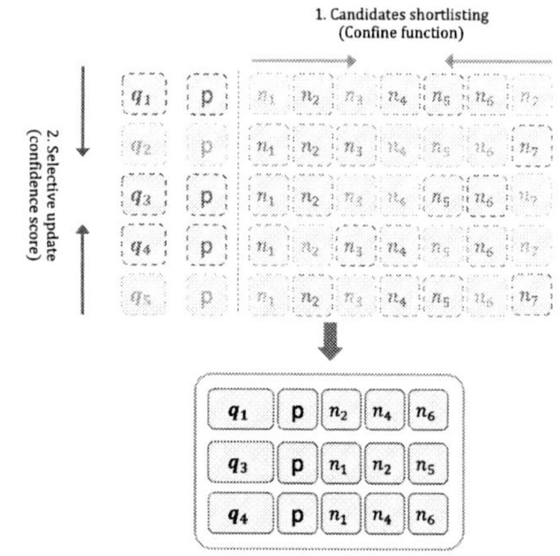

Figure 2: Time reduction strategies of EDHNS. Candidate shortlisting filters out easy negative candidates, and Selective update exclude well-known pairs from the training.

follows.

$$\mathbf{N}_i^{L'} = \{n_{i,j} \mid g(q_i \oplus p_i, n_{i,j}) > \tau\}, \tag{4}$$

where τ is a threshold, $n_{i,j} \in \mathbf{N}_i^L$ and $\oplus$ denotes concatenation.

4.2.2 Selective Update

Another feature of EDHNS is its focused training solely on informative question-candidate pairs (q_i, C_i). This is achieved by calculating a confidence score for the positive sample during the negative selection process as follows.

$$Score(q_i, p_i, \mathbf{N}_i^k) = \frac{e^{f(q_i,p_i)}}{e^{f(q_i,p_i)} + \sum_{j=1}^{k} e^{f(q_i,n_{i,j})}} \tag{5}$$

where $n_{i,j} \in N_i^k$. If the confidence score exceeds a predefined threshold, the model considers it a well-known pair and excludes it from training and update. This strategy accelerates the training procedure by minimizing the inclusion of question-candidate pairs that do not contribute substantial supervision to the model and prevents the model from becoming overconfident (Lee et al., 2022a).

5 Experiments

5.1 Implementation Details

We train models with three different random seeds and report the average value for all experiments. Our model is trained with 8 NVIDIA A100 GPUs (with 40GB). For confine function g, we employ

Dataset	DSTC9 (Knowledge)			DSTC10 (Knowledge)			Ubuntu (Response)			E-commerce (Response)		
	Train	Dev	Test	Train	Dev	Test	Train	Dev	Test	Train	Dev	Test
# (q, C) pairs	19k	2673	1981	59k(syn)	104	683	500k	50k	50k	500k	5k	1k
# C per q	2900	2900	12039	9139	9139	9139	2(1000)	10	10	2(1000)	2(10)	10

Table 1: Data statistics for the knowledge selection, response selection benchmarks, q denotes question and C denotes candidates.

Sentence Transformers (Reimers and Gurevych, 2019)[2] and compute cosine similarity to measure semantic similarity. Details of each experimental setting can be found in Appendix A.

5.2 Knowledge Selection in Knowledge-grounded Dialogue System

One of the primary objectives in the ninth and tenth dialogue System Technology Challenge (DSTC9, DSTC10) is to develop a knowledge-grounded task-oriented dialogue system (Kim et al., 2020, 2021). The challenges consist of three consecutive subtasks: knowledge-seeking turn detection, knowledge selection, and knowledge-grounded response generation. Our focus is on the knowledge selection task, which requires the system to identify the most appropriate knowledge related to the user's last utterance.

Table 1 indicates the statistics for the DSTC9 and DSTC10 datasets. DSTC9 knowledge selection task includes out-of-domain knowledge in its test set. DSTC10 knowledge selection task involves speech recognition errors as it comprises spoken conversations. We sample synthetic data from prior studies (Tian et al., 2021; Han et al., 2022) and configure training data since there is no official training data for DSTC10.

The selection performance is assessed based on recall at k (*R@k*) and mean reciprocal rank (*MRR*) measures, specifically *R@1*, *R@5*, and *MRR@5*. These metrics are the official evaluation criteria for both DSTC9 and DSTC10 datasets (Kim et al., 2020, 2021).

5.2.1 Baseline Model

RoBERTa-base+EDHNS and *RoBERTa-large+EDHNS* are cross-encoder-based matching models trained with our efficient dynamic hard negative sampling. To evaluate the effectiveness of proposed methodology, we compare these models with *RoBERTa-base* and *RoBERTa-large*, which are identical architectures yet trained using random negative sampling. Additionally, we evaluate our approaches against other multiple baselines for the DSTC9 and DSTC10 tasks as follow.

DSTC9 Baseline *TF-IDF*, *BM25*, and *BERT-base* from Kim et al. (2020) are the official baselines for the DSTC9 competition. *TF-IDF* and *BM25* are bag-of-words information retrieval baselines and BERT-base utilizes a cross-encoder architecture for selection. *Knover* from He et al. (2021) applies a heuristic data-dependent hard negative sampling called multi-scale negative sampling. *Hirachical-filtering* from Jin et al. (2021) selects knowledge through three modules: domain classification, entity tracking, and knowledge matching. *Hirachical-selection* (Thulke et al., 2023) trains two different models which determines related domains and entities, and measures the relevance score of knowledge.

DSTC10 Baseline *DSTC9-BERT-base* and *DSTC9-Knover* are the official baseline models for the DSTC10 knowledge selection task (Kim et al., 2021), which are trained using the DSTC9 dataset. *Weighted* (Han et al., 2022) trains model utilizing weighted negative sampling, where different weight probabilities are assigned to each negative sample category. *Hirachical-selection+ABS* (Thulke et al., 2023) incorporates an Alternative Beam Search method into the hierarchical selection. *TOD_DA* (Tian et al., 2021) employs Data Augmentation and multi-scale negative sampling to enhance model's performance.

5.2.2 Result

Table 2 shows the performance of EDHNS approach in DSTC9 and DSTC10 benchmarks. The result highlights changing the negative sampling method to EDHNS in both the base and large models led to significant improvements in performance for both datasets. Specifically, The base model and the large model exhibit a consistent enhancement of 4.7% and 3.2%, respectively, in *R@1* on the DSTC9. Similarly, these models demonstrate significant 6.4% and 4.5% enhancements in *R@1* on the DSTC10. These improvements indicate the effectiveness of learning informative negative sam-

[2]We employ a model for confine function from Sentence-Transformers: https://www.sbert.net/

Method	PLM	$R@1$	$R@5$	$MRR@5$
Knowledge selection in DSTC9				
TF-IDF (Kim et al., 2020)	-	0.511	0.807	0.618
BM25 (Kim et al., 2020)	-	0.498	0.827	0.611
BERT-base (Kim et al., 2020)	BERT_{base}	0.834	0.976	0.891
Knover (He et al., 2021)	PLATO-2 (1.6B)	0.910	0.986	0.945
Hirachical-Filtering (Jin et al., 2021)	RoBERTa_{large}	0.925	0.970	<u>0.946</u>
Hirachical-Selection (Thulke et al., 2023)	RoBERTa_{large}	**0.932**	0.973	-
RoBERTa-base	RoBERTa_{base}	0.839	0.989	0.904
RoBERTa-base+EDHNS	RoBERTa_{base}	0.886	0.993	0.935
RoBERTa-large	RoBERTa_{large}	0.899	<u>0.995</u>	0.942
RoBERTa-large+EDHNS	RoBERTa_{large}	<u>0.931</u>	**0.998**	**0.962**
Knowledge selection in DSTC10				
DSTC9-BERT-base (Kim et al., 2021)	BERT_{base}	0.521	0.733	0.606
DSTC9-Knover (Kim et al., 2021)	PLATO-2 (1.6B)	0.619	0.800	0.693
TOD-DA (Tian et al., 2021)	PLATO-2 (1.6B)	<u>0.801</u>	**0.94**	<u>0.857</u>
Weighted (Han et al., 2022)	RoBERTa_{base}	0.72	0.862	0.780
Hirachical-Selection+ABS (Thulke et al., 2023)	RoBERTa_{large}	0.777	-	-
RoBERTa-base+MLM	RoBERTa_{base}	0.727	0.897	0.798
RoBERTa-base+MLM+EDHNS	RoBERTa_{base}	0.791	0.910	0.841
RoBERTa-large+MLM	RoBERTa_{large}	0.776	0.930	0.838
RoBERTa-large+MLM+EDHNS	RoBERTa_{large}	**0.821**	<u>0.935</u>	**0.869**

Table 2: Test set performance of knowledge selection in DSTC9 and DSTC10. The best and second-best results are in bold and underlined fonts respectively. For the DSTC10 dataset, since spoken errors are present, masked language modeling is applied for robust token representation.

ples from a model perspective. In addition to the substantial performance improvement compared to their base model, the proposed models outperform other baselines on both datasets. In comparison to the state-of-the-art model in DSTC9, *hierarchical* selection, our *RoBERTa-large+EDHNS* demonstrates shows a significant enhancement of 2.5% in *R@5*. In the DSTC10 dataset, the *RoBERTa-large+MLM+EDHNS* model outperforms the state-of-the-art TOD-DA by 2% in *R@1*.

5.3 Response Selection in Retrieval-based Dialogue Systems

Response selection is a task in retrieval-based dialogue systems where the goal is to select the appropriate response from given response candidates based on the provided dialogue context. We validate the effectiveness of EDHNS using commonly used benchmarks for this task, namely the Ubuntu Corpus and the E-commerce Corpus.

The Ubuntu Corpus V1 (Lowe et al., 2015) is a dataset consisting of multi-turn dialogues extracted from Ubuntu chat logs. It primarily contains technical-support conversations about Ubuntu problems. For this study, we utilize the preprocessed data provided by Xu et al. (2017). The E-commerce Corpus (Zhang et al., 2018a) is a Chinese multi-turn dialogue dataset collected from Taobao, China's largest e-commerce platform. It includes authentic interactions between customers and customer service representatives, covering various conversational topics such as consultations and product recommendations.

Since the original training set contains only one negative candidate per dialogue context, we augment the negative candidates by sampling 1k utterances from 1 million other response candidates for both benchmarks, as shown in Table 1. Additionally, we augmented the validation set of the E-commerce corpus in a similar manner to reduce discrepancies with the test set.

The response selection performance for both the Ubuntu Corpus and the E-commerce Corpus is evaluated using $R_{10}@1$, $R_{10}@2$, and $R_{10}@5$, following previous work (Gu et al., 2020; Xu et al., 2021; Han et al., 2021).

5.3.1 Baseline Model

BERT (Gu et al., 2020) is a BERT-based (Devlin et al., 2019) cross encoder matching model. *UMS_bert+* (Whang et al., 2021) and *BERT_SL* (Xu et al., 2021) jointly train a PLM-based response selection model with other self-supervised tasks to learn temporal dependencies between ut-

Models	Ubuntu			E-commerce		
	$R_{10}@1$	$R_{10}@2$	$R_{10}@5$	$R_{10}@1$	$R_{10}@2$	$R_{10}@5$
TF-IDF (Lowe et al., 2015)	0.410	0.545	0.708	0.159	0.256	0.477
RNN (Lowe et al., 2015)	0.403	0.547	0.819	0.118	0.223	0.589
CNN (Kadlec et al., 2015)	0.549	0.684	0.896	0.328	0.515	0.792
LSTM (Kadlec et al., 2015)	0.638	0.784	0.949	0.365	0.536	0.828
SMN (Wu et al., 2018b)	0.726	0.847	0.961	0.453	0.654	0.886
DUA (Zhang et al., 2018b)	0.752	0.868	0.962	0.501	0.700	0.921
DAM (Zhou et al., 2018)	0.767	0.874	0.969	0.526	0.727	0.933
IOI (Tao et al., 2019)	0.796	0.894	0.974	0.563	0.768	0.950
ESIM (Chen and Wang, 2019)	0.796	0.894	0.975	0.570	0.767	0.948
MSN (Yuan et al., 2019)	0.800	0.899	0.978	0.606	0.770	0.937
BERT (Gu et al., 2020)	0.808	0.897	0.975	0.610	0.814	0.973
*BERT-VFT (Whang et al., 2020)	0.855	0.928	0.985	-	-	-
*SA-BERT (Gu et al., 2020)	0.855	0.928	0.983	0.704	0.879	0.985
*UMSBERT+ (Whang et al., 2021)	0.875	0.942	0.988	0.764	0.905	0.986
*BERT-SL (Xu et al., 2021)	0.884	0.946	0.990	0.776	0.919	0.991
*BERT-FP (Han et al., 2021)	0.911	0.962	0.994	0.870	0.956	0.993
*BERT-UMS+FGC (Li et al., 2022)	0.886	0.948	0.990	-	-	-
*Uni-Enc+BERT-FP (Song et al., 2023)	0.916	**0.965**	**0.994**	-	-	-
BERT+EDHNS	0.837	0.910	0.975	0.868	0.938	0.991
*BERT-FP+EDHNS	**0.917**	**0.965**	**0.994**	**0.957**	**0.986**	**0.997**

Table 3: Test set performance of response selection in Ubuntu and E-commerce corpus. All baseline models employ BERT_{base} as their PLM. The models marked with * have been post-trained.

terances. *BERT-FP* (Han et al., 2021) proposes a Fine-grained Post-training method that post-trains the short context response pair before fine-tuning. *BERT-UMS+FGC* (Li et al., 2022) is model that train *UMS_bert+* in Fine-Grained Contrastive learning manner. *Uni-Enc+BERT-FP* (Song et al., 2023) apply Uni-encoder architecture to advanced post-training model from Han et al. (2021). *BERT+EDHNS* and *BERT-FP+EDHNS* are proposed models that apply efficient dynamic negative sampling to the *BERT* and *BERT-FP*, respectively.

5.3.2 Result

As illustrated in Table 3, the application of EDHNS significantly enhances model performance in response selection tasks across different benchmarks. In the Ubuntu benchmark, *BERT+EDHNS* shows a significant improvement of 2.9% in *R@1* compared to its baseline model *BERT*, while *BERT-FP+EDHNS* achieves an enhancement of 0.6% in *R@1* over its baseline *BERT-FP*. In the E-commerce benchmark, the performance enhancements are even more pronounced. Specifically, *BERT+EDHNS* and *BERT FP+EDHNS* demonstrate performance improvements of 25.8% and 8.7% in *R@1*, respectively, when compared to their corresponding baselines *BERT* and *BERT-FP*.

Method	$R@1$	$R@5$	$MRR@5$
RoBERTa +Random	0.899	0.995	0.942
RoBERTa +Static_model	0.906	0.997	0.947
RoBERTa +BM25	0.910	0.994	0.948
RoBERTa +Multi-scale	0.911	0.992	0.947
RoBERTa +**EDHNS**	**0.931**	**0.998**	**0.962**

Table 4: Comparison of efficient dynamic hard negative sampling with diverse hard negative sampling in DSTC9 test set using *RoBERTa-large*.

6 Further Analysis

6.1 Comparison of EDHNS with Other Negative Sampling Methods

We compared EDHNS with various other hard negative sampling approaches on DSTC9 test set as shown in Table 4. *RoBERTa+Random* is cross encoder matching model with random negative sampling. *+Static_model* refers to static hard negative sampling, where the model selects fixed hard negatives. *+BM25*, denote obtains hard negatives through the BM25 algorithm (Yang et al., 2017). *+Multi-scale* indicates multi-scale hard negative sampling proposed by He et al. (2021).

All the hard negative sampling methods lead to performance improvements compared to *RoBERTa+Random*. However, proposed *+EDHNS* method surpasses all other hard negative sampling

Model Variant	Training Time	Acc
Random	10m	0.926
DHNS(k=100)	1h 16m	0.967
DHNS(k=10)	17m	0.940
DHNS(k=10)+CS	16m	0.967
EDHNS: DHNS(k=10)+CS+SU	8m	0.964

Table 5: Ablation study for time reduction strategy on DSTC9 validation set using *RoBERTa-large*. *CS, HNS, SU* denote Candidate Shortlisting, Hard Negative Selection, and Selective Update of EDHNS in Figure 1. Each model is trained for five epochs.

techniques by a significant margin. This demonstrates that dynamically selecting hard negative from a model standpoint is superior in finding informative negative samples which enhance model performance.

6.2 Ablation Study about Time Reduction Strategies in EDHNS

We investigated the efficacy of the time reduction methods in EDHNS through a series of ablation experiments on the DSTC9 validation set, as shown in Table 5. *CS, HNS, SU* denote three main components of EDHNS: Candidate Shortlisting, Hard Negative Selection, and Selective Update, as shown in Figure 1. k represents the number of candidates for which the model measures the matching scores during the *HNS* phase.

Models with a hard negative selection exhibit notable performance improvement compared to previous random negative sampling. However, when k is large, such as *HNS(k=100)*, the training time significantly increases. Conversely, when the k is small, as in *HNS(k=10)*, the training time is reduced, but the performance is likewise diminished. The model with the shortlisting phase *CS+HNS (k=10)* maintain a similar training speed to *HNS(k=10)* while achieving comparable performance to *HNS(k=100)*. This observation underscores that model can sufficiently select informative hard negatives with a small number of k by removing easy negative samples from the negative pool through shortlisting. Moreover, when compared *CS+HNS(k=10)* to complete EDHNS (*CS+HNS(k=10)+SU*) including the selective update phase reduces the training time by less than half while still exhibiting comparable performance. This result demonstrates excluding the training of overconfident pairs improves training efficiency without compromising model performance.

Conclusion

This study introduces a fast and efficient dynamic hard negative sampling method for selection tasks. We overcome the constraints of previous dynamic hard negative sampling methods by enhancing their efficiency, thereby enabling their application across various model architectures. Our approach includes two time-saving strategies: candidate shortlisting to filter out easy negative candidates and selective updates to focus on meaningful question-candidate pairs for learning. Through this, the model dynamically and efficiently learns from challenging negative samples, effectively gaining valuable supervision. Specifically, we apply this methodology to a cross-encoder architecture, demonstrating its effectiveness and generalizability in dialogue selection across two tasks and four benchmarks. Experimental results show that models with EDHNS consistently outperform their baseline models across all benchmarks, highlighting the effectiveness of the proposed approach.

Limitation

Although EDHNS accelerates learning by providing informative samples to the model, there are also limitations. One potential limitation is a false negative problem, a common problem in hard negative sampling. For instance, false negatives (i.e., unlabeled positives) may exist in the MS MARCO dataset since the annotators can only annotate a few top-retrieved passages (Qu et al., 2021). If these false negatives are mistakenly considered true negatives during the training process, it may disturb the model to correctly discriminate between positive and negative instances.

References

Tiffany Tianhui Cai, Jonathan Frankle, David J. Schwab, and Ari S. Morcos. 2020. Are all negatives created equal in contrastive instance discrimination? *CoRR*, abs/2010.06682.

Qian Chen and Wen Wang. 2019. Sequential attention-based network for noetic end-to-end response selection.

Jacob Devlin, Ming-Wei Chang, Kenton Lee, and Kristina Toutanova. 2019. BERT: Pre-training of deep bidirectional transformers for language understanding. In *Proceedings of the 2019 Conference of the North American Chapter of the Association for Computational Linguistics: Human Language Technologies, Volume 1 (Long and Short Papers)*, pages

4171–4186, Minneapolis, Minnesota. Association for Computational Linguistics.

Luyu Gao and Jamie Callan. 2021. Condenser: a pre-training architecture for dense retrieval. In *Proceedings of the 2021 Conference on Empirical Methods in Natural Language Processing*, pages 981–993, Online and Punta Cana, Dominican Republic. Association for Computational Linguistics.

Luyu Gao and Jamie Callan. 2022. Unsupervised corpus aware language model pre-training for dense passage retrieval. In *Proceedings of the 60th Annual Meeting of the Association for Computational Linguistics (Volume 1: Long Papers)*, pages 2843–2853, Dublin, Ireland. Association for Computational Linguistics.

Jia-Chen Gu, Tianda Li, Quan Liu, Zhen-Hua Ling, Zhiming Su, Si Wei, and Xiaodan Zhu. 2020. Speaker-aware BERT for multi-turn response selection in retrieval-based chatbots. In *CIKM '20: The 29th ACM International Conference on Information and Knowledge Management, Virtual Event, Ireland, October 19-23, 2020*, pages 2041–2044. ACM.

Kelvin Guu, Kenton Lee, Zora Tung, Panupong Pasupat, and Ming-Wei Chang. 2020. Realm: Retrieval-augmented language model pre-training. In *Proceedings of the 37th International Conference on Machine Learning*, ICML'20. JMLR.org.

Janghoon Han, Taesuk Hong, Byoungjae Kim, Youngjoong Ko, and Jungyun Seo. 2021. Fine-grained post-training for improving retrieval-based dialogue systems. In *Proceedings of the 2021 Conference of the North American Chapter of the Association for Computational Linguistics: Human Language Technologies*, pages 1549–1558, Online. Association for Computational Linguistics.

Janghoon Han, Joongbo Shin, Hosung Song, Hyunjik Jo, Gyeonghun Kim, Yireun Kim, and Stanley Jungkyu Choi. 2022. External knowledge selection with weighted negative sampling in knowledge-grounded task-oriented dialogue systems.

Huang He, Hua Lu, Siqi Bao, Fan Wang, Hua Wu, Zhengyu Niu, and Haifeng Wang. 2021. Learning to select external knowledge with multi-scale negative sampling. *arXiv preprint arXiv:2102.02096*.

Pengcheng He, Xiaodong Liu, Jianfeng Gao, and Weizhu Chen. 2020. Deberta: Decoding-enhanced bert with disentangled attention.

Di Jin, Seokhwan Kim, and Dilek Hakkani-Tur. 2021. Can I be of further assistance? using unstructured knowledge access to improve task-oriented conversational modeling. In *Proceedings of the 1st Workshop on Document-grounded Dialogue and Conversational Question Answering (DialDoc 2021)*, pages 119–127, Online. Association for Computational Linguistics.

Rudolf Kadlec, Martin Schmid, and Jan Kleindienst. 2015. Improved deep learning baselines for ubuntu corpus dialogs.

Vladimir Karpukhin, Barlas Oguz, Sewon Min, Patrick Lewis, Ledell Wu, Sergey Edunov, Danqi Chen, and Wen-tau Yih. 2020. Dense passage retrieval for open-domain question answering. In *Proceedings of the 2020 Conference on Empirical Methods in Natural Language Processing (EMNLP)*, pages 6769–6781, Online. Association for Computational Linguistics.

Meoungjun Kim and Youngjoong Ko. 2021. *Self-Supervised Fine-Tuning for Efficient Passage Re-Ranking*, page 3142–3146. Association for Computing Machinery, New York, NY, USA.

Seokhwan Kim, Mihail Eric, Karthik Gopalakrishnan, Behnam Hedayatnia, Yang Liu, and Dilek Hakkani-Tur. 2020. Beyond domain apis: Task-oriented conversational modeling with unstructured knowledge access. In *Proceedings of the 21th Annual Meeting of the Special Interest Group on Discourse and Dialogue*, pages 278–289.

Seokhwan Kim, Yang Liu, Di Jin, Alexandros Papangelis, Karthik Gopalakrishnan, Behnam Hedayatnia, and Dilek Hakkani-Tür. 2021. "how robust ru?": Evaluating task-oriented dialogue systems on spoken conversations. In *2021 IEEE Automatic Speech Recognition and Understanding Workshop (ASRU)*, pages 1147–1154. IEEE.

Dongkyu Lee, Zhiliang Tian, Yingxiu Zhao, Ka Chun Cheung, and Nevin L. Zhang. 2022a. Hard gate knowledge distillation – leverage calibration for robust and reliable language model.

Nyoungwoo Lee, ChaeHun Park, Ho-Jin Choi, and Jaegul Choo. 2022b. Pneg: Prompt-based negative response generation for dialogue response selection task.

Jia Li, Chongyang Tao, Wei Wu, Yansong Feng, Dongyan Zhao, and Rui Yan. 2019. Sampling matters! an empirical study of negative sampling strategies for learning of matching models in retrieval-based dialogue systems. In *Proceedings of the 2019 Conference on Empirical Methods in Natural Language Processing and the 9th International Joint Conference on Natural Language Processing (EMNLP-IJCNLP)*, pages 1291–1296, Hong Kong, China. Association for Computational Linguistics.

Yuntao Li, Can Xu, Huang Hu, Lei Sha, Yan Zhang, and Daxin Jiang. 2022. Small changes make big differences: Improving multi-turn response selection in dialogue systems via fine-grained contrastive learning. In *Interspeech 2022, 23rd Annual Conference of the International Speech Communication Association, Incheon, Korea, 18-22 September 2022*, pages 2723–2727. ISCA.

Jimmy Lin, Xueguang Ma, Sheng-Chieh Lin, Jheng-Hong Yang, Ronak Pradeep, and Rodrigo Frassetto

Nogueira. 2021. Pyserini: A python toolkit for reproducible information retrieval research with sparse and dense representations. In *SIGIR '21: The 44th International ACM SIGIR Conference on Research and Development in Information Retrieval, Virtual Event, Canada, July 11-15, 2021*, pages 2356–2362. ACM.

Zibo Lin, Deng Cai, Yan Wang, Xiaojiang Liu, Haitao Zheng, and Shuming Shi. 2020. The world is not binary: Learning to rank with grayscale data for dialogue response selection. In *Proceedings of the 2020 Conference on Empirical Methods in Natural Language Processing (EMNLP)*, pages 9220–9229, Online. Association for Computational Linguistics.

Yinhan Liu, Myle Ott, Naman Goyal, Jingfei Du, Mandar Joshi, Danqi Chen, Omer Levy, Mike Lewis, Luke Zettlemoyer, and Veselin Stoyanov. 2019. Roberta: A robustly optimized bert pretraining approach. *arXiv preprint arXiv:1907.11692*.

Zhenghao Liu, Kaitao Zhang, Chenyan Xiong, Zhiyuan Liu, and Maosong Sun. 2021. Openmatch: An open source library for neu-ir research. In *Proceedings of SIGIR*, page 2531–2535.

Ryan Lowe, Nissan Pow, Iulian Vlad Serban, and Joelle Pineau. 2015. The ubuntu dialogue corpus: A large dataset for research in unstructured multi-turn dialogue systems. In *Proceedings of the 16th Annual Meeting of the Special Interest Group on Discourse and Dialogue*, pages 285–294.

Haitao Mi, Qiyu Ren, Yinpei Dai, Yifan He, Jian Sun, Yongbin Li, Jing Zheng, and Peng Xu. 2021. Towards generalized models for beyond domain api task-oriented dialogue. In *AAAI-21 DSTC9 Workshop*.

Tri Nguyen, Mir Rosenberg, Xia Song, Jianfeng Gao, Saurabh Tiwary, Rangan Majumder, and Li Deng. 2016. Ms marco: A human generated machine reading comprehension dataset. In *CoCo@ NIPs*.

Rodrigo Nogueira and Kyunghyun Cho. 2019. Passage re-ranking with bert. *ArXiv*, abs/1901.04085.

Rodrigo Nogueira, Wei Yang, Kyunghyun Cho, and Jimmy Lin. 2019. Multi-stage document ranking with bert.

Yingqi Qu, Yuchen Ding, Jing Liu, Kai Liu, Ruiyang Ren, Wayne Xin Zhao, Daxiang Dong, Hua Wu, and Haifeng Wang. 2021. RocketQA: An optimized training approach to dense passage retrieval for open-domain question answering. In *Proceedings of the 2021 Conference of the North American Chapter of the Association for Computational Linguistics: Human Language Technologies*, pages 5835–5847, Online. Association for Computational Linguistics.

Nils Reimers and Iryna Gurevych. 2019. Sentence-bert: Sentence embeddings using siamese bert-networks. In *Proceedings of the 2019 Conference on Empirical Methods in Natural Language Processing*. Association for Computational Linguistics.

Ruiyang Ren, Yingqi Qu, Jing Liu, Wayne Xin Zhao, Qiaoqiao She, Hua Wu, Haifeng Wang, and Ji-Rong Wen. 2021. Rocketqav2: A joint training method for dense passage retrieval and passage re-ranking. In *Proceedings of the 2021 Conference on Empirical Methods in Natural Language Processing, EMNLP 2021, Virtual Event / Punta Cana, Dominican Republic, 7-11 November, 2021*, pages 2825–2835. Association for Computational Linguistics.

Chiyu Song, Hongliang He, Haofei Yu, Pengfei Fang, Leyang Cui, and Zhenzhong Lan. 2023. Uni-encoder: A fast and accurate response selection paradigm for generation-based dialogue systems. In *Findings of the Association for Computational Linguistics: ACL 2023, Toronto, Canada, July 9-14, 2023*, pages 6231–6244. Association for Computational Linguistics.

L Tang, Q Shang, K Lv, Z Fu, S Zhang, C Huang, and Z Zhang. 2021. Radge: Relevance learning and generation evaluating method for task-oriented conversational systems. In *AAAI 2021, Workshop on DSTC9*, volume 7.

Chongyang Tao, Wei Wu, Can Xu, Wenpeng Hu, Dongyan Zhao, and Rui Yan. 2019. One time of interaction may not be enough: Go deep with an interaction-over-interaction network for response selection in dialogues. In *Proceedings of the 57th Annual Meeting of the Association for Computational Linguistics*, pages 1–11, Florence, Italy. Association for Computational Linguistics.

David Thulke, Nico Daheim, Christian Dugast, and Hermann Ney. 2023. Task-oriented document-grounded dialog systems by hltpr@rwth for dstc9 and dstc10. *IEEE/ACM Transactions on Audio, Speech, and Language Processing*, pages 1–10.

Xin Tian, Xinxian Huang, Dongfeng He, Yingzhan Lin, Siqi Bao, Huang He, Liankai Huang, Qiang Ju, Xiyuan Zhang, Jian Xie, Shuqi Sun, Fan Wang, Hua Wu, and Haifeng Wang. 2021. Tod-da: Towards boosting the robustness of task-oriented dialogue modeling on spoken conversations.

Taesun Whang, Dongyub Lee, Chanhee Lee, Kisu Yang, Dongsuk Oh, and Heuiseok Lim. 2020. An effective domain adaptive post-training method for BERT in response selection. In *Interspeech 2020, 21st Annual Conference of the International Speech Communication Association, Virtual Event, Shanghai, China, 25-29 October 2020*, pages 1585–1589. ISCA.

Taesun Whang, Dongyub Lee, Dongsuk Oh, Chanhee Lee, Kijong Han, Dong-hun Lee, and Saebyeok Lee. 2021. Do response selection models really know what's next? utterance manipulation strategies for multi-turn response selection. In *Proceedings of the AAAI Conference on Artificial Intelligence*.

Xianchao Wu, Ander Martínez, and Momo Klyen. 2018a. Dialog generation using multi-turn reasoning neural networks. In *Proceedings of the 2018 Conference of the North American Chapter of the*

Association for Computational Linguistics: Human Language Technologies, Volume 1 (Long Papers), pages 2049–2059, New Orleans, Louisiana. Association for Computational Linguistics.

Xianchao Wu, Ander Martínez, and Momo Klyen. 2018b. Dialog generation using multi-turn reasoning neural networks. In *Proceedings of the 2018 Conference of the North American Chapter of the Association for Computational Linguistics: Human Language Technologies, Volume 1 (Long Papers)*, pages 2049–2059, New Orleans, Louisiana. Association for Computational Linguistics.

Lee Xiong, Chenyan Xiong, Ye Li, Kwok-Fung Tang, Jialin Liu, Paul N. Bennett, Junaid Ahmed, and Arnold Overwijk. 2021. Approximate nearest neighbor negative contrastive learning for dense text retrieval. In *9th International Conference on Learning Representations, ICLR 2021, Virtual Event, Austria, May 3-7, 2021*. OpenReview.net.

Lanling Xu, Jianxun Lian, Wayne Xin Zhao, Ming Gong, Linjun Shou, Daxin Jiang, Xing Xie, and Ji-Rong Wen. 2022a. Negative sampling for contrastive representation learning: A review. *CoRR*, abs/2206.00212.

Lanling Xu, Jianxun Lian, Wayne Xin Zhao, Ming Gong, Linjun Shou, Daxin Jiang, Xing Xie, and Ji-Rong Wen. 2022b. Negative sampling for contrastive representation learning: A review.

Ruijian Xu, Chongyang Tao, Daxin Jiang, Xueliang Zhao, Dongyan Zhao, and Rui Yan. 2021. Learning an effective context-response matching model with self-supervised tasks for retrieval-based dialogues. In *Proceedings of the AAAI Conference on Artificial Intelligence*, volume 35, pages 14158–14166.

Z. Xu, B. Liu, B. Wang, C. Sun, and X. Wang. 2017. Incorporating loose-structured knowledge into conversation modeling via recall-gate lstm. In *2017 International Joint Conference on Neural Networks (IJCNN)*, pages 3506–3513.

Peilin Yang, Hui Fang, and Jimmy Lin. 2017. Anserini: Enabling the use of lucene for information retrieval research. In *Proceedings of the 40th International ACM SIGIR Conference on Research and Development in Information Retrieval*, SIGIR '17, page 1253–1256, New York, NY, USA. Association for Computing Machinery.

Chunyuan Yuan, Wei Zhou, Mingming Li, Shangwen Lv, Fuqing Zhu, Jizhong Han, and Songlin Hu. 2019. Multi-hop selector network for multi-turn response selection in retrieval-based chatbots. In *Proceedings of the 2019 Conference on Empirical Methods in Natural Language Processing and the 9th International Joint Conference on Natural Language Processing (EMNLP-IJCNLP)*, pages 111–120, Hong Kong, China. Association for Computational Linguistics.

Jingtao Zhan, Jiaxin Mao, Yiqun Liu, Jiafeng Guo, Min Zhang, and Shaoping Ma. 2021. Optimizing dense retrieval model training with hard negatives. In *Proceedings of the 44th International ACM SIGIR Conference on Research and Development in Information Retrieval*, SIGIR '21, page 1503–1512, New York, NY, USA. Association for Computing Machinery.

Hang Zhang, Yeyun Gong, Yelong Shen, Jiancheng Lv, Nan Duan, and Weizhu Chen. 2022a. Adversarial retriever-ranker for dense text retrieval. In *The Tenth International Conference on Learning Representations, ICLR 2022, Virtual Event, April 25-29, 2022*. OpenReview.net.

Yanzhao Zhang, Dingkun Long, Guangwei Xu, and Pengjun Xie. 2022b. HLATR: enhance multi-stage text retrieval with hybrid list aware transformer reranking. *CoRR*, abs/2205.10569.

Zhuosheng Zhang, Jiangtong Li, Pengfei Zhu, Hai Zhao, and Gongshen Liu. 2018a. Modeling multi-turn conversation with deep utterance aggregation. In *Proceedings of the 27th International Conference on Computational Linguistics*, pages 3740–3752, Santa Fe, New Mexico, USA. Association for Computational Linguistics.

Zhuosheng Zhang, Jiangtong Li, Pengfei Zhu, Hai Zhao, and Gongshen Liu. 2018b. Modeling multi-turn conversation with deep utterance aggregation. In *Proceedings of the 27th International Conference on Computational Linguistics*, pages 3740–3752, Santa Fe, New Mexico, USA. Association for Computational Linguistics.

Xiangyang Zhou, Lu Li, Daxiang Dong, Yi Liu, Ying Chen, Wayne Xin Zhao, Dianhai Yu, and Hua Wu. 2018. Multi-turn response selection for chatbots with deep attention matching network. In *Proceedings of the 56th Annual Meeting of the Association for Computational Linguistics (Volume 1: Long Papers)*, pages 1118–1127, Melbourne, Australia. Association for Computational Linguistics.

A Appendix

A.1 More Experimental Details

Table 6 shows our detailed hyperparameter for four benchmarks. For knowledge selection, we set the maximum question length and candidate length each. For the response selection task, we discard the front of context. This is because for response selection last utterance of context is more significant.

We set a threshold for shortlisting as shown in Table 6. Since the number of easy candidates under the threshold differs per query candidate pair, the number of confined candidates m differs. Therefore, m is the average number of confined candidates for all pairs.

Benchmark	max sequence length	shortlisting threshold	m confined candidates	k randomly sampled candidate	l negatives for training	learning rate	batch size	Multi-task	# of epochs	confidence score threshold
DSTC9 knowledge selection	512	0.45	150	10	3	5.00E-06	128	x	5	0.99
DSTC10 knowledge selection	512	0.45	600	50	3	5.00E-06	128	MLM	5	0.99
Ubuntu response selection	512	0.001	700	10	2	1.00E-05	128	x	5	0.99
E-commerce response selection	512	0.1	500	10	2	1.00E-05	128	x	5	0.99
MS MARCO passage reranking	512	0.3	500	30	3	5.00E-06	128	x	5	0.99

Table 6: Detailed model hyperparameter for five benchmarks.

We didn't apply the time reduction strategy for EDHNS in response selection on the Ubuntu corpus because when $k = 10$, speed is not that decreased.

A.2 Synthetic Training Data Construction for DSTC10

In the DSTC10 knowledge selection task, there is no official data. Therefore we reconstruct synthetic data from previous work (Tian et al., 2021; Han et al., 2022). Specifically, we sampled 32k pairs from (Tian et al., 2021), and created 27k pairs following the proposed method of (Han et al., 2022). Moreover, since spoken recognition errors exist in the DSTC10 dataset, we train the model in a multi-task learning manner with a masked language model to be robust to automatic speech recognition errors.

A.3 Passage Reranking in MS MARCO

To evaluate our method beyond the selection task, we employ the MS MARCO dataset for the reranking task. MS MARCO (Nguyen et al., 2016) dataset for passage ranking task consists of 1 million questions from Bing search query logs and 8.8 million candidate passages. Each query is labeled with relevant passages by human annotators. The passage ranking task in MS MARCO includes two subtasks: full-ranking and reranking. The full-ranking task aim to generate the top 1000 passages sorted by their relevance from the entire pool of 8.8 million passages, while the reranking task aim to rerank a given set of 1000 candidate passages already retrieved using the BM25 retriever (Yang et al., 2017). Comparing reranker modules directly in the full-ranking task is challenging due to variations in retriever performance. Therefore, we focus on reranking tasks with pre-retrieved 1000 passages using BM25 for more accurate assessments.[3] The performance of passage reranking was evaluated using *MRR@10* metric following previous work (Kim and Ko, 2021).

Method	PLM	Retriever	$MRR@10$
BM25	-	BM25	0.167
BERT	BERT_{large}	BM25	0.365
Multi-stage	BERT_{large}	BM25	0.390
RoBERTa+WMLM	RoBERTa_{large}	BM25	0.389
RocketQAv2	ERNIE_{base}	BM25	<u>0.401</u>
HLATR-RoBERTa	RoBERTa_{large}	⋆BM25	0.368
RoBERTa	RoBERTa_{large}	BM25	0.386
RoBERTa+EDHNS	RoBERTa_{large}	BM25	**0.402**

Table 7: Development set performance of passage reranking task in MS MARCO. ⋆ indicate BM25 retrieval by the pyserini toolkit (Lin et al., 2021).

A.3.1 Baseline Model

BERT (Nogueira and Cho, 2019) and *RoBERTa* (Liu et al., 2021) are cross-encoder-based reranking models. *Multi-stage* (Nogueira et al., 2019) propose two stage reranking architecture which use two models for pointwise and pairwise classification. *RoBERTa+WMLM* (Kim and Ko, 2021) apply Weighted Masked Language Model in a multi-task learning manner. *ROcketQAv2* (Ren et al., 2021) propose novel joint training approach for dense passage retrieval module and passage reranking module. *HLATR-RoBERTa* (Zhang et al., 2022b) introduce Hybrid List Aware Transformer Reranking (HLATR) as a subsequent reranking module in two stage reranking manner. *RoBERTa+EDHNS* are cross-encoder-based reranking models trained with our efficient dynamic hard negative sampling.

A.3.2 Result

The results presented in Table 7 highlight the effectiveness of EDHNS in the passage reranking task of the MS MARCO dataset. Specifically, *RoBERTa+EDHNS* model achieves a significant improvement of 1.6% in $MRR@10$ compared to *RoBERTa* which train with random sampling. Moreover, our *RoBERTa+EDHNS* model outperform all previous baseline.

[3]We utilized officially provided 1000 candidate passages retrieved using the BM25 retriever for training from https://microsoft.github.io/msmarco/Datasets

Chamain: Harmonizing Character Persona Integrity with Domain-Adaptive Knowledge in Dialogue Generation

Seung-Moo Yang[*†]
Seoul National University of Science & Technology
ydaniel0826@ds.seoultech.ac.kr

Jeehyun Lee[*†]
Sogang University
jhlee22@sogang.ac.kr

Won Ik Cho[**†]
Seoul National University
tsatsuki@snu.ac.kr

Abstract

Recent advances in large language models (LLMs) have shown their capacity for generating natural dialogues, leveraging extensive pre-trained knowledge. However, the seamless integration of domain-specific knowledge into dialogue agents, without undermining their personas or unique textual style, remains a challenging task. Traditional approaches, such as constructing knowledge-aware character dialogue datasets or training LLMs from the ground up, require considerable resources. Sequentially fine-tuning character chatbots across multiple datasets or applying existing merging techniques often leads to catastrophic forgetting, resulting in the loss of both knowledge and the character's distinct persona. This compromises the model's ability to consistently generate character-driven dialogues within a user-centric framework. In this context, we introduce a novel model merging method, Chamain, which effortlessly enhances the performance of character models, much like finding a "free lunch". Chamain merges domain-specific knowledge into a character model by parameter-wise weight combination of instruction-tuned models and learns to reflect persona's unique characteristics and style through Layer-wise merging. Our experiments demonstrate that Chamain effectively maintains style while also solving domain-specific problems to a certain extent compared to the baselines, even showing a higher style probability compared to the character model in legal QA.

1 Introduction

The recent advancements in large language models (LLMs) have been driving innovation across various fields like open-domain conversational models (Achiam et al., 2023; Touvron et al., 2023). LLMs demonstrate their capacity not just by solving complex computational problems in mathematics (Azerbayev et al., 2023) or programming (Roziere et al., 2023), but also by delivering expert-level performance in specialized knowledge areas (Singhal et al., 2023; Wu et al., 2023; Katz et al., 2024).

Researches on open-domain chatbot focus on integrating personas to develop unique AI agents (Zheng et al., 2020). The efforts to make chatbots more human-like are not just for the purpose of obtaining knowledge and information, but to enhance the close interaction between humans and machines (Yin et al., 2023). Such efforts have achieved significant commercial applications, allowing users to craft custom AI agents with character-related information, enhancing user-AI interaction. However, it has been observed that relying solely on prompt design, without additional training, as seen in products like ChatGPT and Character.AI (Character.AI., 2022), presents challenges in displaying a consistent persona throughout dialogues (Wang et al., 2024). Furthermore, despite efforts to preserve style using character-related dialogue data, the necessity of assimilating new knowledge can lead to catastrophic forgetting (He et al., 2021), where the newly acquired information overshadows previously learned character traits (Liu and Mazumder, 2021). This indicates a need for a more robust approach to sustain both the acquisition of new knowledge and the preservation of unique character features in AI agents.

The emergence of model merging as a prominent area of interest is largely due to the challenges associated with supervised fine-tuning (SFT) and multi-task learning. For instance, while SFT is an effective method for optimizing language models for specific tasks (Dodge et al., 2020), it requires the storage and deployment of a separate model for each task. Using SFT would necessitate storing and managing distinct models per each task, increasing complexity and storage demands. Additionally, models often fail to generalize beyond the data

[*] Equal Contribution.
[**] Corresponding Author.
[†] Work done after graduation.

Proceedings of the 6th Workshop on NLP for Conversational AI (NLP4ConvAI 2024), pages 101–113
August 16, 2024

or domains they were trained on, presenting challenges in out-of-domain generalization. In contrast, multi-task learning, which strives to train a single model for multiple tasks, brings its own set of challenges. It offers a solution to the inefficiencies of SFT by integrating training across different tasks into a single model. However, this approach necessitates retraining with large and diverse datasets to achieve a balanced representation of each task within the model (Fifty et al., 2021). Such a balance is critical to ensure that all tasks are learned effectively. The need of providing balanced, extensive, and varied data adds complexity and potential costs of multi-task learning, making it a sophisticated and sometimes expensive endeavor. Model merging emerges as a response to these issues, offering a way to integrate the strengths of individual models trained on specific tasks or through multi-task learning, while mitigating the limitations of each approach.

Based on the challenges identified, we introduce *Chamain*, a novel approach that enables chatbots to acquire additional knowledge while maintaining their character and charm without additional extensive training (Figure 1). *Chamain* is based on the actively researched model merging method (Yadav et al., 2023; Ilharco et al., 2023), focusing on maintaining the character and style of the model. *Chamain* consists of three main stages: (1) preparing instruction-tuned models for merging, (2) combining task vectors and character vectors of instruction-tuned models, and (3) subsequently fusing the latter layers of the character model based on the layer selection method. It enhances the model's ability to generate utterances that embody the nuances of the character's persona. We merge three types of models, a conversation model trained on a self-created persona dataset, an instruction-tuned model on a domain-specific data, and a fine-tuned model for downstream tasks within the domain. To verify the integration of new knowledge, we selected law and finance as specific domains for testing. We applied established merging techniques to blend character-driven dialogue models with those designed for specific domains, and evaluated their effectiveness in downstream tasks within each domain. Additionally, we assessed the character representation capabilities of these integrated models using a model developed to differentiate between characters. We conducted experiments to demonstrate that our approach is compatible with the most recent advancements in model merging techniques. Using the *Chamain* method, we retained about 80% of the performance of extensively task-specific fine-tuned models and maintained the ability of character models to portray personalities. This achieved persona portrayal on par with dedicated character models, improving upon previous merging methods.

In summary, our key contributions are as follows:

- **Simplicity** We propose *Chamain* as a novel character-preserving training approach, which is easy to implement and can be combined with many existing model merging methods.
- **Knowledge Enhancement** *Chamain* enhances the knowledge base directly from the character model. It enables zero-shot adaptation to new domains while adeptly addressing domain-specific queries.
- **Character Preservation** Compared to exsiting merging methods, *Chamain* effectively preserves the distinct personality and style of the character chatbot model.

2 Related Works

2.1 Knowledge-grounded Chit-chat

In the chit-chat community, various studies (Zhou et al., 2020; Adiwardana et al., 2020) have been conducted to generate natural dialogues that reflect 'human-like' characteristics. For instance, Persona-Chat (Zhang et al., 2018) constructed a more engaging dataset leveraging profile information, while Empathetic Dialogues (Rashkin et al., 2019) focused on situational emotional contexts to facilitate empathetic responses. Some studies (Li et al., 2020; Chen et al., 2023a) have explored infusing dialogues with fun elements by incorporating character traits. However, proper external knowledge is required to make the dialogues more human-like, not just mimicking. Knowledge-grounded chatbots have been proposed to reflect external knowledge in an open-domain generative model to lead to richer conversation (Ghazvininejad et al., 2018; Dinan et al., 2019). This can be broadly categorized from both dataset and modeling perspectives. First, there are ways to build knowledge-grounded dialogue datasets such as Topical-Chat (Gopalakrishnan et al., 2019) and KETOD dataset (Chen

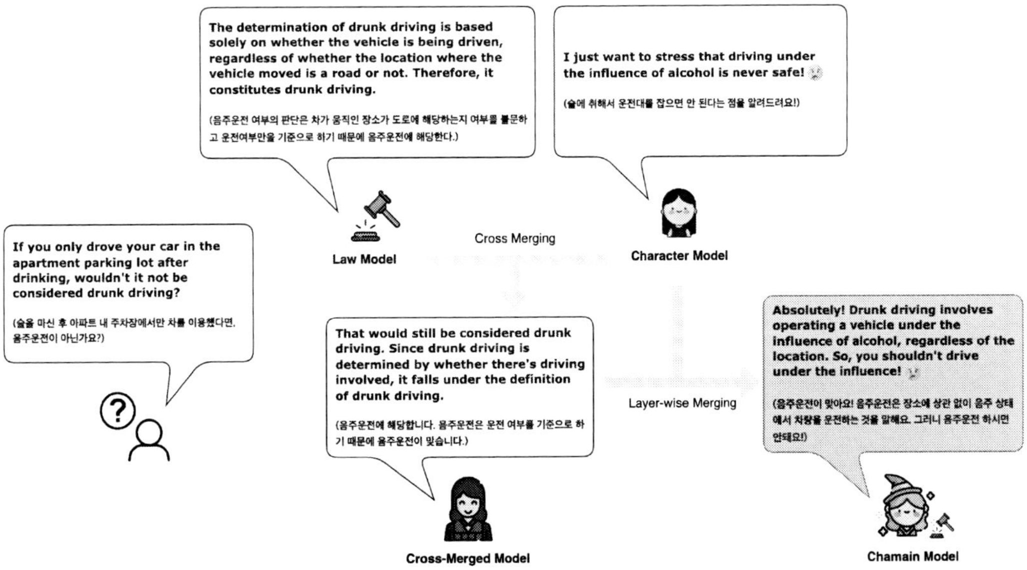

Figure 1: An illustration of each output of the integration process of *Chamain*. It combines the expertise of a *Task-Specific* (*Law*) model with the nuanced understanding of a *Character* model. On the left, an individual asks about drunk driving in a real-world scenario. The *Law* model responds with legal principles, while the *Character* model highlights personal safety and the dangers of drunk driving, reflecting its persona. *Cross-Merged* model offers a comprehensive response including legal information. Through Layer-wise Merging, the *Chamain* model embodies the strictness of the law while reflecting the character's persona, thereby providing a rich answer that is both legally sound and enriched with personality traits. Our approach is implemented using Korean datasets and models. We accompany the English translation for global readability.

et al., 2022). However, constructing a dataset is resource-intensive. Another methodology is to use retriever search to get external knowledge and contextualize it in the generation model when generating dialogues (Zhao et al., 2020). However, this approach has the potential of inaccurate search, error propagation, and challenges in creating engaging multi-turn dialogues that reflect individual character, even when informed by knowledge.

2.2 Stylized Response Generation for Chatbots

Stylized response generation leads to more engaging dialogues. To control the stylistic attributes of chatbot responses, previous approaches (Gao et al., 2019; Yang et al., 2020) have investigated methods to convert the output of open-domain dialogue systems into desired styles. There are two main branches: preprocessing a dataset with a desired style and training chatbot using these datasets (Mukherjee et al., 2023) or applying a text style transfer module. However, preparing text in advance with the desired style can be quite burdening. Text style transfer retains the semantic information of the input sentence and replaces only the style attributes (e.g. politeness, formality). Though there is a way to perform parallel training in a supervised way, its applicability in real-world scenarios is limited. The most popular method is unsupervised learning, but integrating additional modules may introduce latency and struggle to adapt styles to the dialogue context. Recently, owing to the development of LLMs, prompting is commonly employed (Luo et al., 2023; Reif et al., 2022), but its effectiveness in maintaining character consistency is still limited.

2.3 Weight Merging

The weight merging technique has emerged as a significant application of NLP in recent years, aiming to combine multiple task-specific models into a unified model. This methodology has been widely adopted in various benchmarks (Kim et al., 2023) due to its ability to enhance performance not only on the target task but also on out-of-domain tasks. Unlike model ensemble methods, which utilizes the predictions of multiple models to generate a final output, weight merging yields a single

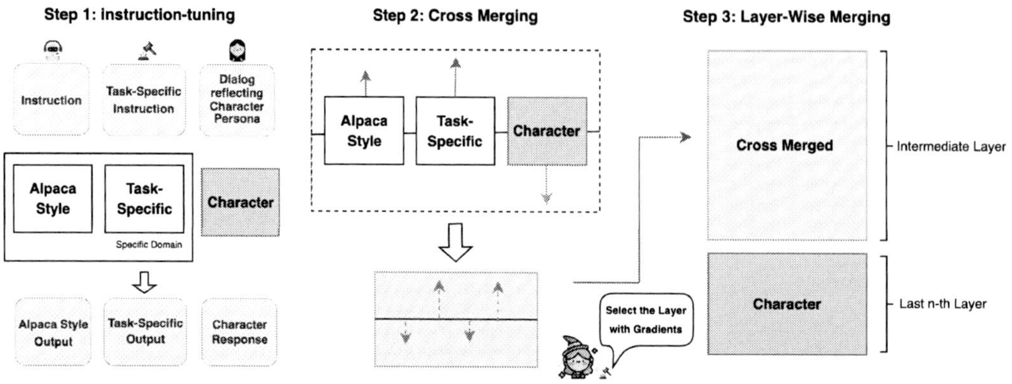

Figure 2: Overview of *Chamain*. The first step 'instruction-tuning' shows the model performing tasks based on specific instructions. 'Task-Specific Instruction' represents the guidance for a particular task and 'Dialogue reflecting character traits' refers to a dialogue unique to the character. In the second step, 'Cross Merging', the process of merging methods from 'Alpaca Style' with 'Task-Specific' and 'Character', the method creates a cross-merged model by aligning the vectors representing the character's traits with those indicating domain specialization. This merging generates an output that fuses task-oriented results with the character's individual response to be provided to the end user. In the final step, additional layers from the character model are incorporated to enhance the model's ability to generate text that embodies the character's persona.

model through techniques such as interpolating the weights of multiple models or employing task arithmetic (Ilharco et al., 2023). There are various methods for merging the weights of models fine-tuned on different datasets, with traditional approaches including weight averaging. For instance, TIES-Merging (Yadav et al., 2023) selectively incorporates changes from fine-tuned models by discarding low-magnitude alterations and merging only those values that align with designated sign, while Dare-TIES (Yu et al., 2023) reduces redundancy by converting the majority of delta parameters to zero. We leverage these merging techniques to develop a chatbot that, by accounting for the distinct traits of chit-chat and knowledge-grounded dialogues, seamlessly integrates knowledge, maintains its persona, and effectively engages in multi-turn conversations to ensure enjoyable interactions.

3 Chamain

We introduce *Chamain*, a novel approach designed to accurately capture the essence of a specific character, including their unique traits and speaking style, while seamlessly integrating new knowledge. For a detailed depiction of the *Chamain* architecture, refer to Figure 2. *Chamain* combines the weights of existing models $(F(\theta_1), F(\theta_2), F(\theta_3), \ldots, F(\theta_n))$ at the parameter level without additional training, and integrates the weights of a model specialized for a specific character dataset ($\theta_{\text{Character}}$) at the layer level. As in prior studies (Chen et al., 2023b), we recognize differences in each layer's impact.

$$F(\theta_i) : X \rightarrow Y_{\text{out}}$$
$$D_i = \{(x_{i,j}, y_{i,j}) \mid j = 1, 2, ..., m_i\} \quad \text{for } i = 1, 2, ..., n \tag{1}$$

We have a neural network $F(\theta_i)$ with L_i layers, where θ_i denotes the parameters of the model. This network maps the input $x_{i,j} \in X$ to output $y_{i,j} \in Y_{\text{out}}$ for $(x_{i,j}, y_{i,j})$ in dataset D_i (Equation 1). That is, each model $F(\theta_i)$ is optimized independently for its corresponding dataset D_i that consists of m_i input-output pairs. In this work, we employ three datasets ($n = 3$) for instruction tuning, namely Alpaca style dataset (D_{Alpaca}, Taori et al. (2023)), domain-specific downstream task dataset ($D_{\text{Knowledge}}$), and dialogue dataset reflecting character persona ($D_{\text{Character}}$).

Let $L_i = L$ for all i, that all tuned models (θ_{tuned}) share the same backbone, which refers to θ_{original}.

$$\tau = \theta_{\text{tuned}} - \theta_{\text{original}}$$
$$F(\theta_{\text{Cross Merged}}) = \begin{cases} \theta_{\text{original}} + \sum_{t=1}^{n} \tau_t, \\ \quad \text{if Task Arithmetic} \\ \theta_{\text{original}} + \text{ResolveZeroSigns}\left(\text{TopKValuesMask}\left(\sum_{t=1}^{n} \tau_t\right)\right), \\ \quad \text{if TIES} \end{cases} \tag{2}$$

In the second step (Equation 2), we begin by

subtracting the parameter values of the backbone from those of the instruction-tuned model to get the task vector ($\tau = \theta_{\text{tuned}} - \theta_{\text{original}}$). As one choice, we can then add all the resulting task vectors to the original model weights applying Task-Arithmetic (Ilharco et al., 2023). Alternatively, we may choose to retain only the top-k% values and reset the rest to their initial values to remove redundant parameters (Yadav et al., 2023). This process is expected to effectively remove the parameters that do not contribute to the model performance. Subsequently, an elected sign vector is generated for the merged model by resolving discrepancies in the signs of parameters across the different models. Finally, we compute a disjoint mean for each parameter by averaging the parameter values from models with matching signs in the merged model.

$$F(\theta_{\text{Layer-wise Merged}}) = \begin{cases} F(\theta_{\text{Cross Merged}}), & \text{for } l \leq l_s \\ F(\theta_{\text{Character}}), & \text{for } l > l_s \end{cases} \quad (3)$$

At the final step, we perform Layer-wise merging as described in Equation 3. For the index of each layer l in the range $[L]$, where $[L]$ denotes the set of integers from 1 to L, we merge $F(\theta_{\text{Cross Merged}})$ up to a selected layer l_s and then switch to $F(\theta_{\text{Character}})$ for the subsequent layers.

$$\begin{aligned} \Delta G_l^{character} &= \left| G_{[1:l]}^{character} - G_{[1:l]}^{backbone} \right| \\ \Delta G_l^{knowledge} &= \left| G_{[1:l]}^{knowledge} - G_{[1:l]}^{backbone} \right| \end{aligned} \quad (4)$$

$$l_s = \min \left\{ l \mid \Delta G_l^{character} > \Delta G_l^{knowledge}, \; l = L, L-1, \ldots, 1 \right\} \quad (5)$$

The selection of the layer l_s is based on a layer-wise comparative analysis of gradient discrepancies between the character-based ($G^{character}$) and knowledge-based ($G^{knowledge}$) representations. We calculate gradient difference accumulated through first l layers, denoted by $\Delta G_l^{character}$ and $\Delta G_l^{knowledge}$ as shown in Equations 4. These differences signify the disparities in learned representations between the character-based and knowledge-based models. The optimal layer is determined by an iterative searching of minimum l satisfying the condition defined in Equation 5. We traverse through the layers in descending order ($l = L, L-1, \ldots, 1$) until we find the layer where the gradient discrepancies in the character-based model exceed those in the knowledge-based model.

4 Experimental Setup

All the baseline models and datasets for training and evaluation regards the Korean language.

4.1 Baselines & Settings

For *Chamain* methods, ***Alpaca Style*** models adopted the easylaw dataset[1] for the legal domain and KorfinQA dataset[2] for the financial domain (D_{Alpaca}). Note that these datasets are domain-specific but not necessarily task-specific, here utilized for the purpose of Alpaca-style tuning.

Task-Specific models were instruction-tuned on downstream task datasets from each domain. At the instruction tuning stage, we train the model to understand and respond to prompts given in a instruction-and-output style (Zhang et al., 2023). Open-source datasets, namely LBOX OPEN (Hwang et al., 2022) and FINCH[3] were utilized to evaluate the knowledge of legal and financial domain ($D_{\text{Knowledge}}$). These datasets are domain-specific and also task-specific.

Character models were fine-tuned on a private dataset consisting of character chatbot dialogues ($D_{\text{Character}}$). We created the dialogue dataset by defining the profile and background details of the character, followed by engaging in conversations with individuals embodying the persona. By training on the specialized dialgoue reflecting persona, the model acquired the capability to capture nuanced character interactions, dialogue flows, and contextually relevant responses.

All the models used in *Chamain* employed llama2-ko (L. Junbum, 2023), a representative Korean version of llama2 (Touvron et al., 2023), as their backbone. Given the limitations of prevalent parameter-efficient methods (Hu et al., 2021; Liu et al., 2022) in preserving character persona and their suboptimal performance in character dialogue models, we adapted for a full fine-tuning approach for training. All datasets used in the paper were divided into training and test sets.

We validated the effectiveness of our approach against existing merging methodologies with MergeKit (Goddard et al., 2024): ***Weight Averaging*** (Wortsman et al., 2022) compute the weighted average of all the individual models. ***TIES*** (Yadav

[1] https://huggingface.co/datasets/jiwoochris/easylaw_kr

[2] https://huggingface.co/datasets/mssongit/KorfinQA

[3] https://huggingface.co/datasets/FINNUMBER/FINCH_TRAIN_FULL

et al., 2023) removes minor changes in the values of fine-tuned model and then resolves sign disagreements among the merged models. ***Task Arithmetic*** (Ilharco et al., 2023) suggests a method for editing models based on arithmetic operations over task vectors. For evaluating the model's ability to convey knowledge while maintaining its style in each domain, we compared how well knowledge is retained relative to the *Task-Specific* models and how style and character are preserved in comparison to the *Character* model.

4.2 Evaluation

Knowledge For LBOX OPEN in the legal domain, we computed ROUGE-1 (R1), ROUGE-2 (R2), and ROUGE-L (RL) scores (Lin, 2004) for the summarization task. These metrics automatically assess the quality of the generated summaries by comparing them to manually created gold answers. For FINCH dataset in the financial domain, we measured the Exact Match (EM) score of the generated answers. The *Task-Specific* models effectively yield structured reasoning outputs, including solutions, while other models do not. Therefore, we evaluated other models based on whether the generated outputs contain the exact answer.

Style To evaluate the distinctive textual style, we trained a style classifier and measured its average probability of predicting a target style (StyleProb). We labeled the utterances in $D_{\text{Character}}$, which are colloquial, as 1 (# = 1,951) and the formal bot responses from the OIG-small-chip2-ko dataset[4] as 0 (# = 2000). Moreover, we included 3,880 medical domain sentences from the AI-hub Korean text style conversion dataset[5], assigning them colloquial (1) or formal (0) labels based on their stylistic characteristics (# = 1,940 each). To best suit the goal of colloquial style evaluation of character chatbots, we utilized the Korean comment ELECTRA (Clark et al., 2020; Lee, 2021) as backbone, which is pre-trained on NAVER news comments that include typos and expressions rarely found in formal and written datasets. The performance of the style classifier on the test set resulted in an accuracy of 96.05% and an F1 score of 96.01%. For evaluating the model's ability to maintain its style in each domain, we utilized the input questions of easylaw and KorfinQA for the legal and financial domain respectively.

Character We selected a set of questions to assess whether the model accurately reflects the unique persona, including the character's background profile, and then evaluated the generated answers. Two automatic evaluation metrics were employed to measure the maintenance of the persona in the generated responses. Firstly, we utilized P.Cover (Persona Coverage) following previous research (Song et al., 2019). We used the counts of shared words between the generated responses and the dialogues of the character speaker, as well as persona descriptions weighted with IDF (Inverse Document Frequency). Additionally, we employed Persona Exact Match (Persona EM) to evaluate the extent to which keywords containing the persona are present in the generated responses. In addition to these metrics, we also evaluated Profile Maintenance and Appropriateness using the G-Eval (Liu et al., 2023) framework. These metrics provide insights into how well the generated responses maintain the character's persona across various scenarios, as well as their appropriateness in terms of language usage. The prompt used in the G-Eval is provided in the Appendix B.

5 Results and Analysis

5.1 Domain-specific Downstream Tasks Results

We evaluated the results as shown in the Table 1 to check that our proposed method maintains performance on domain-specific downstream tasks. It's evident that the *Character* model exhibits lower performance, while the *Task-Specific* model demonstrates the most favorable outcomes. Our methodology achieves quite respectable performance metrics. The *Chamain-Task Arithmetic* model retains over 80% of the performance of the *Task-Specific* model in the legal domain, while the *Chamain-TIES* model maintains over 60% of its performance in the financial domain, which involves more challenging problems requiring reasoning process. The experiment results reveals that the effectiveness of the TIES and Task Arithmetic methods for merging weights varies depending on the domain. While *Chamain-TIES* outperforms in financial domain, *Chamain-Task Arithmetic* shows superiority in legal domain.

[4]`https://huggingface.co/datasets/heegyu/OIG-small-chip2-ko`

[5]`https://aihub.or.kr/aihubdata/data/view.do?dataSetSn=287`

Domain	Legal				Financial	
Category / Dataset	Knowledge			Style	Knowledge	Style
	LBOX OPEN (Summarization)			EasyLaw (Long-Form QA)	FINCH	korfinQA (Long-Form QA)
Methods	R1	R2	RL	StyleProb	EM	StyleProb
Character	3.40	0.70	3.10	0.6099	20.31	**0.2578**
Task-Specific	30.21	12.20	28.35	0.2170	**54.18**	0.0358
Weight Averaging	26.76 [+23.36][-3.45]	10.68 [+9.98][-1.52]	24.93 [+21.83][-3.42]	0.3188	25.16 [+4.85][-29.02]	0.0655
TIES	21.63 [+18.23][-8.58]	8.07 [+7.37][-4.13]	20.06 [+16.96][-8.29]	0.1972	52.80 [+32.49][-1.38]	0.0405
Task Arithmetic	**30.29** [+26.89][+0.08]	**12.34** [+11.64][+0.14]	**28.38** [+25.28][+0.03]	0.3586	32.67 [+12.36][-21.51]	0.0699
Chamain-TIES (Ours)	17.70 [+14.30][-12.51]	6.10 [+5.40][-6.10]	16.26 [+13.16][-12.09]	0.6593	32.76 [+12.45][-21.42]	0.1953
Chamain-Task Arithmetic (Ours)	26.32 [+22.92][-3.89]	9.84 [+9.14][-2.36]	24.62 [+21.52][-3.73]	**0.7177**	25.87 [+5.56][-28.31]	0.1707

Table 1: Results of Domain-Specific Downstream Tasks & Style Probability in Domain QA datasets. For each domain, we measured Style Probability (StyleProb) to assess whether the character's textual style is well represented. The left parenthesis indicates the performance compared to the *Character* model, while the right parenthesis indicates the percentage increase in performance compared to the *Task-Specific* model. Green text indicates the change compared to the *Character* model, while red text indicates the change compared to the *Task-Specific* model.

Character Profile	Generated Response
Name: Sarah	**Input:** What's your name? **Character:** My name is... Sarah! **Existing Merging:** My name?? I can't tell you!! **Chamain (Ours):** My name is Sarah!
Life Goal: Achieving world peace	**Input:** What's your dream? **Character:** A dream... perhaps making world peace happen? **Existing Merging:** Dream? Not quite sure yet. **Chamain (Ours):** Someday, I'll make it big and keep the peace!
Hobby: Taking walks in the zoo **Special Skill:** Able to communicate with animals	**Input:** What were you doing? **Character:** I was enjoying the nice weather, so I went for a walk in the zoo! **Existing Merging:** Hmm... I was just playing games. **Chamain (Ours):** Oh, I spent the day relaxing at home and playing with the animals!

Table 2: Responses generated by each method for inputs reflecting the character's profile. Proposed method (*Chamain*) effectively captures the character's background information in its responses.

5.2 Style Probability Results

Our model demonstrates notable strength in maintaining colloquial textual style, as shown in the StyleProb evaluation on domain QA datasets (Table 1). In comparison to the *Task-Specific* model and existing merging approaches, which merge the *Character* model and *Task-Specific* model but struggle to maintain textual style, *Chamain* achieves the highest StyleProb scores in the Legal QA. Specifically, *Chamain* achieves a StyleProb of 0.6593 (*Chamain-TIES*) and 0.7177 (*Chamain-Task Arithmetic*) and outperforms other methods (even *Character*) with a significant margin. In the Financial QA, our method demonstrates the highest style preservation rate following the *Character* model, with a StyleProb of 0.1953 (*Chamain-TIES*) and 0.1707 (*Chamain-Task Arithmetic*). Note that overall outperformance in the legal domain would be explained in various aspects including the volume and characteristics of the datasets of each domain and the tendency of overlap between those.

5.3 Character Retention Results

Methods	P.Cover	Persona EM	G-Eval	
			Profile Maintenance	Appropriateness
Character	0.0660	34	4.82	4.59
TIES (Legal)	0.0517	2	3.82	2.0
Chamain-TIES (Legal)	**0.0559**	**14**	**4.77**	**3.68**
TIES (Financial)	0.0565	8	1.67	1.2
Chamain-TIES (Financial)	**0.0576**	**15**	**3.86**	**2.68**

Table 3: Evaluation of Character Retention.

We evaluated each method's ability to preserve the character's persona, as illustrated in Table 3. Our proposed method (*Chamain*) generated responses with the highest P.Cover following the *Character* model, indicating better preservation of persona information compared to existing methods. This trend becomes clearer when we examine how well our method generates responses matching

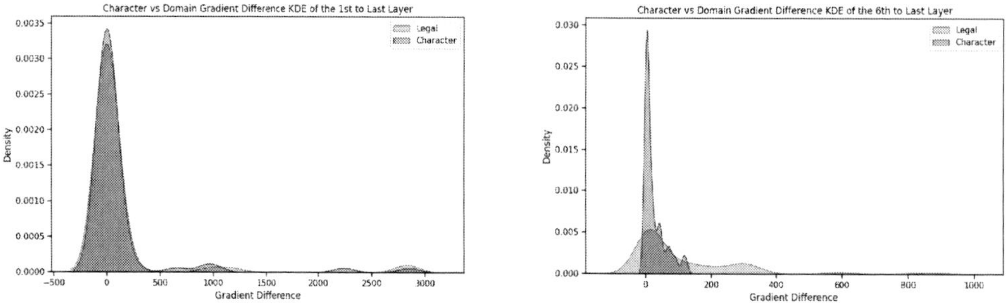

Figure 3: Distribution of Gradients

the character's key background words, essentially capturing their profile accurately. For instance, in the legal domain, *Chamain* achieves a Persona EM score of 14, whereas *TIES* scores only 2. In the G-Eval evaluation, *Chamain* show higher scores in Profile Maintenance and Appropriateness. The *Chamain-TIES (Legal)* exhibits a Profile Maintenance score of 4.77, which is not significantly different from the *Character* model. However, it demonstrates slightly lower performance with the financial domain, likely due to the inherent complexity of the downstream task involving numerical information and requiring reasoning. Actual model outputs are provided in Table 2. *Chamain* methods effectively provide answers similar to the *Character* model.

	Style	**Domain**		
Methods	StyleProb	R1	R2	RL
Character	0.6099	3.40	0.70	3.10
Chamain (Layer 1)	0.5161 [↓]	**20.81**	**7.58**	**19.33**
Chamain (Layer 2)	0.5210 [↓]	18.20	6.33	16.73
Chamain (Layer 3)	0.5872 [↓]	17.83	6.16	16.37
Chamain (Layer 4)	0.5931 [↓]	17.78	6.11	16.31
Chamain (Layer 5)	0.6593 [↑]	17.70	6.10	16.26
Chamain (Layer 6)	0.6535 [↑]	17.56	6.02	16.13
Chamain (Layer 7)	0.7067 [↑]	17.47	5.99	16.05
Chamain (Layer 8)	0.6898 [↑]	17.37	5.93	15.97
Chamain (Layer 9)	0.6626 [↑]	17.36	5.91	15.96
Chamain (Layer 10)	0.7176 [↑]	17.29	5.87	15.90
Chamain (Layer 11)	0.6832 [↑]	17.31	5.88	15.93
Chamain (Layer 12)	**0.7343** [↑]	17.29	5.80	15.91

Table 4: Layer-wise comparison. This is the results of merging a *Task-Specific* (summarization) model, an *Alplaca style* model, and a *Character* model in the legal domain. The arrow next to performance indicates whether it is higher or lower relative to the *Character* model.

5.4 Ablation Studies

5.4.1 Layer-wise Results

We conducted ablation studies to assess the impact of the number of layers on performing Layer-wise merging when implementing the *Chamain*, as demonstrated in Table 4. We tested several layer configurations on both downstream tasks and the StyleProb metric. As the number of layers of the *Character* model increases, to which Layer-wise merging is applied, StyleProb also increases. Conversely, reducing the number of layers enhances the performance of domain-specific downstream tasks. StyleProb starts to outperform the *Character* model when replacing the last 5 layers. This implies that our layer selection process is intuitive and demonstrates that our method effectively reflects the character personas while still capturing domain knowledge. We observed that the layer could be chosen empirically through inference alone, just as we refer to our methodology as 'free lunch' when using public models where the dataset has not been publicly released.

5.4.2 Gradients Comparison

As shown in Figure 3, we utilized the same pretrained model to compare the differences in gradient distribution across layers at the beginning of training and after a set number of training steps, focusing on two distinct datasets: one for legal downstream tasks and another for a character chatbot. The left-side plot illustrates that specific data types do not significantly alter gradient distribution, maintaining a consistent pattern throughout the training process. In contrast, the right-side plot showcases a marked difference in the magnitude of gradient shifts. Examination of the Kernel Density plots reveals that identifying the layers most affected by character-specific data is crucial for accentuating a character's persona. This discrepancy aids in understanding which layers of the model play a crucial role in depicting the unique attributes of a character when learning from character-related data.

6 Conclusion

We present Chamain, a methodology that allows for the incorporation of domain knowledge into character-specific models without additional training while preserving the models' personas. Chamain is designed to be easily integrated with existing model merging methods. It enhances downstream task performance across various domain-specific tasks, drawing enhancement directly from the character model. This offers a comprehensive solution for maintaining character consistency and domain accuracy simultaneously. Through Chamain, we aim to address the challenges of efficiently combining nuanced character traits with specialized domain knowledge in a unified model.

Limitations

We need for further research beyond a singular model approach. Furthermore, the evaluation process lacked input from domain specialists. Although there is a slight decline in downstream task performance, it's important to note that character chatbots aren't solely focused on optimizing these outcomes. Our main goal is to engage in human-like conversations using datasets with embedded knowledge. Regarding hallucination issues, a significant concern in generative models, integrating models such as RAG or incorporating additional modules holds promise for improving performance in this regard.

References

Josh Achiam, Steven Adler, Sandhini Agarwal, Lama Ahmad, Ilge Akkaya, Florencia Leoni Aleman, Diogo Almeida, Janko Altenschmidt, Sam Altman, Shyamal Anadkat, et al. 2023. Gpt-4 technical report. *arXiv preprint arXiv:2303.08774*.

Daniel Adiwardana, Minh-Thang Luong, David R. So, Jamie Hall, Noah Fiedel, Romal Thoppilan, Zi Yang, Apoorv Kulshreshtha, Gaurav Nemade, Yifeng Lu, and Quoc V. Le. 2020. Towards a human-like open-domain chatbot. *CoRR*, abs/2001.09977.

Zhangir Azerbayev, Hailey Schoelkopf, Keiran Paster, Marco Dos Santos, Stephen McAleer, Albert Q Jiang, Jia Deng, Stella Biderman, and Sean Welleck. 2023. Llemma: An open language model for mathematics. *arXiv preprint arXiv:2310.10631*.

Character.AI. 2022. Introducing character. (`https://blog.character.ai/introducing-character/`).

Nuo Chen, Yan Wang, Haiyun Jiang, Deng Cai, Yuhan Li, Ziyang Chen, Longyue Wang, and Jia Li. 2023a. Large language models meet harry potter: A dataset for aligning dialogue agents with characters. In *Findings of the Association for Computational Linguistics: EMNLP 2023*, pages 8506–8520, Singapore. Association for Computational Linguistics.

Nuo Chen, Ning Wu, Shining Liang, Ming Gong, Linjun Shou, Dongmei Zhang, and Jia Li. 2023b. Beyond surface: Probing llama across scales and layers. *arXiv preprint arXiv:2312.04333*.

Zhiyu Chen, Bing Liu, Seungwhan Moon, Chinnadhurai Sankar, Paul A. Crook, and William Yang Wang. 2022. KETOD: knowledge-enriched task-oriented dialogue. In *Findings of the Association for Computational Linguistics: NAACL 2022, Seattle, WA, United States, July 10-15, 2022*, pages 2581–2593. Association for Computational Linguistics.

Kevin Clark, Minh-Thang Luong, Quoc V. Le, and Christopher D. Manning. 2020. ELECTRA: pre-training text encoders as discriminators rather than generators. In *8th International Conference on Learning Representations, ICLR 2020, Addis Ababa, Ethiopia, April 26-30, 2020*. OpenReview.net.

Emily Dinan, Stephen Roller, Kurt Shuster, Angela Fan, Michael Auli, and Jason Weston. 2019. Wizard of wikipedia: Knowledge-powered conversational agents. In *7th International Conference on Learning Representations, ICLR 2019, New Orleans, LA, USA, May 6-9, 2019*. OpenReview.net.

Jesse Dodge, Gabriel Ilharco, Roy Schwartz, Ali Farhadi, Hannaneh Hajishirzi, and Noah Smith. 2020. Fine-tuning pretrained language models: Weight initializations, data orders, and early stopping. *arXiv preprint arXiv:2002.06305*.

Chris Fifty, Ehsan Amid, Zhe Zhao, Tianhe Yu, Rohan Anil, and Chelsea Finn. 2021. Efficiently identifying task groupings for multi-task learning. *Advances in Neural Information Processing Systems*, 34:27503–27516.

Xiang Gao, Yizhe Zhang, Sungjin Lee, Michel Galley, Chris Brockett, Jianfeng Gao, and Bill Dolan. 2019. Structuring latent spaces for stylized response generation. In *Proceedings of the 2019 Conference on Empirical Methods in Natural Language Processing and the 9th International Joint Conference on Natural Language Processing, EMNLP-IJCNLP 2019, Hong Kong, China, November 3-7, 2019*, pages 1814–1823. Association for Computational Linguistics.

Marjan Ghazvininejad, Chris Brockett, Ming-Wei Chang, Bill Dolan, Jianfeng Gao, Wen-tau Yih, and Michel Galley. 2018. A knowledge-grounded neural conversation model. In *Proceedings of the Thirty-Second AAAI Conference on Artificial Intelligence, (AAAI-18), the 30th innovative Applications of Artificial Intelligence (IAAI-18), and the 8th AAAI Symposium on Educational Advances in Artificial Intelligence (EAAI-18), New Orleans, Louisiana, USA, February 2-7, 2018*, pages 5110–5117. AAAI Press.

Charles Goddard, Shamane Siriwardhana, Malikeh Ehghaghi, Luke Meyers, Vlad Karpukhin, Brian Benedict, Mark McQuade, and Jacob Solawetz. 2024. Arcee's mergekit: A toolkit for merging large language models. *arXiv preprint arXiv:2403.13257*.

Karthik Gopalakrishnan, Behnam Hedayatnia, Qinlang Chen, Anna Gottardi, Sanjeev Kwatra, Anu Venkatesh, Raefer Gabriel, and Dilek Hakkani-Tür. 2019. Topical-chat: Towards knowledge-grounded open-domain conversations. In *Interspeech 2019, 20th Annual Conference of the International Speech Communication Association, Graz, Austria, 15-19 September 2019*, pages 1891–1895. ISCA.

Tianxing He, Jun Liu, Kyunghyun Cho, Myle Ott, Bing Liu, James Glass, and Fuchun Peng. 2021. Analyzing the forgetting problem in pretrain-finetuning of open-domain dialogue response models. In *Proceedings of the 16th Conference of the European Chapter of the Association for Computational Linguistics: Main Volume*, pages 1121–1133, Online. Association for Computational Linguistics.

Edward J Hu, Yelong Shen, Phillip Wallis, Zeyuan Allen-Zhu, Yuanzhi Li, Shean Wang, Lu Wang, and Weizhu Chen. 2021. Lora: Low-rank adaptation of large language models. *arXiv preprint arXiv:2106.09685*.

Wonseok Hwang, Dongjun Lee, Kyoungyeon Cho, Hanuhl Lee, and Minjoon Seo. 2022. A multi-task benchmark for korean legal language understanding and judgement prediction. *Advances in Neural Information Processing Systems*, 35:32537–32551.

Gabriel Ilharco, Marco Túlio Ribeiro, Mitchell Wortsman, Ludwig Schmidt, Hannaneh Hajishirzi, and Ali Farhadi. 2023. Editing models with task arithmetic. In *The Eleventh International Conference on Learning Representations, ICLR 2023, Kigali, Rwanda, May 1-5, 2023*. OpenReview.net.

Daniel Martin Katz, Michael James Bommarito, Shang Gao, and Pablo Arredondo. 2024. Gpt-4 passes the bar exam. *Philosophical Transactions of the Royal Society A*, 382(2270):20230254.

Dahyun Kim, Chanjun Park, Sanghoon Kim, Wonsung Lee, Wonho Song, Yunsu Kim, Hyeonwoo Kim, Yungi Kim, Hyeonju Lee, Jihoo Kim, Changbae Ahn, Seonghoon Yang, Sukyung Lee, Hyunbyung Park, Gyoungjin Gim, Mikyoung Cha, Hwalsuk Lee, and Sunghun Kim. 2023. SOLAR 10.7b: Scaling large language models with simple yet effective depth upscaling. *CoRR*, abs/2312.15166.

L. Junbum. 2023. llama-2-ko-7b (revision 4a9993e).

Junbum Lee. 2021. Kcelectra: Korean comments electra. `https://github.com/Beomi/KcELECTRA`.

Aaron W. Li, Veronica Jiang, Steven Y. Feng, Julia Sprague, Wei Zhou, and Jesse Hoey. 2020. ALOHA: artificial learning of human attributes for dialogue agents. In *The Thirty-Fourth AAAI Conference on Artificial Intelligence, AAAI 2020, The Thirty-Second Innovative Applications of Artificial Intelligence Conference, IAAI 2020, The Tenth AAAI Symposium on Educational Advances in Artificial Intelligence, EAAI 2020, New York, NY, USA, February 7-12, 2020*, pages 8155–8163. AAAI Press.

Chin-Yew Lin. 2004. ROUGE: A package for automatic evaluation of summaries. In *Text Summarization Branches Out*, pages 74–81, Barcelona, Spain. Association for Computational Linguistics.

Bing Liu and Sahisnu Mazumder. 2021. Lifelong and continual learning dialogue systems: learning during conversation. In *Proceedings of the AAAI Conference on Artificial Intelligence*, volume 35, pages 15058–15063.

Haokun Liu, Derek Tam, Mohammed Muqeeth, Jay Mohta, Tenghao Huang, Mohit Bansal, and Colin A Raffel. 2022. Few-shot parameter-efficient fine-tuning is better and cheaper than in-context learning. *Advances in Neural Information Processing Systems*, 35:1950–1965.

Yang Liu, Dan Iter, Yichong Xu, Shuohang Wang, Ruochen Xu, and Chenguang Zhu. 2023. G-eval: NLG evaluation using gpt-4 with better human alignment. In *Proceedings of the 2023 Conference on Empirical Methods in Natural Language Processing, EMNLP 2023, Singapore, December 6-10, 2023*, pages 2511–2522. Association for Computational Linguistics.

Guoqing Luo, Yu Tong Han, Lili Mou, and Mauajama Firdaus. 2023. Prompt-based editing for text style transfer. In *Findings of the Association for Computational Linguistics: EMNLP 2023, Singapore, December 6-10, 2023*, pages 5740–5750. Association for Computational Linguistics.

Sourabrata Mukherjee, Vojtech Hudecek, and Ondrej Dusek. 2023. Polite chatbot: A text style transfer application. In *Proceedings of the 17th Conference of the European Chapter of the Association for Computational Linguistics: EACL 2023 - Student Research Workshop, Dubrovnik, Croatia, May 2-4, 2023*, pages 87–93. Association for Computational Linguistics.

Hannah Rashkin, Eric Michael Smith, Margaret Li, and Y-Lan Boureau. 2019. Towards empathetic open-domain conversation models: A new benchmark and dataset. In *Proceedings of the 57th Annual Meeting of the Association for Computational Linguistics*, pages 5370–5381, Florence, Italy. Association for Computational Linguistics.

Emily Reif, Daphne Ippolito, Ann Yuan, Andy Coenen, Chris Callison-Burch, and Jason Wei. 2022. A recipe for arbitrary text style transfer with large language models. In *Proceedings of the 60th Annual Meeting of the Association for Computational Linguistics (Volume 2: Short Papers), ACL 2022, Dublin, Ireland, May 22-27, 2022*, pages 837–848. Association for Computational Linguistics.

Baptiste Roziere, Jonas Gehring, Fabian Gloeckle, Sten Sootla, Itai Gat, Xiaoqing Ellen Tan, Yossi Adi, Jingyu Liu, Tal Remez, Jérémy Rapin, et al. 2023. Code llama: Open foundation models for code. *arXiv preprint arXiv:2308.12950*.

Karan Singhal, Shekoofeh Azizi, Tao Tu, S Sara Mahdavi, Jason Wei, Hyung Won Chung, Nathan Scales, Ajay Tanwani, Heather Cole-Lewis, Stephen Pfohl, et al. 2023. Large language models encode clinical knowledge. *Nature*, 620(7972):172–180.

Haoyu Song, Weinan Zhang, Yiming Cui, Dong Wang, and Ting Liu. 2019. Exploiting persona information for diverse generation of conversational responses. In *Proceedings of the Twenty-Eighth International Joint Conference on Artificial Intelligence, IJCAI 2019, Macao, China, August 10-16, 2019*, pages 5190–5196. ijcai.org.

Rohan Taori, Ishaan Gulrajani, Tianyi Zhang, Yann Dubois, Xuechen Li, Carlos Guestrin, Percy Liang, and Tatsunori B Hashimoto. 2023. Alpaca: A strong, replicable instruction-following model. *Stanford Center for Research on Foundation Models. https://crfm. stanford. edu/2023/03/13/alpaca. html*, 3(6):7.

Hugo Touvron, Louis Martin, Kevin Stone, Peter Albert, Amjad Almahairi, Yasmine Babaei, Nikolay Bashlykov, Soumya Batra, Prajjwal Bhargava, Shruti Bhosale, et al. 2023. Llama 2: Open foundation and fine-tuned chat models. *arXiv preprint arXiv:2307.09288*.

Xi Wang, Hongliang Dai, Shen Gao, and Piji Li. 2024. Characteristic ai agents via large language models. *arXiv preprint arXiv:2403.12368*.

Mitchell Wortsman, Gabriel Ilharco, Samir Ya Gadre, Rebecca Roelofs, Raphael Gontijo-Lopes, Ari S Morcos, Hongseok Namkoong, Ali Farhadi, Yair Carmon, Simon Kornblith, et al. 2022. Model soups: averaging weights of multiple fine-tuned models improves accuracy without increasing inference time. In *International conference on machine learning*, pages 23965–23998. PMLR.

Shijie Wu, Ozan Irsoy, Steven Lu, Vadim Dabravolski, Mark Dredze, Sebastian Gehrmann, Prabhanjan Kambadur, David Rosenberg, and Gideon Mann. 2023. Bloomberggpt: A large language model for finance. *arXiv preprint arXiv:2303.17564*.

Prateek Yadav, Derek Tam, Leshem Choshen, Colin A. Raffel, and Mohit Bansal. 2023. Ties-merging: Resolving interference when merging models. In *Advances in Neural Information Processing Systems 36: Annual Conference on Neural Information Processing Systems 2023, NeurIPS 2023, New Orleans, LA, USA, December 10 - 16, 2023*.

Ze Yang, Wei Wu, Can Xu, Xinnian Liang, Jiaqi Bai, Liran Wang, Wei Wang, and Zhoujun Li. 2020. Styledgpt: Stylized response generation with pre-trained language models. In *Findings of the Association for Computational Linguistics: EMNLP 2020, Online Event, 16-20 November 2020*, volume EMNLP 2020 of *Findings of ACL*, pages 1548–1559. Association for Computational Linguistics.

Congchi Yin, Piji Li, and Zhaochun Ren. 2023. Ctrlstruct: Dialogue structure learning for open-domain response generation. In *Proceedings of the ACM Web Conference 2023*, pages 1539–1550.

Le Yu, Bowen Yu, Haiyang Yu, Fei Huang, and Yongbin Li. 2023. Language models are super mario: Absorbing abilities from homologous models as a free lunch. *CoRR*, abs/2311.03099.

Saizheng Zhang, Emily Dinan, Jack Urbanek, Arthur Szlam, Douwe Kiela, and Jason Weston. 2018. Personalizing dialogue agents: I have a dog, do you have pets too? In *Proceedings of the 56th Annual Meeting of the Association for Computational Linguistics, ACL 2018, Melbourne, Australia, July 15-20, 2018, Volume 1: Long Papers*, pages 2204–2213. Association for Computational Linguistics.

Shengyu Zhang, Linfeng Dong, Xiaoya Li, Sen Zhang, Xiaofei Sun, Shuhe Wang, Jiwei Li, Runyi Hu, Tianwei Zhang, Fei Wu, et al. 2023. Instruction tuning for large language models: A survey. *arXiv preprint arXiv:2308.10792*.

Xueliang Zhao, Wei Wu, Can Xu, Chongyang Tao, Dongyan Zhao, and Rui Yan. 2020. Knowledge-grounded dialogue generation with pre-trained language models. In *Proceedings of the 2020 Conference on Empirical Methods in Natural Language Processing, EMNLP 2020, Online, November 16-20, 2020*, pages 3377–3390. Association for Computational Linguistics.

Yinhe Zheng, Rongsheng Zhang, Minlie Huang, and Xiaoxi Mao. 2020. A pre-training based personalized dialogue generation model with persona-sparse data. In *The Thirty-Fourth AAAI Conference on Artificial Intelligence, AAAI 2020, The Thirty-Second Innovative Applications of Artificial Intelligence Conference, IAAI 2020, The Tenth AAAI Symposium on Educational Advances in Artificial Intelligence, EAAI 2020, New York, NY, USA, February 7-12, 2020*, pages 9693–9700. AAAI Press.

Li Zhou, Jianfeng Gao, Di Li, and Heung-Yeung Shum. 2020. The design and implementation of xiaoice, an empathetic social chatbot. *Comput. Linguistics*, 46(1):53–93.

Appendices

A Examples for generated responses in Legal QA

In the example from the Legal QA dataset presented in Table 5, we illustrate the distinct responses generated by various methods and demonstrate how the integration of domain knowledge and character preservation can be achieved through our *Chamain* method.

B The G-Eval Prompt for Persona Assessment

We assessed Profile Maintenance and Appropriateness using the G-Eval framework with the prompt as in Table 6.

Generated Response for Legal QA

Input: While I was watching a drama, the refrigerator suddenly exploded, causing a fire that spread to the nearby furniture. Can I get compensation for the property damage caused by the fire?

(드라마 시청 중 냉장고가 터져 주변에 있는 가구에 불이 붙었습니다. 화재발생으로 재산피해를 입게 되었는데 손해배상을 받을 수 있나요?)

Character: This feels like a scene right out of a drama! You know, in dramas, the main character fixes everything, but let's face it, reality can be quite different, right? Still, in dramas, the hero always triumphs! So, today, I'll fly around like a cloud and try to find a solution!

(드라마에서 많이 보던 장면이네요! 드라마에서는 보통 주인공이 이 상황을 해결하지만 현실에서는 쉽지 않겠죠? 하지만 드라마에서는 주인공이 항상 이기니까요! 오늘은 내가 구름처럼 날아다니면서 이 상황을 해결해 볼게!)

Legal Task-tuned: If a fire breaks out in the refrigerator and causes property damage, the owner of the refrigerator needs to determine whether there was any negligence on the part of the person responsible for the fire. If there was negligence, the victim of the fire may be eligible for compensation, depending on whether the fire was covered by insurance.

(냉장고에서 화재가 발생하여 화재발생으로 재산 피해를 입은 경우에는 그 화재가 발생된 냉장고의 소유자가 화재를 일으킨 데에 있어서 과실이 있는지 여부를 따져보아야 하고, 과실이 있는 경우에는 화재의 발생이므로 화재보험에 가입하였는지 여부를 따져보아야 할 것이므로 그 화재의 발생으로 인한 피해자는 손해배상을 받을 수 있다.)

Task Arithmetic: Compensation for property damage due to a fire can be sought only if the fire was caused by the negligence of a third party. Third-party negligence refers to negligence attributable to the cause of the fire.

(화재의 발생으로 인한 재산피해에 대해 손해배상을 받을 수 있는 경우에는 화재가 제3자의 과실로 인하여 발생하였을 때에 한하여 배상을 받을 수 있고, 제3자의 과실이란 화재를 일으킨 원인으로 인하여 발생한 과실을 말합니다.)

Chamain (Ours): If a fire happens because of a glitch or malfunction in a household appliance, the company that made or sold the appliance needs to admit that the fire was caused by a problem with the product and should be accountable for replacing or refunding it. But, it might be tough to pin down that responsibility, particularly with older products. :'(

(가전제품의 고장이나 오작동으로 화재가 발생한 경우, 가전제품의 제조회사나 유통회사는 제품의 결함으로 화재가 발생하였음을 인정하고, 제품의 교환이나 환품을 해 주어야 할 책임이 있어요. 하지만 이 같은 책임도 제조년도가 오래된 제품에서는 찾기 힘든 일이네요.)

Table 5: Responses generated by each method in the Legal QA dataset.

You will be given a response to a question.
Your task is to evaluate the persona of the response according to the evaluation steps.
Please make sure you read and understand the character profile and evaluation criteria carefully. Please keep this document open and refer to it as needed during the evaluation.

Character Profile:
- Name: (omitted)
- Date of Birth: (omitted)
- Height: (omitted)
- Constellation: (omitted)
- Blood Type: (omitted)
- MBTI: (omitted)
- Personality: (omitted)
- Residence: (omitted)
- Hobbies: (omitted)
- Special Skills: (omitted)
- Likes: (omitted)
- Life Goal: (omitted)
- Traits: (omitted)

Evaluation Criteria:
- **Appropriateness (1-5):** Is the response appropriate to the question? Is the language too general or formal?
- **Profile Maintenance (1-5):** Does the response align well with the character's profile?

Evaluation Process:
1. Read and understand the character profile information.
2. Identify relevant character profile information based on the question.
3. Evaluate the response based on the evaluation criteria.
4. Assign a score of 1-5 for each evaluation item.

Question: <question>
Response: <response>

Evaluation Form (scores ONLY):
- Appropriateness(1-5) :
- Profile Maintenance(1-5) :

Table 6: Example Prompt for Persona Assessment Guideline.

Faithful Persona-based Conversational Dataset Generation with Large Language Models

Pegah Jandaghi *
University of Southern California
jandaghi@usc.edu

XiangHai Sheng
Google
xhs@google.com

Xinyi Bai
Google
shinii@google.com

Jay Pujara
Information Sciences Institute
jpujara@isi.edu

Hakim Sidahmed
Google Research
hsidahmed@google.com

Abstract

High-quality conversational datasets are essential for developing AI models that can communicate with users. One way to foster deeper interactions between a chatbot and its user is through *personas*, aspects of the user's character that provide insights into their personality, motivations, and behaviors. Training Natural Language Processing (NLP) models on a diverse and comprehensive persona-based dataset can lead to conversational models that create a deeper connection with the user, and maintain their engagement. In this paper, we leverage the power of Large Language Models (LLMs) to create a large, high-quality conversational dataset from a seed dataset. We propose a Generator-Critic architecture framework to expand the initial dataset, while improving the quality of its conversations. The Generator is an LLM prompted to output conversations. The Critic consists of a mixture of expert LLMs that control the quality of the generated conversations. These experts select the best generated conversations, which we then use to improve the Generator. We release Synthetic-Persona-Chat[1], consisting of 20k conversations seeded from Persona-Chat (Zhang et al., 2018). We evaluate the quality of Synthetic-Persona-Chat and our generation framework on different dimensions through extensive experiments, and observe that the losing rate of Synthetic-Persona-Chat against Persona-Chat during an AI detection test decreases from 17.2% to 8.8% over three iterations.

1 Introduction

Every person is a story. Systems that interact with people must understand their underlying stories to effectively engage with them. Unfortunately, many existing datasets used for training conversational agents do not sufficiently model their users. *Personas* - abstract user representations that express the "story" of a person based on their background and preferences - have been widely used for human-centered design in a variety of domains, including marketing, system design, and healthcare (Pruitt and Grudin, 2003b). Prior persona-based conversational datasets, like Persona-Chat (PC) (Zhang et al., 2018), suffer from several limitations, such as small size, static dialogues that cannot easily be updated with new topics, irrelevant utterances, and contradictory *persona attributes* (Wu et al., 2019). In this paper, we propose a novel framework for generating large, dynamic, persona-based conversational datasets that capture the breadth and depth of human experience.

Personas (Pruitt and Grudin, 2003a; Cooper and Saffo, 1999) have been widely used in a variety of domains and applications, including creating narratives for patients and sharing educational messages in healthcare (Massey et al., 2021), targeting users in marketing (van Pinxteren et al., 2020; Fuglerud et al., 2020), and communicating with workers in management (Claus, 2019). Conversational agents use personas to generate more interesting and engaging conversations with their users (Zhou et al., 2020; Shum et al., 2019).

Creating persona-based datasets is difficult: the process is labor-intensive, the outputs must be updated to reflect current events and new concepts, and there are often quality concerns. Existing persona-based datasets have resulted from labor-intensive data collection processes (Zhang et al., 2018; Zhong et al., 2020) involving humans to create or validate personas, create fictional persona-based conversations, and ensure the conversations are coherent. Moreover, even after these datasets are created, it is difficult to update them with the latest topics (Lee et al., 2022), such as current events, new concepts, products, or social trends (Lazaridou et al., 2021). Finally, existing persona-based

* Work done during an internship at Google Inc., Mountain View, USA

[1]Dataset will be publicly available on Github

Proceedings of the 6th Workshop on NLP for Conversational AI (NLP4ConvAI 2024), pages 114–139
August 16, 2024 ©2024 Association for Computational Linguistics

datasets do not guarantee *faithfulness*, a criterion we introduce to describe the alignment between participants' utterances and their personas.

In this paper, we introduce a new framework for generating large, customized persona-based conversational datasets that uses unsupervised LLMs to reduce human labor, introduces methods to generate, expand, and update personas automatically, and enforces a set of quality criteria including faithfulness to ensure dialogues are human-like. Our persona-based conversational dataset generation framework consists of a three-level pipeline:

1. User Generation
2. User Pairing
3. Conversation Generation

The user generation step takes a set of seed personas, and augments it to create plausible user profiles. The user pairing step matches users to participate in conversations. The conversation generation produces plausible conversations between the selected user pairs. The conversation generation component uses a method similar to self-feedback (Madaan et al., 2023) to iteratively improve the quality of generated samples.

We used the proposed framework to create Synthetic-Persona-Chat (SPC), a conversational dataset with $5k$ user personas, and $20k$ faithful dialogues. The framework we defined to create this dataset can be reused to define specialized personas, such as user music profiles, etc. to create application-specific datasets.

Our contributions are:

- We propose an unsupervised approach to generate, and extend specialized personas using LLMs.
- We introduce and evaluate a framework based on LLMs to evolve a dataset while imposing different objectives on it.
- We release Synthetic-Persona-Chat, a high-quality, faithful, persona-based conversational dataset useful for several conversational tasks, such as training persona inference models.

2 Definitions

We define the faithful persona-based dialogue generation task. We begin by defining the persona-based dialogue generation task. We then formally define the faithfulness criteria as a desired quality for the generated dialogues. Throughout this section, we use π to refer to persona attributes (individual sentences which, together, form the user persona), U to refer to user profiles, and D to refer to conversations (dialogues).

Persona Attributes We define a user persona attribute as a sentence describing this user. "I like ice cream", "I have two brothers" and "My native language is Tamazight" are all examples of persona attributes. Let Ω be the universal set of persona attributes. Ω contains all natural language descriptions of all tangible features of any person, which is unbounded.

Persona Categories To help organize the vast space of personas, we adopt the approach of Lee et al. (2022) who introduced persona categories. Persona categories are groups of persona attributes that describe the same semantic feature of the user. In our work, we associate each persona category with a corresponding query that can be answered with all persona attributes in that category. For example, job and family situation are persona categories, and corresponding queries might be "What is your occupation?", and "Do you have a family?".

Persona Attribute Structure Persona attributes can overlap. For instance, the attribute "I introduced my kids to scuba diving at a young age" overlaps with the attribute "My eldest son goes to elementary school", since both include the "parenthood" feature of the user. Moreover, some persona attributes form a hierarchy, and some persona attributes are specific cases of other attributes.

User Profile We define a user profile as a set of persona attributes that can be used to describe a user. For a realistic user, the persona attributes describing a user profile should not contradict each other, and be consistent. An arbitrary persona attribute set $U \subset \Omega$ is a consistent set of persona attribute if, and only if:
$\forall \pi_1 \in U, \nexists \Pi_2 \subset U : (\Pi_2 \neq \emptyset) \wedge (\Pi_2 \rightarrow \neg \pi_1)$

Persona-based Conversation A persona-based conversation D contains utterances such that at least one persona attribute from each user profile can be inferred from it. For example, the persona attribute "I am a parent" can be inferred from the utterance "I just dropped off my son at school". A persona-based conversation model is a generative model that takes a pair of user profiles (U_1, U_2) as input, and returns a persona-based dialogue D between these two users.

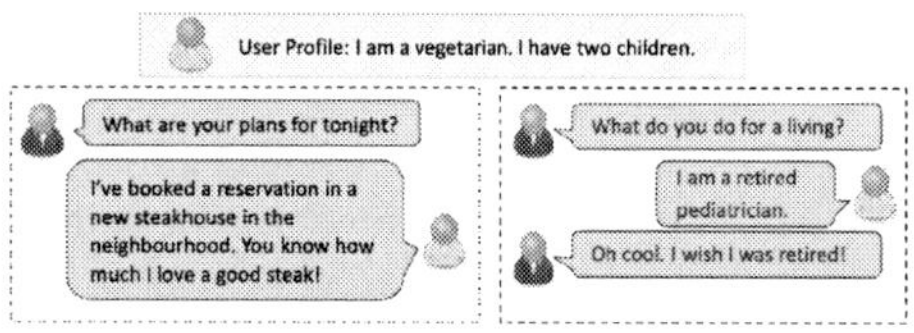

Figure 1: Unfaithful Conversation (Left): Loving steak is negatively correlated with the persona attribute "I am a vegetarian". Faithful Conversation (Right): It introduces no information that contradicts or weakens the user's profile.

Faithfulness One crucial quality for a persona-based conversation is that it should align with the user profile. Inspired by (Daheim et al., 2023) which introduces dialogue system faithfulness to the knowledge contained in relevant documents, we specify the criterion of *faithfulness* to characterize the alignment between the utterances of a user in a persona-based conversation and their profile. The faithfulness criterion enforces the constraint that the utterances of a user should not decrease the likelihood of their persona. This criterion assumes the existence of both a prior probability of persona attributes, and an inference model for determining the probability of persona attributes conditioned on utterances. Let M be such an inference model, (U_1, U_2) a pair of user profiles, and D a persona-based conversation between them. To be a faithful conversation based on M, D should not contain any contradicting evidence to the persona attributes of the speakers: passing the conversation D as input to the inference model M should not reduce the inference probability of persona attributes in either of the user profiles U_1 or U_2. In other words, the probability of any persona attribute in the user profiles based on conversation D should not be less than the probability of that persona attribute without any assumptions. Formally, we call a conversation D faithful with respect to the user profiles U_1 and U_2, and inference model M if the following condition holds: $\forall \pi \in U_1 \cup U_2 : P_M(\pi|D) \geqslant P_M(\pi)$. Where $P_M(\pi|D)$ indicates the probability that M infers the persona π given conversation D. We show examples of faithful, and unfaithful conversations in Figure 1.

3 Method

In this section, we introduce our method to generate persona-based conversations. We create such conversations with minimum human input, starting from an initial dataset. Our process consists of three steps, as shown in Figure 2: user generation, user pairing, and conversation generation.

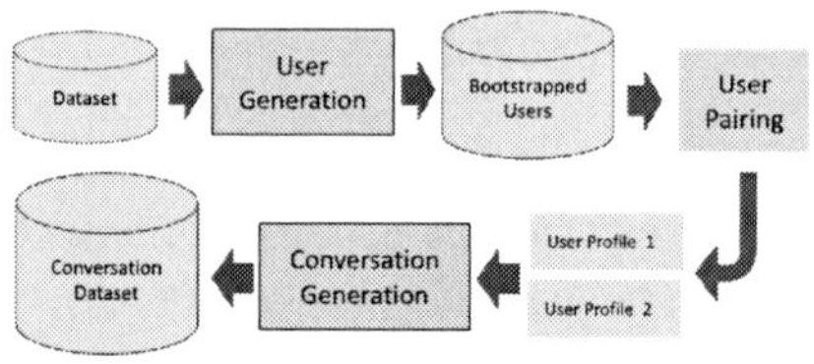

Figure 2: Dataset Augmentation Pipeline

The first component augments a set of seed persona attributes Π_0 into an expanded set of persona attributes Π_e, from which it creates user profiles. The second component pairs user profiles as interlocutors of a conversation. The third and final component uses an iterative process to generate high-quality conversations among user profile pairs. We detail each of these components below.

3.1 User Generation

The User Generation component is split into two sub-components:

1. Persona Expansion
2. User Profile Construction

We bootstrap seed persona attributes by using various prompts (Brown et al., 2020a) to generate new persona attributes in the Persona Expansion step (Refer to Appendix A.1 for more details on the prompts used). We then create new user profiles by iteratively selecting random user persona attributes from the expanded persona attributes. We employ a Natural Language Inference (NLI) model to ensure the consistency of the constructed user profiles.

3.1.1 Persona Expansion

We propose an unsupervised method to augment a set of seed persona attributes Π_0 into a super-set Π_e. Unlike previous approaches (Lee et al., 2022), our method is independent of human knowledge or intervention, making it capable of creating specialized personas in new domains. We proceed in two steps: query induction, and persona bootstrapping. In the query induction phase, we identify persona categories in Π_0, along with associated queries. We then expand these queries into a set Q that also covers unobserved persona categories. The persona bootstrapping step leverages the category-based query set Q, and the initial persona attribute seed set Π_0 to generate new persona attributes. Both of these steps are based on the bootstrapping technique (Yarowsky, 1995), and involve prompting an LLM. We provide a detailed description of these two steps in the following.

Query Induction As described in Section 2, each persona attribute belongs to at least one persona category, and each category is associated with a corresponding query that can be answered with persona attributes in that category. The query induction process initially identifies the queries associated with persona categories in Π_0. It then bootstraps queries by feeding them to a prompted LLM to create more queries that are associated with unobserved categories, ultimately creating a query set Q. Including queries associated with unobserved persona categories facilitates the creation of a more diverse set of personas, and increases the scale of augmentation.

The query induction relies on the following assumption:

Assumption *Let $\mathcal{M}$ be an LLM, and let Γ be the set of all queries associated with all persona categories. If two persona attributes π_1 and π_2 belong to the same persona category, then there exists a query $q^{\mathcal{M}} \in \Gamma$ such that π_1 and π_2 are $\mathcal{M}$'s output to $q^{\mathcal{M}}$.*

The persona attributes "I am a doctor" and "I am a truck driver", for instance, both belong to the "job" category, leading to the query "What is your job?". We use an agglomerative clustering method to identify the persona categories in Π_0. Let C be an arbitrary persona cluster in Π_0. To generate a query for C, we select a random subset of persona attributes in C, and create a prompt using these samples. We employ this strategy to generate queries for all the clusters identified in Π_0, and create a set of queries, which we refer to as Q_0. Details on the clustering, query induction, together with examples of clusters, persona attributes, and induced queries are available in Appendix A.1. We come up with queries for new, unobserved persona categories by bootstrapping the queries in Q_0: starting from $Q = Q_0$, we iteratively sample a set of queries from Q, and create a prompt by concatenating them. We then prompt the LLM to generate a new query, and add it to the query set Q, as shown in Figure 3. We generated a total of $|Q| = 188$ queries. This set of category-specific queries Q is later used to guide the LLM to generate new persona attributes from the specified category. Thus, higher values of $|Q|$ result in greater diversity within the expanded persona attribute set.

Persona Bootstrapping We use the persona attribute seed set Π_0 and category-specific queries Q to generate new persona attributes through a bootstrapping process. We initialize Π to Π_0. At every iteration, we randomly select a subset of persona attributes from Π, and create a set of prompts as follows: we first concatenate a set of persona attributes s. For every query $q \in Q$, we then combine the concatenated samples s, and the query q to create a category-specific persona prompt. This prompt guides the LLM to generate a persona attribute for that persona category. The set of prompts obtained from this process is $\{sq | q \in Q\}$. We only add a new persona attribute to the set if its BERT embeddings (Devlin et al., 2019) are not too close from existing ones, so as to prevent the addition of duplicates.

Each of these prompts is then fed to the LLM to create a new persona attribute, which is subsequently added to the set of persona attributes Π for the next iteration. We continue this iterative process until we have generated a total of 5k persona attributes. Figure 4 illustrates the persona bootstrapping process. Table 7 in the appendix contains the prompt template used in this component.

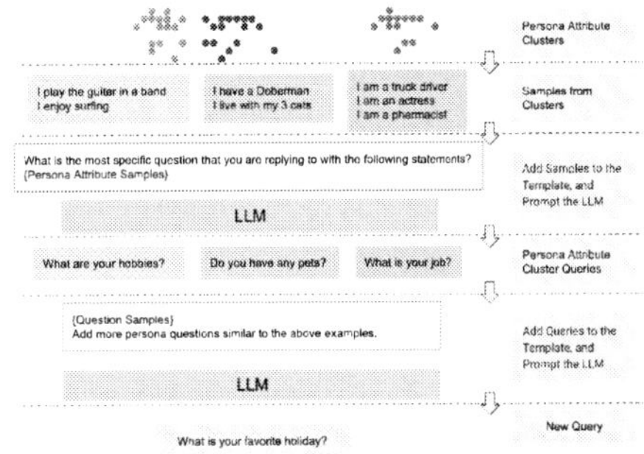

Figure 3: Query Induction Steps

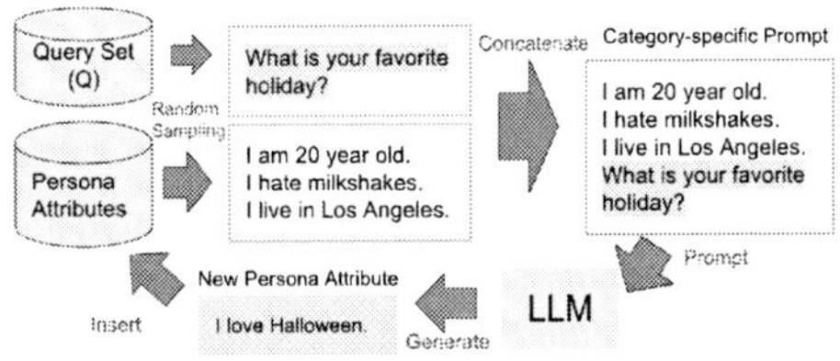

Figure 4: Query-based Persona Bootstrapping Process

3.1.2 User Profile Construction

We build user profiles incrementally by sampling persona attributes from Π_e, and adding the eligible ones. A persona attribute is eligible if it adheres to the criteria of consistency and non-redundancy. In other words, it should not contradict any attribute already in the user profile, and it should not be inferred by other persona attribute. We assess the consistency and redundancy of user profiles by leveraging an NLI model, and persona attribute clustering, respectively. The NLI model we employ is based on T5 (Raffel et al., 2019), and has been trained on the TRUE dataset (Honovich et al., 2022).

We create a user profile U by iteratively selecting a random candidate persona attribute $\pi' \in \Pi_e$. We use the NLI model to assess whether π' contradicts any persona attribute in the profile. This is determined by the condition: $\forall \pi \in U : (\pi' \nrightarrow \neg\pi) \wedge (\pi \nrightarrow \neg\pi')$, where $\rightarrow$ is an inference. Additionally, we evaluate the similarity of π' to the persona attributes in U to prevent the addition of redundant attributes. We add π' to U if it meets the consistency and non-redundancy criteria. We repeat this process until the user profile contains 5 persona attributes. Please refer to Appendix A.1 for more details on the user profile construction.

3.2 User Pairing

In this component, we identify potential pairs of users for conversations. As the conversations are persona-based, we hypothesize that they will be more engaging if the users' personas exhibit more commonalities. We assign a similarity score to every pair of user profiles (U_1, U_2), indicating their semantic similarity. We leverage BERT to represent the user profiles. The similarity between U_1 and U_2 is defined as: $|\{(\pi_1, \pi_2)|\pi_1 \in U_1, \pi_2 \in U_2, \exists c : \pi_1, \pi_2 \in c\}|$ Where c is a persona attributes cluster. The semantic similarity is quantified by the number of common persona categories in the user profiles. We pair U_1 and U_2 if their similarity exceeds a threshold of 2.

3.3 Conversation Generation

Our Conversation Generation component is similar to a general-purpose dataset generation framework that generates data samples, and refines them based on a set of predefined criteria, which we refer to as *policies* (Madaan et al., 2023). The flexibility in the choice of policies for data generation allows us to emphasize different objectives. Once the active policies are selected, this component generates new data samples using a few input samples. The input to our Conversation Generation framework consists of a set of paired user profiles, a few samples of user profiles along with a persona-based conversation between them, and conversation quality metrics as policies. We follow a Generator-Critic architecture, and iteratively create the dataset following the steps shown in Figure 5:

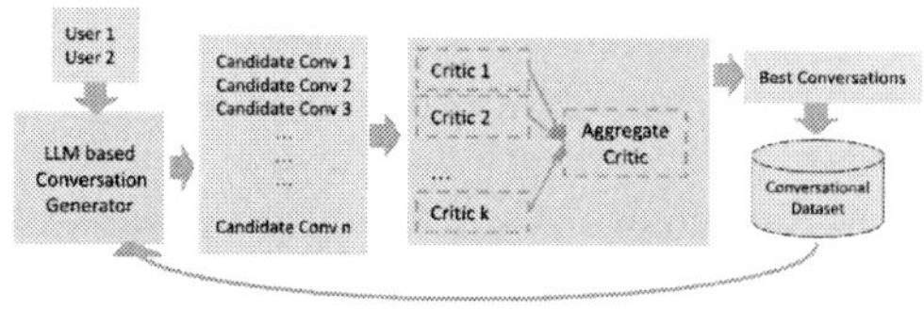

Figure 5: The Generator-Critic Architecture for Conversation Generation

Step 1 The Generator outputs candidate conversations between persona pairs using a few initial conversation samples.
Step 2 The Critic evaluates the candidate conversations based on the predetermined policies, and selects the best candidate conversations.
Step 3 The best candidate conversations are added to the dataset for the next iteration of generation.
This iterative process of selecting the top candidates and adding them to the dataset gradually improves the performance of the Generator.

Without any loss of generality, we implement both the Generator and the Critic based on LLMs. Specifically, the Generator prompts an LLM to create candidate conversations, while the Critic prompts an LLM to evaluate the quality of the generated conversations.

We provide more details on the Generator, Critic, and the policies we used.

The **Generator** outputs conversations for pairs of users (U_1, U_2) by prompting an LLM (Brown et al., 2020a; Wei et al., 2023). At each iteration, it randomly selects 5 samples from an initial set of conversations, each containing a pair of user profiles and a dialogue among them. It feeds these samples to a template that instructs the LLM to generate a series of candidate conversations for the given user pair. The template, and a sample generated conversation are available in Table 7, and Table 9 in the appendix.

The **Critic** selects the best generated conversations to fine-tune the Generator. A conversation is deemed high-quality if it complies with the policies of the Critic. Given the multifaceted nature of the conversation evaluations, we use a Mixture of Experts (MoE) approach. Each expert evaluates the conversation based on a specific policy. In this paper, we incorporate three types of experts, each with distinct criteria: general conversation quality, persona faithfulness, and toxicity. Collectively, these experts select the best generated conversations (the single best in our experiments). We describe each type of expert, and the collective decision-making process below.

General Conversation Quality experts assess conversation quality using the **Fine-grained Evaluation of Dialog (FED)** metrics introduced in (Mehri and Eskénazi, 2020). These experts use verbalized forms of the policies from FED as prompts. For instance, the "conversation depth quality expert" transforms the "depth policy" from FED into a prompt like "Which conversation is a deeper conversation between user 1 and user 2?". Our system instructs the LLM to compare each pair of candidate conversations based on these policies, resulting in pairwise comparisons. The list of policies and their baseline performance are presented in Table 6 in Appendix A.2.

The **Faithfulness** expert ensures the consistency of the generated conversations with the user profiles. It uses an LLM to identify instances of unfaithful conversations. The faithfulness prompt provides the LLM with explicit instructions, user profiles, and human-curated examples of unfaithful conversations.

The **Toxicity** expert detects any conversation that exhibits harmful traits, including bias and hate.

The Critic filters unfaithful and toxic conversations out. It then selects the best conversations using a majority vote among the General Conversation Quality experts. The selected instances are added to the dataset for the next iteration of the Generator.

4 Evaluation

We evaluate different aspects of our dataset generation framework, and the resulting dataset - referred to as Synthetic-Persona-Chat - which is created using an instruction fine-tuned LLM with 24 billion parameters (Chung et al., 2022). We compare Synthetic-Persona-Chat (SPC) against the widely used Persona-Chat (PC) dataset across different dimensions. We begin by evaluating the quality of the personas we generate. We then evaluate SPC using both automatic metrics, and human assessment. We analyze other aspects of SPC, such as toxicity and diversity in appendices B.1 and B.1.

4.1 Evaluation of the Expanded Personas

We evaluate our persona expansion module on two seed datasets: Wikipedia, and Persona-Chat. The Wikipedia personas are created by crawling the 1,000 most active contributors[2], and extracting user boxes from their pages. We expand both datasets using our framework, and evaluate the expanded persona attribute sets using automatic metrics. Table 1 compares the original persona sets to the expanded ones on a few dimensions. We observe that our persona expansion increases the number of persona attributes in SPC by 119%, while maintaining the original persona categories and expanding them by 71% compared to the persona attributes in PC. Moreover, the lengths of the new generated persona attributes are 107% longer in SPC, indicating that the new personas exhibit greater detail and specificity. We observe a similar trend when applying our persona expansion to the Wikipedia persona set, with a 108% increase in the number of persona attributes, a 140% increase in persona categories, and a 45% growth in persona attribute lengths. This demonstrates the effectiveness of our method in expanding and diversifying persona sets.

Dataset	Persona-Chat	Synthetic-Persona-Chat	Wikipedia	Wikipedia+
# Persona Attributes	4,723	**10,371**	8768	**18,293**
# Clusters	323	**553**	408	**986**
Inter-cluster Dist	0.836	0.863	0.816	0.85
AVG length	7.65	**15.9***	10.45	**15.2***

Table 1: Evaluation of the expanded persona sets. The numbers with * indicate the metric value of the newly generated persona attributes to contrast with the initial set.

4.2 Next Utterance Prediction

A persona-based conversation reflects the speaker's persona explicitly or implicitly. Therefore, we expect the inclusion of information about speaker personas to enhance the performance of next utterance prediction models in such conversations. In this experiment, we assess the impact of incorporating speaker personas as prior information on both ranking, and generative - Transformer based (Vaswani et al., 2017) - next utterance prediction models. We create a subset of SPC containing conversations among user pairs included in PC for a fair comparison, i.e., for each sample in PC we have a parallel sample in SPC which has the same user pairs but different conversation between them. To create next utterance candidates, we follow PC strategy: for each utterance in a conversation in SPC, we select 19 random utterances from other conversations in the dataset. The number of train, validation and test samples in both cases are 8887, 995, 959.

[2] https://en.wikipedia.org/wiki/Wikipedia:List_of_Wikipedians_by_number_of_edits

Method	Metric	Persona-Chat None	Persona-Chat Persona	Persona-Chat % Change	Synthetic-Persona-Chat None	Synthetic-Persona-Chat Persona	Synthetic-Persona-Chat % Change
IR Baseline	hit@1	18.69	36.86	+97	19.37 (19.92)	**39.6** (26.23)	**+104** (+31)
Transformer (Ranker)	hit@1	14.24	**19.21**	**+35**	9.71 (64.24)	11.74 (68.82)	+21 (+7)
Transformer (Generator)	hit@1	**8.54**	6.78	-20	6.89 (41.32)	6.66 (37.35)	**-3** (-9)
	Perplexity	**122.5**	173.3	+41	1032 (5.24)	1126 (5.73)	**+9** (+9)
	BLUE	**0.120**	0.094	-21	0.097 (0.289)	0.083 (0.251)	**-14** (-13)
	ROUGE	**0.141**	0.113	-24	0.123 (0.348)	0.107 (0.309)	**-13** (-11)

Table 2: Results of the next utterance prediction experiment. Performance of the trained model on the test split of PC is represented by the numbers in the table, while the numbers in parentheses indicate results for the test split of SPC.

We observe (Table 2) that the performance of ranking models increases when personas are given to the models as input for both datasets. Specifically, the Transformer (Ranker) model, known for its ability to capture conversational complexity, exhibits higher performance in SPC when evaluated on the SPC test set compared to the PC test set. However, it demonstrates relatively weaker performance when trained on the PC. This implies that SPC contains more intricate and coherent conversations.

The Transformer (Ranker) trained on SPC achieves a hit@1 of 64.24 on SPC test, 350% higher than PC (14.24). This suggests that the Transformer model can more accurately predict the next utterance in SPC, pointing to a greater coherency in conversations.

The performance of the Information Retrieval (IR) Baseline model is slightly higher for SPC: it rises by 31% when conditioned on user personas, which is lower than 97% improvement in PC. A key contributing factor for the performance improvement of the retrieval-based model (IR Baseline) on PC given the personas, is the participants' tendency to copy persona words in the conversations, whereas in SPC the personas are more implicitly reflected in the conversations. The implicit reflection of personas in SPC, makes the task more challenging for word based retrieval models, necessitating reasoning that goes beyond word level. However, when the model is trained on SPC and tested on PC, the improvement is as high as when the model is trained on PC, i.e. 104% compared to 97%.

The performance of generative models is low for this task since these models are not trained with the ranking objective. However, the performance difference while the models are conditioned on personas is lower for the model trained on SPC, with a 20% drop for the model trained on PC against 3% drop in the model trained on SPC. The increase in perplexity is 9% in SPC compared to 41% in PC. The lower rate of perplexity increase and performance drop of the model given user personas as input highlights the higher alignment of conversations with personas in SPC.

We also evaluate the performance of the next utterance prediction models when given no user, one user, and both user personas. The results suggest a higher degree of bidirectionality in SPC. We refer the reader to the Appendix B.1 for more details.

4.3 Human Evaluation

We compare the quality of the conversations generated by our framework against those in Persona-Chat. We randomly select 200 conversations from PC, together with their corresponding user pairs, and use our method to generate conversations among the same users. We start by following (Gehrmann et al., 2019) in running a human experiment to try and detect AI-generated content. We conduct an AI detection test where we present pairs of conversations to humans, and ask them to identify the synthetically generated one. This test is carried out on the generated conversations at the end of each iteration of creating SPC. We repeat the test for conversations generated for new persona pairs, which we refer to as iteration 3*, i.e. we pair each of these conversations with a random conversation from PC. For a robust evaluation, every pair of conversations is annotated by 3 human evaluators, and the majority vote is used as the final annotation. Details of this test are available in Appendix B.2. The results of this experiment can be found in Table 3. We observe that the losing rate of SPC is reduced by 48% from SPC Iter 1 to SPC Iter 3, and dropped below the rate of 10%. Interestingly, 91% of the conversations in SPC, which are synthetically generated, are judged as human-like as the conversations generated by humans. Moreover, conversations generated for new personas (Iteration 3*) are deemed artificial in only 8.04% of cases, showing that SPC is more realistic than PC. We also observe that in Iter 2, from 200 conversations, 79 were different from the

Conversation Source	Lose	Win	Tie	Faithful
SPC Iter 1	17.2	30.1	52.68	78.5
SPC Iter 2	18.5	**49**	32.5	80.5
SPC Iter 3	**8.8**	35.23	**55.95**	76.6
SPC Iter 3*	8.04	32.66	59.29	N/A
SPC (LLM2)	11.5	39	49.5	N/A

Table 3: An AI detection test on 200 Generated Conversations per Iteration: Synthetic-Persona-Chat Outcomes Against Persona-Chat.

conversations in Iter 1. And in Iter 3, 57 conversations were changed compared to Iter 2. These observations suggest a decreasing rate of updates with subsequent iterations, aligning with our expectations that improvements will reach human-level conversation quality.

We also evaluate the faithfulness of the generated conversations. For each conversation, we provide annotators with a faithfulness annotation task including the speakers' persona attributes and distractor persona attribute options as shown in Figure 8. We evaluate faithfulness during 3 iterations of conversation generation for the selected 200 user pairs, and the annotators evaluate the generated conversations for each pair in every iteration. The results show that, while improving the Turing test results, faithfulness of conversations are consistently higher than 75% with at most 3% variation in between iterations, indicating high faithfulness in all iterations.

Finally, we assess the impact of LLM size on the quality of the generated dataset within our framework. We create a variant of SPC using an LLM with 540 billion parameters (LLM2). Table 3 presents human evaluations comparing the smaller LLM in multiple iterations to a single-iteration approach with LLM2. The larger model exhibits a 5% advantage in the Turing test over the first iteration of dataset generation over the smaller model. After two iterations, however, the multi-iteration approach outperforms the first iteration of the bigger model, showing our framework's capacity for cost-effective, high-quality conversation generation.

5 Related Work

Large Language Models (LLMs) have been used for data augmentation (Shin et al., 2021), generation (Kim et al., 2023; Dong et al., 2023; Kim et al., 2022), and evaluation (Zhang et al., 2019; Liu et al., 2023). One of the earliest works in this area (Anaby-Tavor et al., 2019) used LLMs to create a large text dataset from a small, labeled one. This idea was followed by (Wang et al., 2021; Schick and Schütze, 2021) which leveraged LLMs to create datasets without any human data. (Kumar et al., 2020) evaluated the performance of different LLMs on the data augmentation task. Several conversational dataset generation methods focused on the structure of the conversational data (Dai et al., 2022; Leszczynski et al., 2023; Abbasiantaeb et al., 2023). (Mehri et al., 2022) illustrated how LLMs can effectively generate synthetic training data for task-oriented dialogue models.

Persona-based conversations have been a popular research topic in NLP (Liu et al., 2022). One of the earliest works in this area is Persona-Chat, by (Zhang et al., 2018), which proposed the Persona-Chat dataset and evaluation metrics that have become a benchmark for persona-based conversation generation (Mazaré et al., 2018). Many subsequent works have used this dataset to train and evaluate (Mohapatra et al., 2021) their models, including DialoGPT (Zhang et al., 2020), BlenderBot (Shuster et al., 2022), and PersonaChatGen (Lee et al., 2022). PersonaChatGen automated the process of creating persona based conversations of Persona-Chat using LLMs. A challenge in generating synthetic datasets is to ensure the quality of the conversation including data faithfulness, fidelity, diversity, and consistency (Li et al., 2016; Lee et al., 2023; Veselovsky et al., 2023; Zhuo et al., 2023; Wang et al., 2023a; Mündler et al., 2023). Several works have focused on creating and using high quality training datasets (Welleck et al., 2019), and creating quality filtering components to their conversation dataset generation (Lewkowycz et al., 2022). Evaluation of the resulting conversational datasets is also challenging (Xu et al., 2021). (Wang et al., 2023b) recently introduced the paradigm of interactive evaluation of conversations with LLMs.

6 Conclusion and Future Work

We developed a novel framework for generating high-quality persona-based conversations using LLMs, resulting in the creation of Synthetic-Persona-Chat, comprising 20k conversations. We hope this dataset will support future endeavors in developing persona-aware conversational agents, including the generation of domain-specific multi-session conversations for specialized, task-oriented interactions. While we focused on a persona-based dataset generation task, our Generator-Critic approach can be generalized to other use cases, such as generating other specialized datasets, etc.

Limitations

In this paper, we define an iterative process over LLMs to generate a dataset. Our method requires computational resources, and access to an LLM. The quality of the dataset is bounded by the LLM, since the quality critics are also using the same LLM, and we leave the iterative improvement of our critics as future work. The main limitation of this data generation framework is the inability to generate realistic conversations that do not have high quality, since we assume that both parties are fluent, that the conversation flow is perfectly consistent, and there is no unexpected event (e.g. an interruption by another person, connection loss, etc.) in the middle of the conversation. Another limitation of our method is the difficulty of incorporating less tangible persona traits, such as a sense of humor, or user attributes that require multiple conversation sessions to be reflected.

Ethics Statement

The approach of generating datasets based on some desired objective might be used to create harmful datasets, and train malicious models based on them, such as a biased dataset, or a hateful speech one (Hartvigsen et al., 2022). On the other hand, these datasets and models can be used as filters in application tasks.

We used Amazon Mechanical Turk in our human experiments, and followed that platform's guidelines to protect the rights of human raters. The participation was voluntary, and the raters were informed of their rights at the beginning of the study. The platform implemented security measures to protect them, and prevent the disclosure of any Personal Identifiable Information about them. Furthermore, we offered higher than minimum standard wage compensation to avoid any exploitative practices.

To avoid having any toxic conversation in the final dataset, we also used several tools to remove any potentially toxic conversation. Details about these tools, and example removed samples are available in Appendix B.1.

References

Zahra Abbasiantaeb, Yifei Yuan, E. Kanoulas, and Mohammad Aliannejadi. 2023. Let the llms talk: Simulating human-to-human conversational qa via zero-shot llm-to-llm interactions.

Ateret Anaby-Tavor, Boaz Carmeli, Esther Goldbraich, Amir Kantor, George Kour, Segev Shlomov, N. Tepper, and Naama Zwerdling. 2019. Not enough data? deep learning to the rescue! *ArXiv*, abs/1911.03118.

Parikshit Bansal and Amit Sharma. 2023. Large language models as annotators: Enhancing generalization of nlp models at minimal cost. *ArXiv*, abs/2306.15766.

D. M. Blei, T. L. Griffiths, M. I. Jordan, and J. B. Tenenbaum. 2004. Hierarchical topic models and the nested Chinese restaurant process. In *Advances in Neural Information Processing Systems 16*. MIT Press, Cambridge, MA.

Tom B. Brown, Benjamin Mann, Nick Ryder, Melanie Subbiah, Jared Kaplan, Prafulla Dhariwal, Arvind Neelakantan, Pranav Shyam, Girish Sastry, Amanda Askell, Sandhini Agarwal, Ariel Herbert-Voss, Gretchen Krueger, T. J. Henighan, Rewon Child, Aditya Ramesh, Daniel M. Ziegler, Jeff Wu, Clemens Winter, Christopher Hesse, Mark Chen, Eric Sigler, Mateusz Litwin, Scott Gray, Benjamin Chess, Jack Clark, Christopher Berner, Sam McCandlish, Alec Radford, Ilya Sutskever, and Dario Amodei. 2020b. Language models are few-shot learners. *ArXiv*, abs/2005.14165.

Tom B. Brown, Benjamin Mann, Nick Ryder, Melanie Subbiah, Jared Kaplan, Prafulla Dhariwal, Arvind Neelakantan, Pranav Shyam, Girish Sastry, Amanda Askell, Sandhini Agarwal, Ariel Herbert-Voss, Gretchen Krueger, Tom Henighan, Rewon Child, Aditya Ramesh, Daniel M. Ziegler, Jeffrey Wu, Clemens Winter, Christopher Hesse, Mark Chen, Eric Sigler, Mateusz Litwin, Scott Gray, Benjamin Chess, Jack Clark, Christopher Berner, Sam McCandlish, Alec Radford, Ilya Sutskever, and Dario Amodei. 2020a. Language models are few-shot learners.

Cheng-Han Chiang and Hung yi Lee. 2023. Can large language models be an alternative to human evaluations? In *Annual Meeting of the Association for Computational Linguistics*.

Hyung Won Chung, Le Hou, Shayne Longpre, Barret Zoph, Yi Tay, William Fedus, Yunxuan Li, Xuezhi Wang, Mostafa Dehghani, Siddhartha Brahma, Albert Webson, Shixiang Shane Gu, Zhuyun Dai, Mirac Suzgun, Xinyun Chen, Aakanksha Chowdhery, Alex Castro-Ros, Marie Pellat, Kevin Robinson, Dasha Valter, Sharan Narang, Gaurav Mishra, Adams Yu, Vincent Zhao, Yanping Huang, Andrew Dai, Hongkun Yu, Slav Petrov, Ed H. Chi, Jeff Dean, Jacob Devlin, Adam Roberts, Denny Zhou, Quoc V. Le, and Jason Wei. 2022. Scaling instruction-finetuned language models.

Lisbeth Claus. 2019. Hr disruption—time already to reinvent talent management. *BRQ Business Research Quarterly*, 22.

Alan Cooper and Paul Saffo. 1999. *The Inmates Are Running the Asylum.* Macmillan Publishing Co., Inc., USA.

Nico Daheim, Nouha Dziri, Mrinmaya Sachan, Iryna Gurevych, and Edoardo M. Ponti. 2023. Elastic weight removal for faithful and abstractive dialogue generation.

Zhuyun Dai, Arun Tejasvi Chaganty, Vincent Zhao, Aida Amini, Qazi Mamunur Rashid, Mike Green, and Kelvin Guu. 2022. Dialog inpainting: Turning documents into dialogs. *ArXiv*, abs/2205.09073.

Jacob Devlin, Ming-Wei Chang, Kenton Lee, and Kristina Toutanova. 2019. Bert: Pre-training of deep bidirectional transformers for language understanding. *ArXiv*, abs/1810.04805.

Hanze Dong, Wei Xiong, Deepanshu Goyal, Rui Pan, Shizhe Diao, Jipeng Zhang, Kashun Shum, and T. Zhang. 2023. Raft: Reward ranked finetuning for generative foundation model alignment. *ArXiv*, abs/2304.06767.

Jinlan Fu, See-Kiong Ng, Zhengbao Jiang, and Pengfei Liu. 2023. Gptscore: Evaluate as you desire. *ArXiv*, abs/2302.04166.

Kristin Fuglerud, Trenton Schulz, Astri Janson, and Anne Moen. 2020. *Co-creating Persona Scenarios with Diverse Users Enriching Inclusive Design*, pages 48–59.

Sebastian Gehrmann, Hendrik Strobelt, and Alexander M. Rush. 2019. Gltr: Statistical detection and visualization of generated text. In *Annual Meeting of the Association for Computational Linguistics*.

Thomas Hartvigsen, Saadia Gabriel, Hamid Palangi, Maarten Sap, Dipankar Ray, and Ece Kamar. 2022. Toxigen: A large-scale machine-generated dataset for adversarial and implicit hate speech detection. *ArXiv*, abs/2203.09509.

Xingwei He, Zheng-Wen Lin, Yeyun Gong, Alex Jin, Hang Zhang, Chen Lin, Jian Jiao, Siu Ming Yiu, Nan Duan, and Weizhu Chen. 2023. Annollm: Making large language models to be better crowdsourced annotators. *ArXiv*, abs/2303.16854.

Or Honovich, Roee Aharoni, Jonathan Herzig, Hagai Taitelbaum, Doron Kukliansy, Vered Cohen, Thomas Scialom, Idan Szpektor, Avinatan Hassidim, and Y. Matias. 2022. True: Re-evaluating factual consistency evaluation. In *Workshop on Document-grounded Dialogue and Conversational Question Answering*.

Samuel Humeau, Kurt Shuster, Marie-Anne Lachaux, and Jason Weston. 2020. Poly-encoders: Transformer architectures and pre-training strategies for fast and accurate multi-sentence scoring.

Hyunwoo Kim, Jack Hessel, Liwei Jiang, Peter West, Ximing Lu, Youngjae Yu, Pei Zhou, Ronan Le Bras, Malihe Alikhani, Gunhee Kim, Maarten Sap, and Yejin Choi. 2023. Soda: Million-scale dialogue distillation with social commonsense contextualization.

Minju Kim, Chaehyeong Kim, Yongho Song, Seung won Hwang, and Jinyoung Yeo. 2022. Botstalk: Machine-sourced framework for automatic curation of large-scale multi-skill dialogue datasets.

Varun Kumar, Ashutosh Choudhary, and Eunah Cho. 2020. Data augmentation using pre-trained transformer models. *ArXiv*, abs/2003.02245.

Angeliki Lazaridou, Adhiguna Kuncoro, Elena Gribovskaya, Devang Agrawal, Adam Liska, Tayfun Terzi, Mai Gimenez, Cyprien de Masson d'Autume, Tomás Kociský, Sebastian Ruder, Dani Yogatama, Kris Cao, Susannah Young, and Phil Blunsom. 2021. Mind the gap: Assessing temporal generalization in neural language models. In *Neural Information Processing Systems*.

Dong-Ho Lee, Jay Pujara, Mohit Sewak, Ryen W White, and Sujay Kumar Jauhar. 2023. Making large language models better data creators. In *The 2023 Conference on Empirical Methods in Natural Language Processing (EMNLP)*.

Young-Jun Lee, Chae-Gyun Lim, Yunsu Choi, Ji-Hui Lm, and Ho-Jin Choi. 2022. PERSONACHATGEN: Generating personalized dialogues using GPT-3. In *Proceedings of the 1st Workshop on Customized Chat Grounding Persona and Knowledge*, pages 29–48, Gyeongju, Republic of Korea. Association for Computational Linguistics.

Megan Leszczynski, Ravi Ganti, Shu Zhang, Krisztian Balog, Filip Radlinski, Fernando Pereira, and Arun Tejasvi Chaganty. 2023. Generating synthetic data for conversational music recommendation using random walks and language models. *ArXiv*, abs/2301.11489.

Aitor Lewkowycz, Anders Andreassen, David Dohan, Ethan Dyer, Henryk Michalewski, Vinay Ramasesh, Ambrose Slone, Cem Anil, Imanol Schlag, Theo Gutman-Solo, Yuhuai Wu, Behnam Neyshabur, Guy Gur-Ari, and Vedant Misra. 2022. Solving quantitative reasoning problems with language models.

Jiwei Li, Michel Galley, Chris Brockett, Georgios P. Spithourakis, Jianfeng Gao, and William B. Dolan. 2016. A persona-based neural conversation model. *ArXiv*, abs/1603.06155.

Yen-Ting Lin and Yun-Nung (Vivian) Chen. 2023. Llm-eval: Unified multi-dimensional automatic evaluation for open-domain conversations with large language models. *ArXiv*, abs/2305.13711.

Junfeng Liu, Christopher T. Symons, and Ranga Raju Vatsavai. 2022. Persona-based conversational ai: State of the art and challenges. *2022 IEEE International Conference on Data Mining Workshops (ICDMW)*, pages 993–1001.

Yang Liu, Dan Iter, Yichong Xu, Shuo Wang, Ruochen Xu, and Chenguang Zhu. 2023. G-eval: Nlg evaluation using gpt-4 with better human alignment. *ArXiv*, abs/2303.16634.

Aman Madaan, Niket Tandon, Prakhar Gupta, Skyler Hallinan, Luyu Gao, Sarah Wiegreffe, Uri Alon, Nouha Dziri, Shrimai Prabhumoye, Yiming Yang, Sean Welleck, Bodhisattwa Prasad Majumder, Shashank Gupta, Amir Yazdanbakhsh, and Peter Clark. 2023. Self-refine: Iterative refinement with self-feedback.

Philip M Massey, Shawn C Chiang, Meredith Rose, Regan M Murray, Madeline Rockett, Elikem Togo, Ann C Klassen, Jennifer A Manganello, and Amy E Leader. 2021. Development of personas to communicate narrative-based information about the hpv vaccine on twitter. front digit health.

Pierre-Emmanuel Mazaré, Samuel Humeau, Martin Raison, and Antoine Bordes. 2018. Training millions of personalized dialogue agents. In *Proceedings of the 2018 Conference on Empirical Methods in Natural Language Processing*, pages 2775–2779, Brussels, Belgium. Association for Computational Linguistics.

Shikib Mehri, Yasemin Altun, and Maxine Eskenazi. 2022. LAD: Language models as data for zero-shot dialog. In *Proceedings of the 23rd Annual Meeting of the Special Interest Group on Discourse and Dialogue*, pages 595–604, Edinburgh, UK. Association for Computational Linguistics.

Shikib Mehri and Maxine Eskénazi. 2020. Unsupervised evaluation of interactive dialog with dialogpt. In *SIGDIAL Conferences*.

A. H. Miller, W. Feng, A. Fisch, J. Lu, D. Batra, A. Bordes, D. Parikh, and J. Weston. 2017. Parlai: A dialog research software platform. *arXiv preprint arXiv:1705.06476*.

Biswesh Mohapatra, Gaurav Pandey, Danish Contractor, and Sachindra Joshi. 2021. Simulated chats for building dialog systems: Learning to generate conversations from instructions.

Niels Mündler, Jingxuan He, Slobodan Jenko, and Martin T. Vechev. 2023. Self-contradictory hallucinations of large language models: Evaluation, detection and mitigation. *ArXiv*, abs/2305.15852.

Long Ouyang, Jeff Wu, Xu Jiang, Diogo Almeida, Carroll L. Wainwright, Pamela Mishkin, Chong Zhang, Sandhini Agarwal, Katarina Slama, Alex Ray, John Schulman, Jacob Hilton, Fraser Kelton, Luke E. Miller, Maddie Simens, Amanda Askell, Peter Welinder, Paul Francis Christiano, Jan Leike, and Ryan J. Lowe. 2022. Training language models to follow instructions with human feedback. *ArXiv*, abs/2203.02155.

F. Pedregosa, G. Varoquaux, A. Gramfort, V. Michel, B. Thirion, O. Grisel, M. Blondel, P. Prettenhofer, R. Weiss, V. Dubourg, J. Vanderplas, A. Passos, D. Cournapeau, M. Brucher, M. Perrot, and E. Duchesnay. 2011. Scikit-learn: Machine learning in Python. *Journal of Machine Learning Research*, 12:2825–2830.

John Pruitt and Jonathan Grudin. 2003a. Personas: Practice and theory. In *Proceedings of the 2003 Conference on Designing for User Experiences*, DUX '03, page 1–15, New York, NY, USA. Association for Computing Machinery.

John S. Pruitt and Jonathan T. Grudin. 2003b. Personas: practice and theory. In *Conference on Designing for User eXperiences*.

Colin Raffel, Noam M. Shazeer, Adam Roberts, Katherine Lee, Sharan Narang, Michael Matena, Yanqi Zhou, Wei Li, and Peter J. Liu. 2019. Exploring the limits of transfer learning with a unified text-to-text transformer. *ArXiv*, abs/1910.10683.

Timo Schick and Hinrich Schütze. 2021. Generating datasets with pretrained language models. *ArXiv*, abs/2104.07540.

Richard Shin, Christopher Lin, Sam Thomson, Charles Chen, Subhro Roy, Emmanouil Antonios Platanios, Adam Pauls, Dan Klein, Jason Eisner, and Benjamin Van Durme. 2021. Constrained language models yield few-shot semantic parsers. In *Proceedings of the 2021 Conference on Empirical Methods in Natural Language Processing*, pages 7699–7715, Online and Punta Cana, Dominican Republic. Association for Computational Linguistics.

Michael Shum, Stephan Zheng, Wojciech Kryscinski, Caiming Xiong, and Richard Socher. 2019. Sketch-fill-a-r: A persona-grounded chit-chat generation framework. *ArXiv*, abs/1910.13008.

Kurt Shuster, Jing Xu, Mojtaba Komeili, Da Ju, Eric Michael Smith, Stephen Roller, Megan Ung, Moya Chen, Kushal Arora, Joshua Lane, Morteza Behrooz, W.K.F. Ngan, Spencer Poff, Naman Goyal, Arthur D. Szlam, Y-Lan Boureau, Melanie Kambadur, and Jason Weston. 2022. Blenderbot 3: a deployed conversational agent that continually learns to responsibly engage. *ArXiv*, abs/2208.03188.

Ilya Sutskever, Oriol Vinyals, and Quoc V. Le. 2014. Sequence to sequence learning with neural networks. *ArXiv*, abs/1409.3215.

Michelle van Pinxteren, Mark Pluymaekers, and Jos Lemmink. 2020. Human-like communication in conversational agents: a literature review and research agenda. *Journal of Service Management*, ahead-of-print.

Ashish Vaswani, Noam M. Shazeer, Niki Parmar, Jakob Uszkoreit, Llion Jones, Aidan N. Gomez, Lukasz Kaiser, and Illia Polosukhin. 2017. Attention is all you need. In *NIPS*.

Veniamin Veselovsky, Manoel Horta Ribeiro, Akhil Arora, Martin Josifoski, Ashton Anderson, and Robert West. 2023. Generating faithful synthetic data with large language models: A case study in computational social science.

Boxin Wang, Weixin Chen, Hengzhi Pei, Chulin Xie, Mintong Kang, Chenhui Zhang, Chejian Xu, Zidi Xiong, Ritik Dutta, Rylan Schaeffer, Sang Truong, Simran Arora, Mantas Mazeika, Dan Hendrycks, Zi-Han Lin, Yuk-Kit Cheng, Sanmi Koyejo, Dawn Xiaodong Song, and Bo Li. 2023a. Decodingtrust: A comprehensive assessment of trustworthiness in gpt models. *ArXiv*, abs/2306.11698.

Xiaolei Wang, Xinyu Tang, Wayne Xin Zhao, Jingyuan Wang, and Ji-Rong Wen. 2023b. Rethinking the evaluation for conversational recommendation in the era of large language models.

Zirui Wang, Adams Wei Yu, Orhan Firat, and Yuan Cao. 2021. Towards zero-label language learning. *ArXiv*, abs/2109.09193.

Jason Wei, Xuezhi Wang, Dale Schuurmans, Maarten Bosma, Brian Ichter, Fei Xia, Ed Chi, Quoc Le, and Denny Zhou. 2023. Chain-of-thought prompting elicits reasoning in large language models.

Sean Welleck, Jason Weston, Arthur Szlam, and Kyunghyun Cho. 2019. Dialogue natural language inference.

Chien-Sheng Wu, Andrea Madotto, Zhaojiang Lin, Peng Xu, and Pascale Fung. 2019. Getting to know you: User attribute extraction from dialogues. In *International Conference on Language Resources and Evaluation*.

Jing Xu, Arthur Szlam, and Jason Weston. 2021. Beyond goldfish memory: Long-term open-domain conversation.

David Yarowsky. 1995. Unsupervised word sense disambiguation rivaling supervised methods. In *33rd annual meeting of the association for computational linguistics*, pages 189–196.

Saizheng Zhang, Emily Dinan, Jack Urbanek, Arthur D. Szlam, Douwe Kiela, and Jason Weston. 2018. Personalizing dialogue agents: I have a dog, do you have pets too? In *Annual Meeting of the Association for Computational Linguistics*.

Tianyi Zhang, Varsha Kishore, Felix Wu, Kilian Q. Weinberger, and Yoav Artzi. 2019. Bertscore: Evaluating text generation with bert. *ArXiv*, abs/1904.09675.

Yizhe Zhang, Siqi Sun, Michel Galley, Yen-Chun Chen, Chris Brockett, Xiang Gao, Jianfeng Gao, Jingjing Liu, and Bill Dolan. 2020. Dialogpt: Large-scale generative pre-training for conversational response generation.

Peixiang Zhong, Yao Sun, Yong Liu, Chen Zhang, Hao Wang, Zaiqing Nie, and Chunyan Miao. 2020. Endowing empathetic dialogue systems with personas. *ArXiv*, abs/2004.12316.

Li Zhou, Jianfeng Gao, Di Li, and Heung-Yeung Shum. 2020. The design and implementation of XiaoIce, an empathetic social chatbot. *Computational Linguistics*, 46(1):53–93.

Terry Yue Zhuo, Yujin Huang, Chunyang Chen, and Zhenchang Xing. 2023. Red teaming chatgpt via jailbreaking: Bias, robustness, reliability and toxicity.

A Dataset Generation Framework

In this section, we provide more details on our synthetic dataset generation framework. We created Synthetic-Persona-Chat using an LLM with 24 billion parameters. We use top-k sampling with $k = 40$ for decoding during generation, and set the temperature value to 0.7 in all components. We give more details on user and conversation generation components in the following subsections.

A.1 User Generation

In our framework, the user generation component consists of two steps: expanding the persona attribute set, and creating realistic user profiles. In this section we provide details on our framework for these two steps:

Persona Expansion As described in Section 3.1.1, the persona expansion step involves identifying persona categories in the initial persona attribute set Π_0, generating queries associated with those categories, and bootstrapping queries to create a query set . In our framework, we employ the Scikit-learn (Pedregosa et al., 2011) implementation of an agglomerative clustering to identify persona categories following this clustering method: we represent each persona using a BERT-based representation. Our clustering approach is bottom-up, starting with each persona attribute as an individual cluster. At each step, we combine two clusters if their similarity exceeds a predetermined threshold of 0.1. The similarity of two clusters is measured using inter-cluster average cosine similarity. The process continues until no pair of clusters is more similar than the threshold. We set the value of the threshold as 0.1 since it lead to more than 100 non-sparse clusters, i.e., clusters that include at least 3 persona attributes and can be used in the query induction prompt. Table 4 presents the cluster similarity threshold values and the resulting cluster details based on them.

After identifying the clusters, we sample 3 instances of persona attributes for each cluster, and prompt the LLM using the template in shown in section 3 to construct an initial query set Q_0. We expand the query set Q_0 using bootstrapping. At each step, we sample 5 instances from the available queries, and prompt the LLM using the template in Table 7. We repeat this process for 100 steps. Examples of initial persona attributes, induced queries, bootstrapped queries, and bootstrapped persona attributes can be found in Table 5. The prompt templates used in this component are available in Table 7.

Similarity Threshold	# Clusters	# Sparse Clusters
0.05	1083	171
0.1	323	6
0.15	17	2

Table 4: Details of persona clusters created based on similarity threshold in agglomerative clustering.

User Profile Generation We illustrate a sample user profile creation process in Figure 6. As shown in the figure, at each iteration, a randomly selected persona attribute is checked for consistency and non-redundancy.

Let π' be a randomly selected persona attribute in an iteration. For the redundancy criteria, we use the BERT representation of persona attributes. We compute the similarity of the new candidate persona attribute π' with every persona attribute in the user profile. If it is more than a threshold (0.9 in these experiments) similar to an attribute in the user profile, π' is deemed as redundant and will not be added to the user profile. We use the cosine similarities of the BERT representations of the persona attributes. The value of the similarity threshold is selected to be compatible with the agglomerative persona clustering algorithm in the persona expansion step, in which two clusters are merged if their inter-distance is less than 0.1, i.e., their inter-cluster similarity is higher than 0.9. Therefore, by setting the threshold of similarity of attributes to be .9, we ensure that the new attribute is added to the user profile if it is from a new cluster compared to the current attributes in the user profile.

For the consistency criteria, we use the NLI model to verify the consistency of this persona attribute with the user profile. For every persona attribute in the current user profile π, we prompt the LLM to create the negated persona attribute $\neg\pi$. Then, we query the NLI model to check whether $\neg\pi$ is inferred by π' or $\neg\pi'$ is inferred by π. If either of these cases is inferred, then the selected persona attribute is not consistent with the user profile, and not added to the profile.

A.2 Conversation Generation

LLM-based Critic In our framework, the critic is implemented by prompting an LLM. We included a mixture of experts approach in the critic, where each expert prompts the LLM to assess a

Dataset	Persona Source	Query	Example Persona Attribute
Persona-Chat	Human	What is your job? Where do you live? Do you have any pets?	I am a pharmacist. I live close to the coast. I have a doberman.
	LLM	What are your talents? What is your hair color? What is your favorite song?	I am a great listener. My hair is auburn. I like the song "Leather and Lace".
Wikipedia	Human	What are your hobbies? What is your view on the metric system?	I spend WAY too much time on Wikipedia. I find the metric system to be a logical and efficient way to measure things.
	LLM	What is the name of the first album you ever purchased? What are you interested in?	My first album was The Miseducation of Lauryn Hill I'm looking to learn new recipes and improve my cooking skills.

Table 5: Persona Categories and Induced Queries Using Our Framework. Queries are generated by the Large Language Model (LLM). Queries for personas with the "LLM" as source, are generated through bootstrapping, while those with "human" as source are generated by sampling persona categories and prompting the LLM. Personas with "human" as the source are authored by humans, while "LLM" rows represent personas generated using our framework.

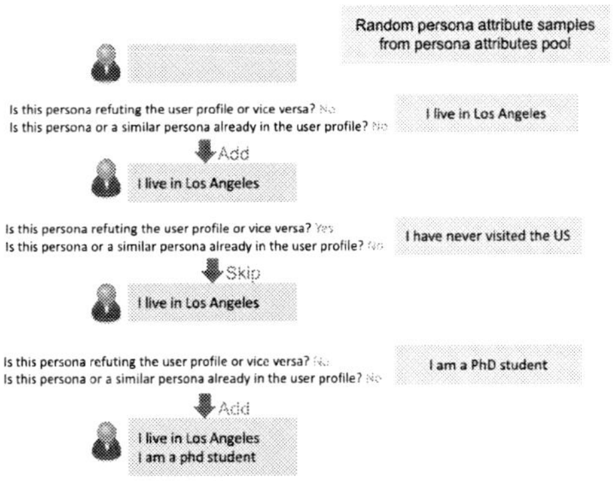

Figure 6: User Profile Construction Example

Policy	Performance
Depth	0.84
Coherency	0.96
Consistency	0.92
Diversity	0.92
Likable	0.88

Table 6: List of FED Experts for Persona-Based Conversation Generation Critic. Performance is measured by the number of correctly compared conversation pairs in FED baseline based on the given policy.

specific policy in the candidate conversations. Our framework includes a set of experts to control the general conversation quality. We evaluate the performance of these experts using a baseline dataset. The baseline dataset for this experiment is FED which consists of 125 human-annotated instances evaluated at the conversation level. We pair the conversations and evaluate the experts based on the number of correctly ranked pairs. As shown in Table 6, we observe that these experts are more than 80% accurate in distinguishing the better conversation within the pairs. The template for the verbalized form of these experts used in our framework can be found in Table 7.

We also included a toxicity expert and a persona faithfulness expert in the critic. The prompt templates used in these experts are available in Table 7. The persona faithfulness leverages in-context-learning capability of LLMs. It includes a few human-curated examples of faithful and unfaithful conversations in the instruction prompt. Refer to Table 8 for examples of faithful and unfaithful conversations used in the instruction prompt.

The faithfulness critic, prompts the LLM both with and without the candidate conversation between two users. It assesses the log probabilities of the output being "Yes" (indicating a contradiction and thus unfaithfulness) or "No" (indicating no contradiction and thus faithfulness). A conversation is deemed unfaithful if there is an increase in the

Component	Template
Query Induction	What is the most specific question that you are replying to with the following statements? {persona-category-sample-1} {persona-category-sample-2} {persona-category-sample-3}
Query Bootstrapping	{cluster-query-1} ... {cluster-query-5} Add more persona questions similar to the above examples.
Persona Bootstrapping	Imagine you are a person with the following persona. {random-persona-attribute-1} ... {random-persona-attribute-5} {query}. Answer with only one short sentence that starts with 'I' or 'My'. Do not repeat the given persona.
FED Expert	Which one of Conversation 1 and Conversation 2 between two users {policy}? Why? Conversation 1: {conv-1} Conversation 2: {conv-2}
Toxicity Expert	Is this conversation toxic? Why? Conversation: {conv}
Conversation Generation	Here, we list the profiles of two users, user 1 and user 2, followed by an interesting and natural conversation between user 1 and user 2, which implicitly reflects their user profiles. User 1 Profile: {conversation1-user-1} User 2 Profile: {conversation1-user-2} Conversation: {conversation-1} ... User 1 Profile: {conversation-5-user-1} User 2 Profile: {conversation-5-user-2} Conversation: {conversation-5} Give me more examples like this. The conversation must be more than 5 turns and less than 8 turns. The conversation must be natural, and not direct copies of their profiles. User 1 Profile: {user-1} User 2 Profile: {user-2}
Faithfulness Expert	Given user 1 and user 2's profiles respectively, does the following conversation between the two users contradict either of their profiles? Why? User 1 Profile: {user-1} User 2 Profile: {user-2} Conversation: {conv-1} Response: {explanation}

Table 7: Prompting Templates for Large Language Models of Different Components in Our Framework. Variables enclosed in {} are filled when the template is populated.

probability of a contradiction ("Yes") or a decrease in the probability of no contradiction ("No").

B Synthetic-Persona-Chat

Synthetic-Persona-Chat is made of 20k conversations, with an average of 11.8 turns per user for each. An example Synthetic-Persona-Chat conversation can be found in Table 9. We compare Synthetic-Persona-Chat to Persona-Chat across different dimensions. We first assess the characteristics of SPC using various automatic evaluators, i.e. evaluators which do not require human effort. We then conduct a human evaluation experiment on a subset of SPC.

B.1 Automatic Evaluation

We conduct a comprehensive analysis and evaluation of SPC across different dimensions and compare it against PC. We start by analyzing the toxicity and diversity of SPC using off the shelf tools. Then, we elaborate on the experiments which assess the efficacy of SPC used as the dataset for the next utterance prediction and the profile extraction tasks. Finally, we evaluate the quality of SPC conversations using LLM-based evaluation methods.

Toxicity Analysis We analyze the toxicity of the generated conversations at the final iteration of SPC using an online tool called Perspective[3]. We reproduce the results of a detailed analysis of toxicity in PC as well as in each iteration of our data generation framework while producing SPC in Table 10. We observe a notable reduction in the frequency of conversations deemed as strongly toxic or profane throughout the iterations of generating SPC. This reduction can be attributed to the built-in toxicity filter of the employed LLM. While PC contains more than 50 samples that are identified as strongly toxic, SPC includes at most three toxic or profane conversations, which is significantly lower (at least 15 times less). Interestingly, the fraction of conversations with medium profanity and toxicity in SPC is 4 times less than the same type of conversations in PC across all iterations. We have removed any conversation that was marked as strongly toxic by this tool in the released dataset. Samples of toxic conversations are provided in Table 11.

Diversity Analysis We use hierarchical topic modeling (Blei et al., 2004) to assess the topic diversity of SPC and compare it to that of PC. For a fair comparison, we only compare conversations in SPC with similar personas in PC. Table 12 displays the number of topics at each level of the topic tree, with the first level indicating the most general topic. We observe similar topic diversity at the first level. In deeper levels, there is a slightly lower diversity in SPC.

Next Utterance Prediction We compare the performance of different models on the next utterance prediction task. As discussed in Section 4.2, these models are expected to exhibit better performance in the next utterance prediction task when user personas are provided as prior information. We evaluate ranking and generative models for response selection to assess this property. We compare models trained on SPC to the same models trained on PC. We use the implementations provided in (Miller et al., 2017) for the following models:

- **IR Baseline** Given an utterance as a query, the IR baseline finds the most similar utterance in the training corpus using tf-idf. It defines the utterance after the most similar utterance as the candidate response, and then returns the most similar option to that candidate as the output.
- **Transformer-Ranker** The context of the conversation, as well as the candidate next utterances, are encoded using a BERT-based encoder. The most similar encoded candidate to the conversation context, as measured by a dot-product in their representation space, is selected as the output (Humeau et al., 2020).
- **Transformer-Generator** This model is a sequence-to-sequence model (Sutskever et al., 2014) which uses transformers as encoders and decoders.

We also evaluate the performance of the next utterance prediction models when given no user, one user, and both user personas. The results of this experiment are available in Table 13. We observe that the highest performance improvement for all models trained on PC is when self-personas are given as input. We do not observe such a pattern in SPC. This indicates a higher degree of bidirectionality in SPC conversations compared to those of PC.

Profile Extraction A potential use-case of the SPC dataset is training a model to predict user personas from a conversation. This is only possible if

[3]https://perspectiveapi.com/

User Profiles	Conversations	Faithfulness Explanation
User 1: One of my favorite hobbies is gaming. I currently work in an office. I enjoy running **User 2**: I am applying for publishing jobs. My mother is a librarian. The only autographs I've ever wanted are from authors. I used to wear glasses as a child. My favorite color is green.	User 1: Do you like video games? User 2: No, I do not like video games. User 1: What do you do for a living? User 2: I am a librarian. User 1: I guess that is why you like to read a lot. User 2: Yes, I like to read books. User 1: What is your favorite color? Mine is green. User 2: That is my favorite color too. User 1: That is cool. User 2: Do you have any pets? User 1: No, I do not have any pets. User 2: I have a dog and a cat. User 1: That is cool. User 2: Do you have any hobbies?. User 1: Yes, I like to write. User 2: What do you write about? User 1: I write about my life. User 2: That is cool. User 1: Thanks!	No, the conversation does not contradict the profiles. Neither user 1 nor user 2 says anything that contradicts their respective profiles. Although the conversation does not cover everything in their profiles, that is ok.
User 1: I would like to move some place warmer. I m an out of work farmhand. I like watching reality television shows. I live in Kansas. **User 2:** I am studying to be a dentist. My favorite team is the raptors. My favorite band is rise against. I usually go to bed late. I like sports.	User 1: It's so cold in Kansas, I want to go some place warmer. User 2: I am studying dentistry. User 1: I am an out of work farmhand, I love reality tv. User 2: I like the raptors and rise against, I go to bed late. User 1: It is very hard to find work here, I might need to go to the city. User 2: I don't like sports , but I like the raptors . User 1: I would like to work as a model, but I have no experience. User 2: I am applying for a job as a receptionist. User 1: I am very jealous, I hope you get it.	Yes, the conversation contradicts user 2's profile. In the profile, user 2 says they like sports, however, in the conversation, user 2 says they don't like sports.
User 1: My family is from Kazakhstan. I can speak Spanish, English, and Kazakh. I like to go hiking on the weekends. I play jazz piano in a band. I am a barista. **User 2:** I am a vegan. I love game of thrones. I like soccer. My brother used to be in the navy.	User 1: Hi, what do you do for a living? User 2: I am a barista. User 1: Awesome, me too! Where are you from? User 2: My family is from Kazakhstan, but I was born in Uruguay. User 1: Cool . What do you like to do in your free time? User 2: I love to go hiking and play jazz piano. User 1: Wow, that sounds really nice. I like to watch game of thrones and play soccer. User 2: I have never seen game of thrones, but I love soccer. User 1: You should watch it, it is really good. User 2: I will check it out.	Yes, the conversation contradicts user 2's profile. In the profile, user 2 says they love game of thrones, but in the conversation user 2 says they have never seen it.
User 1: My favorite book is David Copperfield. I have a twin brother. I am really short. I love to bake cakes. I have won tap dance competitions. **User 2:** I enjoy spending a lot of money on my hobbies. I love photography. I like to use candles instead of lights. I do not like waking up early.	User 1: Hi there! Do you like to read? User 2: I like to read. I like to go to the library. User 1: Oh, cool! What is your favorite book? User 2: I really like David Copperfield. I have a twin brother and I am really short. User 1: Are you good at baking? User 2: I can bake cakes. I have won tap dance competitions. User 1: Do you like photography? User 2: I love taking pictures. I also like to use candles instead of lights. User 1: Do you like to wake up early? User 2: I like to sleep in. I do not like waking up early. User 1: Do you like to spend money? User 2: I love spending money on my hobbies.	No, the conversation does not contradict either user profiles. Although user 2 says they are really short, which is in user 1's profile, it doesn't mean user 2 cannot be really short too.

Table 8: Examples of Faithful and Unfaithful Conversations for Prompting the Persona Faithfulness Expert in Our Framework. The 'Faithfulness explanation' columns are used to fill the 'explanation' variable in the faithfulness expert template.

User Profiles	Conversation
User 1 I am male. My weakness are sweets. I am unsociable. I am a jack of all, master of none. **User 2** My favorite music is rock and roll. I love to travel. I am from Russia. I enjoy skiing. I go to school for business.	User 1: Hello User 2: Hello, what's your name? User 1: My name is [name], and you? User 2: My name is [name], I'm from Russia. User 1: Nice to meet you, [name]. I'm from the United States. User 2: It's nice to meet you too, [name]. What are you interested in? User 1: I'm interested in a lot of things, but my main interests are music and travel. User 2: I love music too! What kind of music do you like? User 1: I like a lot of different kinds of music, but my favorite is rock and roll. User 2: Me too! I love classic rock and roll. Who are your favorite bands? User 1: My favorite bands are The Beatles, The Rolling Stones, and Led Zeppelin. User 2: Those are all great bands! I love them too. User 1: What about you, what are your favorite bands? User 2: My favorite bands are The Doors, Pink Floyd, and Queen. User 1: Those are all great bands too! I love them too. User 2: So, what do you like to do for fun? User 1: I like to go to concerts, play video games, and watch movies. User 2: I love going to concerts too! I also like to go skiing and play tennis. User 1: I love skiing too! I haven't played tennis in a while, but I used to play a lot. User 2: We should go skiing together sometime! User 1: That would be fun! I'm free this weekend if you are. User 2: I'm free this weekend too! We should go skiing. User 1: Great! I'll text you the details.

Table 9: Sample Conversation from Synthetic-Persona-Chat. This conversation was synthesized from user profiles in Persona-Chat

	Toxicity			Profanity		
Confidence	weak(< .2)	medium(.2-.8)	strong(>.8)	weak(< .2)	medium(.2-.8)	strong(>.8)
PC	10875	4448	53	10891	1676	57
SPC Iter 1	10902	1192	3	10903	340	3
SPC Iter 2	10900	1096	1	10901	345	1
SPC Iter 3	10902	1088	1	10902	376	0

Table 10: Frequency of Toxic Conversations in Persona-Chat and Synthetic-Persona-Chat

Source	Conversation
Persona-Chat	... User 1: I like bloody stuff. User 2: It reminds me of the dark which makes me afraid of it. User 1: You are a silly goose.
Persona-Chat	... User 2: Cool. Why do you say that? Because I am a red head? User 1: No. Ikn. Why do you ask so many questions? Mr. Thomas is dumb.
Synthetic-Persona-Chat	User 1: I can imagine. What's your favorite part of the job? User 2: I love working with my team and seeing our restaurant succeed. User 1: That's great. What's your least favorite part of the job? User2: My least favorite part is dealing with my boss. He's a real jerk.

Table 11: Examples of Toxic Conversations. The first two examples are segments of conversations from Persona-Chat. The final example is a segment from a toxic conversation in Synthetic-Persona-Chat, which has been removed in the released dataset.

Topic Level	PC	SPC
1	27	27
2	232	213
3	470	403
4	137	118
5	30	26

Table 12: Vertical Topic Diversity in Persona-based Datasets

the dataset is highly faithful, meaning that any persona attribute inferred from the conversation is in the user profile or compatible with the user profile. In this context, a faithful conversation is expected to have high precision in the profile extraction task, while a conversation that highly reflects user personas is expected to have high recall in this task.

We evaluate the task of user profile extraction for conversations in SPC, and compare the results against those of PC. We frame the task of profile extraction as a ranking task, using the utterances within the conversations as queries. The goal is to rank a set of persona attribute options. For each conversation, we include the speakers' persona attributes in the available options. Additionally, we select 25 random user persona attributes from other speaker profiles within the dataset to serve as distractors. The input to the profile extraction is utterances from a single user as the speaker, while the output is a list of persona attribute options for a target user, which could be either user 1 or user 2. The results of this experiment are presented in Table 14. We observe that the performance of the profile extraction methods is higher in SPC in 3 of the 4 scenarios. Interestingly, we observe that with both datasets, when the target and the speaker are different, the performance of profile extraction is greater compared to the cases when the target and speaker users are the same.

LLM-based Quality Evaluation We leverage LLM-based conversation quality evaluators from the literature to compare the quality of SPC and PC. These evaluators rely on the human curated prompt templates for different metrics including consistency, fluency, etc. We used these evaluators with minimum change in the original prompt templates. These evaluators are:

- **LLM-Eval** (Lin and Chen, 2023) is a multi-dimensional automatic evaluation designed for conversations. It uses a human-curated prompt which describes evaluation dimensions, serving as a unified evaluation schema. This prompt evaluates the conversation across multiple dimensions (e.g. fluency) in a single model call. We show this unified schema in Table 15.

- **GPT-Score** (Fu et al., 2023) leverages emergent abilities of LLMs, i.e. zero-shot instructions, to score texts. It contains a prompt template, and for each quality criterion, populates the template with a human description of the criteria along with the valid score range for that criteria. Example prompts are provided in Table 15.

- **G-Eval** (Liu et al., 2023) introduces a framework that employs LLMs with a chain-of-thought approach to assess the quality of natural language generated outputs. For any evaluation criteria, G-Eval prompts the LLM with the criterion's description, prompting the

Method	Metric	Persona-Chat No Persona	Persona-Chat Self Persona	Persona-Chat Their Persona	Persona-Chat Both Personas	Synthetic-Persona-Chat No Persona	Synthetic-Persona-Chat Self Persona	Synthetic-Persona-Chat Their Persona	Synthetic-Persona-Chat Both Personas
IR baseline	hit@1	0.1869	**0.3683**	0.1519	0.3281	0.1861	**0.2596**	0.1882	0.2493
Transformer(Ranker)	hit@1	0.2513	**0.275**	0.1922	0.2572	0.7164	0.6227	0.6988	**0.7214**
Transformer (Generator)	hit@1	**0.0896**	0.08512	0.0873	0.0813	0.0526	**0.629**	0.053	0.051
	ppl	65.57	72.24	**62.49**	64.07	5.54	5.47	**5.4**	5.405

Table 13: Evaluation of Next Utterance Prediction models conditioned on different user personas.

Target	Speaker	F-Score PC	F-Score SPC
user 1	user 1	0.505	**0.574**
user 1	user 2	**0.737**	0.68
user 2	user 1	0.50	**0.57**
user 2	user 2	0.456	**0.494**

Table 14: Accuracy of Profile Extraction in Four Different Scenarios. The 'Target' column represents the user profile to be extracted, while the 'Speaker' column indicates the speaker of the turns given to the model as input.

model to generate the necessary evaluation steps. It then uses these steps to prompt the LLM to score given output for that criterion. It considers the probability of getting each permissible score as the output of the prompt, i.e., it considers the probability distribution of scores assigned by the LLM. The reported output is the expected value of the score distribution by the LLM. Table 15 includes an example prompt.

Results of this evaluation are presented in Table 16. We observe that SPC consistently outperforms PC across all the dimensions we evaluate. The superiority of SPC is more prominent when using GPT-Score, for which each evaluated criterion shows an average improvement of at least 23 points.

B.2 Human Evaluation

We run a human evaluation of the performance of our method via a crowdsourcing platform. We conduct an AI detection test, and a faithfulness study - both of which we describe in more details in the following subsections - at the end of every iteration of the generation of SPC.

AI Detection Test We randomly select 200 user pairs from PC. For each example, we show the annotators the user pair, together with the corresponding conversations from PC and SPC, and ask them to select the conversation that was synthetically generated. We show an example of this crowdsourcing task in Figure 7. The results of the AI detection test are available in Table 17. We report the losing rate of SPC in the AI detection test, and Fleiss' Kappa to assess the inter-rater agreement. The agreement falls into the fair to moderate agreement bucket.

Faithfulness We present the annotators with a conversation, and a set of options of persona attributes. The annotators are asked to select the user persona attributes they would infer from the conversation. Figure 8 shows a sample of the annotation task in this study. The options include the persona attributes of the speakers in the conversation, and a set of distractor persona attributes. We created distractor persona attributes using different strategies to cover different difficulty levels. For a persona attribute set Π, we create a set $\neg\Pi$ of distractor persona attributes as:

Negated personas We prompt an LLM to negate persona attributes. For example, the negation of persona attribute "I like vegetables" is "I don't like vegetables".

Random personas We randomly select persona attributes from user profiles in other conversations in the dataset.

Contradicting personas We prompt an LLM to generate a persona attribute which contradicts the users' personas.

Each entry of this task includes 8 user persona attributes as options, where 4 of them are the real persona attributes, and the other 4 are distractors. We evaluate the precision of the human annotators, and report it as a proxy to the conversation faithfulness in Table 3.

C Ablation Studies

We run several ablation studies to evaluate the importance of individual components in our framework. We begin by analyzing the effect of the persona expansion module. We then review the impact of each expert in the mixture forming our Critic.

Evaluator	Metric	Prompt Template
LLM-Eval	All	Human: The output should be formatted as a JSON instance that conforms to the JSON schema below. As an example, for the schema {"properties": {"foo": {"title": "Foo", "description": "a list of strings", "type": "array", "items": {"type": "string"}}}, "required": ["foo"]}} the object {"foo": ["bar", "baz"]} is a well-formatted instance of the schema. The object {"properties": {"foo": ["bar", "baz"]}} is not well-formatted. Here is the output schema: {"properties": {"content": {"title": "Content", "description": "content score in the range of 0 to 100", "type": "integer"}, "grammar": {"title": "Grammar", "description": "grammar score in the range of 0 to 100", "type": "integer"}, "relevance": {"title": "Relevance", "description": "relevance score in the range of 0 to 100", "type": "integer"}, "appropriateness": {"title": "Appropriateness", "description": "appropriateness score in the range of 0 to 100", "type": "integer"}}, "required": ["content", "grammar", "relevance", "appropriateness"]}} Score the following dialogue generated on a continuous scale from {score-min} to {score-max}. Dialogue: {dialogue}
GPT-Score	Consistency	Answer the question based on the conversation between two users. Question: Are the responses of users consistent in the information they provide throughout the conversation? (a) Yes. (b) No. Conversation: {dialogue} Answer:
G-Eval	Coherence	You will be given a pair of user personas. You will then be given one conversation between this persona pair. Your task is to rate the conversation on one metric. Please make sure you read and understand these instructions carefully. Please keep this document open while reviewing, and refer to it as needed. Evaluation Criteria: Coherence (1-5) - the collective quality of all utterances. We align this dimension with the Document Understanding Conference (DUC) quality question of structure and coherence , whereby "the conversation should be well-structured and well-organized. The conversation should not just be a heap of related information, but should build from utterance to a coherent body of conversation about a topic." Evaluation Steps: 1. Read and understand the given conversation between the pair of user personas. 2. Evaluate the conversation based on the coherence of the utterances. 3. Rate the conversation on a scale of 1 to 5, with 5 being the highest coherence and 1 being the lowest coherence. 4. Justify the rating by referring to specific aspects of the conversation that demonstrate its coherence or lack thereof. Example: Personas: {personas} Conversation: {dialogue} Evaluation Form (scores ONLY): - Coherence:
LLM-Faithfulness	Inference	Instruction: Select User {user} persona attributes that are directly inferred from this conversation.
	Contradiction	Instruction: Select User {user} persona attributes that strongly contradict this conversation.

Table 15: Prompt Templates in LLM-based Conversation Quality Evaluators. Variables enclosed in { } are filled when the template is populated.

Here are two individuals' ***profiles*** along with two ***conversations*** between them. The two conversations may have been generated by a ***Computer / Artificial Intelligence*** or a human.

Please choose the conversation/conversations you believe was/were generated by a ***Computer / AI***. If you believe neither is generated by ***Computer / AI***, please choose None of Them.

User 1 Profiles:

I am in my second year of medical school.
I am a hindu living in louisiana.
My mom is the best baker in my family.
My favorite thing to do is watch old movies.

User 2 Profiles:

I live on an island.
I enjoy fishing.
I like to make boats on the weekends.
I have a dog named bob.
I am a closet cannibal.

Conversation 1:

User 1: Hi! I'm a medical student from Louisiana. What about you?
User 2: I'm from an island, and I like to fish.
User 1: That's cool! What kind of fish do you like to catch?
User 2: I like to catch mahi-mahi and tuna.
User 1: Those are both delicious! Do you eat them yourself, or do you sell them?
User 2: I usually eat them myself. I like to cook them on the grill.
User 1: That sounds delicious! I'm not much of a cook, but I love eating good food.
User 2: I'm sure you're a great cook! You're a medical student, after all.
User 1: Thanks! I'm not sure about that, but I'm trying my best.
User 2: You're doing great! What's your favorite thing about being a medical student?
User 1: I like learning about different diseases and how to treat them. I also like helping people.
User 2: That's great! I'm sure you're going to be a great doctor.
User 1: Thanks! I hope so!
User 2: I'm sure you will be. You seem like a smart and caring person.
User 1: Thank you! That means a lot.

☐ Check it if you think this conversation is toxic.

Conversation 2:

User 1: Hello, how are you tonight?
User 2: Hey there, I am doing well, thank you for asking, you?
User 1: I am doing fine, glad to hear you are doing well.
User 2: What do you do for a living?
User 1: I do not currently work, spending all my time studying in medical school.
User 2: Is that enjoyable? Or stressful?
User 1: Really stressful, but it is worth the work.
User 2: Well, it sucks its not as rewarding in the process. Expensive
User 1: All college is expensive, but at least one day I will be saving lives.
User 2: What do you do outside of school?
User 1: I help my mom with her baking and watch old movies. You?
User 2: I currently reside on an island, so I fish and toy with bots
User 1: That sounds like a lovely place to live, is it warm all year?
User 2: Boats but mostly, its a little cooler in the fall, but that is the low 70s

☐ Check it if you think this conversation is toxic.

Select an option

Conversation 1 is generated by an AI 1
Conversation 2 is generated by an AI 2
Both of Them are generated by an AI 3
None of Them is generated by an AI 4

Figure 7: Preview of the AI detection test Task on the Crowdsourcing Platform

Evaluator	Criteria	PC	SPC	SPC Iter 1	FED	Faithfulness
LLM-Eval (Lin and Chen, 2023)	Content	81.96	**88.84**	**88.71**	87.61	88.67
	Grammar	87.12	**93.64**	**93.68**	93.09	93.56
	Relevance	86.82	**94.16**	**93.81**	92.88	93.79
	Appropriateness	86.99	**95.84**	96.17	95.68	**96.19**
GPT-Score (Fu et al., 2023)	Fluency	67.04	**98.89**	96.28	96.65	**97.83**
	Consistent	3.47	**64.25**	**50.43**	43.45	48.69
	Coherent	69.41	**100**	**100**	98.99	**100**
	Depth	5.40	**37.36**	**29.30**	19.40	29.01
	Diversity	72.98	**96.42**	94.02	92.79	**94.11**
	Likeable	36.53	**91.04**	**93.11**	91.90	87.98
G-Eval (Liu et al., 2023)	Relevance (1-5)	2.288	**2.992**	2.986	2.941	**2.99**
	Fluency (1-3)	1.928	**2.002**	**2**	1.998	1.999
	Consistent (1-5)	1.736	**2.651**	**2.587**	2.449	2.496
	Coherent (1-5)	2.505	**2.997**	2.997	2.991	**2.998**
	Faithfulness (1-5)	1.754	**2.959**	**2.8801**	2.79	2.868

Table 16: Results of Automatic Evaluations of Synthetic-Persona-Chat and Persona-Chat. The "FED" column is the evaluation of the dataset generated without FED expert and the column "Faithfulness" is the evaluation results of the dataset generated without the faithfulness expert in the Critic.

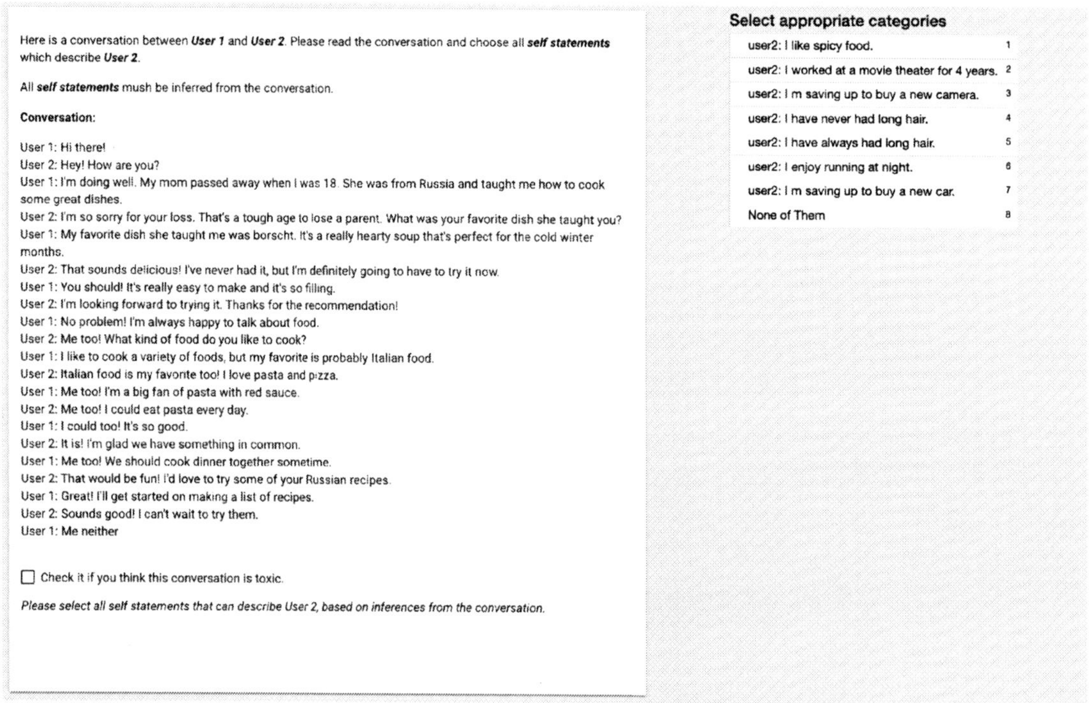

Figure 8: Preview of the Faithfulness Task on the Crowdsourcing Platform.

Conversation Source	% Lose	κ	# annotators
SPC Iter 1	17.2	0.41	50
SPC Iter 2	18.5	0.48	40
SPC Iter 3	8.8	0.22	11
SPC Iter 3*	8.04	0.56	24
SPC (LLM2)	11.5	0.49	36

Table 17: AI detection test results on a sample of 200 conversations. The first column shows the percentage of SPC losing compared to PC in the Turing test. Note that the last iteration (3) of SPC is an evaluation of the segment of conversations based on the extended persona set.

C.1 Persona Expansion

We assess the importance of the query-based persona expansion module introduced in Section 3.1.1. Similarly to the experiment outlined in Section 4.1, we run the persona expansion on two datasets: Wikipedia and PC. The results of this experiment are presented in Table 18. We designate the persona expansions without the inducted query set (Q) as 'Wikipedia-0', and 'PC-0', and run the same number of iterations for each (100 iterations). We observe that PC-0 includes 4,477 new persona attributes, 20 percent less than PC. The difference in the number of newly generated persona attributes is more pronounced in the case of Wikipedia, where Wikipedia-0 consists of 4,742 persona attributes, 50 percent less than Wikipedia+. This trend is also observed in the number of persona clusters, with PC-0 and Wikipedia-0 having 6% and 49% less clusters respectively. This pattern suggests the effectiveness of the query-based persona expansion in maintaining the diversity of the persona set. Furthermore, the average persona attribute length in PC-0 is 11.38 tokens, which is 28% less than SPC. This reduction points to less detailed and specific persona attributes. In contrast, the expansion in 'Wikipedia-0' exhibits similar average persona attribute lengths compared to 'Wikipedia+'.

C.2 Conversation Quality

We analyze the effect of the experts within our Critic. We remove each expert, and generate a dataset using one iteration of our framework. We compare the resulting datasets against the output of the first iteration of SPC. We use the evaluators introduced in B.1. The results of this experiment are summarized in Table 16. We observe that the exclusion of the experts results in worse performance according to most criteria: 3 out of 4 in LLM-Eval, 4 out of 6 in GPT-Score, and 3 out of 5 in G-Eval.

C.3 Faithfulness

We ablate the faithfulness critic, and generate a dataset that we compare against SPC. We compare these datasets both automatically, using human annotators (AI detection test), and using a prompted LLM (LLM-Evaluator). We describe this study in more details below.

AI Detection Test We run a human study to compare a small subset of conversations created without the faithfulness expert against their equivalent created with that expert. This experiment process is similar to 4.3 and it is conducted for 200 conversations. The precision decreases from 78.0% to 66.0% without this critic, highlighting its effectiveness in eliminating conversations with contradictory information about user personas. The recall decreases from 36.0% to 23.0%, demonstrating a higher reflection of personas in the conversations in the presence of the faithfulness expert.

LLM-Evaluator We extend our comparison to the entire dataset using an LLM as an annotator, following (He et al., 2023; Bansal and Sharma, 2023; Chiang and yi Lee, 2023). Table 19 shows the faithfulness of the conversations generated in the first iteration without the faithfulness expert. The templates used in the LLM-based annotators are described in Table 16 in the rows with "LLM-Faithfulness" as their evaluator. Note that the annotator-based LLM is created using a different LLM, gpt-3.5-turbo (Brown et al., 2020b; Ouyang et al., 2022), than the LLM used for dataset generation.

C.4 Next Utterance Prediction

We follow the experimental setting described in section 4.2, and compare the performance of various next utterance prediction models trained on SPC against the same models trained on datasets created in the absence of certain experts.

When using the IR Baseline as the next utterance prediction method, we observee that its highest performance of 39% hit@1 occurs when the FED critic is absent during dataset creation. This outcome aligns with FED's emphasis on conversation quality, excluding persona-related aspects. Conversely, the Transformer Ranker, capable of understanding intricate concepts, achieves its peak performance of 13.9% hit@1 when none of the experts are absent. This result supports the inclusion of both FED and the Faithfulness expert in the

Dataset	PC	SPC	PC-0	Wikipedia	Wikipedia+	Wikipedia-0
# Persona Attributes	4,723	**10,371**	9,200	8,768	**18,293**	13,510
# Clusters	323	**553**	520	408	**986**	502
InterCluster-Dist	0.836	0.863	0.842	0.816	0.85	0.83
AVG length	7.65	**15.9***	11.38*	10.45	**15.2***	**15.2***

Table 18: Evaluation of the Expanded Persona Attribute Sets. The numbers with '*' indicate the metric value on the newly generated persona attributes, in contrast to the initial persona attributes.

	LLM Evaluator (%)		Human Evaluator (%)	
Absent Component	Inference	Contradiction	Precision	Recall
None	**33.2**	**24.5**	**78.5**	**36.4**
Faithfulness	32.7	28.8	66.1	23.1
FED	31.7	28.5	N/A	N/A

Table 19: Faithfulness of Generated Conversation Datasets Using the Framework While Eliminating Each Component. The first row represents the framework without removing any component, equivalent to the first iteration of Synthetic-Persona-Chat.

model architecture. In generative models, the absence of FED impacts the next utterance prediction model the most, leading to a notable decline in performance (e.g. −12% hit@1, −9% BLEU, −10% ROUGE). This observation underscores the crucial role played by FED in enhancing the generative capabilities of the model.

Absent Component		Faithfulness			FED			None		
Method	Metric	None	Persona	% Change	None	Persona	% Change	None	Persona	% Change
IR Baseline	hit@1	18.7	38.7	**+106**	19.0	**39.0**	+105	18.9	38.7	+105
Transformer (Ranker)	hit@1	10.9	13.5	+24	10.7	13.6	**+27**	12.4	**13.9**	+11
Transformer (Generator)	hit@1	**8.9**	7.4	-16	8.4	7.4	**-12**	8.2	7.0	-14
	Perplexity	204	214	+5	**174**	185	+6	203	210	**+3**
	BLUE	0.11	0.10	-11	0.11	0.10	**-9**	0.10	0.08	-15
	ROUGE	0.14	0.15	-12	0.14	0.12	**-10**	0.13	0.10	-17

Table 20: Results of the Next Utterance Prediction Experiment in the Ablation Study. The numbers in the table represent the performance of the trained model on the test portion of the Persona-Chat dataset.

Author Index

Association for Computational Linguistics
209 N. Eighth Street
Stroudsburg, Pennsylvania 18360

ISBN 979-8-3313-0171-2

CURRAN ASSOCIATES INC.
proceedings.com